INFORMATION TECHNOLOGY AND THE HUMAN SERVICES

INFORMATION TECHNOLOGY AND THE HUMAN SERVICES

Edited by
Bryan Glastonbury
University of Southampton, UK

Walter LaMendola
University of Denver, USA

and

Stuart Toole
Polytechnic of Birmingham, UK

JOHN WILEY & SONS
Chichester · New York · Brisbane · Toronto · Singapore

Copyright © 1988 by John Wiley & Sons Ltd.

British Library Cataloguing in Publication Data available

ISBN 0 471 92127 0

Printed in Great Britain by St. Edmundsbury Press, Bury St. Edmunds.

Contents

Contents

PART II
AGENCY FOCUS

Contents

Contents

Contributors

Jan L. Ames	Washington Library for the Blind & Physically Handicapped, Seattle, USA.
Alan Anciaux	Sociological Institute, Free University of Brussels, Belgium.
Donald F. Bellamy	Faculty of Social Work, University of Toronto, Canada.
Alan R. Benston	Washington Library for the Blind & Physically Handicapped, Seattle, USA.
Edis B. Bevan	Disability Study Research Centre, The Open University, Milton Keynes, England.
Evelyn Blennerhasset	Institute of Public Administration, Dublin, Ireland.
Catherine Cassell	MRC/ESRC Social & Applied Psychology Unit, University of Sheffield, England.
Ram A. Cnaan	Bob Shapell School of Social Work, Tel Aviv, Israel; and, School of Social Work, University of Pennsylvania, USA.
M.J. Coleman	School of Information Science, Portsmouth Polytechnic, England.
Elizabeth S. Cordingley	University of Surrey, Guildford, England.
Les Cowan	Central Regional Council Social Work Department, Stirling, Scotland.
J. Christopher Daniel	Madurai Institute of Social Work, (affiliated to Madurai Kamaraj University), Madurai, India.
Rochelle D. Denke	Washington Library for the Blind & Physically Handicapped, Seattle, USA.
Paul Dolan	Social Services Department, University of Birmingham, England.
Joyce Epstein	Research Institute for Consumer Affairs, London, England.
Judith M. Feinstein	School of Social Work, University of Connecticut, USA.

Contributors

Richard J. Fiene	Behavioural Science & Education Division, Pennsylvania State University at Harrisburg, USA.
Mike Fitter	MRC/ESRC Social and Applied Psychology Unit, University of Sheffield, England.
Donald J. Forgie	Faculty of Library and Information Science, University of Toronto, Canada.
Jan Forrest	Capita Limited, London, England.
Joyce E. Frakes	School of Accountancy, University of Denver, Colorado, USA.
Bryan Glastonbury	Department of Social Work Studies, University of Southampton, England.
Judy A. Goodrich	College of Communications, University of Kentucky, Lexington, USA.
James Gripton	University of Calgary, Alberta, Canada.
Leo de Groot	Alberta Children's Hospital, Calgary, Canada.
Hugh Grove	School of Accountancy, University of Denver, Colorado, USA.
Kevin A. Harris	Community Projects Foundation, London, England.
Garry Homer	Wolverhampton Polytechnic, Wolverhampton, England.
K.R. Howey	Human Reliability Associated Ltd., Wigan, England.
Salvatore Imbrogno	College of Social Work, Ohio State University, USA.
Paul Licker	University of Calgary, Alberta, Canada.
Robert J. MacFadden	Faculty of Social Work, University of Toronto, Canada.
Nancy Marlett	Disability Information Services of Canada, Calgary, Canada.
Tom McKinlay	Excelsior Youth Centers Inc., Aurora, Colorado, USA.
Walter LaMendola	University of Denver, Denver, Colorado, USA.

Contributors

Diane Metzendorf	Hands-On Community Computer Center Inc., Haverford, Pennsylvania, USA.
Simon Mielniczuk	Faculty of Social Work, University of Toronto, Canada.
Clive Miller	National Institute for Social Work, London, England.
Shelley Mills-Brinckley	School of Social Work, University of Connecticut, USA.
Jan Monasso	Dutch Council for Higher Education, Amsterdam, Holland.
William O'Connor	Ombudsman, Older Alaskans Commission, Anchorage, Alaska.
Lars Qvortrup	Odense University, Odense, Denmark.
Peter Petrella	School of Social Work, University of Connecticut, USA.
Linda A. Porter	College of Communications, University of Kentucky, Lexington, USA.
Vidya Rao	Tata Institute of Social Sciences, Bombay, India.
Hy Resnick	University of Washington, Seattle, Washington, USA.
Graham Rodwell	Department of Social Administration, University of Lancaster, England.
Ramona R. Rush	College of Communications, University of Kentucky, Lexington, USA.
Dick Schoech	University of Texas at Arlington, Arlington, Texas, USA.
Elizabeth B.Shear	College of Communications, University of Kentucky, Lexington, USA.
Joaquin G. Tan	Quegon City, Philippines.
S.B.N. Thompson	School of Information Science, Portsmouth Polytechnic, England.
Stuart Toole	Birmingham Polytechnic, Birmingham, England.
Albert Visser	Council for Higher Professional Education, The Hague, Holland.

Contributors

Sandra Williams	Policy Studies Institute, London, England.
Sarah L. Wilson	Royal Hospital and Home for Incurables, London, England.
Stanley L. Witkin	Florida State University, Tallahassee, Florida, USA.
Janrose C. Zingg	College of Communications, University of Kentucky, Lexington, USA.

Acknowledgements

The editors are extremely grateful to the following individuals and organisations who contributed to the success of HUSITA 87. Inevitably, where so many people were involved, some names will slip through unmentioned. To those we offer our apologies, and we would stress that we have had to trace back through some scrappy records covering more than two years in order to identify as many of the helpers and sponsors as possible.

Mauricio Andres
Henrick Backmann
Colin Barnes
Floyd Bolithio
Carlton Bott
Ruth Brack
Syngen Brown
Pamela Burgess
Bill Cohen
Betsy Cordingley
Hein de Graaf
Paul Dolan
Maria Dossi
Ellis Envall
Mike Ferriter
Jan Forrest
Derek Gardiner
Fritz Gruendger
Lars Gunner
Garry Homer
Steve Johnson
Brian Klepinger
Jo Landstrom
David Lansky
Mark Law
Marco Mazeland
Anne McAnne
Rob McFadden
Vera Mehta
Clive Miller
Jan Mlejnic
Mike Monk
Menachem Monnichen
Tom Neudecker
Liv Opdol
Ian Robinson
Eunice Schatz
Dick Schoech
Buddy Silberman
Norman Smith
Jake Tan
Toshio Tatara
Hazel Toole

Acknowledgements

Tom Tossyn
Albert Visser
Annette Warner
Douglas Warns
Sara Wilson

Apple Computers
Astrography Software, France
Austin Rover
Birmingham Convention & Visitor Bureau
Birmingham Polytechnic
British Association of Social Workers
British Council
British Tourist Authority
Central Council for Education and Training in Social Work
Centre for Urban Education, Portland
City of Birmingham
CASW Limited
Computer Users in Social Services Network
Council for Social Work Education
Danish Social Work Union
Denver University
Finnish Social Work Union
Haworth Press
IASSW and Vera Mehta (Secretary General)
IBM
International Federation of Social Workers
Information Technology Resource Centre, Chicago
Ministry of Social Welfare, Health & Culture, Netherlands
Norwegian Social Work Union
Pan Am
Price WaterHouse
Public Welfare Organisation
Social Services Insight
Social Work Today
Southern Californian Centre for Non Profit Management
SRB (Dutch Research Organisation)
Technology Learning Centre of the Non Profit Manage-
        ment, Dallas
Trendwatch Publications
United Way of America

CHAPTER 1

Introduction

According to personal preference, Information Technology (IT)
either has its origins in the work of Charles Babbage a century
or so ago, in the development of census data processing at the
start of the current century, with the push for computing to aid
military management in the 1940s, or in the new technologies of
semiconductors and microprocessors during the last few decades.
Whatever the chosen start point, and however desirable it might
be to give IT a longer and hence more venerable history, reality
for the vast majority of computer users begins with the
microchip. IT is the invention of our age, and we are the first
to become dependent on it for the conduct of our lives. The
application of IT is all around us – we cannot any longer book
a holiday, shop at a supermarket, use a credit card or put
petrol in the car without IT. As a society we have not approved
or opposed the full flow of this deluge of technology: quite
simply we have not been consulted, and have accepted, albeit
with some cynicism, the view that such changes are necessary if
we are to operate on a bigger scale, do tasks more quickly,
have extensive communications, increase productivity, or generally be more efficient. The implementation of IT in our lives has
had teething problems, and continues to cause occasional guilt
and frustration from time to time, but for such a massive
transition the process has been relatively painless.

Such generalisations cannot, however, be made about every
possible sector in which IT might have a role to play. This book
is about IT in the human services, or personal social services,
to use the nearest British equivalent, or health and social
welfare services, to use more of an international perspective,
and the path to progress has been littered with obstacles,
failures, resistance, and a more than usual dose of apathy. It
is possible to trace early applications back to the late 1960s in
North America, or a few years afterwards in Europe. What has
emerged since that time, alongside a solid block of successful IT
developments, is a vast agenda of issues which any practitioner,
professional, technician or policy-maker in the human services
has to take into consideration. They include issues about ethics
and social values – can IT ensure confidentiality? Is it an
invasion of personal privacy? How will it affect the consumer of
services? Will it cause unemployment? Will it compromise the
professional standards and values of social workers, clinical
psychologists and a host of others who work face-to-face with
clients? There are issues about professionalism and the client/
worker relationship – will IT undermine professional activity by
automating decision-making? Will it replace the warmth and

therapeutic potential of the relationship by some kind of cold, inflexible robot? There is a fundamental question about human service work – will IT take away the flexibility and intuitiveness of response which is so vital to helping people? Added to all of these items is the scepticism about the utility, accuracy and efficiency of IT in human service work.

The first message, then, for the apostle of IT in human servicing is that the technology comes together with a great deal of additional baggage, much of which presents as a series of obstacles to easy development. The context is a sensitive one, and the task that much harder in consequence. Perhaps the second message concerns the apathy, occasionally fearfulness, of potential users, such that IT applications are unlikely to sell themselves, and in contrast need diligent, imaginative presentation. The reasons for apathy are not the proper subject matter of this book, though they are easy to identify and, indeed, are discussed in some of the papers contained here. Most human service workers have well established servicing or therapeutic procedures which they see no grounds for altering. Fear is, perhaps, on the decline, but the basic assumption remains that computers require users with numeracy skills, while the human services are a refuge for the non-numerate.

To apathy, fear and 'wider issues' must be added a substantial degree of insularity and isolationism about IT developments among practitioners in the human services. There has been a conspicuous shortage of self-initiated discovery and application, national co-ordination, standardisation and leadership over the two decades of activity. International collaboration has been minimal. Overall it is tempting, as previous paragraphs have shown, to take a thoroughly pessimistic viewpoint. Yet a pause for reflection will show that there are also many reasons for optimism. Certainly the task is a difficult one, characterised as it is by intrinsic and self-imposed problems; but at the same time it is an observable fact that most welfare agencies in the wealthier parts of the world, and some in the poorer parts, now have IT applications working well and indispensably.

Nevertheless, there remain a larger set of intriguing unanswered questions. Is there a way to implement a model of technology transfer that is based upon technical expertise which originates within the professional disciplines involved in carrying out human service work? One that is firmly built upon human service ethics and values? One that advocates for the recipients of service? One that empowers the user? Is America ahead of the rest of us? Are the human service systems of some countries more amenable to technological intervention than in others? Have some countries and some human services moved forward with technology because they have solved the 'unsolvable' problems, or because they have chosen to ignore them? Most fundamentally, has the fragmentation and isolation of developments resulted in progress along a range of very different paths, or has a broad pattern emerged to link together schemes from across the world?

In Autumn 1987 many of these questions were addressed at the first International Convention of HUSITA (the acronym for Human

Services Information Technology Appliations). This book is a compilation of papers presented to HUSITA 87. As the Introduction has implied, HUSITA 87 was not a gathering of narrowly focused technology specialists, but of a wide range of workers from human services, educational and research institutions around the world. In addition to their training in a human service profession, some were specialists in the technology: others had particular knowledge of practical applications, agency circumstances and client needs. Some were wholly committed to the benefits of IT: others were more sceptical, and a few downright hostile. Most presenters came from North America, the UK and other industrialised countries, where IT applications have made most progress in the human services: but there were significant minorities from third world countries, as well as some representation from Eastern Europe. What they had in common was an enthusiasm about IT, whether motivated by positive or negative views, and an urge to know what everyone else was doing. We hope that there will be a growing volume of publication in this subject area, and some widely known names (almost all with papers in the following pages) participated, but HUSITA 87 was the first international opportunity to get together and share developments which have, too often, been pursued in isolation.

Later sections of this introductory chapter will give more background to HUSITA and signpost the reader through the chapters and structure of the book. A preliminary task, however, is to define important terms, and to draw attention to some of the conceptual and linguistic distinctions between American English and British English.

CLARIFYING TERMS

The title of the book contains two labels which need some definition. *Information Technology* (IT) is widely understood (or misunderstood), with no cross-cultural nuances. IT is the use of computer and communication technologies to receive, handle, store, retrieve, transmit, process, update, analyse, and present data for the purpose of deriving meaning from it; in other words, IT supports the human acts which surround the activity of informing ourselves. Therefore, these technologies can facilitate making calculations, drawing conclusions, taking decisions, making inferences, and adding to the scope and sophistication of applications. Within the context of the human services, the information being handled is likely to be about actual or potential clients of the services (identity data, problems/needs, service links, etc.), agency resources (places on programmes, in residential or day care units, money grants, etc.), accessible external resources (facilities of other agencies), agency staff (numbers, qualifications, salaries, etc.), or agency procedures (child abuse regulations, for example).

The other label is *Human Services* . This is an American concept, grouping together services for and staff dealing with social welfare activities. The term is not used much in other countries and, despite its widespread use in the States, has no clear definition. For the purposes of this book, we define it as 'the set of organizations whose primary function is to define or alter the person's behavior, attributes, and social status in order to maintain or enhance his well-being . . . These organizations are differentiated from other bureaucracies by two fundamental characteristics: (a) their input of raw material are human beings with specific attributes, and their production output are persons . . . and (b) their general mandate is that of "service", that is, to maintain and improve the general well-being and functioning of people' (Hasenfield and English, 1974, p.1). The nearest British label is 'personal social services', which can be defined as 'those services whose primary focus is the meeting of individual and special needs arising from the relationship between individuals and the social environment and from intra personal stress' (BASW, 1977, 15).

Following on the title of the book itself, the reader is next likely to notice that both American and British spelling and language use is included. An editorial decision has been made not to try to translate all contributions into one style or spelling, so for the most part papers have been left just as they were presented in their written form. There will be some difficulties of comprehension, but all can be overcome by a little thought and imagination. The language of IT varies across cultures, as do some of the terms in social welfare. There are widely differing writing styles, regardless of the origin of the author, and there is no attempt to introduce homogeneity. This one and the last chapter have both British and American authors, so the result is American English with a Southampton accent, or English English as spoken in Denver, or whatever you, the reader, perceive it to be!

BACKGROUND TO HUSITA

The interest and movement toward the idea of an international gathering came for reasons already discussed and from several directions at once. In the United States and Canada there had been a number of successful local efforts which highlighted the work being done in this area. The *Computer Users in Social Services* (CUSS) group, led by Richard Schoech and long a force in US human service computing, saw a steady growth in membership and developed an electronic bulletin board network across the United States. The network of bulletin boards was later extended to include membership groups in other countries. These efforts were followed by a very successful regional conference in Seattle, sponsored by the USA Federal Department of Health and Human Services and the United Way of America, on Microcomputers in the Human Services, during the Fall of 1985, and an equally compelling meeting on Computers and Community Organization in New York the following year. In England, a newsletter, which later became the journal *Computer Applications in Social Work* was well received, and the editorial group have sponsored two UK conferences on social welfare computing, the last of which, in 1986, attracted delegates from the Netherlands, Germany, and Belgium. Principals involved in these events felt that an international convention was now timely and could allow practitioners in different countries to develop an understanding of the variety, diversity and commonality of efforts taking place in different countries. It also seemed at that point that the various countries were at different stages of development, some specializing in areas that other countries had little activity in application development. A mutual interchange of applications and thinking had not yet taken place: many people working in the same areas of development in different countries were unaware of each other's work.

In the Summer of 1985, Stuart Toole, from the Birmingham Polytechnic (Birmingham, England, that is!), and Walter LaMendola and Brian Klepinger of the University of Denver, agreed to pursue the idea of an international gathering. By that Fall, the University of Denver and Birmingham Polytechnic had agreed to support, respectively, the efforts of Walter LaMendola and Stuart Toole to organize such a gathering. The prospective convention was to have five goals:

1 to share applications work
2 to begin the process of technology transfer
3 to promote strategies of empowerment for populations at risk
4 to examine the ethical and value basis for information technology in human services
5 to examine the basis for a continuing international organization concerned with the conduct of this work.

An early attempt was made to gather sponsors. While many sponsors were indeed gathered, initial financial participation was not forthcoming from any but Denver and Birmingham. The journal *Computer Applications in Social Work* (by this time edited by Bryan Glastonbury) and the British based conference programme were incorporated as CASW Limited, in order to limit risks, and took on HUSITA as a project. In most ways, our situation mirrored the problem of funding anything to do with human services, as reflected in cutbacks in the various countries for actual service delivery. We fared no differently in that regard. Without the support of the University of Denver and the Birmingham Polytechnic, the dedicated, mostly voluntary work of persons individually and in national planning groups from a number of countries, and the registration monies of the participants – almost one half of which were presentors – HUSITA could not have taken place.

A special note should be taken of the participation of the City of Birmingham. Early in 1987, the City contributed funds and services to the Convention, and became the venue for the gathering. It is appropriate that Birmingham should have been the site of the Convention. As the home of the Industrial Revolution and its consequences, the problems and opportunities of the British Midlands provided a context which fitted well with the theme of HUSITA ('A Technology to Support Humanity'), and the aspirations of its participants. Other organizations contributed finances, effort, and goods, enough to allow us to go on and meet in September, 1987. The support of the Central Council for Education and Training in Social Work (CCETSW) was an important psychological boost. All of them deserve the grateful thanks of the human service field. During the Convention HUSITA was also able to recognize the contribution of Samuel Silberman of the Silberman Fund for his leadership in beginning the exploration of the conjunction of information technology and human service work in the United States.

STRUCTURE OF THE BOOK

After the call for papers, the resulting set of abstracts were examined and were judged by readers to fall into nine general areas. Those areas are:

1 information systems and the consumer
2 direct use with clients, automated assessment, and treatment decision-making
3 education and training
4 policy development and administration
5 electronic networks and electronic communication
6 system design and development
7 empowerment
8 information ownership, privacy, and codes of practice
9 technology transfer and third world countries.

These nine areas appear within the framework of this book as Chapters 2 to 10. After an introductory chapter, those chapters are structured into four parts, to reflect the differing angles of approach from service consumer, agency, technology, and value systems.

Part 1, with a consumer focus, has chapters looking at some of the concerns facing consumers in the use of IT, and at some applications of IT which draw clients directly into processes of automated assessment and treatment decision making.

Part 2 moves the focus towards service agencies, firstly to take up matters connected with education and training for staff, as well as the notion of computer assisted learning; then it offers papers discussing the development of agency IT policies, and systems for their administration.

Part 3 is concerned with technological aspects of human service developments, with material on communicating and networking between staff and between agencies, and on the design and development of systems, whether that term is used to describe total IT systems, or specific items of programming.

Part 4 picks up the major political and ethical issues which have overlayed many of the earlier contributions. The powerless-ness (or need for empowerment) of members of the public, including the disabled, is discussed, alongside matters of privacy, information ownership, and the standards which should cover IT practices. Lastly this part turns to the idea of technology transfer, and the particular problems faced by third world countries.

Each chapter consists of a choice of papers (made by the editors) to reflect the variety of offerings on the subject. A number of criteria were used in the difficult task of deciding which papers to offer the reader. Forty-two papers (from a total of 136) are proposed for the volume, mostly complete, though in order to accommodate that number the editors have been forced to reduce the longer ones.

Several criteria were used for selection.

1 Quality

2 Applicability to a wide readership. Several high quality papers which were also highly specialized have been held back

3 'Fit' within the chapter structure of the book, and the maintenance of a reasonable balance. Some themes offered more good material than could be accommodated, and again these have been held over

4 Geographic spread of authors. The editors aimed for a good balance of material between Europe and North America, within European countries, and between the developed and third world. In practice Britain and the USA have the largest number of papers (as was true of the whole 136). It has not always been easy to maintain both high quality and a strong third world representation, mainly because for third world contributors English is a second language.

Other than for essential shortening, editorial intervention in the preparation of these papers is limited to necessary grammatical corrections, with the exception of those submitted by non-English speakers (mostly continental Europe and third world), where sufficient editing has been undertaken to ensure reasonable grammar and comprehensibility. English and American spellings have been left as in the originals.

The final chapter, 11, seeks to draw together the major themes of the preceding papers, and discusses the future for IT in the human services, both in the specific context of an investigation of the possibilities and potentials of an International Organization, and more broadly in the areas of development and innovation which we can all anticipate during the coming years.

It is our feeling, along with many of the participants, that the next few years are critical when taken from the point of view of information technologies and human services. Certainly it can be argued that criticality pales in the face of the austere redefinition of welfare services in many countries, or the failures of third world development; but information technologies are being used as a powerful instrument of economy, politics, polity, and progress. The ability to wage war, to propagandize a population, and to teach our children commercial idioms, intemperate violence, and compliant sensibilities are well publicized, negative aspects of the present uses of this technology. In fact, the use of IT seems to be monopolized by both people and corporate interests whose values and social ideas are apparently quite different from those found in the human services. It is our stewardship of human service ideals that motivates us to raise the discussion now and lend our

voices to this important debate. We invite you to join us, and
offer the information, ideas and views expressed in this book
as a reference point.

REFERENCES

BASW (1977). *The Social Work Task*, British Association of Social
    Workers, Birmingham. UK.
Hasenfield, Y. and English, R.A. (eds.) (1974). *Human Service
    Organizations*, University of Michigan Press, Ann Arbor, USA.

PART I

CONSUMER FOCUS

CHAPTER 2

Information Systems and the Consumer

The development of information technologies has largely been in the hands of specialized technicians and, at least until very recently, has been unresponsive to what has euphemistically been called the *User*. This chapter is not necessarily about the direct 'hands on' user of the technology; instead it focuses largely upon those who are at the receiving end. For example, the clerk at the grocery store has no more understanding of the device that reads the bar codes on products than the person who buys the product. We are concerned here with what would be comparable to the person who buys the product, not with the clerk. In the case of the human services, it is often true that the consumer of services has a different relationship to the product than the person at the grocery store. The choice of the grocery store buyer is often between and among products that vary widely in price, quality, or offering. The consumer of a public service has a choice to accept an available service or to refuse it. This type of choice is certainly a forced one. It is also true that often human service consumers are unaware of alternative services, some of the information about which may actually be hidden from them in a rather deliberate manner; or, in other cases, they may be punished for advocating changes in service type, quality, or quantity. In most countries the consumer of human services may also be a member of the organization which serves them. The Boy Scout is a member of the scouts as much as the elderly person is a member of the local recreation centre; the Gypsy is a much a citizen as the welfare recipient, or as the business person.

This Chapter deals with the human service consumer on four different levels. The Epstein paper begins by looking at the human service consumer in terms generally accepted to apply to any consumer. Joyce Epstein uses a list of general characteristics which should apply to analysing any good consumer oriented service, and adapts them to an analysis of the situation of the consumer of human services who has been subjected to some degree of computerization. She finds, in a collection of studies in different countries, that computerization has meant less sensitivity to consumer problems, and recommends that public sector service providers acknowledge and implement the special responsibility they have to take the lead in experimenting with effective consumer oriented services.

Evelyn Blennerhasset follows with a report on the specific findings of a study conducted for the European Foundation for the Improvement of Living and Working Conditions. The study looked at the effects of the introduction of information technologies on the quality of service in eight different European countries. The findings indicate that while innovation has occurred, public agencies have taken a fairly conservative and narrow view of the use of information technology, one that serves the bureaucracy, not the consumer. An astonishing finding is the cavalier attitude toward access to public data banks taken by major public organizations in different countries. The problems of individuality in service determination make up another signifi- cant point, particularly in the example of a job placement service that cannot accommodate specific skill and location preferences.

Kate Howey's study of factors affecting the access to work aids focuses the effects evident in the larger studies upon a specific population, those with physical disabilities. While her study found that the physically disabled as a consumer group are more technically qualified and interested than other population groups, and that devices, experts, and help exist, there is no organizational structure, public or private, which sets out to further development, assist in job placement and retention, or to enable the co-ordination required to make employment a reasonable goal. Social attitudes toward disability are viewed by the disabled themselves as the biggest problem that they face.

The final paper of this chapter looks at the family as the consumer of information technologies. The author, Alain Anciaux, speaks in an engaging and creative manner of his experiences as a social worker/video technician in French-speaking Belgium. Taking a family viewpoint, the author looks at the consequences of information technology consumption upon family life. He discusses thirteen effects, ranging from unwilling togetherness to unwilling isolation. As he argues, the conception of the family as a consumer of information technology clarifies the power of a consumer approach: not only are social service recipients, the public, and the disabled disenfranchised consumer groups, as the first three papers cogently argue, but more powerful and widespread effects can be specified when the family is examined in the same manner.

INFORMATION SYSTEMS AND THE CONSUMER

Joyce Epstein

The purpose of this paper is to look at information technology applications solely from the point of view of the end user – the client, customer, patient, applicant, consumer, member of the public – whatever it is that different agencies care to call that person for whom the whole structure of human services is presumably to aid.

ISSUES FOR CONSUMERS

What do people want out of a public service? That is, of course, a very large question over which there is some considerable public debate, both professionally and politically. But it is possible to produce a fairly uncontroversial list of general characteristics of a good consumer-orientated service, simply as a broad, generally-acceptable framework for discussion. The list would include:

> speed
> access
> accuracy
> reliability
> comprehensiveness
> choice
> comprehensibility
> good relations with staff
> privacy

The service should be available when and where people need it, and should be delivered in a timely fashion. A service that comes after great delay, or takes place too far away to get to easily, or that is available 9 to 5 but the client can only get there after work at 6, is not a good service from the consumer point of view. It should be correct (wherever that term is relevant – for example in giving out advice, or paying out cash benefits). It should be reliable, always there when you need it. It should be comprehensive. That is, it should recognise that real people's needs do not come in conveniently discrete administrative categories, but are experienced as an unpleasant 'whole', and it is the whole person that needs service. There ought to be some real choice for the consumer. That is one of the major cornerstones of consumerism. Too often, consumer choice in the public social services means 'take it or leave it'. But there should be at least some areas where people can choose the type of service that they feel they want. People must be able to understand the service, know what it consists of and what it can do for them. The service should be provided in a user-friendly manner. A service that is fast, convenient, clear, but that is delivered in a way that is, at best, impersonal, and at worst, downright rude, is not usually what people prefer. Clients may also prefer the service to be delivered with some privacy and to know that personal details about them will be secure. With that kind of consumer perspective in mind, let us turn to information technology. Has the introduction of computers been beneficial for public services, from the customers' point of view?

Speed

In many instances, clients are now served much more quickly in government agencies where an on-line benefit inquiry service has been introduced. Procedures that might have taken days before, can now be completed in seconds, and of course that is good for the client. But that is not the whole picture. Computerisation unquestionably speeds technical process, but its introduction does not always speed service. The distinction is an important one to bear in mind, from the point of view of the consumer.

A good example is to be found in a local authority in West Germany where the rent allowance department was computerised. The technical process of assessing claims took only seconds to complete. But because of the way the technology was applied, with only twice-monthly batch processing of applications, claimants still had to wait six weeks to hear the results of a claim. A researcher who evaluated the German project from the client viewpoint, about two years ago, noted with supreme understatement: "Such a long delay seems unacceptable . . . nor can it be considered at all 'sensitive' to the need of the citizen . . . ".

There is also some irony in this particular case, because while the counter clerk takes the claimant's details on the application form for batch processing, he could say with some accuracy whether or not the person would be entitled to an allowance and at least the approximate amount of it. In fact, the researcher noted it would be simple for the clerk to calculate the amount exactly, on the spot. Instead, the calculation is done by central computer, and the client ends up with a 6-week wait. Information technology can equal delay, not speed.

But even where service is faster, that does not always make it better. In the UK Employment Service, a job vacancy can now, thanks to computers, be advertised within 30 minutes of its availability, instead of the previous one hour. Since the increased speed has been accompanied by disadvantages as well, such as reduction in the amount of information about vacancies, and reduced staff support services, we may well question the consumer value of a 30-minute gain in finding out about a vacancy.

Access

It has to be noted, from the start, that the best, certainly the most major, application of information technology to improve consumer access to services comes in the private sector, not public social services, and that is: cash machines in banks. Or, more properly, *outside* of banks. They have improved customer access to bank services enormously, and so have been taken up very readily by the vast majority of bank customers. These computers have, as the former director of the UK National Consumer Council put it, relieved the consumer of "the twin tyrannies of time and place". People can use the service whenever it suits them and regardless of the status of the bank building - i.e. open or closed.

There is no equivalent, so far, on that grand a scale, in the field of public sector human services. A few - a very few - government agencies are just beginning to experiment, on a small scale, and in isolated instances, with placing computer terminals in the foyers of public buildings and in shopping centres, railroad stations and so on, that people can use on their own to get service - for example to find out what vocational training courses are available, or to get job leads. But such instances of improved direct access, so that clients can get to services on their own, are still very limited in the public sector.

Information technology is improving another form of access. A London local authority, for example, has just started a mobile office scheme that, with on-line terminals in a fleet of vans, brings all of the Council's services down to neighbourhood level; and of course the more usual form of decentralisation of local authority services is often accompanied by - supported by - a network of on-line terminals to make city hall services somewhat more accessible to consumers. But these decentralisation and mobile schemes still do not do the equivalent of what the cash machines do - and that is improve consumer access to services by eliminating the necessity for an intermediary - in the case of banks, the bank teller. They do not improve *direct* access, relieved of those 'twin tyrannies of time and place'. The paper will return to this issue later, in describing a major public sector technology experiment that took place in the UK.

Accuracy

"The only opportunities pensioners have had of detecting changes resulting from computerisation have been the incorrect payments . . . ". This rather negative finding, in relation to social services in Denmark, represents an important and recurrent theme. So-called 'computer error' is a continuing problem, for the consumer. A review of a number of studies shows that it is not, contrary to popular belief, limited only to the earlier stages of the introduction of information technology; it persists throughout. In part this is because 'computer error' is usually no such thing. 'Computer errors' are usually human errors, made by people who design, program, or use computers. And even in cases where errors are fewer after the introduction of new technology, the significant factor is that they are certainly more difficult to prove, trace, and correct, than the old-fashioned kind of errors. For example, misspelling a name in some public sector agencies can make it impossible to retrieve the client's record in a computerised file, whereas with the old card indexes, you just thumbed through it and found it eventually.

It should be made very clear at this point that speaking from the point of view of consumers does not mean calling for a return to a pre-computer era. It does mean, though, that service providers – professional and counter staff – must be sensitive to the extreme frustration, anger and injustice that can be suffered by consumer victims of computer error, when that error can be so difficult to identify. In the example given, about misspelled names, in fact, computers can be programmed to accept approximate spellings as well; technology can and will no doubt change. Staff sensitivity to client/victims of computer error must, however, be developed.

One final thing about the 'new generation' of computer mistakes that are so difficult to pinpoint: research has found that the persistent problem of computer error tends to mitigate the one great computer advantage to consumers of speed. A number of studies of public sector service computerisation projects have had to conclude that the work simply could not be speeded up due to the frequent errors.

Reliability

There are few instances of service computerisation that are not plagued, to a greater or lesser degree, by 'system downtime'. It always happens and yet it always seems to come as a surprise. That is, no systematic preparations are made in advance for servicing the consumer to meet those inevitable occasions when the computer is down. The problems created can be merely annoying or inconvenient. For example, in one public agency (an employment service that was examined in a research project) the computer is down *at least* twice a week, every week. And what happens when the computer is down? Clients are told to come back another day. Is that an alternative back-up: "Come back some other time"?

Computer breakdown can have more than mere nuisance value. Computerised monitoring equipment can fail in hospital intensive care units. The effect is, as described by one Dutch nurse, " . . . dreadful. The alarm kept on going and it spat out paper. It howled along the whole corridor and people are fully aware that when it howls something is really wrong . . . it's very stressful, hectic and confusing". The point is, as a review of hospital computerisation showed, that it's not rare. It's a frequent, recurring problem. That particular review of hospital use of information technology made the point that it is in fact the unreliability of the equipment that solves another potential problem: that nurses could become de-skilled by its use. De-skilling is unlikely to happen because the equipment breaks down so often. This is perhaps a gain of doubtful value, in view of the patient stress caused by breakdown.

Comprehensiveness

Computers can handle instructions for a great many different operations and can therefore make available to consumers more comprehensive services. There is certainly evidence that this is beginning to happen. Information technology has enabled a wider range of existing services to be made easily available very often under one roof, and there is increasing interest, and development, in the approach to service delivery coming to be known as the 'one-stop shop'.

Staff access to a greater range of information through computerised programmes is beginning to eradicate the old divisions of service that were based on real administrative needs but had little relevance for consumers, and could make dealings with authorities a nightmare from the consumer point of view. Information technology is erasing those old demarcations and introducing greater flexibility of job content which means that, at least in theory, and increasingly in practice, every member of staff in an authority can do any of the authority's work. At the 'One-Stop Shop' in London's Westminster Council, people can renew their residents' parking permit, apply for housing benefits, pay their rates, enquire about parks facilities, and so on, all in one spot. This is proving very popular with the consumer; and the Council has been receiving interested visiting officials from all over the world, from as far afield as Japan, to see how it works and whether the idea could be adapted in their own authorities. The range of services that can now be offered in one place is very wide, potentially creating whole new living patterns. In Sweden, what are called 'telecentres' are being developed that can provide neighbourhood services to cater to practically every need, from library services to electronic voting.

But what is so far not being developed very much at all is the capacity of information technology to co-ordinate services for consumers *across* authority boundaries. Unemployed people, for example, need services not only from employment departments. Unemployment usually brings with it a whole range of problems – in health, housing, social security, family stress, maybe even legal problems. Each of these is usually dealt with by separate statutory authorities as well as by a variety of voluntary agencies. Computers could ease the way to shared information about needs and to joint planning. There is very little evidence that that is happening. We all know the difficulties of such a co-ordinated approach to service provision. Here in Birmingham, an inter-agency mental handicap register is being developed to promote co-ordination of services across the health authority, social services, education, and a voluntary agency. The project is reported to be still in its developmental stages.

Choice

Computers' increased capacity to handle more bits of information at once should enable a greater choice of service to be offered to consumers as well as more comprehensive services. Services should be able to handle and keep track of more options and provide more individualised service. But this does not appear to be happening to any significant extent. There are what appear to be exceptions, of course. In Ireland, information technology has meant that housing allocation processes can now keep track of clients' first, second and third neighbourhood preferences, whereas the previous manual system allowed clients to state only one preference.

In general, though, just the opposite of greater individual choice seems to be happening. Computer programmes may be forcing a process of increasing standardisation in which people who do not fit the standard pattern dictated by the computer package are not well served. This is happening, it is perhaps interesting to point out, in many aspects of the commercial sector, as well as public sector services. For example, in the insurance industry it is more and more the case that packaged programmes do an injustice to the individual nature of claims. Claims settlements are coming to depend on the software, and not the other way round. And in the public services we see the same thing happening. For example, in Denmark, computerisation of the job placement service meant that all clients had to be placed in predetermined categories according to work experience and job aspirations; job seekers who could not conform to the computer's categories were placed at a disadvantage.

The point to bear in mind is that what is being standardised is always technically capable of being more varied. The capacity of new technology to provide more individual choice of services, rather than more anodyne, standard packages, already exists, but it has not been in the interests of service providers to exploit this capacity. This paper will return to this theme later.

Comprehensibility

Official communications from government to consumers have always been a problem – at times even a joke. But with computers, the situation seems to have got even worse. The problem lies in the failure to adapt computer information to human consumption. And sometimes these failures can be quite horrific reflecting an amazing lack of sensitivity to the client. In the Netherlands, after computerisation in one welfare agency, explanations about benefit were sent out in computer code, rather than words, with no key provided as to what the code meant. In Germany, suddenly much more information could be made available to applicants for benefit; and so it all was. The result was that claimants got *ten* pages of precise and very accurate information, but had no idea which was the crucial bit of information telling them how much money they would get.

Good Relations with Staff

Information technology eliminates the need for workers to perform many of the time-consuming repetitive tasks that used to be part of their work. The theory is that this removal of drudgery will enable staff to spend more time, and more 'quality' time, in direct client services and develop better staff/client relations. This almost never proves to be so. Freed staff time is disposed of in entirely different ways, which this paper will deal with later, and relieving staff of tedious work is not being used in any way to promote more customer-orientated services.

The DHSS and Department of Employment spent several years and many millions of pounds on their Terminal Replacement and

Enquiry Service, and it provides, through an on-line network, an evidently efficient and much faster service for the public. In 1987, a customer satisfaction survey found that many claimants remain unhappy with their treatment. We must never forget that counter clerks can treat claimants just as badly whether they have a keyboard in front of them or a paper file. Technology does not automatically make things better, and it should not be assumed that it does.

Privacy

This is a very important area, with potentially high significance for consumers. That is why virtually every state has passed data protection legislation, but unfortunately civil servants and other public employees have at best only very limited knowledge of the relevant regulations. At worst, staff attitudes were characterised by a German researcher in this way: " . . . data protection is considered to be an irritating obstacle to 'orderly' staff administration".

* * * *

Having gone through the consumer issues to see how information technology fits in, some general comments are now in order.

The reasons why service organisations are bringing in computers are related to strategic considerations that have little to do with the consumer. They do not even, in many fields, have much to do with concern to exploit technical potential. They are to do mainly with greater control – over operations and decision-making – in order to maximise efficiency. It is important to emphasise that technology is itself not a cause of rationalisation. It is a tool that has enabled management to achieve already determined goals. Technology is deeply implicated in the need to rationalise, and to cut costs and improve productivity, and it acts to facilitate these management goals.

One of the more obvious ways in which this issue is manifest is in the failure to transform freed resources – created by computers doing a lot of the drudgery – into resources to provide more intensive personal service to the public. Rather the immediate reaction is to cut back on staff. Authorities are under pressure to make savings by rationalisation. In almost every instance in fact the freed time is used to limit the costs of service, not to improve the service. It could have been the means of providing a more supportive service.

The capacity for new technology to bring about positive change in what is offered to the public is being developed hardly at all. The way in which ordinary consumers are affected by the introduction of new technology and what technology should be introduced is rarely, if ever, taken into account. Decisions are in effect impervious to the feelings and views of clients, because client responses do not usually feed through into executive action until after the technology is installed, if at all, and there is then little opportunity of going back. The systems in use are designed, planned and implemented by technicians charged with promoting rationalisation and control. Improvement in consumer service is rarely on the agenda.

The consequences of the introduction of new technology into service organisations are rarely simple and clear-cut. Every technological advance has both advantages and disadvantages for the consumer of services. There is not enough consideration of how change will affect consumers. It is probable that changes that have both advantages and disadvantages for consumers may have good reasons for coming anyway and so will come. The options may refer, not to whether consumers want to have this new technology or not; the options may be, rather, largely reactive: the technology must come, but how should decision-makers respond in order to cushion the disruptive effects? Two points are crucial.

1   The power of the computer must be brought to bear much more directly on the interests of consumers, not management. The public services are there to serve the public, not to provide a stage for efficient bureaucracies. Efficient bureaucracies are merely an intermediate goal to an end purpose, serving the customer.

2   Whatever technology is introduced, for consumer or management purposes, it must be carefully evaluated to see whether that end purpose *is* well served, i.e. what actually happens to client services.

For example, recent developments in the field of new technology raised the possibility of bringing the advantages of computerisation to bear on the problems of benefit information. In the past few years, systems have been developed which provide professional staff access to accurate information on a comprehensive range of their clients' personal entitlements; which provide public access to general factual information about benefits (e.g. Prestel); or which provide public access to personal entitlement information in a single benefit area.

THE SURREY BENEFIT INFORMATION SYSTEM

One system combined all the above features: direct public access to information on a comprehensive range of personalised entitlements. Developed at Surrey University in 1980, this system permitted people to get accurate information on their own entitlement from among a wide range of benefits, without having to approach an agency, without having to wait to be seen, and without having to divulge personal, embarrassing information to staff.

Between September 1982 and September 1983, the DHSS installed nine experimental micro-computers in various locations throughout Britain. These computers – in two local offices of the DHSS, two Unemployment Benefit Offices (UBs), two Citizens' Advice Bureaux (CABx), a Social Services Department (SSD), a Neighbourhood

Centre, and a Hypermarket – were programmed to enable members of the general public to find out, by themselves, exactly which of a range of national and local non-contributory benefits they personally were entitled to, how much money they could get, and how to claim.

The computers were set up in public areas – usually the waiting room, or other public reception area – of these sites. Anybody who wished to could go up on their own, bypassing the agency and its staff, and use the computer to find out their entitlement. The DHSS issued no specific instructions to the sites as to how they should or should not make use of the computers. In essence, the nature of the project was to install the computers and see what happened, both in terms of the public and staff. The computer program was designed so as to require no prior training to operate it. Approximately the first five to ten minutes of the program was devoted to explaining how to operate the machine, giving people practice at making entries, correcting mistakes, and so on. A message, permanently flashed on the video display unit when the computer was not in use, stated:

25 minutes to spare?
Find out if you can claim
Supplementary Benefit * Rate Rebate * Free School Meals
and many more

To find out how to get information on these and other benefits
just press the button marked START

When START was pressed the program displayed a series of questions about the person's economic circumstances, family status, living arrangements – basically imitating an ordinary DHSS assessment interview – which the machine user answered by pressing the relevant keys on a specially adapted alphabetical keyboard, usually the YES or NO key or some number or amount. People could operate the program at their own pace. Only when the user pressed the NEXT button did a new screen of instructions or questions appear.

At the end of the series of questions the machine calculated the entitlement and the person was then told, on the screen, what their entitlement was and how to claim. A print-out of the information was also produced, so that the machine user could take it home with him or her. Users were informed that none of the information they fed in was retained by the computer.

The Research Institute for Consumer Affairs (RICA) was commissioned by the DHSS to evaluate the experiment. The aims of the research were to assess the computer experiment in terms of the reaction of users and of the agencies in which the computers were placed, and to assess its potential as a public service. Details of the research methodology are given in a published report available from RICA, and this paper will not go into that, except to say that about 400 computer users were interviewed, as well as 60 staff members at the various agencies.

The results were very interesting. It turned out, contrary to many predictions, that all kinds of people tried the computer – young and old, male and female. Computer users were not a middle class elite either: the vast majority were working class people in difficult economic circumstances, with no higher education, no previous experience with computers and, usually, no job. And they liked using the computer; more than merely 'liked' it – they came away from the computer positively euphoric. Here are a few representative quotes:

"Super, easy as pie. First time we used one. No problems at all."

"Interesting, enjoyable. I've never used a computer before and I really enjoyed it."

"I think it's great. I just think it's good to find out your rights. You can do it yourself. It gives you the feeling you're doing something."

"Very good. If I can use it, anybody can. I phoned up twice and all I got was a load of abuse . . ."

"It was good. I found out something I hadn't known about."

The research then went into details of people's experience of using the computers – what difficulties they experienced, how they compared it with other ways of getting information (e.g. leaflets, asking at the welfare agency, asking voluntary advice workers, and so on), and of course whether they found out anything useful, by using the computer.

The results were uniformly positive. Most people experienced no difficulty using the computer and did not need or ask for any staff help. (It should be noted that the project had been several years in development, with a fairly substantial pilot period, to produce a system that would be easy to use – it was very carefully developed with the end user in mind.) People much preferred using the computer to any other way they had ever tried to get information about benefits. The results were not marginal, either, but rather very striking.

Assessment of Computer Compared to Other Means of Getting Information

	DHSS	Leaflet	UBO	CAB	Friend/ relation	Soc. Serv./ Council
	%	%	%	%	%	%
Computer is:						
better	85	83	76	61	91	58
worse	6	7	10	9	3	28
not sure	9	9	10	27	6	14

The reasons for preferring the computer included: easier to understand exactly what was coming to them; enabled people to have access to the information, while avoiding disliked agency staff, or avoiding bothering busy staff members; it gave them confidence they were getting accurate, reliable information; and they liked the speed of service.

This last is interesting. The computer was preferred to the agency because it was faster. In the staff interviews most of the office managers cited the length of time required at the computer as being its main drawback. They expressed incredulity that anyone would want to sit at the computer for as long as half-an-hour to get information. While there is little doubt that staff could do an assessment in less than 30 minutes, the managers evidently discount the two hours people told us they have to wait until they can be seen by a member of staff. So the computer does provide faster service.

There is another important point. Many of the people who used the computer *had* tried other ways of getting information, and had some basis for comparison, which has already been described. But quite a large proportion of computer users – about 40% – said they had never approached a person, a welfare worker, to find out if they were entitled to anything. And why not? Because they could not bear the thought of divulging what they regarded as embarrassing details about their life to another person, whereas they evidently felt quite comfortable 'asking' a computer. This was especially true of older people and of women, the very groups that many claim prefer personal service and shun or fear computers. The computer expanded the service choices available to consumers.

The bottom line though is, however much they preferred the computer, was it effective, i.e., did it improve information for clients? The answer is yes. The research went into some fairly detailed analysis of who found out what sort of information, but here let us look at just one important finding. Almost a third of people who used the computer for some specific reason found out that they may be entitled to a totally separate benefit that they hadn't even been enquiring about. This is very important because of what emerged in the staff interviews. It was common for staff at all agencies to say that when clients came in with a question, it was easier and faster simply to give them a direct answer to that question, rather than going through a half-hour session with the computer (or making the client go through a half-hour session with the computer). The research shows that allowing the client to define the information needed can mean, in a significant proportion of cases, that benefit may be lost. The computer is much more thorough, and therefore improved the service people got.

Overall, nearly two-thirds of computer users found they were entitled to something they were not receiving; and of those, one month later, half had actually followed through by filing a claim, of which nearly all were successful.

So, from the consumer point of view, the computers were a pretty good thing: they liked it, found it easy and enjoyable to use, it improved their access to service and they derived financial gain from it. But what about staff perception, social workers in particular?

They hated it. Perhaps hate is too strong a word. They actively ignored it. One was asked if she had ever tried the computer. There's an expensive piece of relevant machinery two minutes away from her office. Have you ever been at all interested in trying it? This was her response:

" . . . never . . . I wouldn't use the machine. I have never used it. I never would. I don't like it. I've never seen how it works."

Here is another social worker's comments. This one has also never tried it, but was more apologetic:

"I feel terribly guilty. Often felt I should do it for my mother, but never did."

Here are a few more:

"My clients are mostly on benefit and getting all they're entitled to anyway. I am aware of what needs to be done . . ."

"There's no need to use the machine . . . I feel I can assess social security needs and entitlement."

The interesting thing here is, when we talked to the clients, the very reason why they said, specifically, they preferred the computer to the social worker was that they felt social workers give unreliable, inaccurate information, a view which clearly does not accord with the view of social workers themselves. And I'm afraid the facts bear out the client view. People seen by social workers *don't* have the information they need, and found out things that were new to them after trying the machine.

Here's another social worker, on why he hasn't used the machine:

"I haven't come across an appropriate case (for the computer). Clients need a mediator . . . a lot of personal help."

In all the clients this social worker saw he didn't find any of them 'appropriate'. But all kinds of people considered *themselves* appropriate. "Clients need a mediator" - yes, sometimes. But it's a matter of choice. Nobody is saying computers instead of social workers. But computers and a whole lot more can be on offer in delivering services, to meet a range of consumer needs. Some people do not want to talk to a staff member.

This was fairly common too:

"People don't like using machines . . . most of our clients aren't the brightest."

* * * *

In conclusion, then, service organisations should devote more research and development resources to experimentation with other than administrative record-keeping applications of technology. There is a special onus on public sector service providers who, as public servants, ought to be taking the lead in experimenting with technology to provide effective client services.

Even if the goal is exclusively efficiency, organisational efficiency and consumer effectiveness are not necessarily mutually exclusive. Technology can be implemented in ways that are more sensitive, than we have so far seen, to consumer considerations. But in order to do that decision-makers must first be made more aware of the need to aim both for efficiency and effectiveness. There needs to be more empirical research on the implications of computerisation from the end user point of view. Technological change must be monitored and assessed, so that assumptions about effects on consumers can be tested.

CONSUMERS, COMPUTERS AND THE PUBLIC SERVICE:
AN OVERVIEW OF EUROPEAN TRENDS

Evelyn Blennerhassett

(The views expressed in this paper are those of the author, and not necessarily those of the Institute of Public Administration, Dublin, Ireland.)

INTRODUCTION

This paper is based on the findings of a cross-national research study commissioned by the European Foundation for the Improvement of Living and Working Conditions. The study was undertaken in 1984 and looked at the effects of technology on the quality of service rendered to the public in eight countries of the European Community: Belgium, Denmark, France, Germany, Ireland, Luxembourg, the Netherlands, and the United Kingdom. Each country undertook a small number of in-depth case studies of technological change, principally in the areas of social security, employment services, and population registration. (A list of the case studies undertaken in each country is given at the end of this paper. The consolidated report and the individual nation reports were published in 1986 by the Office for Official Publications of the European Communities, Luxembourg, as "New Technology in the Public Service".)

The research findings should be viewed as indicative rather than conclusive for two reasons: (i) major areas of public sector activity (e.g. health, education, public utilities) were not covered; and (ii) the technological picture is dynamic, not static – consequently, research studies become quickly out-of-date. In this regard, we are conscious that the main emphasis in the case studies is on traditional data processing applications, that is, on the processing of large volumes of routine data. These types of applications are currently the most important in the public service computerisation portfolios of all countries. In future years, however, other types of applications are likely to be of more interest, e.g. office automation and new IT-based services to the public.

IMPACT OF TECHNOLOGY ON SERVICE TO THE CONSUMER: SUMMARY OF MAIN FINDINGS

In almost all of the case studies, computerisation had *only marginal effects on the quality and kind of service provided to the client population.* However, this statement masks the fact that some significant changes did take place, particularly in the field of social security. It must also be borne in mind that some of these so-called marginal changes may have long-term consequences, the character of which is only beginning to emerge. Basically, two kinds of changes accompanied the process of computerisation: (a) the obvious, viz. changes which were immediately visible and apparent to both employees and clients of the public service; and (b) the subtle, viz. changes which were not immediately apparent to individual clients who had only intermittent contact with the particular public service, but which were apparent to staff who work constantly with the system.

Obvious Changes

The most frequently encountered 'obvious' changes in client service were:

> changes in methods of payment
> changes in speed of payment or service
> changes in frequency of personal attendance at public offices.

Most of these obvious changes related to social security payments rather than to personal social services such as employment or population registration services. The changes brought about by computerisation in these latter areas tended to be more subtle and less immediately observable.

Changes in Methods of Payment

In most of the case studies involving financial compensation, there was a distinct trend for computerisation of the administrative process to be accompanied by a change in payment method. Cash payments were being phased out and replaced by electronic funds transfer (EFT) and/or computerised cheque payment. This development was welcomed by the majority of social security claimants. However, it created some difficulties in some situations. For example, in Luxembourg, the withdrawal of the cash payment option in relation to reimbursement of medical expenses has increased the average waiting period for insured persons from 8 to 15 days (over 21 days, if the person fails to give the correct registration number in the first place). To the extent that this longer waiting period creates cash flow problems for individuals (particularly those in the weaker sections of society), computerisation could be said to have disimproved the quality of service. In some countries, the proportion of unemployed persons without personal bank accounts is quite high. These people often experience difficulties in cashing cheques with third parties. Consequently, they preferred the old method of cash payment.

Changes in Speed of Payment or Service

Where payments were regular and unvarying in amount, computerisation generally resulted in faster payment. However, where payments were once-off, or fluctuated from payment period to payment period, there was generally no improvement in speed of payment. At best there was no deterioration, at worst a substantial disimprovement. Differences in the mode of data processing accounted in large part for the differences in speed of payment: batch processing (run once or twice monthly) was the usual method for processing once-off claims or monthly claims; on-line data processing being used for processing regular weekly payments.

Speedier service was also apparent in the non-financial area. For example, most of the case studies on population registration showed a significant improvement in speed of service. In the Netherlands, a passport can be issued by a computerised local authority in 15 minutes. Yet another good example of improved speed of service was given in the British study of employment services, where a high speed national network enables job vacancies notified to one local office to be on public display in another local office on the regional network within 15-30 minutes (an improvement of 15 minutes on the previous norm) and in non-local offices nationally within one hour (previously up to two days by post).

Changes in Frequency of Personal Attendance at Public Offices

There was a definite trend for computerisation in the social security area to be associated with less frequent personal contact between public service organisations and their clients. In some instances, personal contact had been reduced to one initial meeting to establish eligibility; therafter, contact tended to be by letter or telephone. The changeover to non-cash methods of payment was a significant factor in this regard. This change was welcomed by the majority of unemployed persons, many of whom found the weekly or fortnightly ritual of signing on and queueing in overcrowded public offices personally humiliating and inconvenient. They preferred the anonymity of postal or electronic payment.

Although face-to-face contact tended to be lower, the frequency of telephone and written contact tended to be higher following computerisation, due mainly to claimants' queries and requests for clarification. Forms designed more for data input purposes than easy understanding, the complexity of the rules and regulations governing most social security payments and inadequate explanatory leaflets all contributed to clients' lack of understanding and confusion. Only in a minority of instances could the increase in personal queries be traced directly to inadequacies in the computer system itself, e.g. in relation to the UK housing benefits case study, where lack of integration of accounting systems resulted in clients receiving different amounts of money each week or month or being notified that they owed money when in fact the amount owing would be taken up by the next month's benefit. Slowness in payment (whether perceived or actual) also gave rise to a substantial number of written and, especially, telephone enquiries, creating what the Belgian report called a "vicious circle", viz. delays in payment producing enquiries which take up staff time, thereby delaying payments further.

Subtle Changes

Unlike the obvious effects, which were felt most keenly in the social security field, the subtle effects of technology were experienced in both the financial and personal social services areas. Among the most frequently mentioned of these less apparent but nonetheless real effects were:

> Faster information/enquiry service for the majority of clients
> Poorer quality service to 'non-routine' clients
> More formalised, business-like service
> Greater equitability of treatment
> Difficulty in tracing and correcting errors in records
> Difficulty in understanding forms.

Faster Information/Enquiry Service for the Majority of Clients

Where the computer system was on-line, introduction of technology always resulted in a faster information service to clients. Although the volume of queries usually increased substantially following computerisation, in most cases so had the organisation's ability to cope. The case studies indicate, however, that few individual clients are aware of the improvements in information services. In some instances, the only visible evidence of computerisation to the general public was a change in the type of form they received or had to complete. Even then, they were scarcely aware that the service had been computerised. The extent to which the existence of computer systems is made public varied from country to country. In Ireland, for example, enquiry screens and other pieces of computer equipment are not placed in full public view. In Denmark, which has more of a 'computer culture', the public is accustomed to computer systems and employment service counsellors are in the habit of showing job-seekers, willingly and often without being asked, the information that they encode about them.

Poorer Quality Service to 'Non-routine' Clients

In all case studies, the majority of clients were relatively satisfied with the quality of service, although few had noticed any visible improvement following the introduction of technology. Where a deterioration in quality of service was detected, it was generally in relation to non-routine cases or applicants. Compartmentalisation of the work and job fragmentation (whereby employees are familiar with only aspects of the administrative procedure or regulations governing the particular public service) rather than technological factors, were the main reasons for the inability of the staff to handle non-routine enquiries or to give full explanations to clients. The Danish case study on employment services illustrates how computer systems can, inadvertently, disadvantage some types of client. In this study, the person-job matching system requires a precise description of the type of job sought by the job-seeker. Thus it was not enough for a person to say that he was "interested in any kind of job";

areas of interest had to be defined exactly in accordance with a
pre-coded reference system. This preciseness worried some
job-seekers, who felt that their chances of employment were
affected adversely by being 'pigeon-holed in a certain occupational category'.

More Formalised, Business-like Service

Less frequent personal contact, combined with an increase in the
speed of service, affected the quality of service in that contacts
became "briefer and more business-like although not unfriendly"
(Dutch report). This greater efficiency was usually appreciated
by the public. There was no indication in the reports that staff
were less personally helpful following computerisation. In many
instances they shielded clients from the vagaries of the computer
system, e.g. by preparing cheques manually during systems
breakdown and by helping clients complete computer-coded forms.

Greater Equitability of Treatment

Computerisation did not affect equitability of treatment in the
social security field, where eligibility is governed by statutory
rules and regulations. In the personal social services area, the
evidence from the national reports is conflicting. In the Danish
employment services, as noted previously, there was some
indication that computerisation had disadvantaged certain categories of job-seekers. However, in the UK study of employment
services, the opposite was the case. Computerisation had
improved equity of treatment in that job vacancies were now
displayed almost simultaneously in all offices in a district or
region, thereby giving each job-seeker 'an equal bite of the
cherry'. This development was welcomed particularly by those
advising disabled job-seekers; they felt that their clients had a
better chance of getting a job, the quicker they heard about the
job vacancy. Jobs which were filled were also cancelled more
quickly, thus lessening the frustration of unsuccessful job-
seekers.

Difficulty in Tracing and Correcting Errors in Records

As long as information is input correctly, computerised records
are generally accepted as being more reliable than manually-kept
files. Difficulties arise, however, when data is input incorrectly.
For example in the German case study on population registration,
one employee stated: "If you mis-spell a name, you might never
find it again in the system; when we had paper files and
microfiche, you leafed through and found it eventually". In the
Netherlands case study on social assistance, more than 50% of
clients interviewed claimed that they had come across mistakes in
their dealings with the social services. Of these, about a
quarter said they had experienced difficulty in having the errors
corrected - a time lag of up to several months was not
exceptional. A similar picture emerged in the Netherlands case
study on population registration. Although such precise data
were not given in any of the other national reports, these

findings indicate that errors in coding and data input may be more frequent than realised or admitted.

Difficulty in Understanding Forms

Regarding forms, the German study echoes the sentiment implied in many other reports: "The whole notion of forms has always been a lamentable chapter in the public service". With computerisation, the situation seems to have deteriorated – especially in the social security area where clients have difficulty completing very comprehensive forms or understanding the details given on payment slips (Netherlands, Denmark, Ireland, UK, Germany). In the German rent allowance case study, the comment is made that the wealth of detail contained in forms is really for the benefit of the administration: it shows staff in the local office exactly how the amount to be paid was derived.

The important role played by public service employees in determining the extent and nature of 'computer impact' on client service was identified clearly in the Danish report:

"It is not possible to isolate the relationship between the EDP system and clients without taking the staff into consideration as a kind of intermediate variable . . . We are in no doubt that it is the employees and their behaviour who determine primarily the nature of the service given to the general public and, therefore, the public's attitude towards the EDP system."

Employees are seen as an important *buffer* between the technology and the client system, e.g. shielding clients from the effects of a system breakdown by writing out cheques manually, helping individuals understand and complete forms, and so on.

BROADER SOCIAL ISSUES

In addition to the client service changes, both positive and negative, that arose in relation to particular public services, three issues of broader social concern are highlighted by the research:

Data protection and privacy
Technology as a mechanism of social control
Low priority being given currently to client service issues in computerisation of the public services.

Data Protection and Privacy

The importance of placing information technology in its proper political and social context was very evident in the treatment of data protection and privacy issues in the various national reports. The problem is seen with different degrees of urgency in different countries. The most stringent laws exist in Germany and Denmark. In Belgium, rules have been drawn up in relation to the use of the National Register and a general law on individual privacy is anticipated. In the Netherlands, the situation is less advanced - at best municipalities had created (or were in the process of creating) privacy statutes. Rules of one sort or another also exist in the UK, France, Luxembourg and Ireland.

Public Servants' Lack of Knowledge
and Awareness of Data Protection

It is clear from the various reports that data protection laws alone are not sufficient to safeguard individual rights. Strict organisational controls and administrative measures as well as statutory regulations will be needed, given the relatively low level of awareness among public servants dealing with the public of data protection legislation and the importance of privacy and confidentiality of individual data. The general impression was that there was a certain degree of complacency, born largely out of ignorance, among both public servants and the general public. As stated in the German report: "There is an underdeveloped sensitivity towards data protection on the part of public service organisations". A concrete example of this insensitivity is given in the Dutch case study of a computerised social assistance system where the computer supplier had direct access to the computer system via a telephone line and a modem, thereby increasing the danger of unlawful access to social security records. To many public service employees, data security means nothing more than having to use a password to access a computer terminal. Even this elementary security precaution becomes trivialised with constant use. Although mentioned explicitly in only one report, the informal use of other colleagues' passwords when one has forgotten one's own probably occurs in most countries.

The case studies indicate that the majority of public servants have little knowledge or interest in the uses to which public data banks are put. This lack of knowledge means that employees are not in a position to advise citizens of their rights. Nor are these rights explicitly set out in the various forms members of the public have to complete. For example, in the German population registration office studied, the only reference to a person's rights in the data protection field was contained in a short note on the back of the form which stated: "These data are collected in accordance with articles 13, 16 and 18 of the Bavarian registration law. The citizen is informed of his/her right to veto" - a cryptic message which was not readily understood by either the public or employees of the office.

The only example of a spontaneous concern and interest in data protection and privacy on the part of public servants was given in the Belgian report. A local authority which had not linked its population register to the National Register when participation was optional now found itself in a position where it was being forced to computerise. Staff in this office were extremely wary of the introduction of information technology. As stated by one respondent: "Who knows where technology will stop?" Among their concerns were: (a) What information will appear on the new identity card? Would it be possible to have a secret code showing an individual's political tendencies? (b) Would not the nine items of information currently demanded grow to 15 or 20 tomorrow? (c) Was it in the national interest to have details of the whole population available in a readily accessible form? *There would have been no need for informers if a National Register had existed during the Second World War.*

Technology as a Mechanism for Social Control

Concern about the linking up of social, regional and national databases was mentioned in several reports (Belgium, Denmark, Germany, Luxembourg, Netherlands). The most serious reservations were expressed in the German report. The researchers express concern about: (a) possible violation and abuse of individuals' democratic rights inherent in the trend towards the creation and amalgamation of databases containing a vast amount of information on individuals; and (b) the use of technology as a social control mechanism, e.g. to disclose abuses of the social security system by cross-checking taxation records with social security records. The Danish report indicates that the use of technology to detect social crime in this way is not permitted.

The German researchers are particularly sceptical about the adequacy of data protection laws in controlling the use of advanced technologies in the public service – especially in a climate where public bodies are being forced to rationalise and reduce expenditures. Current data processing arrangements are also cited as a factor contributing towards the "erosion of presently valid data protection law". In a situation where data are processed centrally but stored locally, responsibility is "blurred and deferred". Whether the increased use of advanced information technologies in the public sector will or will not lead to greater state control of the individual citizen is a matter for speculation. The Luxembourg report strikes an optimistic note: "Security and protection of computer data does not appear to constitute a problem: there is a law guaranteeing protection and there appears to be no doubt that it is strictly applied". By way of contrast, the German report expresses a pessimistic view, indicating cause for concern.

Impact on Client Service: A Secondary Consideration?

An issue of social concern arising from the research is the relatively low priority being given currently to client service aspects of computerisation in the public service, both at the level of service to the individual and at a more macro, national level. It is clear from the case studies that computerisation is viewed in all countries primarily as a means of cutting costs and increasing administrative efficiency. The main objective is to reduce administrative costs (usually labour costs) associated with providing existing services rather than to create new services or improve current services in any fundamental way. Social and client service considerations seem, at best, to be of secondary importance in the decision to computerise. Priority setting as between cost efficiency and client service objectives in computerisation inevitably poses difficulties for decision-makers. Advantages for the citizen may be seen as disproportionate to the running cost of the service. As stated by one German public service manager: "We have to reflect whether we can continue to spend thousands of marks just to save five minutes of the citizen's time".

The financial pressures being experienced by public service organisations everywhere, combined with a rising demand for public services (especially in the social security and health areas), are undoubtedly important factors explaining the current emphasis on computerisation as a tool for rationalising and optimising internal administrative procedures. However, lack of finance only partially explains the relatively low level of attention paid to client service aspects in computerisation projects generally. It is not the total explanation of why client outcomes (both positive and negative) often seem more like by-products of the computerisation process than one of the primary products. Nor does lack of finance adequately explain why changes in client outcomes are as likely to be accidental and unexpected as they are to be planned and deliberate. To some extent at least, these indicators of a lack of sensitivity to and awareness of the importance of client service issues reflect more general structural characteristics of public service organisations, namely, their tendency to be more internally-orientated than externally-orientated.

This concern with the internal workings of the organisation is a characteristic feature of that form of organisation we call 'bureaucratic'. It existed before the advent of computer technology and, in spite of predictions to the contrary, shows little sign as yet of being replaced by alternative ways of organising. To many ears, the following description of the pattern of civil service administration in the UK, made 28 years ago in 1959 by Arnold Tonybee, still has a ring of truth about it today:

> "In the world of civil service, plunging into action is the arch crime. When you sight an objective you must not head straight for it. You must consult a thousand colleagues who have the right to file objections in the names of a hundred other government departments who are great powers, and you must not feel frustrated or guilty when you find yourself bogged down. The civil servant's duty is not to achieve desirable results; it is to follow the correct procedure."

Toynbee's description encapsulates both the spirit and content of what people mean when they complain of public service 'bureaucracy' or 'red-tape'. Complaints about 'bureaucracy' are made not only by citizens and those outside the administrative apparatus, but also by public servants themselves. The victim in Toynbee's scenario above is not a member of the public; it is a well-intentioned, motivated official trying his best to get things done despite the odds against him. Many of the negative effects on client service reported in the various studies can be traced to the hierarchical impersonal bureaucratic form of organisation rather than to faults in computer systems or bad work attitudes of officials.

Indeed, the willingness of public service employees to go out of their way to protect the public from the more negative aspects of bureaucracy, and/or overcome problems associated with computer systems, is stressed in many of the national reports. Although there is an understandable tendency on the part of members of the general public to blame individual public servants for any red-tape, 'buck-passing' or impersonal treatment they encounter (whether computer-related or not), it is important to remember that the bureaucratic mode of operation is an organisational attribute and not an individual personality trait. Bureaucracy has survived (some might say flourished) for decades, despite major changes in the social, economic and political environment. Its demise will not be caused by technology, which cannot of itself force public service organisations to abandon long-established ways of relating to their environment. Technology has not, and cannot, force the public service to become more responsive to client needs. This will only happen when the ideology or set of beliefs underlying the bureaucratic model of organisation is replaced by a different ideology - one which places a greater emphasis and value on innovation, change, results and service to the customer.

CONCLUSION

Information technology is clearly a double-edged sword. It has both liberating and controlling potential, depending on how and for what purpose it is implemented. It may be used to reinforce existing policies and organisational arrangements or it may be used as a vehicle for promoting change, either internal organisational change or external, client service change. While there are some signs of innovation in public service provision (e.g. the movement towards 'self-service' in certain public service areas), in general, public service policy-makers and decision-makers have adopted a conservative and fairly narrow view of the use of information technology.

Technology is seen primarily as a means of maintaining the status quo, of doing an existing job cheaper or faster. It is not often realised that its introduction also offers the opportunity to assess the strengths and weaknesses of existing policies and procedures, to discuss whether the whole area of information processing could or should be approached in quite a different way. Plans and strategies tend to focus on operational technical matters, to the detriment, sometimes exclusion, of policy and client service aspects.

Lack of finance, lack of awareness and knowledge of information technology, and social and political pressures are undoubtedly important factors explaining the relatively low impact of computer systems on the public service to date in most countries. The bureaucratic structure of public service organisations is, however, an equally important factor. It emphasises stability, conformity and impersonality and focuses on the 'how' aspects of doing something rather than the 'what', 'why', or 'whether at all' aspects. As such, it does not marry easily with the concepts of innovation and change implied by the new information technologies.

Whether the public service can continue indefinitely to adapt technology to suit existing practices and procedures is open to question. Most commentators think it unlikely in the long-term. As computerisation becomes more pervasive and public service managers become more skilled and knowledgeable in managing the process of technologically-stimulated organisational change, significant change can be expected in the nature and number of public service jobs, in organisational structures and processes, and in the type and quality of services offered to the public.

LIST OF CASE STUDIES UNDERTAKEN IN EACH PARTICIPATING COUNTRY

BELGIUM

Population Registration

(i) at **national level** via a study of the National Register;

(ii) a **before/after comparison at the local level** of two local authority population registers – one computerised and linked to the National Register; the other a manual system not linked to the National Register.

Occupational Diseases Fund

A national organisation with responsibility for the prevention of occupational diseases and for the payment of industrial compensation to workers with specific occupationally-contracted illnesses.

Research undertaken by the Institute for the Improvement of Working Conditions (Institut pour l'Amelioration des Conditions de Travail).

DENMARK

Employment Services

Computer system for supporting the filling of job vacancies in two local employment offices.

Sickness Benefit

Administration in a large municipality.

Pensions

Administration in a large municipality.

Research undertaken by the Institute for Informatics and Management Accounting, Copenhagen School of Business (Institut for Informatik og Okonomistyring, Handelshojskolen i Kobenhavn).

FRANCE

Unemployment Benefits and Employment Services

The GIDE project: computerisation as an aid to co-operation between agencies in the unemployment/employment field.

Research undertaken by the National Agency for the Improvement of Working Conditions (Agence Nationale pour l'Amelioration des Conditions de Travail).

GERMANY

Rent Allowances

Administration in a local office.

Social Assistance

Administration in a local office.

Population Registration

In a large town.

Research undertaken by the Social Sciences Project Group, Munich (Sozialwissenschaftliche Projektgruppe, Munchen).

IRELAND

Unemployment Assistance

Administration in a local office of a central government department.

Disability/Sickness Benefit

Administration in a central government department.

Allocation of Public Housing

In a large local authority.

Research undertaken by the Institute of Public Administration, Dublin.

LUXEMBOURG

Social Security Administration at national level:

Administration of **family allowances.**
Administration of **sickness benefits.**

Research undertaken by the Centre for the Study of Population, Poverty and Socio-Economic Policies (Centre d'Etudes de Populations, de Pauvreté et de Politiques Socio-économiques).

THE NETHERLANDS

Population Registrations

Comparison of two local population registers: one manual, the other computerised.

Social Assistance

Administration in two municipal offices.

Research undertaken by Delft University of Technology (Technische Hogeschool Delft, Vakgroep Techniek, Arbeid en Organisatie).

UNITED KINGDOM

Employment Services

Computerised vacancy circulation system in two local employment offices: experienced user vs inexperienced user.

Housing Benefits

Administration in two local authorities: contrast of two different computer systems in use.

Research undertaken by the Social Policy Research Unit, University of Sussex and the Innovation Research Group, Brighton Polytechnic.

FACTORS AFFECTING THE USE OF INFORMATION TECHNOLOGY AND COMPUTER SYSTEMS AS WORK AIDS FOR THE PHYSICALLY DISABLED

K R Howey

INTRODUCTION

This paper outlines some of the research findings of a one year study, funded by the European Commission, on the effects of the increasing use of information technology devices and other computer systems in the workplace, on the employment prospects of physically disabled people in the EEC countries.

The study reported on many facets of the employment problems of physically disabled people, and on some existing technological solutions to them. Two major conclusions drawn from the study form the basis of this paper.

1 Although some of the current changes in employment which have resulted from the increased use of computer and information technology systems in the workplace (such as the increase in jobs requiring computer skills and the decrease in jobs requiring physical dexterity) may be beneficial to the physically disabled, this has not resulted in greater job opportunities.

2 Although many new technology devices have been developed to assist the physically disabled with a wide range of physical, social and vocational difficulties resulting from different impairments, there is little evidence to suggest that such devices are being widely used to help them to improve their communications ability or to perform other tasks at work.

Evidence from the study showed that the factors influencing the effective use of new technology devices to improve the employment conditions of disabled people at work in the EEC countries are largely social, political and economic ones. These factors include:

1 the effectiveness of EEC directives and national employment legislation (and of special schemes or government initiatives) aimed at promoting the integration of the physically disabled into the workforce by the use of computer-based systems to enhance their skills

2 current employment services for the physically disabled, with regard to arrangements for the purchase, distribution and selection of appropriate new technology devices

3 the availability of expertise to assess the need for communication and other computer-based systems in relation to job demands

4   the   availability   of   financial   resources   to   support   the
    development,   manufacture   and   purchase   of   new   technology
    aids

5   the attitudes of society, and especially of employers, toward
    the   abilities   of   physically   disabled   people,   and   their
    willingness to consider them in relation to available employ-
    ment opportunities.

THE STUDY

The study aimed to gather comparative data from the ten EEC
countries selected to take part in the study (UK, France, West
Germany,   Italy,   Belgium,   Denmark,   Eire,   Luxembourg,   Netherlands and Greece). However, only general findings and case-
study material from the UK are reported here.

Research Methods

A number of different methods were used to gather data from a
sample   of   government,   research   and   rehabilitation   agencies
within   the   selected   countries.   Industrial   employers,   micro-
electronic   aids   manufacturers,   employment   and   rehabilitation
advisers   for   the   disabled   and   designers   of   equipment   were
contacted, and some handicapped workers were interviewed.
   In addition to a review of existing documentation relating to
the handicapped populations of each country, the following main
methods of data collection were used:

1   a limited postal survey of government institutions, research
    and   rehabilitation   agencies   and   industrial   organisations
    within the EEC

2   interviews of individual specialists in the design, adaptation
    and selection of technological aids in the UK and EEC

3   postal survey of new technology aids manufacturers.

RESULTS OF THE STUDY

Objective data and subjective opinion on policy issues relating to
the use of new technology aids in the employment of handicapped
people was obtained mainly from the literature review, from the
EEC postal survey and from personal interviews. A summary of
the   main   findings   from   these   combined   sources   is   presented
below.

Awareness of Employment Legislation
and its Perceived Effectiveness

Data was collected on the perceived effects of EEC or national
government   legislation   promoting   the   use   of   new   technology
devices, in addition to subjective opinion on the effectiveness of

employment legislation. The UK is used here as a case-study, to illustrate some of the more general points made by respondents.

The overall picture gained from this data was that of a very low level of awareness throughout the EEC countries amongst those in government departments and amongst others concerned with the employment of physically disabled people, about EEC or national initiatives encouraging the use of new technology. Only 21 (40%) of respondents reported an awareness of government legislation or policies concerning the employment of the physically disabled within their countries.

Although it is difficult to measure the outcomes of legislative provision or the effects of government intervention on behalf of the handicapped at work, when asked how legislation works in practice, 17 of the 21 respondents pointed to some weaknesses in current legislation.

Some respondents felt that the generally high unemployment levels of most western nations has reduced the effectiveness of special legislation aimed at encouraging the integration of the handicapped into the workforce, because of increased competition with the able-bodied for jobs. Its effectiveness is further reduced by the lack of awareness of special schemes or allowances for encouraging the use of technology, and for adapting premises to suit the needs of physically disabled employees.

Other problems in the implementation of employment laws concern variations in their interpretation which can lead to inequities in the provision of local services. This is especially the case in the UK where the Chronically Sick and Disabled Persons Act, 1970 enables local authorities to exercise discretion over the provision of welfare services for disabled people. In particular, there are few sanctions which can be applied to reinforce the recommendations of either employment legislation or requirements to assess disabled people for aids or other services.

Although many countries have a legal requirement to protect the employment of handicapped people (i.e. 'quota' regulations requiring employers of a certain size to employ set percentages of handicapped people as part of the workforce), non-compliance with these schemes by industrial and government employers was frequently cited as an example of the inadequacies of employment law. It was felt that opportunities to increase the participation of disabled people in the workforce by the greater use of technological aids would not come about until such non-compliance is reduced.

Recent legislation in the UK (i.e. section 4 of the Disabled Persons [1986] Act) does attempt to make enforcement of the Local Authorities' requirement under the Chronically Sick and Disabled Persons Act to assess all disabled people for services less discretionary, but has not been in force long enough yet to make an impact on this situation.

The Provision of Technological Aids

The need for a uniform code of practice for the provision of technical aids was expressed by many respondents during personal interviews. No country in the EEC has created a system whereby all or part of the cost of rehabilitation aids are covered by a single body or law (Maron, 1979).

The decentralisation of aids supply has effects on both the criteria used by different local authorities to determine eligibility for an aid, and upon the procedures by which they are obtained. As previously indicated, this has resulted in an uneven distribution of the help available. In the UK, provision is made for the supply of work aids under the Employment and Training Act 1973, via the Manpower Services Commission (MSC). The MSC are also responsible for adaptations to the work environment. However, the cost of technological aids is generally extremely high, and may be thought to be prohibitive where low-technology alternatives exist. Knowledge of suitable technological solutions to communication or other difficulties at work also requires a specialist help not always available at the local level, where the need for assistance is assessed.

Under some circumstances, the purpose for which an aid is required may be in doubt; in this case responsibility for its supply may be transferred to another agency. In the UK responsibility is divided between central and local government agencies, according to the purpose for which the aid is required. For example, the Department of Health and Social Security supply some technical aids (such as wheelchairs and environmental controls); Local Health Authorities provide aids for medical and rehabilitative purposes (such as surgical appliances, hearing aids and low vision aids); Local Authorities supply, via the Social Services, 'aids to daily living' (such as bathing aids, chairs, and hoists). Adaptations to the workplace and the provision of equipment are the responsibility of the Manpower Services Commission, but adaptations to the home are within the remit of Local Authority Housing Departments.

This fragmentation of responsibility, coupled with the complexity of procedures for finding the appropriate agency and for making formal applications for assistance can thus affect the supply of work aids. This makes it difficult for people to obtain appropriate help from official agencies, and can result in long delays in obtaining assistance. For these and other reasons, it was felt by some respondents that the application of current legislation is often unsuited to individual circumstances.

Additionally, it was felt that government policy toward the provision of pre-employment training, rehabilitation and job placement in the UK is not geared toward training in the use of new technology aids. This is mainly because such aids, and the use of information technology systems in general, were not widely available at training and rehabilitation centres.

Only ten EEC respondents reported an awareness of initiatives in which their governments were encouraging the use of computer technology for such purposes, and of these few were widespread. Initiatives cited included the setting up of computer-skills training centres and financial help from government in installing computer technology, research funds for the development of specific applications, and the provision of technological aids.

Very few technological applications were reported as being directly used in the employment of disabled people. Most examples of suitable technological devices (7 in all) were from research centres of various types, and these applications were generally still at a very early stage of development.

Problems with Current Services for the Supply of Work Aids

As previously described, the state makes provision for the supply of some work aids in most of the EEC countries surveyed. However, the services tend to overlap, and the distribution of such aids can be subject to limited resources and delays. As a result, voluntary bodies play a significant part in the distribution of aids, both in the UK and the EEC (Uyttendale, 1980).

In the UK, for example, aids to work are generally supplied through the Manpower Services Commission on the recommendation of Disablement Resettlement Officers (DROs). Due to the limited availability of resources for this purpose, and the high cost of most information technology devices, there is often a shortfall between the needs for assistance and their fulfillment. Voluntary organisations and charities, however, also offer advice and organise the loan or exchange of equipment to people who would otherwise have difficulty in obtaining help.

Data from the EEC survey indicated that the structure of current services for supplying aids for handicapped people are inadequate for the purpose and therefore under-utilised. It was indicated during interviews that many problems relate to cost. Restrictions on the finance available to government services for the purchase and allocation of aids can result in an unacceptable choice between helping one person with a high technology aid or providing several people with less expensive forms of help. Expertise in the selection of appropriate aids is also lacking, with regard to information systems and computerised communication devices. A report published by the Manpower Services Commission (1982) in the UK found:

" . . . a lack of expertise amongst most DROs as to what aids and adaptations are available . . . because no structured system exists for the dissemination of information about employment aids and adaptations."

The report also showed that the various special schemes aimed at encouraging the employment of handicapped people were not greatly used by employers:

"Last year the number of 'retention' cases (where a DRO is called upon to advise when a disabled person is in danger of losing his job) was around 3,000, and there were only about 300 cases of aids and adaptations being arranged by DROs, yet probably around 300,000 people a year lose or leave their jobs for health reasons."

The report also found that:

"In general, employers had a poor knowledge of the advice

and aids available from DROs", and that "it is questionable whether the present system (of aids supply in the UK) is well geared to providing specialist advice to employers or to disabled people at work."

Since this study was conducted, a number of 'Aids Centres' funded by the DHSS have been set up by the Disabled Living Foundation throughout the UK, to provide assistance to the disabled. Information and assistance is becoming more available through government services at the local level. However, there is still a sizeable proportion of physically handicapped people who could be greatly assisted in finding and keeping work in the UK than are currently receiving appropriate help.

Techniques for Assessing the Need for Technological Devices

Data from the interviews showed that the provision of communication aids or aids to self-sufficiency at work can be a complicated task. The main requirement is for communication aids, to help with either written communication (reading or writing) or with speech and hearing. There is also a need for devices which provide access to computer systems for people with motor control impairments. Such assistance can be provided via special interfaces or operating controls. Thus, at an occupational level, individuals have to be assessed for the functional implications of their loss in relation to job demands, before suitable technological devices can be suggested. The overall needs of the individual for communication, mobility and environmental control have to be taken into account. The selection of appropriate aids therefore requires an extensive knowledge of both disability and technology.

One approach to this task is the attempt to combine the use of job classification schemes and person assessment techniques to analyse the needs of individuals. A review of existing techniques of job and disability assessment (McCormick et al, 1969; North and Rohmert, 1981; Singleton, 1979) showed that these are often medically based, rather than functionally oriented. There are very few compatible techniques for person and job assessment, as many of the schemes used are very different in approach. An exception is the Activity Matching Ability Systems (AMAS) Scheme, developed by Whalley and Watson which provides compatible techniques for assessing job demands and personal ability.

In addition, a lack of technical guidelines or functional evaluations of available information technology systems or devices means that there is no systematic way of selecting appropriate disability aids to ensure the optimisation of the abilities of disabled people in different work situations (although several large databases have been set up which hold listings of suppliers and manufacturers of technical aids). There are limited opportunities in practice for disabled people to try out an aid to test its suitability. There is also a lack of experienced people to make adaptations to equipment if necessary.

Interviews with those responsible for selecting aids for handicapped people revealed that no uniform techniques were used for this purpose. Reliance is more often placed on the personal knowledge and technical skills of individual therapists.

Most of those interviewed who specialise either in the design, adaptation or selection of occupational aids were working in isolation from others in the area. As a result, existing knowledge is largely unco-ordinated. Because of this a wider distribution of the available guides to aids for particular disabilities (see Schofield, 1981, for example) may be a more useful immediate solution to the selection of disability aids than the approaches to assessment described above.

The Design, Production and Supply of New Technology Work Aids

In addition to the high cost of purchasing new technology work aids, other problems of supply are related to the design and manufacturing process. Government restrictions on finance not only affect the purchase of aids, but also the support given to research initiatives for the development and production of new kinds of aids.

The main obstacle to the manufacture of new technology aids is their specialised nature. The numbers of people who could benefit from a particular technological device have to be large enough to make commercial manufacture profitable. However, the proportion of the handicapped population who are likely to benefit from the use of technological devices is comparatively small (Kuppers, 1980). This is because a high percentage of the physically disabled population suffer from age-related disabilities likely to affect daily living. By contrast, the requirement for the disabled workforce is mainly for communication devices.

An additional difficulty is that of estimating the potential size of the market for aids designed for particular impairments. Although statistics can provide some information on the incidence and severity of various impairments, these are not related to the characteristics of the working population or the functional implications of different impariments for the performance of jobs. Thus the provision of particular aids for 'sub-populations' of the disabled workforce requires an analysis of the demand for different kinds of aid (e.g. communication aids for the hearing impaired, the visually impaired and the speech impaired; interface aids for providing access to computer systems for the motor impaired).

Thus the individual nature of impairments often requires specialised solutions for a relatively small part of the market. The production of such aids can be seen as uneconomic by larger manufacturers, who are more likely to be interested in the manufacture of 'universal' aids reaching greater numbers of people. They can also be reluctant to support 'untried' new ventures developed by smaller-scale, more innovative designers. Although these are more likely to produce the specialised aids required, many of the smaller designers interviewed reported difficulty in finding the finance to support the production of their designs.

Government departments too can be unwilling or unable to risk financing the production of new designs. Consequently, contracts for the supply of aids can be monopolised by larger, more established firms, producing a diversity of equipment.

Evidence gathered during the interviews suggests that there is enough technical expertise and interest by the handicapped themselves, by associations operating to further their interests, by researchers, designers and rehabilitation engineers, to enable experts in different aspects of handicap to co-operate with large-scale manufacturers to generate a range of products to suit almost every need. What is needed is the willingness to finance the development of such aids, and the establishment of an appropriate structure to enable the co-ordination of activities and exchange of information and expertise.

Social Attitudes towards the Employment of Handicapped People

Data from the EEC postal survey, interviews and literature review showed that a major factor in encouraging the use of work aids is the willingness of employers and others to understand the problems of the handicapped workforce and to make appropriate help available.

Interviews with handicapped people indicated that their biggest problem is often the attitudes of others towards them. The distinction between an 'impairment' (a functional loss) and a 'handicap' (something which prevents one from carrying out particular activities) was often made in this context, to illustrate how labelling by able-bodied people can lead to an under-estimation of the abilities of the physically disabled. (There is often also a confusion between mental and physical disability.) This can be more of a handicap than the functional limitations of the impairment itself.

The use of technology and other work aids can reduce the handicap effect of many impairments, by improving communication and the performance of other tasks previously requiring physical skills, but this is not often realised by those in a position to help the disabled.

The attitude of employers is crucial in supporting the use of aids to widen the opportunities of the handicapped at work. Employers can be encouraged to promote the participation of the handicapped in the workforce by government allowances to supply aids or to adapt premises to make them more accessible. Unfortunately, data from the survey showed a great lack of awareness by employers of the kinds of help available and a consequent reluctance to take advantage of the special government schemes promoting the supply of technological aids or the adaptation of workplaces to the needs of handicapped people.

RECOMMENDATIONS

It is suggested that, in the UK at least, social education resulting from government initiatives and increased information dissemination to employers and to the general public is a pre-requisite for increased awareness of the difficulties faced by physically disabled people seeking work, and for change in the attitudes of employers and others. This may result in the greater integration of handicapped people into the workplace and into society.

Employment legislation needs to be improved to make it more effective and enforceable. In the UK, for example, the Manpower Service Commission (1982) recommended that the existing Quota Scheme be replaced by a general statutory duty, backed by a code of practice, on employers to take reasonable steps to promote equality of employment opportunity for handicapped people. This would involve more active enforcement of compliance with regulations and following-up of complaints. Since then, further legislation (the Disabled Persons Act of 1986) has been brought in to reinforce Section 2 of the 1970 Chronically Sick and Disabled Persons Act, wherein the Local Authority is required to assess and make provision for the needs of disabled persons, including the provision of technical aids. It is still too early, however, to assess the effects of this legislation.

A uniform code of practice to reduce variations in the interpretation of the law relating to the supply of aids is needed, so that handicapped people receive more equal treatment. At the moment, the new legislation means that the onus is on disabled people to appeal against decisions made by the Local Authority if they feel that their needs have not been met. Variations in treatment will persist as long as it is up to the individual to seek redress if they feel their needs have not been met.

The responsibilities of different government departments for the supply of aids should be clarified and centralised so that 'aids for work' are easier to obtain.

Increased support for the development and extension of existing 'Aids Centres' or 'Communication Aids Centres' could provide disabled people with a local forum for identifying and fulfilling their requirements for technological aids, and with opportunities to try out and to obtain appropriate devices. This would also help in the co-ordination of expertise, by allowing the establishment of multi-disciplinary teams to assess the need for services. Thus disabled people would be more likely to receive help according to their needs. The further development of such centres would also make it easier for manufacturers to identify the needs of the market for particular technological devices, and thus to produce designs which are more closely tailored to those needs.

CONCLUSIONS

Data from the literature review, from personal interviews and the EEC postal survey shows that, clearly, there is an important role for technology to play in extending the job opportunities of physically impaired people.

*   Technological innovation in offices and industry has resulted in the expansion of some areas of work in ways which could be advantageous to the handicapped because computer-related

work requires less physical dexterity and more use of intellectually based skills than many traditional jobs.

* Current and developing technological devices not only provide physically impaired people with improved methods of communication and help with other problems such as mobility and environmental control, but also enable access to computer facilities.

* By extending their abilities to perform a wider range of tasks, computer technology can help handicapped people to compete on a more equal basis with the able-bodied in areas of the job market requiring computer and communication skills.

* This may promote a more integrated workforce and increase the participation of the handicapped in some jobs which were not previously open to them, thus giving a greater chance for self-sufficiency and independence.

All of the above can be of benefit to physically impaired people seeking more equal opportunities to become part of the workforce, and could potentially ease their assimilation into new areas of work. However, as we have seen, although the technological feasibility to ameliorate a wide range of problems experienced by handicapped people at work exists, there are many factors described in this paper which inhibit the use of new technology work aids by those who could benefit from them.

REFERENCES

Chronically Sick and Disabled Persons Act, 1970. HMSO, London.
Disabled Persons Act, 1986. HMSO, London.
Employment and Training Act, 1973. HMSO, London.
Howey, K.R. (1986). 'New Technology Work Aids for the Physically Disabled', in M.D. Harrison and A.F. Monk (eds.) *People and Computers: Designing for Usability*. Proceedings of the Second Conference of the BCS Human-Computer Interaction Specialist Group. University of York. 23-26 September, 1986.
Kuppers, H.J. (1980). 'Working Aids for the Office Environment', in J. Bray and S. Wright (eds.) *The Use of Technology in the Care of the Elderly and the Disabled*. Francis Pinter, London.
McCormick, E.J. et al (1969). 'Position Analysis Questionnaire'. Purdue Research Foundation, Occupational Research Centre, Indiana.
Manpower Services Commission (1982). 'Review of Assistance for Disabled People'. A Report to the Commission by the Employment Service. Manpower Services Commission, Sheffield.
Maron, A. (1979). 'Analysis of the Procedures in Use in the Community to Support the Cost of Aid to Disabled Persons'. Commission of the European Communities, Berlin.
North, K. and Rohmert, W. (1981). 'Job Analysis Applied to the Special Needs of the Disabled'. University of Technology, Institute of Ergonomics, Darmstadt.

Schofield, J.M. (1981). 'Microcomputer-Based Aids for the Disabled'. Monographs in Informatics. Heyden, London.
Singleton, W.T. (1979). 'Current Problems in Occupational Disability Research'. Document No. 2977/79e, Commission of the European Communities, Luxembourg.
Uyttendale, D. (1980). 'The Distribution of Aids for the Disabled', in J. Bray, and S. Wright (eds.), op.cit.

PART I CONSUMER FOCUS

THE USE OF INFORMATION TECHNOLOGY IN HUMAN SERVICES: STRATEGIES, BORDERS AND EFFECTS IN THE FRENCH-SPEAKING PART OF BELGIUM

Alain Anciaux

INTRODUCTION

New communication technologies seem to bear a double valency. On the one hand, they produce social problems because of their impact on labour and employment. On the other hand, they favour social relationships since they can favour information and communication. Information technologies not only involve elements of cultural and social conflicts but they also take part in a political and economical world-wide system summed up in the following four logics.

1   The ecomomic logic: the market of electronic components lies in the hand of some multinational companies (Texas, Toshiba, National, etc.). To use a new technology makes us become an actor in the world-wide economic game.

2   The military logic: a large number of technological innovations in the communication field are related to research work undertaken in the framework of military development. For instance, the first complete computer, ENIAC, was set up in 1946 for the US Navy.

3   The financial logic: the use of new technologies also leads to changes in commercial and manufacturing enterprises. The pursued objective is to diminish employers' costs (by reducing staff) and to increase the profit margin.

4   The classifying logic: the setting up of data banks is not always related to a legislative approach regulating them.

Recognition of these logics confronted me with the following question: in relation to social work, was it important for me to study the impact of these new communication technologies on families . . . or was it more important for me to try and manipulate these new technologies with a social prospect and to study their effects afterwards? I chose to use them. The three examples used in this paper (the electronic eye and the children, the screwdriver and the women, the camera and the Gypsies) describe the elements of this use. The examples are followed, from a theoretical point of view, with a discussion of the effects of these technologies by comparing my ideas with those of other researchers from Berlin and New Delhi. Finally, I suggest possibilities for new research about the impact of these new technologies on families, starting with a reflection on the video column of the Belgian weekly magazine *Moustique*.

ACTION

The Electronic Eye and the Children

In 1978, a trainee social worker was working with a group of children aged from 8 to 13 in the animation centre of the Viaduc neighbourhood of Charleroi. The children showed neither interest nor motivation for traditional activities (painting, weaving, pottery, etc.), so he decided to develop a 'video workshop' with these youngsters. They enthusiastically welcomed the idea. With the help of an animator from the cultural centre, I agreed to the request from the trainee and the children and organised an activity based on video for two afternoons a week over three months. At that time, I was the only permanently employed animator and was responsible for the management of community television.

The Viaduc neighbourhood, located near the centre of Charleroi, was suffering from isolation because of the building up of the west ring road and the works involved by the setting up of the semi-tube network: works, dust, reduction of green spaces as always in such cases. The neighbourhood was sinister and children had little space to exert themselves physically. In order to keep the children motivated, we organised sessions of shooting and sessions of viewing by turns. In the beginning, they all wanted to participate in the shooting of a film either on karate or on the landing of Martians in their neighbourhood. This 'science fiction' project imagined by the children can be interpreted in two complementary ways: it corresponded with a series watched on television but it also represented a flight from the reality of the appalling state of the neighbourhood. The high-rise building where most of them lived was located near a 'park', covered with trees and bushes, where they could not play. It had become a real clandestine rubbish dump: it was full of broken bottles, old boxes, and even old cars, preventing any secure movement. Together with the children, we made a video film on this park. The children acted as journalists and were holding the microphone, or rather pulling it out, which resulted in the need to solder the wires over and over again after each session. The children described the state of the park. After that, we explained to the children that it could be interesting to interview people living in the neighbourhood on the appalling state of this park, on the possibilities of cleaning it, and on whether they would help to do it.

Once finished, the video film was shown to the members of the neighbourhood committee, who were struck by the urgent character of the problem. The committee then contacted the local authorities concerned to organise a cleaning operation. On a Saturday morning, the park was cleaned by the children, volunteers, and workers from the City of Cherleroi. Five trucks were needed to take away the rubbish and old cars. In this type of activity, the main result was not that we made a video film, but that we emphasized the use of the video as a form of communication between the children on the one hand, and the adults on the other hand.

The Screwdriver and the Women

In 1982 and 1983, the social service of the housing department in Brussels asked me to develop a video animation in a deprived area of the City, the Botanique neighbourhood, where light renovation was being implemented but the inhabitants did not have to move. It was a small neighbourhood made up of seventy three- or four-storey buildings near the northern station. It was mainly inhabited by Moroccan and Turkish immigrants. Video was meant to be used for making films on fire prevention, water maintenance, gas and electricity installations, and the preservation of renovated buildings.

Video equipment was put at my disposal by the City. Unfortunately, the equipment was only meant for shooting and not for editing a definitive film. It took six months, at the rate of two afternoons per week, with a social worker, to make the first film on the circulation of water in the buildings.

The video was shown to the neighbourhood inhabitants and was eventually translated into Arabic and Turkish. But the use of the video equipment required too much time and we decided to organise electricity and plumbing courses for the neighbourhood inhabitants. This was implemented in collaboration with Logazel, an association specialising in this type of training. Video was then used to motivate the neighbourhood inhabitants and inform them of the organisation of these sessions. A small room was arranged in a renovated building to welcome the people interested in this training. To our great surprise, the first course was attended by Turkish women! They considered this room as a 'free' social space, enabling them to get together, sometimes with their young children. At the request of the trainers in plumbing and electricity, the women bought or managed to find an indispensable tool: a screwdriver. They thus were taught to do some concrete odd jobs, such as how to take a tap apart and descale it, and to assemble electrical mountings, etc. Later on, Turkish and Moroccan men came and attended training sessions reserved for them. As far as I was concerned, I had abandoned the video camera and simply made coffee for the afternoon break. In this example, which is the new technology? Is it the camera? The training? Or the screwdriver? It is also important to underline the transfer from one technique to another (from the video to the training session). It is a strategic approach centred on the choice of the most appropriate technique.

The Camera and the Gypsies

A social worker of the City of Brussels was faced with a problem relating to gypsies. A plot of land located in the Anderlecht commune near the canal was used as a stopping place. However, the site had never been arranged for welcoming nomads - it had no electricity, no water, and the frequent rains often transformed it into a slough. Some small works could have been undertaken, but they had to be accepted by the local authorities concerned.

In order to provide the locally elected people with a view of the situation, the social worker suggested that I film the disastrous state of the place and equipment, but not the gypsies who would have rejected me as an intruder. Fifty caravans were there. In the past, the Social Services of the City also had a caravan on this piece of land where a social worker could listen to the needs of this specific group. The social worker, who knew them well, introduced me to the natural leaders and I was authorized to film, although the Sintes, gypsies of Yugoslav origin, expressed strong reservations. At the sight of my video camera, several men called me, not to prevent me from filming, but to invite me inside their caravans to show me that they had a video recorder but no camera. They gave me film and, at their request, I filmed them, their wives and children, and their cars, while the microphone recorded their comments on, for instance, how they managed to get their Mercedes cars. I formally and orally promised them that this film would be handed back to them and only used by them. When the social worker went back to the field, the gypsies asked him whether I could come back, with my camera. They had gone beyond the mediator towards the media.

*   *   *   *

Through these three examples, data appear which link media and the family universe. In the first case, the children communicate with their parents through the video; in the second one, the women react to the use of training sessions in plumbing and electricity, with an indirect impact on housing and thus on the family; in the third example, the video is turned away from its initial objective to film a stopping place to become the nearly photographic reflection of family life.

THEORISATION

The following reflections arose.

1 The new communication technologies offer the possibility of developing activities of social reintegration and training. However, the experimental character of their use involving still not well-assessed psycho-social effects and the financial, legal, ethical and technical problems related to the acquisition and use must be underlined. For instance, I met a social worker developing a literacy project in Saumur, thanks to micro-dataprocessing. He was faced with the lack of software devoted to such an activity.

2 Social relationships, and more particularly community relationships, can use media as an active and favourable element. However, in Belgium most community television has become local television. Is this the sign of failure in the social use of a media?

3   The appeal of micro-dataprocessing can be powerful, notably within the social services centred on families. Nevertheless, it is necessary to implement a feasibility study considering the available time, the resources, the available staff, the family motivations, etc. But I have the impression that this operation is often skipped; a given service buys equipment, such as a video and computer, and then wonders how it could possibly be used.

4   The secret of mediation rarely lies in the technical means being used but rather in the knowledge base of the mediator, in this instance, the social worker. To use a new communication technology is neither a refuge, nor a flight. The media is only an inert object. Only the mediator livens it up.

5   The most important or determining changes which can be noticed within the family and society result from human behaviour but not from the introduction of new technologies.

6   But new technologies engender new conditions and opportunities which may give birth to changes.

7   We must not talk of either positive or negative changes because they depend on man's will and may change according to each family's living conditions.

8   The existence of new technologies is related to the problem of access and distribution. Everything seems to indicate that groups of marginal people will appear in relation to the access to these new technologies.

These conclusions were discussed during the International Conference of Sociology in New Delhi (1986). Two reactions in particular provided me with new information. On the one hand, Serge Proulx (Quebec University of Montreal), in his approach related to the personal uses of the micro-computer, insisted upon the introduction of labour within the private life circle of the family: "Some people will even go as far as occasionally carrying their personal computer to their working place. On the other hand, some employees will bring the institutional computer back home - in this case the institutional will, beside being used at work, occasionally serve within the practical framework of family life and/or leisure activities." He also underlined the dynamics of male and female appropriation of the computer: "It looks as though the micro-computer has also been, until now, an object of psychological/emotional investment mostly privileged by men. Even if it first appears as belonging to a male universe, its penetration in prviate homes favoured publicities based on a family image which, together with other factors, partly participated in and favoured the symbolic access of the technical object to children, teenagers and women."

Moreover, Hans Peter Peters, Program Group Technology and Society, FRG, informed us of the results of his research work on the social consequences of the use of new communication technologies in terms of its impact on life styles and time budgets. He stressed the importance of the following effects of new communication technologies on people.

1 Loss of reality: the individual no longer has direct information relating to reality, but he receives information expressed through the media, and the media is impersonal.

2 Increasing lack of knowledge: the use of new technologies would only be profitable to the people already having a good knowledge beforehand. As for less trained (or under-educated) people, the use of these new technologies would not fill in the gap but would, on the contrary, enlarge it.

3 Fragmentation of social reality: the news items conveyed, for instance, through either radio or television, are submitted to a preliminary selection. They do not reflect all the current affairs but a daily or even an hourly section. Social reality loses its homogeneous character.

But how are these new communication technologies presented to the family and, more particularly, in magazines meant for families? I shall take the example of the French-speaking Belgian weekly magazine *Télémoustique*, for two reasons: firstly I have been buying this weekly magazine for about 12 years and know the evolution of its headings, and secondly, it seems to be a significant example of a review meant for the whole family.

Let us examine one issue and enter into details: it is number 3185 of 12 February 1987. I shall not analyse its traditional contents but mention that the magazine contains headings for young people (pp.151–155), for women (for instance, an article on women aged 40, pp.20–23), for men ('The Sand Convoy', pp.29–32), and for the whole family radio and TV programmes, leisure activities, games, etc.

The first striking feature is that the image of the family mainly appears through comments on TV series. For example, in an article on 'Dallas' (pp.5–6): "Barbara Carrera: a woman standing up to JR – and on equal terms – it had never been seen before." Looking at the actress' photograph on the cover and on page 5, a doubt remains as for the 'terms'. She looks more like a praying mantis than the mother of a family! Other similar articles deal with 'Monte Carlo' and 'Falcon Crest'. It must be said, however, that this weekly magazine does not fall into the trap of easiness and clichés. For instance, the article on 40-year-old women explains in a clear, detailed and modest way the case of women living with younger men. Bernard Lanssens writes: "American studies prove that couples involving women older than men are much more stable than others."

A striking element shows that the family is the target group of this weekly magazine: there is a column on cooking, one on domestic animals and a legal one, dedicated in this issue to life annuity, which often examines problems relating to family life.

The articles devoted to mass media are the most numerous: radio, television, music, and for the last few years, a video heading. I shall solely concentrate on the video item: technical innovations and new video films are commented upon. The 'Microtex' exhibition on micro-computers is announced. An article attracted my attention: it contained the results of the video-poll launched by the magazine. The viewers were asked to give their opinion about the projection of films in the original language, or dubbed ones, about the 'Pan and Scan' (films in cinemascope projected in the video lose part of their image, on the left and right sides), about black and white films, about remakes (new versions of a subject already dealt with in another film). It was only an analysis of technical problems. Video is a technique and only examined as such (in this issue): the psycho-social effects were entirely neglected. However, concerning the impact of video in the family, which is the most important issue: the partial loss of the image through the 'Pan and Scan' effect, or the possibility of the video isolating members of the family in front of the screen, and taking them out of the family dynamics? Video impact is not limited to the technical effects but also (and perhaps especially) to psycho-social effects. A new research area appears when translating a whole series of technical effects into psycho-social ones.

This examination allows me to distinguish thirteen effects characterising the impact of new communication technologies on the family.

1 The convex effect: mass media provides us with the opportunity to open our eyes to the world. Television, for instance, is a window opened to the world.

2 The concave effect: paradoxically, although television is open to the world, it keeps us at home, within the family cell, sometimes unwillingly united (everybody watches the same programme).

3 The analysing effect: the introduction of one or several communication technologies in the family can strongly reveal social relationships inside it. For instance, to introduce either a video or a micro-computer at home may lead to reactions of rejection or discussion. But when problems arise within a family 'because a new technology has been introduced', it means, in fact, that there was already a tension or a conflict situation in latency within the family. In such a case, the arrival of a media simply corresponds with a stimulus favouring the outbreak of a pre-existing conflict.

4 The 'Pan and Scan' effect: the 'Pan and Scan' means that we lose part of the image on the left and right sides when projecting a film in cinemascope on the video. Television or the video games may also have a 'Pan and Scan' effect on people and families by cutting out a certain vision of the world. The huge absorption of a media may isolate us, make us go through life in blinkers, and leave us in a universe with a 'reduced image'.

5 The transcolour effect: in France, they use the Secam system for television and video. A videogramme filmed and edited in colour in Belgium can only be shown in black and white in France, on the local television sets. Similarly, images seen on a television within the family may lose part of their 'colour', for instance, their serious character, and become ordinary. There may be a certain disconnection from reality, reducing the serious character of some events. Let us give a classical image: to see corpses in the news does not prevent the viewer from eating his meal while watching.

6 The panoptic effect: 'Panoptic' means 'to see everywhere'. The increasing use of new communication technologies may create a fear or phobia effect. There are many public places where cameras follow people's movements, such as at crossroads, large department stores, or covered galleries. This normative vision of 'God's eye' pursuing Cain is taking place in our homes: the use of a monitoring camera makes it possible, for example for the mother to work in her kitchen and, at the same time, watch over her baby sleeping in its bedroom upstairs. Is our intimacy threatened?

7 The hypnotic effect: some people are captivated, 'hypnotised', by the media. A family watching television can sometimes be compared with a group of apathetic salt statutes so much overstimulated by the media that any outside communication is considered as a 'breach of the right of concentration'. I know families where it is impossible to talk while the television is on. If you speak, you will be asked, not to keep quiet, but to listen to the television, which one-sidedly monopolises communication.

8 The aggressive effect: some images shown on television may increase people's aggression. Violence is present everywhere and often reproduced by children.

9 The subliminal effect: some fleeting and quick images, which are not directly perceived by the individual, get printed in his unconscious and can influence his behaviour. This effect, well known in the field of advertisement, can be found in all types of programmes. The individual's personality is affected by it without choice.

10 The uchronic effect: this effect is related to the movements within time. In the past, radio and television programmes were limited in time and used to finish by 11.00 p.m. or midnight. Nowadays, an English channel received through cable television broadcasts 24 hours a day. Moreover, the use of the video has 'altered' leisure times. I know elderly people who spend part of their nights watching films on the video.

11 The utopic effect: this is related to movements within space. For instance, to watch a film can project the televiewer in

the media, where the action takes place. This effect is largely responsible for the success of the Belgian programme 'Le Jardin Extraordinaire' (the extraordinary garden). In fact, more than showing images on nature, this programme projects viewers into nature during 30 minutes. But it is an artificial shift. What would be better for the family: either never miss this programme or spend an afternoon walking in a natural site?

12 The tribal effect: this is a gathering effect. For instance, I sometimes listen to conversations taking place in this inexhaustible mine of sociological observation which is public transport. On Monday morning, for example, people talk of the programmes they have watched during the weekend. If, by 'accident', someone has missed 'the film' or 'the programme' that the others have watched, he/she is excluded from the discussion. He/she is the victim of the 'tribal' effect.

13 The taboo effect: this is a specific effect relating to the fear engendered by new communication and other technologies. If one has not been made familiar with such devices or if one does not have faculties of plasticity and of adaptation, resistance to change appears. For instance, in the household, who is able to correctly use the hi-fi system or the video-recorder, not only to broadcast but to record? During an introductory session to micro-dataprocessing organised in Paris for social workers, I made a very short presentation which was followed by a demonstration on consoles put at our disposal by a large French manufacturer. After my lecture, I asked the ladies to come and work on the keyboards of the micro-computers. Most of them hesitated, some even refused, giving arguments relating to a curtailed image of women: "I am not able to manipulate this"; "Well, you know, I do not know anything about electronic devices"; "I shall not be able to manage". The strongest resistances were expressed by older women.

* * * *

These 13 effects (which are not exhaustive) provide new research areas because they are not now based on quantitative data. They can only work as hypotheses, but could be supported through a research approach centred on, for instance, the impact of new communication technologies on the family.

CONCLUSION

Through these few reflections, I examined the bases of what could be researched within the family on the impact of new communication technologies. It is a preliminary approach, but makes it possible to draw a whole set of variable elements, the effects, which would provide the basis of a questionnaire. This approach is important because it offers prospects and hypotheses conditioning the whole research process. In this respect, I think that the different 'effects' described provide us with more subtle keys than just statistics limited to, for instance, the time spent in front of television or to the number of communication electronic devices in the family: it is thus an introduction to the psycho-social effects of information technology upon the family.

Information Technology and the Human Services
Edited by B. Glastonbury, W. LaMendola and S. Toole
© 1988 John Wiley & Sons Ltd

CHAPTER 3

Using Technology with Clients: Automated Assessment and Treatment

INTRODUCTION

There are five papers offered in this chapter. One of them (Cowan) makes the point that in Britain IT has developed extensively in the context of service administration, but that much less software development has occurred in the areas of use by social workers, psychologists, and others with their clients, or for direct use by clients. Indeed, Cowan's work reflects an important characteristic of the situation in Europe – that while work on administrative systems has been reasonably well supported at the corporate level, client applications have depended on small scale initiatives, often pioneered by isolated individuals. Cowan is a social worker who saw an opening for using computers to help troubled children, and worked on it in his spare time: only when he could demonstrate a valuable working program did he begin to get recognition and support. In one sense the picture in North America is similar; for example in Canada, as the paper from Gripton, Licker and de Groot makes clear, human service professional use of computers in automated assessment and treatment has tended to lag somewhat behind the growth of administrative systems. In contrast, however, the project that they carried out in Alberta, 'The Digital Social Worker', is one where there has been a significant flurry of investment and information technology application developments.

The chapter begins with Sarah Wilson's overview of the issues involved in using computers directly with clients. Her work setting is the Royal Hospital and Home for Incurables in London, and not surprisingly, therefore, she gives some emphasis to methods of linking technology to clients who may lack the skills to use a conventional keyboard or joystick. She is concerned to ensure that the relevant questions are asked about employing technology in sectors where previously the dominant force has been human judgement. As a result she offers negative as well as positive views about the potential of IT, and concludes by suggesting that there needs to be a clearly established balance of benefits if IT applications are to gain wide acceptance.

Thompson and Coleman present an example of the kind of benefits which Wilson demands. Their paper, 'Making the Therapist's Prognosis of Stroke a More Scientific Process', argues that computer-assisted visual feedback is one of the most significant current clinical applications of microcomputer graphics. The authors base their developments on the potential usefulness of 'biofeedback' as a means of therapy for those who wish to control or modify bodily functions, in this case stroke victims who have some resultant paralysis. The technique of biofeedback is to offer the patient an immediate indication of the extent to which an effort to achieve a desired function (for example, muscular relaxation) is succeeding. By linking the 'feedback' measurement to a computer display, patients receive a vivid and easily understandable view of progress, with a corresponding boost to motivation.

The paper from Gripton, Licker and de Groot is also set in a hospital context, perhaps indicating the extent to which IT developments in the human services can draw on work in the health sector. The paper describes the outcome of a three-year research and demonstration project on microcomputer applications to clinical social work practice. The project, the Digital Social Worker, was conducted in the Alberta Children's Hospital, Calgary, Canada. The paper locates the project in the history and current context of micro-computer applications to clinical social work, describes the structuring of an integrated software package to support clinical social work and its role in family therapy, and considers issues surrounding the implementation of project software.

The work of Gripton, Licker and de Groot, like that of Thompson and Coleman, has a formal research structure tied in with an experimental or trial application, prior to wider usage. Cowan, in contrast, offers more of an 'on the job' project, based directly on his own experience of communicating with children and young people. He felt that there was often a 'communication gulf' between worker and young client when attempting to talk about past, present and future patterns of behaviour. He came to the view that this could be eased by introducing a 'games' type of computer activity, which took a real problem (like poor school attendance) and traced the effects of such behaviour by asking the client to choose from a menu of possible attitudes or courses of action. From writing specific games, Cowan tells how he eventually moved on to producing a shell within which any social worker can place a particular problem for consideration by a chosen client.

Resnick's *Busted*, like Cowan's *Optext*, is a game based on posing the players a series of questions and responding to the sorts of answers given. Whereas Cowan prefers to focus more single-mindedly on following through the effects of a particular choice of answers, Resnick has set up Busted as a computerised board game, in which chance (the roll of a die) is interspersed with the underlying seriousness of the questions and answers. By tracking the impact or giving a score to positive and negative responses, both games seek to indicate to the players the benefits of responding to problematic situations in ways which are enabling rather than disabling, likely to generate support and approval rather than criticism and disapproval.

Resnick has another valuable offering, an overview of computerised therapeutic games in North America, which shows how important they have become to personal social servicing, especially in work with children and young people. His review allows us to conclude that development has passed beyond trying out prototypes into full-scale applications, and this is perhaps one sector on information technology which is well set for a major expansion during the next few years.

DIRECT USE WITH CLIENTS:
AUTOMATED ASSESSMENT, TREATMENT, AND DECISION-MAKING

Sarah L. Wilson

INTRODUCTION

The purpose of this paper is to highlight issues likely to be raised by the contributors to this topic. The authors of the papers come from a diversity of professions and deal with a wide range of client populations. It is therefore something of a mammoth task to review the issues for all the different applications to be discussed. I shall therefore focus this paper on the common issues and problems.

As the title of this topic suggests, it can be divided into three sections: assessment of clients, treatment of clients and making decisions about intervention. The first two categories involve direct interaction between client and computer system and, therefore, particularly in terms of issues concerning design and development, have more in common with each other than with the third category.

ASSESSMENT AND TREATMENT

One of the first problems that must be considered in automated assessment or treatment is the suitability of the system for use with the client population in question. The prime issue here is the means of communication between clients and computer. The computer's own QWERTY keyboard may be judged to be insufficiently resilient for use by the client group in question or to contain too much information for the clients to deal with, so an alternative response medium may well be desirable. A number of alternatives are available, such as joysticks, keypads, light pens and touch screens to name a few. The selection of the alternative has to be made in accordance with the nature of the information the client has to convey to the computer and also within the limitations of the clients' physical and mental abilities. For example, the use of a touch screen is feasible when dealing with dementing elderly people but has obvious limitations for use with people with severe physical disabilities. Other ergonomic factors such as position of screen, size and brightness of screen, the position, size and labelling of response media and the seating and environment of the subject may all affect the performance of the individual.

There are also issues concerning the presentation of material, which is usually done via the monitor. The first question is whether the resolution is adequate to produce clearly the material to be represented. Generally speaking, the greater the complexity of graphic material that is required the higher the resolution that is needed. Presentation of text needs careful consideration; selection of letter size, spacing, sentence length, how the text should be divided if several pages are needed, the use of colour and highlighting to enhance rather than distract from the meaning, and if there are several pages of text whether they should be 'turned' automatically or under client control. If aural presentation of material is used, the quality of the synthetic speech in terms of its comprehensibility to the clients should be considered.

The reaction of and effect on the client population to the application of computers is another issue: both immediate and long term effects should be considered. In some instances the client may find it preferable to interact with a human; in others the computer may prove to be the preferable medium for the client. After all, computers don't take lunch breaks and may be perceived as being less intimidating than the human professional. Perhaps one of their most endearing features is that they can be switched off!

Assessment

Computers can be used as a medium for a number of forms of assessment, from electrophysiological measures to questionnaires. For some forms of assessment such as electrophysiological measures, automation has always been involved, for others such as cognitive testing, alternative approaches have long existed and it is the low cost and high accessibility of the microcomputer which has spurred on the development of computer-based approaches.

For 'pen and paper' type tests there are two strategies; the first is to take existing tests and automate their presentation, the second is to develop tests specifically for computer-based assessment. In the first instance the comparability between automated and standard form of the test should be established. If the forms are comparable then when normative data has been gathered for the standard form of the test, it can be used in the interpretation of data from the automated version of the test. When new tests are developed for computer presentation, as with any new test, validation of the measure should be carried out, and if normative data is required it should be collected, which can be a time-consuming process. However, if the purpose of the test is to compare the performance of individual subjects on sequential occasions then the collection of normative data may not be necessary.

There are, as has already been discussed, limitations on the type of material that can be presented by computer such as those on graphic material. In the use of expert systems for assessment by interview, limitations are imposed by the lexicon available to the system for the interpretation of answers. For example, a medical diagnostic program may be able to infer nausea from statements such as "I have been sick" or "I have vomited", but it may not have in its lexicon expressions such as puke, throw-up or spew to name but a few of the possible colloquialisms. The matter is further complicated if the system is to be used in different regions or countries where the language is officially the same but there may be marked variations in usage, spelling or even meaning. For example, in the UK the expression 'going like a bomb' means something is going well. In the USA a converse interpretation would be made.

In some circumstances the client's ability to interpret the question can be part of the assessment, in others it is essential that the client understands the question properly. Particularly in matters that they find embarrassing to discuss, people may have learned to use euphemisms and may not understand the correct terminology.

In non-expert systems, if responses are to be scored then the use of material with answers that can be strictly defined are the most practicable, such as answer options in multiple choice questions, numbers or spellings. Scoring assessments by computer can save considerable amounts of time and should lead to greater accuracy in their interpretation.

The use of computers as a medium for assessment has a number of advantages; one is that they give a standardised presentation of the test material, they have no body language and therefore can not unwittingly prompt the client by changes in gesture and posture. They also permit the analysis of different aspects of performance such as response times and error patterns which are not always feasible when the test is being administered by human hands. The process of assessment can also be speeded up by applying adaptive models which speed the client through the sections of the material where the client has no difficulties and concentrate assessment in areas which the client finds problematic.

Apart from the limitations of the material that can be used in automated assessment, which have already been mentioned, the present state of technology limits us to use of material in two dimensions only. There may also be a loss of the information that can be gained from the examination of written answers such as spelling and positioning of answers. Another problem is that if an automated test is developed for one make of computer and necessity requires the transfer of the test to another computer system, then the second version of the test may look different from the first, which requires that the validation procedure be followed again.

Finally questions that apply to all forms of assessment: if the assessment is to be used in other centres should it be developed on the minimum configuration possible for the computer system in question, e.g. single disc drive, monochrome monitor, etc., so as to allow the most widespred use? Also, is there a case for agreement amongst co-professionals to use a common format for data management systems so as to facilitate data collection about the assessment procedure? One issue which is shared with the next section is that of instructions to clients. They can be presented by computer or by the professional or by a combination of both. Certain types of material or certain clientl groups may call for particular strategies in this respect, practice items may be used and, of course, the idiom used for instruction must be an appropriate one.

Treatment

Computer-based treatment can be broadly divided into two areas: games which simulate real life situations; and activities where repeated practice of a particular skill is carried out. In all events the major issue must be whether the therapy program is actually treating the desired aspect of behaviour and whether performance on the computer task generalises into daily life.

The principle behind simulation games is that by allowing clients to experience a simulation of a real life situation and the consequences of different actions, when the real life situation actually occurs they will be able to cope with it more competently. The essential part of the game is to get the client to make decisions and to feed back the consequence of the decision. The decisions can be collected in one of two ways. The easier approach is probably to present the client with a multiple choice array of possible decisions. The other approach is expert systems based where the client enters the decision in his or her own words. As those of us who play text-based adventure games will know, much frustration can be caused by the program not recognising what the player feels to be an appropriate word or phrase, or worse still only recognising the word or phrase in a certain context. As with assessment, the problem is to ensure that the vocabulary available in the software corresponds with the vocabulary of the clients. The multiple choice approach also presents problems, as individual clients may feel that the options proffered at a particular point may all be inappropriate. Such problems may necessitate the presence of the professional, which may also be desired to permit the professional to discuss the clients' decisions with them.

The use of computers for practice in or retraining of basic skills or functions such as may be carried out, for example, in cognitive therapy, presents a number of advantages to both professional and client – chiefly that the client can receive therapy on routine tasks without the presence of the profes- sional, but the professional can still be in a position to monitor the client's performance. The therapy can take place in the client's own home. The processional has to decide, in accordance with the client's needs and abilities, the frequency and duration of the sessions, whether alternative forms of the program should be used to vary the stimuli, and whether forms with increasing difficulty are appropriate.

DECISION-MAKING

For this process interaction between the client and the computer is not directly required, although information gathered as the result of interaction between client and computer may be used in the decision making. The decisions in question concern interven- tion with the client. The major issue in this area must be whether decisions made using a computer should be acted on as they stand or whether they should be supported by or used as an adjunct to decisions made by professionals.

The effectiveness of the computer as a decision-making tool must depend on the program used. It must be effective at eliciting the necessary information, able to ensure that it has collected all the information, and should be capable of weighting the information appropriately when required to do so. Just as with assessment and treatment programs, the validity of the decision-making model should be evaluated. The more systematic approach engendered by computer-based decision-making should lead to more reliable results since, for whatever reason, the human decision maker can fail to accumulate all the necessary information or fail to consider all possible options. On the other hand, when exceptional circumstances occur which are not allowed for in the computer-based model, the professionals can adjust their own decision-making processes accordingly.

In the final analysis, computer-based decision-making is dependent for its effectiveness on the abilities of the individuals who produced the model on which the decision-making is based and also the abilities of those who use the system and the care they exercise when doing so.

CONCLUSION

Having examined each application individually, there is one major question shared by all three. This is quite simply: are there overall benefits either for the professional or the client in applications of information technology to assessment, treatment, and decision-making?

PART I CONSUMER FOCUS

MAKING THE THERAPIST'S PROGNOSIS OF STROKE
A MORE SCIENTIFIC PROCESS

S.B.N. Thompson and M.J. Coleman

INTRODUCTION

The modern interpretation of 'biofeedback' is the technique of using electronic equipment to reveal instantaneously to patients and therapists particular physiological events, and to teach patients to control these otherwise involuntary events by manipulating the displayed signals (usually visual and/or acoustic). As it is now being practiced, biofeedback is a scientific technique rather than a separate science, but the basic concept has led to almost a revolution in medical science which encompasses both medical and paramedical approaches. This new approach has often been termed 'behavioural medicine'.

The use of behavioural techniques is emphasised in behavioural medicine and has been used for the treatment of a host of disturbances, ranging from recurring headaches (Johnson and Turin, 1975) to severe cardiovascular problems (Basmajian, 1981). Patients with physical handicaps of varying degrees have been sharing the benefits of biofeedback techniques for some time now but it is only recently, with the advent of microcomputer technology, that the range of benefit is being assessed.

Probably the most significant current clinical application of microcomputer graphics is with hemiplegic patients (for example, suffering paralysis as a result of a stroke during rehabilitation (Bazzini et al, 1984). The potential of computer-assisted feedback therapies has not been fully recognised, with many established therapies remaining denied of the range and versatility of computer technology. Such is the case with oscilloscope-based therapies like electromyography (Wolf and Binder-MacLeod, 1983; Thompson, Coleman and Yates, 1986; Thompson, 1987).

In an attempt to resolve this situation, a pilot study was conducted at the School of Information Science, Portsmouth Polytechnic, to assess the usefulness of computer-assisted visual feedback with adult hemiplegics. Further developments were tested at Queen Alexandra Hospital, Cosham, using electromyographical techniques (Thompson, 1985) with one area of pursuit being the development of biomedical devices for use in paramedical therapies.

RATIONALE

Since motivation is an important factor in determining the recovery progress of a stroke patient, a microcomputer was considered an ideal device for presenting motivating displays to aid in the recovery process. Following the issue of Acorn BBC microcomputers by the Department of Trade and Industry (DTI) Scheme to over 50 rehabilitation departments throughout the

United Kingdom, this system was adopted for this research in preference to others to ensure the usability of any developed software that may arise from this study. Identification was then made of how best such a system could be used, and in which areas of stroke rehabilitation there was a need for quantification and objective assessment. This led to the following proposals:

(a)   to find a way of motivating the stroke patient to both produce and improve upon a particular *useful* and *measurable* response (possibly physiological);

(b)   measure the response accurately;

(c)   ensure that this response can be both repeated and measured consistently;

(d)   record this response;

(e)   compare this response with a previous one or with those of similarly disposed patients;

(f)   make conclusions and recommendations for future rehabilitation.

By testing and modifying a range of specially written computer programs and from investigating the effectiveness and ease-of-use of conventional electromyographical feedback techniques, an assessment battery was developed that essentially comprised these three components:

(a)   an accurate detection and storage of the electrical activity of the incompletely innervated leg muscle on the damaged side of the stroke patient (by an electromyograph-microcomputer link);

(b)   an opportunity for the stroke patient to attempt control over the affected muscle by manipulating a feedback loop involving a visual display;

(c)   an indication of the improvement or deterioration in performance over several trials and over several patients using database storage techniques.

The quadriceps muscle group was chosen for investigation for its large size and significance in ambulation. Being important for overall hip adduction and lateral rotation, it is one of the most important muscle groups in terms of emphasis for therapy following a stroke. The quadriceps tendon was chosen specifically for electromyographical analysis because of its prominence just above the patella, and because of its use during conventional therapeutic activities, such as with a quadriceps switch and in sitting-to-standing exercises.

THE THERAPEUTIC SOFTWARE

The microcomputer displays that were found to be most effective in terms of fulfilling the main aims of the research were as follows:

(a)   figure 3.1 - an opening and closing drawbridge display which clearly indicated relaxation and contraction of the quadriceps muscle group

(b)   figure 3.2 - a rising and falling thermometer display which enabled the stroke patient to attempt control over the changing electrical activity of the incompletely innervated muscle site

(c)   a time-recorded task involving a set of microcomputer-generated auditory cueing signals to test the stroke patient's muscular reactions in the affected leg.

DATA ANALYSES

Medical histories, statistical measures from the electromyographical monitoring of leg muscle, and reaction time responses for each patient were carefully encoded and stored onto floppy disc for later interrogation and comparison by the therapist.

In order to collect as much data as possible from a cross-section of stroke patients, a national stroke survey was also conducted. From the survey and test sample data several stroke factors were identified as being most commonly included in occupational therapists' prognoses of stroke patients.

Extensive analyses were performed on these data: conventional statistical tests, an automatic interaction detector, and multi-dimensional scaling (run on an ICL mainframe). Results of these analyses enabled a better understanding of stroke recovery and the formulation of a model for stroke prognosis.

A list of stroke factors was therefore produced which were considered as likely predictors of a 'poor' or 'good' prognosis. With reference to Bayesian mathematics, the following conditional probability formulae were used to calculate the observed and estimated probability of occurrence of each stroke factor considered to be a likely predictor of stroke recovery:

(a)   Observed probability (which was the frequency of association of a given stroke factor, B, with a 'poor' or 'good' prognosis, A, in the study sample):

$$P(A|B) = \frac{P(A,B)}{P(B)}$$

(b)   Estimated probability (which was an estimate of the association of any *two* given stroke factors, A and B, based on the study data, for the wider 'unknown' stroke population):

$$P(A,B) = P(B|A).P(A)$$

Relaxation− Contraction Feedback Display

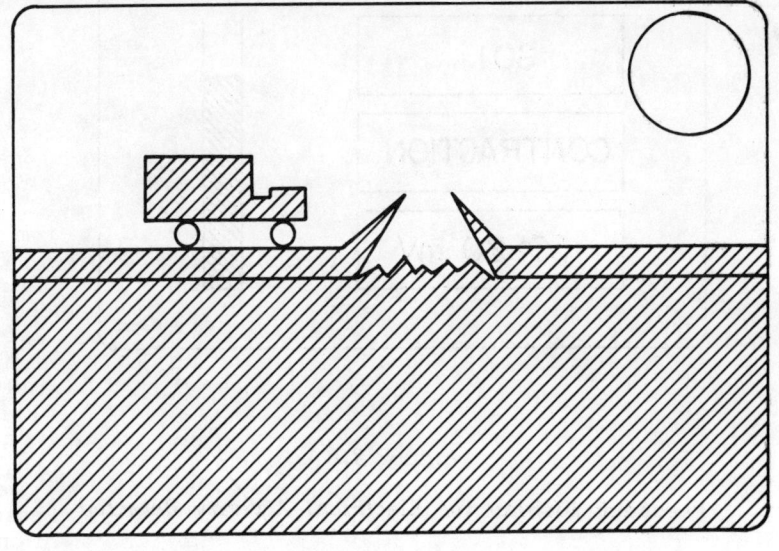

Figure 3.1

Relaxation–Contraction Feedback Display

Feedback Display for Electrical Activity Detected

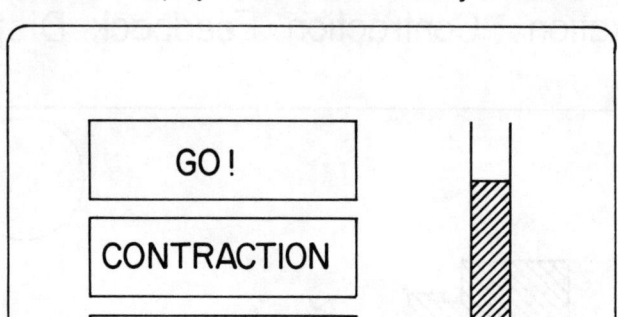

Figure 3.2

Feedback Display for Electrical Activity Detected

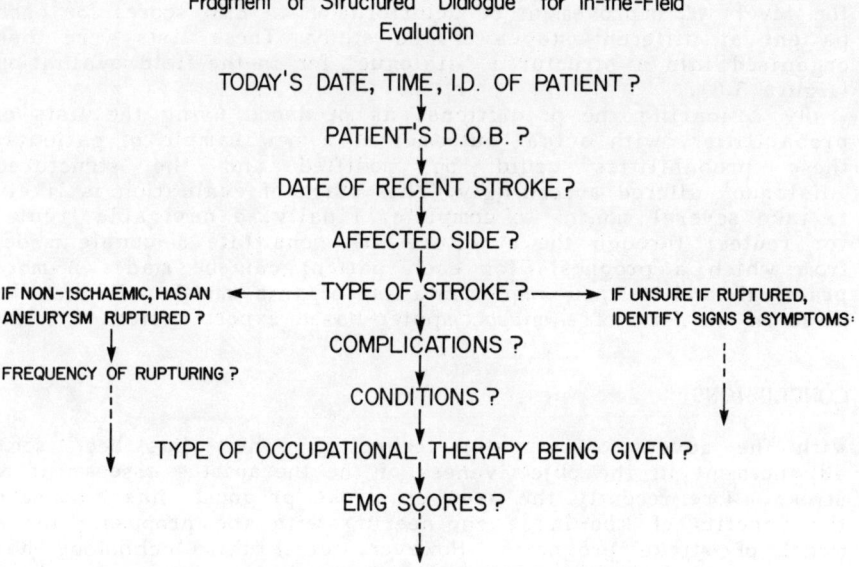

Fragment of Structured "Dialogue" for In-the-Field
Evaluation

TODAY'S DATE, TIME, I.D. OF PATIENT ?

PATIENT'S D.O.B. ?

DATE OF RECENT STROKE ?

AFFECTED SIDE ?

IF NON-ISCHAEMIC, HAS AN ⟵ TYPE OF STROKE ? ⟶ IF UNSURE IF RUPTURED,
ANEURYSM RUPTURED ?   IDENTIFY SIGNS & SYMPTOMS:

FREQUENCY OF RUPTURING ?   COMPLICATIONS ?

CONDITIONS ?

TYPE OF OCCUPATIONAL THERAPY BEING GIVEN ?

EMG SCORES ?

Figure 3.3

fragment of Structured "Dialogue"
for In-the-Field Evaluation

A STOCHASTIC MODEL OF STROKE PROGNOSIS

The following variables were proposed as being most likely predictors of stroke recovery: affected side (right vs left); complications (e.g. arteriosclerosis, contracture, double vision, hemianopia, hypertension, left verticular failure, speech loss) and combined with high, medium or poor motivation; conditions (e.g. angina, diabetes, epilepsy); drugs administered (e.g. atenolol, diazepam, digoxin, heparin, inderetic, nifedipine) and combined with high, medium or poor motivation; severity of stroke (i.e. mild or severe); type of stroke (i.e. ischaemic vs non-ischaemic). The observed and estimated probability of occurrence of each of these factors was found in association with the therapist's 'poor' or 'good' prognosis of each patient in the study. In addition, a list of probabilities was produced of all the levels of improvement or deterioration in EMG scores for each patient at different stages of the study. These lists were then organised into a structured 'dialogue' for in-the-field evaluation (figure 3.3).

By comparing the predictions, as produced using the lists of probabilities, with actual outcomes of a new sample of patients, these probabilities could be modified and the structured 'dialogue' altered accordingly. This stage of evaluation is likely to take several months to complete. Finally, a navigable 'route' (or routes) through the structure will constitute a usable model from which a prognosis for each patient can be made. A more practical and refined implementation of this model will then be made in the form of a microcomputer-based expert system.

CONCLUSIONS

With the advent of computer technology, there has been some advancement in the objectiveness of the therapist's assessment of stroke. More recently the area of stroke prognosis has also seen the benefits of knowledge engineering with the proposals for a model of stroke prognosis. However, until this technology has become second nature among the paramedical professions, there cannot be the progress that is possible from using such techniques. As Sartre (1948) so aptly remarked: "Man is . . . a project which possesses a subjective life"; but let us hope that falling victim to a stroke is one area of life that can at least be assessed objectively despite its quality being undoubtedly subjective.

ACKNOWLEDGEMENTS

The authors would like to thank Miss J Yates (Head Occupational Therapist), Dr K M Shaw (Consultant) and their staff and patients at Queen Alexandra Hospital, Cosham, Portsmouth. This paper is dedicated to Anne Christine Cornec who tragically died of anorexia nervosa, and who would have been pleased with the success of this work.

REFERENCES

Basmajian, J.V. (1981). 'Biofeedback in Rehabilitation'. *Arch Phys Med Rehab*, **62**, 469–475.

Bazzini, G., Guarnascelli, C., Casale, R. and Zelaschi, F. (1984). 'Studio di un Feedback Visivo sui Momento Massimo Volotario di Flessione Dorsale della Tibio-Tarsica in Pazienti Emiplegici'. *Boll Soc Ital Biol Sper*, **60**(2), 375–381.

Johnson, W.G. and Turin, A. (1975). 'Biofeedback Treatment of Migraine Headache'. *Behav Ther*, **6**, 394–397.

Sartre, J.-P. (1948). *Existentialism and Humanism*. (Translated by P. Mairet). Methuen, London.

Thompson, S.B.N. (1985). 'Computerised Therapy for Leg Injuries'. *Ther Wkly*, **12**(11), 4.

Thompson, S.B.N. (1987). 'A System for Rapidly Converting Quadriceps Contraction to a Digital Signal for Use in Microcomputer-oriented Muscle Therapy and Stroke Patient Assessment Schedules'. *Comput Biol Med Int J*, **17**(2), 117–125.

Thompson, S.B.N. and Coleman, M.J. (1987). 'An Interactive Microcomputer-based System for the Assessment and Prognosis of Stroke Patients'. Paper presented at the Special European Conference of the American Society for Cybernetics, 15–19 March 1987, University of St Gallen, Switzerland.

Thompson, S.B.N., Coleman, M.J. and Yates, J. (1986). 'Visual Feedback as a Prognostic Tool'. *J Microcomput Appl*, **9**(3), 215–221.

Wolf, S.L. and Binder-MacLeod, S.A. (1983). 'Electromyographic Biofeedback Applications to the Hemiplegic Patient. Changes in Upper Extremity Neuromuscular and Functional Status'. *Phys Ther*, **63**(9), 1393–1403.

PART I CONSUMER FOCUS

MICROCOMPUTERS IN CLINICAL SOCIAL WORK

James Gripton, Paul Licker and Leo de Groot

This paper is based upon "The Digital Social Worker", a three-year research and demonstration project conducted in the Family Therapy Program, Alberta Children's Hospital, Calgary, Canada (Gripton, 1984). The goal of the project was to demonstrate the contribution that microcomputers can make to clinical social work practice, especially in relation to semi-structured decisions regarding eligibility, referral, treatment planning and intervention.

THE DEVELOPMENT OF MICROCOMPUTER APPLICATIONS TO SOCIAL WORK

The computerization of social work agencies was in its infancy when the Digital Social Worker project was initiated in 1982. The literature consisted of fewer than a dozen articles, mostly conjectural and general in nature, and one small book (Taylor, 1981) that described straightforward administrative applications in support of management functions.

Little consideration had been given to applications that would support clinical practice and would involve the clinician as primary user. In the years since, the utilization of computers in social work has expanded rapidly and the literature has developed accordingly. A newsletter, *Computer Users in Social Services*, was introduced in 1981 and the journal, *Computers in Human Services*, began publication in 1985. Discussion of administrative applications no longer predominates; over one half of the articles in the first four issues of *Computers in Human Services* relate directly to clinical practice. During the past two years several social work journals have published special issues on computer applications to specific practice domains. As yet, however, there has been little reporting of well-tested applications to practice that are transferable to other settings. Completed applications tend to be specific to the situation in which they were developed. In summary, the current status of the development of microcomputer applications to social work may be described as highly active and multidirectional. Comments on the major components of this development are as follows.

(a) **Management Information Systems**

Sophisticated microcomputer-based management information systems designed for small and medium sized social work agencies and for specific services are available, either commercially or in the public domain. This development has been made possible by the greatly increased memory and hard disk storage of personal computers and the development of powerful relational database software.

(b)   **Agency Ownership and Use of Microcomputers**

Recent surveys indicate that from one-third to one-half of all social service agencies own microcomputers, and the acquisition curve indicates that within five years the non-owning agency will be the exception. These same surveys also report, however, that microcomputers are used predominantly for word processing, administrative and financial management functions. Less than five percent of agency computers are used directly by clinicians for case management or clinical decision-making. Applications to clinical practice are still primarily under development.

(c)   **Computer Literacy of Professional Social Workers**

Five years ago, most social workers viewed computers as an alien, dehumanizing technology that had no place in social work. This situation has changed remarkably. A substantial minority of social work students now have computer knowledge and skills acquired in high school of undergraduate courses. As a group, they approach computer courses with the same range of attitudes and expectations with which they approach other courses in the curriculum. Furthermore, the emphasis of courses has shifted from teaching basic computer knowledge and skills to the understanding and use of social service and clinical practice information systems.

(d)   **Computer Assisted Client Assessment**

The most highly developed and extensively utilized applications of computers to clinical practice relate to clinical assessment. Standardized psychosocial measurement, used extensively in clinical psychology practice, can be readily computerized. Well over one hundred of these instruments have been programmed for computer administration, scoring, and interpretation. Research indicates that most clients prefer being tested by the computer to being tested by a counsellor; and that data provided to the computer is more complete and less subject to impression management. Social workers have been hesitant to use standardized psychosocial measurements or quantitative measures of any kind in their practice. This is partly because the most popular clinical social work theories emphasize qualitative data and partly because testing has been considered by social workers as the exclusive domain of the psychologist. In the past decade, however, a large number of well-constructed instruments that can be appropriately applied, scored and interpreted by any well-trained, responsible counsellor have become available (Saxman and Brandt, 1987). Some of them have been developed specifically for social work practice, most notably the clinical scales developed by Hudson (1984). Consequently use of such instruments by social workers has become

much more widespread. Those who have found them useful
in their practice will undoubtedly embrace the computerized versions because of the advantages of ease of
administration, rapid and error-free scoring, and effort-
less interpretation.

(e)   **Computerized Clinical Records**

On the face of it, computers have the potential to improve
radically the quality of clinical social work records, the
efficiency of practice recording, and the use of recorded
data by clinicians for practice decisions and practice
accountability and evaluation. The first step is realizing
this potential is the design of a clinical record that
includes all relevant clinical data in formats that can be
readily processed by the computer. This task requires
clinical social workers to make fundamental shifts in how
they think about cases, observe clients, and record
clinical events. It means developing new taxonomies,
redefining concepts, deciding upon measurement procedures, and obtaining consensus on these matters among
all those who will compile, maintain, and use the new
standardized record. This is the most demanding part of
the data discipline that is imposed by the computer. The
other is the necessity to maintain complete and up-to-date
records. The promise of the standardized clinical record
rests in the ease with which the computer can manipulate
cross-case data. In so doing, it overcomes the obstacles
of tedium, time, and the computational limits of human
data processing that have stood in the way of effective
use of data stored in paper clinical files. This capacity
of the computer is compromised, however, if case records
are incomplete or out of date.

Many computerized clinical social work records are now
being developed and marketed, but predictions about their
contribution to practice must be guarded. There is a
history of failure of very costly and carefully designed
computerized medical and mental health treatment records.
In some instances the failure has been attributed to not
involving professional end-users sufficiently in the design
and installation of the system. In other cases, systems
have failed in spite of extensive participation of
clinicians in their development. It appears that human
service professionals' habitual ways of processing clinical
data are very difficult to alter. It is not easy to design
user-relevant and user-friendly software for clinical
practice and then persuade the counsellors to use it.

The contribution which clinical data make to the
quality of practice is limited by quality. This is true
regardless of whether or not the data are computerized.
With computerized data, these limits become more evident
because the benefits of computerization are realized
through more extensive and elaborate data manipulation.
There are two formidable tasks that follow upon the

design of a computerized clinical record and determination of the component data items:

(i)   establishing the validity, reliability and sensitivity of the clinical observations, measurements and judgements that comprise the elements of the computerized record

(ii)   training clinician users to improve these parameters of their clinical data gathering.

Little work has yet been undertaken on these tasks.

(f)   **Software for Clinical Social Work Practice**

The development of software to support clinical social work practice during the past five years has been energetic, creative and chaotic. Some software has been developed specifically for social work, much of it for other human service professionals. Until recently it has been difficult to locate or assess because of the many sources of such information. Two major efforts have been made to rationalize knowledge about and access to these programs – the compilation and maintenance of an annotated bibliography on computer applications to mental health by Hedlund and his associates and the formation of a directory and library of social work related software by the Spellman Computing Centre at the Graduate School of Social Work, University of Denver.

(g)   **Computerized Support for Clinical Decisions**

Developing computerized support for professional practice decisions is the most challenging, and potentially the most rewarding, aspect of recent computer applications to clinical social work. Such systems are exceedingly costly and time-consuming to develop, especially in a field such as social work that does not operate from a limited set of explicit theories, that lacks a strong empirical base, and that involves the manipulation of variables that are difficult to quantify.

(h)   **Computerized Report Writing**

One tedious task in clinical social work is preparation of reports on clients. Computers can be programmed to prepare readable clinical reports that are superior to clinician-prepared reports in at least two respects: they are based on more consistent and complete use of the recorded clinical data; and there are fewer errors committed in transposing recorded clinical information from computerized clinical records to reports. The quality of computer generated reports depends upon the completeness and organization of the computerized clinical record upon which it is based, and on the quality of the clinical data recorded.

(i)   **Use of On-Line Databases**

Several surveys have indicated that few clinical social workers consult the professional journal literature relevant to their practice on any regular basis. In this regard, they may be no different from other professionals. It would be unreasonable to expect individual social workers to subscribe to the range of major journals that relate to their practice. Furthermore, conventional retrieval of information from a library is not feasible for most practitioners. Few social agencies maintain well-equipped libraries and many clinicians do not have access to a library that has a comprehensive collection related to their professional interests. Even with access to such a library, retrieval can be awkward, time-consuming, costly, and non-productive. It is not surprising, therefore, that social workers make limited use of professional literature. It would, in most instances, not be cost-effective for them to do so.

Another obstacle is the degradation of conventional libraries. Recent economic constraints have forced most libraries to reduce their paper document holdings, and to limit acquisitions to the leading publications in a field. These curtailments have only been partially offset by technologies such as microfiche.

Finally, the problems of accessing relevant professional literature are exacerbated for clinical social workers because the practice knowledge base extends to a wide range of professional, applied and basic scientific disciplines.

One means to easier and more efficient access to professional literature is the on-line database. There are a number of major on-line systems, each of which provides access to information stored in a wide range of subject databases. Many of these are bibliographic databases, which enable users to locate speedily and precisely the literature that meets specified search criteria. The documents ultimately selected can then be browsed, downloaded to disk, or ordered by mail. The costs of conducting searches and retrieving documents are considerable, but must be weighed against the hidden costs of time spent in less efficient and less productive conventional searches, and the costs of poorer service that may result from failing to consult the published knowledge base of practice.

THE PROJECT RATIONALE

The Digital Social Worker project sought to overcome two conditions. The first related to the history of computer applications to social work and social welfare. Until the mid-seventies, applications were almost exclusively mainframe-based data processing operations designed to serve administrative and management functions. Data of interest to clinicians were either not collected or, if included in the system data base, were likely to be of poor quality or not accessible to clinicians (Dery, 1981). Offsetting the negligible benefits to clinicians were the significant costs of data entry and the threat of closer surveillance and deprofessionalization of practice (Gripton, 1981).

The second condition was the limited application of computers to clinical social work in contrast to the numerous applications to the related disciplines of psychiatry and clinical psychology (Schwartz, 1984). This difference can be attributed to four conditions that have facilitated applications in these other disciplines: the lost cost, flexibility, and appropriate capacity of microcomputers that make their use feasible for the private practitioner; the control exercised by the private practitioner over application of the computer to his or her practice; the high proportion of psychologists and psychiatrists engaged in private practice; and the commitment of psychiatry and psychology to science and their use of psychometrics and other quantitative measurements (Gripton, 1983).

A third reason for initiating the project in 1981 was that certain developments in social work seemed likely to override social workers' misgivings about computers. Demands for service accountability have stimulated the installation of computerized service information systems, even in small agencies. Methods of clinician self-evaluation of practice have been developed that involve use of standardized psychosocial measures and other procedures that generate quantitative clinical data (Bloom and Fischer, 1982). Clinical interventions that require more systematic and efficient clinical records, such as behavior modification (Fischer and Gochros, 1985) and task-centred casework (Reid and Epstein, 1977) have become more widely practiced.

Main Characteristics of the Project

In the light of the history of computer applications to social work and the recent trends described above, the Digital Social Worker project was based on four principles. First, micro-computers were used because they are better suited than the mainframe computer to the development of flexible, 'user friendly' systems. Second, the applications developed were to be exclusively oriented to the needs of clinical practitioners. Third, clinicians were fully supported in the development and use of the system. State-of-the-art hardware and software were to be made available. The project programmer/analyst was hired as much on the basis of ability to work with clinicians as on technical qualifications. A clerk was hired to assist clinicians with data entry. Fourth, software development was oriented to support clinical decision-making.

A major activity of the start-up phase of the project was an analysis of the information requirements of the family therapists. What clinical data did they collect? How did they store, organize, manipulate, retrieve and dispose of them? It was concluded from this analysis that the central component of the software package developed should support important semi-structured clinical decisions related to eligibility, referral, assessment, treatment planning, intervention, and evaluation of practice. Some characteristics of semi-structured decisions are: they are made at irregular intervals and unpredictable times; the decision process is heuristic rather than prescribed; and the data items selected to inform such decisions, the way in which these items are combined, and the decision alternatives vary from decision to decision.

A secondary emphasis was on the development of interactive programs to administer standardized psychosocial measurements and carry out other procedures for collecting clinical data and monitoring, measuring and evaluating practice. The project de-emphasized but did not exclude data-processing and management information system (MIS) applications for better caseload management and the production of structured clinical reports.

Analyzing how Family Therapists make Clinical Decisions

A critical phase of any decision support system (DSS) development is the analysis of how users make the decisions the system is intended to support. Two approaches were used in this project. One was to apply a framework developed for DSSs for relatively unspecified and unstructured decision environments, such as family therapy practice (Sprague and Carlson, 1982, pp.95-107). This analysis was conducted by interviewing each of the family therapists about how they make clinical decisions, and the results were used in developing the project DSS software. Besides identifying the information and information handling procedures that therapists use in making clinical decisions, this analysis also confirmed that there was sufficient uniformity among therapists in the way that they practiced to justify the development of a system that could be expected to serve all of them. Individual therapist practice was not as idiosyncratic as was anticipated.

Group Supervision as a Decision-making Mechanism

The second analysis of family therapists' decision-making was based upon audiotape and videotape recordings of their group supervision sessions. The therapists meet weekly for group supervision, when cases are presented for group discussion and decision. The cases presented are families with which the presenting therapist is having difficulty. Observation of these meetings revealed that the structure and process of group supervision is analogous to the structure and process of computer decision support systems.

The Integrated Software Package

The structure and operation of the integrated software package developed in the project is depicted in Figure 3.4.

At the centre of the system is the Clinical Data Base Program. This is implemented under dBASE III+, a commercial off-the-shelf relational data base management program. The principal content is the set of files that contain the records of families served by the program. The family therapists developed a case record of more than 300 items organized in sections on family description, psychosocial assessment, intervention and evaluation.

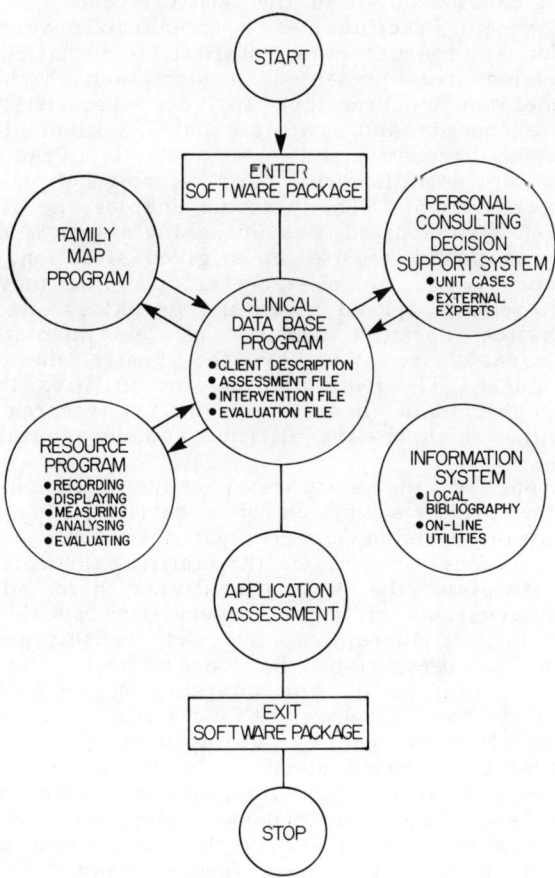

Figure 3.4

*An Integrated Software package
for Clinical Social Work*

A second component of the package is a Family Map Program. This program constructs a family map from descriptive data on the family and the family therapist's ratings of the relationships and interactional patterns between family members on several dimensions. The family maps can be printed as well as displayed, and can be stored in the family record.

A third component Practique, is a computerized version of the procedures, forms, measurements, statistical operations, guidelines and decision trees presented in Bloom and Fischer (1982). The forms generated by Practique includes checklists, behavior records, self-anchored and rating scales, client logs, post interview session reports and line charts. Practique also provides computer administration and scoring of standardized psychosocial measurements. The program enables the clinician to choose the best standardized measure, single-system design, or data analysis procedure to use in a given situation. Practique resides in Lotus 1-2-3, an off-the-shelf program that combines data base management, spread sheet and graphics capabilities.

The Information Package consists of: an annotated family therapy bibliography compiled by the family therapists and stored as a dBASE III+ file; and on-line utilities that access other bibliographic data bases. Continuing research is being done to determine which on-line utilities and data bases are most cost-effective.

The component of the software package with the greatest potential is the project's version of a decision support system, Personal Consultant Decision Support System (PCDSS), a consultant system that provides advice to the family therapists. It is designed to stimulate the way consultants give advice. The analysis of observations of group supervision revealed that the participating family therapists act as consultants to the colleague who is presenting the case under discussion by recalling cases similar to it, and advising on the basis of what interventions they had found to be successful with such cases. PCDSS simulates this provess by acting upon the clinical data base to retrieve cases, based upon similarity functions which are elicited from consultants. The interventions used with these similar cases are then examined to determine their relative effectiveness. For example, a family therapist might ask PCDSS: "What should I do with the Jones family, headed by a single mother who was abused as a child and whose daughter is acting out in school?" The therapist can request advice from a number of consultants; suppose she seeks advice from Mr Oracle.

In a previous session, Oracle has informed PCDSS that similarity judgements are made on the basis of family size (+/- 2 members), presenting problems (in eight classes), age of head of household (+/- 6 years), and a number of other traits. Let us ignore these others for the moment. The therapist has already entered information to a case data file describing the Jones family, their problem, and a host of other factors. This file of therapeutic events contains information on what interventions were tried with each family and what the judgement of 'success' was on a variety of dimensions. Oracle then proceeds, under control of PCDSS (and therefore under control of dBASE III+) to examine all therapeutic events on file, seeking those which fall into a certain range of family size (the size of the Jones family +/- 2), experience problems Oracle judges as similar to 'acting out', and have the same age of head of household as the Laporte family (+/- 6 years). The capabilities of the data base manager are such that this search is easy and rapid.

Since the case data file links families, assessments, interventions and treatment outcomes, the results of this search provide a set of cases in which the families are similar to the Jones and problems are similar to 'acting out' (see Figure 3.5).

Given this set of cases, PCDSS proceeds to sort it by interventions and provide an average outcome rating for each such intervention. An example of such a list appears below.

Effectiveness of Interventions
with Families similar to Jones

Interventions	Number of Families	Percentage Success
Milan therapy	27	44%
Systemic therapy	14	50%
Strategic therapy	3	67%
Behavioral therapy	19	79%
	63	54%

Important constraints in applying PCDSS must be overcome if its potential is to be realized in clinical social work practice in general, and family therapy in particular. The characteristics of clinical data and information and the ways that these are processed by the social worker in clinical practice must be substantially modified for effective computer applications. This transformation may be an interesting challenge for the computer systems designer and the programmer/analyst; it is both a formidable intellectual demand and a time-consuming task for the clinical social worker, and one not likely to be assumed without convincing demonstration of the practice gains that will be forthcoming.

A second constraint concerns the reliability, validity, and accuracy of clinical social work measurement data, and especially measurements of practice effectiveness. The current uneven quality of these data limits the usefulness of PCDSS.

Finally, the underlying logic of PCDSS applications is a linear model of cause and effect, whereas popular theories of family therapy are based upon cybernetic models. This difference presents an obstacle to the use of PCDSS by family therapists.

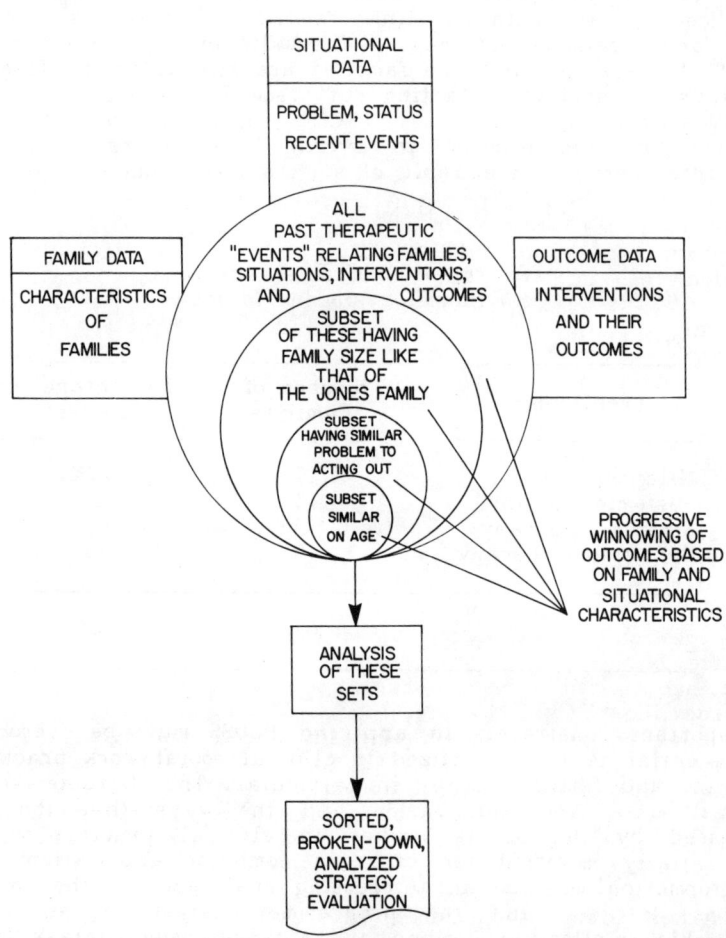

Figure 3.5

How PCDSS Creates Advice

PCDSS is a complex software system aimed at simplifying the process of describing families and obtaining advice from consultants in a fairly straightforward mode. It provides an easy-to-use consulting facility for family therapists built around a simple model of consulting while providing powerful data capture, reporting and advising functions.

The PCDSS developed by the project is a 'shell'. The contents of current family therapy clinical data can be emptied and replaced by another agency's clinical records. The program can thus be adapted to the requirements of other clinical social work services.

Clinical Practice and Computer Expertise

Two recent trends have been noted elsewhere in this report: the wider exposure of social workers and social work students to microcomputers, and the greater prominence of clinical practice applications in the development of software for the social services. These raise the issue of an appropriate stance for the clinical social worker toward microcomputer technology.

Despite the growing proportion of social workers who have some familiarity and competence with respect to computers, there is evidence from studies of social workers' values, attitudes, and aptitudes that suggest that few would find the technical aspects of computers intrinsically interesting. If this is the case, then what position should clinical social workers take toward this rapidly changing technology? A strategy for social workers to use in relating to microcomputers is described below. It involves locating oneself in a continuum of involvement with computers, and acquiring the knowledge and skills that are specific to that position.

At one end of the continuum is the design and development of applications software. The person at this position, the *toolsmith*, must acquire high levels of knowledge and skill in computer programming and computer languages, and a comprehensive knowledge of hardware and software development. For toolsmiths, the marginal value of each increment of new knowledge or skill is high. To maintain their position, they must compensate for the rapid obsolescence that characterizes this technology and stay close to the cutting edge of new developments. It would be the rare clinical social worker who would aspire to the toolsmith role.

Further along the continuum, is the person who designs clinical information systems. This person, the *systems designer*, must have information system analysis competence and a good understanding of the domain of the system – in this instance, clinical social work practice and social service organization. Familiarity with the components and capabilities of microcomputers is also important, but this level of knowledge of the technology is not as susceptible to change as the knowledge required by the toolsmith. Continuing development of clinical information systems and clinical practice applications will require a growing number of social agency administrators and clinical social workers at this position on the continuum.

Toward the other end of the continuum are *active users* who regularly use the computer and who are interested in further exploration of the technology for their practice. This will probably be the modal position of clinical social workers within five years. Maintaining this position on the continuum requires a much more modest understanding of the technology. More important is a clear understanding of the requirements of a clinical information system, and the information processing needs of their practice. Two skills are paramount to this position:

(a)   communicating these needs clearly to system designers; and

(b)   making sound decisions or securing sound advice on the acquisition of clinical practice support software.

At the non-computer end of the continuum are the *non-users*, and those who use the computer only because they are required to do so by their employers. Non-users obviously need not know or do anything with respect to computers. Involuntary users, and these will increase in number, should acquire basic computer literacy – a rudimentary understanding of how a computer works, modest keyboard skills, and the ability to use basic system commands and manuals. These clinicians should expect to be provided with good computer literacy instruction, user-friendly software, and accessible technical assistance whenever they encounter difficulty. They should be effectively shielded from other than modest requirements to upgrade their technical knowledge and skills in response to technological changes, and it is the responsibility of toolsmiths and system designers to provide that shielding.

INTRODUCING COMPUTERS TO CLINICAL PRACTICE: ADMINISTRATIVE AND HUMAN RELATIONS ISSUES

The Rationale for Computerization

Practitioners or administrators who ask "Why computerize?" should consider the following conclusions derived from our project experience and consultations with others involved in developing computer applications to clinical practice.

(a)   Performance – computers can store voluminous data in very little space, sort and retrieve it with great speed, and present it in varying formats to suit the needs of the user. They can easily answer 'what if' queries. Furthermore, they can almost instantaneously share such information with the world at large through the use of electronic communication systems.

(b)   Accuracy and reliability – a properly functioning computer is unerringly consistent in its digestion and reproduction of data. As a result, such a device can avoid many of the human errors in the recording, storage and retrieval of information. Attaining such error-free functioning, however, involves a significant investment in developmental programming.

(c)   Productivity – knowledgeable users of computer systems can accomplish considerably greater amounts of information processing than would be possible without this technology, but this benefit is not obtained without the costs of learning to harness this computational power.

(d)   Revelation – since they extend human information processing capacity, computers permit exploration of relationships among disparate items of information that would not be feasible with the 'naked brain'. Before these benefits of computerization can be realized, prospective users must first wrestle with the issue of *purpose*. Clinical service agencies perform many functions in their daily operation that are amenable to computer support. The question of purpose must be addressed in relation to the users of the system as well as at the level of the individual task that is to be automated. A broad distinction can be made between *management staff*, who generally use computers to automate administrative tasks, and *line employees*, who may wish to use computers to assist them as practicing clinicians. Each user group will be less inclined to use a computer system developed primarily to meet the needs of others.

Although systems can be built to meet the requirements of each staff group in equal measure, this can only be achieved with a corresponding increase in development and maintenance costs. Consequently, agencies with limited resources may be faced with robbing Peter to computerize Paul. Evidence suggests that computerized systems must be tailored carefully to the user's requirements if they are to be well utilized.

At the level of individual tasks, further issues of purpose revolve around the decision as to whether the computer system should directly automate presently performed functions, or innovate in the performance of tasks that were heretofore too time-consuming or computation-intensive. For example, the introduction of word processing is a use of computer power that does not introduce any new functions but serves to enhance efficiency. On the other hand, the introduction of a clinical decision support system may reshape practice in truly novel ways.

Table 3.1 presents possible uses of computers in clinical agencies, based on the above considerations. Particular uses of computer systems are classified according to their interest to management or line staff. The uses are listed in descending order according to whether they primarily enhance the efficiency of task performance, or whether they lead to a modification of the task's performance. This list by no means exhausts the possible uses of computers in clinical agencies.

Table 3.1: Applications of Computers in Social Work Practice

Use	Management Staff	Line Staff	All Staff
Word processing:			
- correspondence	X		X
- agency	X		X
- client records			X
Caseload management		X	X
Caseload reporting		X	X
Financial tracking/ projections (spreadsheets)	X		X
Scheduling:			
- workloads		X	X
- room/equipment bookings			X
Administration/interpretation of scales of psychological/ social functioning		X	X
Treatment outcome monitoring and documentation	X	X	X
Client and service descriptions to aid in planning resource development (e.g. problem typologies, service parameters, referral routes all through database management	X		X
Clinical Decision Support Systems guiding treatment		X	X

A further primary consideration in planning for the computerization of a clinical service agency is the resources available to the agency to realize any such plan. Computerization entails the obvious costs of hardware, and software. Additional expenses are usually incurred for consultants to advise on which items of hardware and software to acquire. Once these items are on site the task begins of developing viable applications that serve the needs of the agency. This can vary in complexity from the simple use of off-the-shelf software for word processing to the construction of an elaborate, tailor-made data base management system. Complex applications involve extended time frames and substantial investments of money and expertise. Computer experts are required to construct, test, and help implement the system. The costs associated with such an installation can be expected to greatly exceed the combined costs of the basic software onto which the specific application is built and the computers themselves.

It is only after the system is in place and functioning that the costs that are least visible at the outset are incurred. These include expenditures for staff training, maintenance and upgrading of hardware, and, most importantly, the costs of maintaining and developing the software system. Computer programs often appear to be thoroughly error-proofed on first implementation, but may contain subtle 'bugs' that only appear after a protracted period of actual use. Furthermore, whatever the positive attributes of computer systems, they are inflexible to a high degree. As a result, individually tailored software systems typically incur ongoing maintenance costs involving the reprogramming of newly surfaced errors, and redesign of the system in whole or in part in order to make it better meet the evolving needs of the agency.

The process of decision-making relating to the acquisition of a computer system is represented in Figure 3.6.

The first consideration is whether there is sufficient interest in computerization on the part of either management or clinical staff. If at least one of these groups is interested, then the next issue is availability of resources. If there are both sufficient interest among clinical staff and the resources available to computerize, the next consideration is the degree of standardization of practice among prospective clinician users. If standardization is low and unlikely to be developed, then computer application will be limited to 'static' data use systems that passively store data on client and service parameters. Such applications are likely to be of greater value to managers than clinicians. Agency-wide clinical applications demand some consistency in how practice is conducted, described and defined across practitioners. Such standardization permits the development of 'dynamic' systems that can render judgements as to how service is best provided. Dynamic systems are capable of reshaping the information that they store. Such is the case of the Personal Consultant Decision Support System described above.

The chart also depicts the sub-process whereby the design of a dynamic data base system develops through cycles of refinement, and may never reach a fully final form. This type of applications development, involving continuous close collaboration between computer personnel and clinician users, is called 'prototyping' (Sprague and Carlson, 1982). The maintenance of this cyclical process is dependent upon dependable operation of the computer system, the level of support provided to facilitate clinicial utilization, the availability of resources to maintain the refinement process, and the level of enhancement to practice that its use provides to clinicians. Failure to meet these conditions

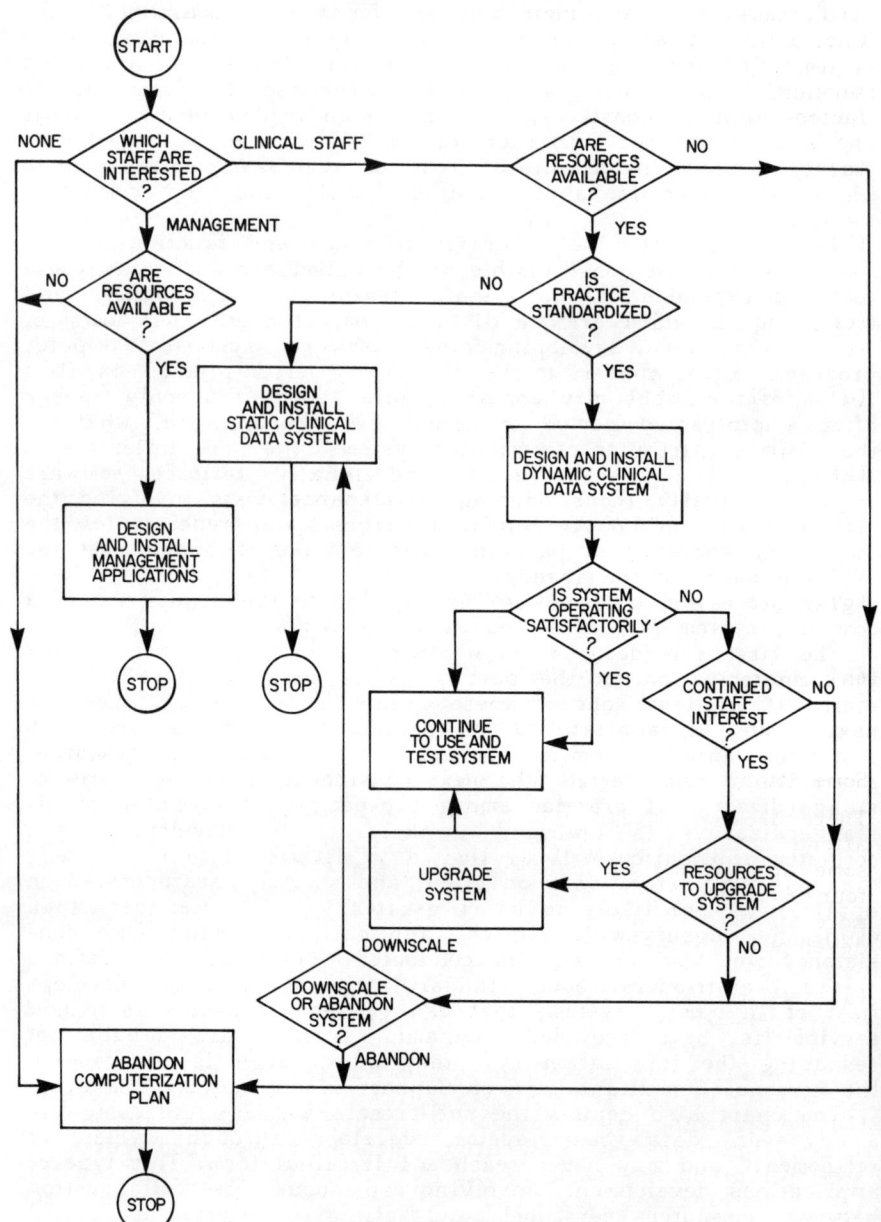

Figure 3.6

Steps in Planning a Computerised Information System

will result in abandonment of the system (Hedlund, Vieweg and Cho, 1985), or downscaling to a static system.

In summary, the process of computerization of a clinical service agency will proceed most productively if the following factors obtain:

(a)   The agency's administration supports the value of computerization

(b)   In the case of clinical applications, the line staff also are supportive and are open to technological innovation

(c)   The necessary budgetary resources are available to finance hardware, software, and technical expertise

(d)   There are adequate consulting, technical support, and training personnel

(e)   Adequate investment is made in staff training

(f)   Users receive on-going support from data entry personnel, and prompt trouble-shooting is available

(g)   Use of the system is perceived by the users as significantly enhancing their practice

(h)   In the case of clinical applications, the clinicians jointly adhere to a common theoretical perspective on practice and use the same repertoire of therapeutic interventions.

Some Impacts of Computerization - Good, Bad, and Indifferent

There are some further impacts on clinical service agencies that attend computerization. Some are readily apparent, others not; some are clearly desirable, others potentially noxious. The first four apply to computer applications in general. The others refer more specifically to the kind of clinical decision support software developed in the project.

(a)   Time will *not* be saved by computerization and the amount of data stored will be increased. Initially, time will be lost until the system is properly operational and staff have accommodated themselves to its functioning.

(b)   Lightning-fast storage of information goes along with lightning-fast eradication. Hence, proper procedures for reproducing back-up copies of data banks become crucial. Fortunately, this task is easily and reliably performed by modern computer systems.

(c)   The secure protection of confidential data becomes a paramount concern as theft of this information can also occur at lightning-fast speed.

(d)   Overdependence on computerized data processing can lead to crippled operations when software or hardware malfunctions. The impact of this can be minimized through building competent technical support networks. Similarly, the selective reproduction on paper of digitally stored information will permit the agency to continue to function at some measure of effectiveness should such a malfunction occur.

(e)   Obsolescence in hardware and software will be totally unavoidable and mercilessly swift. It will be measured in months rather than years. The resulting depreciation of the original financial investments should be expected at the outset of the computerization process. The only absolute defense against this reality is to perpetually postpone computerization until the next, more powerful computer is introduced.

(f)   Deification of the computer can lead to dangerous over-reliance on its calculations. One of the oldest and truest adages about computers is 'garbage in - garbage out'. It succinctly captures the fact that computers are nothing more than incredibly fast and reliable morons. The machine cannot convert items of data into meaningful information in the sense in which Bateson defines this term as being "A difference that makes a difference". The transformation of fact to import must still be performed by the user of the system.

(g)   Users of software systems designed to improve clinical practice will be obliged to engage in conceptual clarification of the nature of their practice. Computer representations of therapy process do not yet capture its subtleties and complexities. Nor can they resolve ambiguities or correct faulty logic.

(h)   Clinical practice will come to be viewed more in digital/scientific terms than in analogic/artistic terms. Practice will be analyzed more atomically according to its subcomponents, rather than holistically according to its overarching design. This development results from the fact that dissection is more amenable to computer-assisted processing than is the expression of global patterns. It is a direct concomitant of the triumph of digital computers (which represent percepts as sequences of bits of data) over analogic computers (which represent percepts as data wholes).

(i)   Practice will tend to become more standardized within any given agency. Because any computer representation of clinical practice will enforce a parsimony of ideas about practice in order to enhance computational manageability, all participating staff members will tend to underuse some of their earlier conceptualizations about practice in accommodating to the new computer system. This will be a consequence of a system that requires certain data from the user which previously may not have been valued highly, and that ignores other data which the user may consider highly important. Hence, the agency as a whole may experience a 'regression to the mean', a clustering of ideas and practice about the new definition of reality imposed by the computer system. Since individual clinical service agencies can easily share their data through the use of telecommunications, the effect of such networking may be to extend standardization beyond the boundaries of any particular agency to the larger system of psychosocial services.

(j)   Computerized agencies may more strongly resist change. Computer systems tend to develop considerable inertia because of the major investment in creating them. Redesign entails reprogramming costs, retraining, and further error-proofing. For a clinical service agency the initial investment in computerization is likely to consume all of the resources allocated for this purpose, and the agency may be unwilling to commit the additional resources required to modify or upgrade the system. Hence, it is anticipated that new developments in the practice professions will be expected to fit existing clinical computer systems, rather than the reverse. An installed system may thereby retard the agency in incorporating therapeutic innovations.

REFERENCES

Bloom, M. and Fischer, J. (1982). *Evaluating Practice: Guidelines for the Accountable Professional*. Prentice Hall, Englewood Cliffs, New Jersey.

Codd, E.F. (1970). 'A Relational Model of Data for Large Shared Data Banks'. *Communications of the ACM*, **13**(6), 377–387.

Dery, D. (1981). *Computers in Welfare: the MIS-match*. Sage, Beverley Hills, California.

Fischer, J. and Gochros, H.L. (1975). *Planned Behavior Change: Behavior Modification in Social Work*. Free Press, New York.

Gripton, J. (1981). 'Microcomputers and Wordprocessors: their Contribution to Clinical Social Work Practice', in G.E. Lasker (ed.), *Applied Systems and Cybernetics Vol. 3, Human Systems, Sociocybernetics, Management and Organizations*. Pergamon, New York.

Gripton, J. (1983). 'How to Computerize your Practice'. *Practice Digest*, **6**(3), 16–20.

Gripton, J. (1984). 'The Digital Social Worker: Microcomputer Applications to Clinical Practice'. Presented at Council of Social Work Education Annual Conference, Detroit.

Hedlund, J.L., Vieweg, B.W. and Cho, D.W. (1985). 'Mental Health Computing in the 1980s: General Information Systems and Clinical Documentation'. **1**(1), 3–34.

Hudson, W.W. (1984). *The Clinical Measurement Package.* Delsey, Homewood, Illinois.

Keen, P.G.W. and Scott-Morton, M.S. (1978). *Decision Support Systems. an Organizational Perspective Reading.* Addison-Wesley, MA.

Licker, P. and Thompson, R. (1985). 'Consulting Systems: Group Decision Support by One Person'. Presented at 18th Annual Hawaii International Conference on Systems Sciences, Honolulu.

Reid, W. and Epstein, L. (eds.) (1977). Colombia, New York.

Saxman, D. and Brandt, J. (1987). *Mental Health Personal Computers.* Psychological Research Associates, Houston, Texas.

Schoech, D. (1982). *Computer Use in Human Services: a Guide to Information Management.* Human Sciences, New York.

Schoech, D., Hennings, M., Schkade, L. and Kooper-Russell, C. (1985). 'Expert Systems: Artificial Intelligence for Professional Decisions'. *Computers in Human Services.* **1**(1), 81–115.

Schwartz, M.D. (1984). *Using Computers in Clinical Practice.* Haworth, New York.

Sprague, R.H. and Carlson, E.D. (1982). *Building Effective Decision Support Systems.* Prentice-Hall, Englewood Cliffs, New Jersey.

Taylor, J.B. (1981). *Using Microcomputers in Social Agencies.* Sage, Beverley Hills, California.

OPTEXT ADVENTURE SYSTEM
SOFTWARE DEVELOPMENT IN PRACTICE - A CASE HISTORY

Les Cowan

Although the presence of computers within social work and social service departments has been a reality for over a decade now (Glastonbury, 1985), for the most part this still seems to remain largely a feature of management control with relatively little of this processing power available to the social work practitioner in direct work with clients. Functions available include data management, statistical analysis, and database handling, but only rarely can a practising social worker call on computer facilities to assist in everyday casework tasks.

At the same time there has been a dramatic growth in the popular appeal of microcomputers, particularly in the guise of the 'home computer'. Young people particularly are in many cases much more at ease with the medium than their elders – including their social workers.

Throughout this period there remains the perennial problem of communication with clients. Particularly in work with children and young people, social work clients often lack the written and verbal skills taken for granted by their allocated workers. Hence, when it comes to discussion of present patterns of behaviour, future choices of action, or review of past events there can develop a disconcerting gulf between worker and client to do with how to even begin discussing these things. Younger clients particularly are well used to being lectured about their conduct and to this extent social workers may not be seen as very greatly different from the host of other authority figures telling them what to do. When it comes to counselling about both past events and future changes, as for example with children in care, the subject matter can be both hypothetical and highly abstract. How then can the worker creatively engage a client who may lack many of the skills basic to such a discussion?

Given the growth in computer systems in the personal social services, widespread and growing familiarity with the medium amongst the general population, the obvious appeal of the games computer for certain age ranges and the continuing needs of our client groups, there would seem to be a considerable scope for bringing these many factors together to help in the daily tasks of communication, counselling and therapy faced by social work practitioners.

The theoretical problems of client communication became particularly real within my own practice in field social work with the needs of a 13-year-old boy in residential care. 'Tony' had already been in a children's home for more than a year following an adoption breakdown, when the question of an alternative family placement came up. Prior to this it had been felt that to force the issue might be detrimental given his previously poor experiences of family life.

Due to the development of a programme of Community Care within Central Regional Social Work Department (involving professional family care for older children on a contract basis), Tony had seen other children from the home moving on and expressed an interest in the scheme for himself. A meeting was soon arranged between Tony, his link worker within the home, the local co-ordinator of the scheme and myself, and the decision of all concerned was that the time was now right to proceed to alternative family placement.

As part of the planning and preparation for such a move the Community Carers scheme already had available a range of preparation exercises for children and their social workers to work through in an effort to anticipate what going to a new family might feel like, and what obstacles might have to be overcome in the process. This included guidance on discussion topics, e.g. "Will they throw me out if I'm bad?" "What will be the easy things and the hard things?", and written exercises like getting different people in the child's life to write down three things about him or her, to help the child consider different aspects of personality which might come into play in moving to a new family.

Additionally, the 'preparation pack' included a number of short scenarios about children recently moved to Community Carers and now facing some sort of problem or dilemma. The child was asked to think with the social worker about what Billy or Janet or Harry should do next and the consequences of that choice. In conversation about these exercises the scheme co-ordinator mentioned his long term hopes of getting some of these exercises onto computer but without any clear idea at that stage of how this might be accomplished.

In software design terms what seemed to be called for was a program which would be able to simulate the circumstances of family life such as a child might experience moving to Community Carers, putting the child in control of the action but able to see the consequences of different choices. It has been noted that: "The type of simulation program which is useful in group work programmes and similar are ones which try to simulate real life (or at least quasi-real life situations!) and allow the user to offer responses and take control of the outcomes." (Dearling, 1986, p.7). The emphasis must be on matching the simulation or game to 'real life' i.e. to the real circumstances of the move, not to some vague or generalised set of circumstances divorced from the personality of the child and the realities of his own background and experiences.

The first attempt at programming something along these lines produced a multiple choice 'adventure' type game similar to some commercially available (such as adventures based on Sue Townsend's 'Adrian Mole' books). At each stage of the game a text 'introduction' on screen summarised the current situation including events as a result of the last user choice. New options for action were then displayed while the program paused for the next choice to be made.

For example, in an adventure entitled 'Billy Hates School', in which the consequences of repeatedly truanting from school are considered in terms of their impact on the success of a family placement, the screen display at a given point in the program might be as follows:

Introduction: Billy still refuses to go back to school. He and his Carers are referred to the Children's Panel. The Panel chairman asks Billy what the problem is.

What next . . .

Option 1: Billy isn't interested in talking about why he isn't going to school. He tells the panel he can't be bothered going.

Option 2: He doesn't believe anyone is really interested in why he isn't going. He makes something up.

Option 3: Billy realises they are trying to make things better for him and that not going to school could mean he'll get sent away. He explains how he's always teased about being in care.

Choosing Option 1 would produce a new introduction perhaps explaining the reaction of the panel of Billy's 'couldn't care less' attitude – they discuss making a residential order. Option 2 might have a similar outcome, while option 3 leads to a discussion of how Billy can be helped to realise that succeeding with his new family is the first step to getting out of care, and going to school, even if it means putting up with silly remarks, is part of making the placement succeed.

Although the child is in control of the action, the program was never conceived of as being for purely individual use. For the maximum benefit to be obtained it was realised from the start that such a simulation needed both child and worker together to consider the alternatives, thinking and talking together about the results of any proposed course of action, and how easy or hard it might be to actually put some of the choices into action. It is readily acknowledged that pressing the 'right' button is a great deal easier than sustaining the 'right' perspective in the face of pressures from peers, parents and past experiences.

Nevertheless it was found that game play of this sort did allow an easier, more productive discussion of the issues. Introducing a third party – the central character of the adventure – helped to avoid the child feeling merely lectured to about what he or she should or should not do. Keeping the subject matter personally relevant but with this degree of detachment also seemed helpful in freeing the child to look at issues otherwise too close for comfort. The game element itself easily surpassed any formal written or verbal exercise in terms of attention and concentration spans.

While programming specifically for the child in question did allow the game scenario to deal with issues felt to be specific to that individual, since all text was held within a stand alone program, there was no scope at this stage for either extending the scope of the adventure, changing details or reconsidering the suitability of a consequence to a particular choice of action. Any change in gameplay involved altering the program listing. Hence if a particular scenario did not exactly fit the needs of the child or did not seem to be 'working' in practice, the programmer would be the only person who could improve things, and that only by breaking into the code of the program. Clearly something a great deal more versatile was called for if the advantages of such a system were ever to be available to more than one child and one worker over a very limited number of topics.

The solution to these problems first presented itself from the code of the programs already written. In each case the structure of the program was almost identical. All that differed was the data. Would it be possible to retain the structure in a system program while merely loading in such data as was required for a particular adventure scenario? If this could be achieved, the main program would also have to permit the writing of the adventure with all text, option numbers and consequence connections by the user without resorting to hard code. In other words, instead of being merely a user system, the program would also have to become an authoring system. Instead of a stand alone game, what was required would be much more like a word processor with game scenarios stored in separate files and loaded in as required. Writing a new adventure or altering a given file would have to be as easy for the non-specialist as writing a letter or report.

Approximately one year and many alterations later OPTEXT now functions as intended. Whether that intention is itself adequately conceived is not for the author to say, but comments from disinterested users have been positive to date. Refinements of the original design include joystick control of all the functions required to load and play an adventure scenario, the option to begin an adventure midway through if a previous session has perhaps not exhausted the possibilities, and the option of linking a given choice back to the same introduction and choices to show how certain courses of action can be circular in their outcome, until that particular pattern of behaviour is broken. A library of some 20 or 30 different scenarios can be held on disc and are immediately available to the user.

Given that "software must encourage exploration and play to be successful" (La Mendola, 1986, p.6) the question of simply 'what happens next' or 'what happens if I do this' has been catered for in allowing the user to try out an option, observe the consequences and then withdraw that choice to have another go if the result is not as expected. OPTEXT can also link either a rising or falling tone to any particular 'cell' to indicate a positive or negative choice leading to that cell to make more of the gameplay desire to 'win' as well as the worker's hope that the user will learn from the experience.

In terms of the needs of the authoring user, adventure scenarios can be written a complete cell at a time, i.e. all text for introduction and options with any associated tone required. To link cells together in an ordered way, allowing any choice to link correctly to its associated 'destination', cells are numbered and options have a destination cell number linked to them. As an additional programming aid, full screen editing is available cell by cell and a 'data map' can be called up to draw on screen the tree diagram of all cell connections. A number of HELP pages are available within the program should instructions additional to the on screen prompts be required.

As the full flexibility and versatility of the system began to become evident as program development continued, it became clear that the original function of preparation for family placement might be only one of a whole range of applications. In line with this, demonstrations were arranged within other departmental settings where direct work with clients involved consideration of options and choices. Adult Training Centre staff found that: "It's great strength is in it's simplicity of operation and (the) variety of situations in which it could be used . . ". Following on from a program demonstration, it was noted that:

"The reaction of staff then and subsequently has been one of increasing excitement at the potential use of computers and this system in particular at Kerse Road. Subsequent discussions have led to many and varied suggestions for the system's use some of which are: with (the) members committee, with profoundly handicapped people, with independent living training groups, with social skills training groups, in group discussions, in health and hygiene, with work discipline groups, etc." (Butler and Tovt, 1987).

Not only has a program demonstration apparently led to some wide ranging thinking on the use of such a simulation system, but it also seems to have brought about a rethink of the use of computers as such within this particular setting.

Other applications implemented to date have included foster parent training, work with children subject to home supervision orders, and in a social work open day where members of the public had the opportunity to try their hand at a simulation of social work practice.

One of the problems long associated with the introduction of computer systems into social work practice has been the issue of practical and observable benefit to the social workers being asked to implement the systems. As has been observed:

"The early developments of computing in the personal social services, with their strong slant towards management uses, had limited appeal to front-line staff because there seemed to be no immediate advantages . . . It remains pertinent for social workers to ask - 'What's in it for us?' - and to go further and wonder about the impact on professional standards and practices, as well as on day-to-day social work activity." (Glastonbury, 1985, p.6)

With it's origins firmly rooted in that very "day-to-day social work activity" it is to be hoped that the OPTEXT ADVENTURE SYSTEM may go some way towards answering the question posed above. Any tool which will assist the social worker in communicating, in counselling and in enabling the client to reassess behaviour should be of benefit. At the same time it must be remembered that no tool can function without the skills of the user behind it, and in this no computer system is better than the worker utilising it.

In terms of OPTEXT as a case history in software design and implementation, lessons learned have been to do with matching the capabilities of the system to the needs of the recipient rather than the reverse, and in frequent and open-ended consultation with the eventual end users. Perhaps this way there will be some likelihood of computer power contributing positively to "professional standards and practice" rather than remaining by and large in service management rather than front-line practice.

REFERENCES

Butler, M. and Tovt, G. (1987). Appraisal of Visit from Mr. L. Cowan, Social Worker, Denny Area Office to Kerse Road Day Centre Demonstrating the Potential of a Computer System. Internal Social Work Department Report. Unpublished.

Dearling, A. (1986). 'Computers in IT and Associated Settings – a View from Scotland'. *Programmes in Practice Newsletter*, Autumn 1986, University of Sheffield.

Glastonbury, B. (1985). *Computers in Social Work*. Macmillan, London.

LaMendola, W. (1986). 'Software Development in the U.S.A.', *Computer Applications in Social Work and Allied Professions*, 3, No.1, CASW Ltd.

"BUSTED", A COMPUTERIZED THERAPEUTIC GAME:
DESCRIPTION, DEVELOPMENT, AND PRELIMINARY EVALUATION

Hy Resnick

This paper describes a computerized therapeutic simulation game designed for troubled youth. The hope, not yet an hypothesis, is that this game, 'Busted', will reduce antisocial behavior. The paper also provides a brief evaluation of the game, which is still in its prototype stage, and offers a perspective on electronic therapeutic games in the helping professions.

Traditional therapies and educational programs have not proven successful with troubled, acting-out adolescents. These young people do not enter easily into therapeutic relationships, often mistrusting the therapist as an authority figure, and they frequently drop out of treatment (Grotevant and Cooper, 1983; Clark and Schoech, 1984). Labeled as 'the problem', they resist therapeutic talk. Working through electronic therapeutic games can take the spotlight off the adolescents as troubled individuals and may bring the therapists closer to the youths' experiences. In this way, such games may increase the benefit adolescents derive from therapeutic experiences (Lepper, 1985).

GAMES, COMPUTERS, AND COMPUTERIZED GAMES IN THE HELPING PROFESSIONS

The helping professions have long recognized the potential of games as a tool in therapeutic work. Scholars and practitioners such as Freud, Bettelheim (1984), Gardner (1973), Axline (1947), and others have written about the therapeutic uses of young people's games.

Games have been used in a variety of ways to assist in the therapeutic process. They can be used to develop therapeutic alliances; to aid diagnosis; to enhance a youthful ego; to develop cognitive skills such as concentration, consequence awareness and problem solving; and to develop social skills Schaefer and Reid, 1986). Games have been used to establish situations in which players can confront and work through anxiety about certain conditions (Nickerson and O'Laughlin, 1983). For example, the game Monopoly can be used to master the anxiety created by game conditions of poverty, competition and helplessness (Capell, 1968). Playfulness and creativity may emerge, and win-win games can create a safe environment in which to explore new behaviors (Nickerson and O'Laughlin, 1983).

Games can be used to teach societal norms and values. Schaefer and Reid (1986) describe one of the earliest board games, called Mansion of Happiness, which appeared during Victorian times. The object of this game was to reach an ethereal mansion by avoiding vice and temptation. Piaget (1962) has written about games as vehicles for children to practice

rules that compose a social order. Delinquency has been
described as a failure to learn socialized behavior (Cressy and
Ward, 1969; Serok, 1986), and certain games may have the
potential to teach more acceptable behavior.

Serok (1986) conducted a study about delinquents' game
preferences and found, not surprisingly, that delinquents
preferred games of chance over games of strategy. She posited
that games of chance require less need for assessment of
behavioral consequences, decision-making, or acting within
societal norms. She also found that delinquents preferred games
with fewer rules, requiring less conformity or obedience and
that they also liked games of aggression. Following implications,
a program of games for this population could include gradually
introducing those which have rules, reduce aggression, and
reward achievement of societal norms.

Some creative games have been developed using these
principles. Corder (1986) developed a board game based on the
general categories of 'knowing yourself', 'understanding each
other', and 'problem solving'. Players move along a board
using a dice and choose cards that relate to the three
categories, depending on which square they land. This game has
been used in outpatient mental health settings, residential
treatment centers, group homes, classrooms of emotionally
disturbed teens, and detention centers. Participants have
reported a positive experience using this game.

Another game which has been used with acting-out youth is
the Etiquette Olympics game (Corder et al, 1981). After
structured training with role modeling and didactic materials,
each group member role-plays a specific task, such as making
introductions, admitting a mistake or making an apology. Other
group members act as judges showing points or ratings and
members are assigned homework for practice of social skills.
They can then accumulate points for successful completion of
homework, which will earn them rewards. Many other games have
been developed and used with adolescent acting-out youth
including 'Stacking the Deck' (Foy and McMorrare, 1984);
'Ungame', developed by the Ungame Company; and the 'Talking,
Feeling, and Doing Game', published by Creative Therapists.

In general, board games have been used successfully with
many populations and for many purposes, including therapy.
However, despite their strengths as relatively low-cost transport-
able media, they have certain features which may reduce their
desirability in a treatment or educational setting. Paper
shuffling, organizing, score keeping, and retrieval are distract-
ing, complicated, and inefficient. Variety and complexity of
game exercises are limited to two dimensions. Finally, the
printed word in board games makes it difficult to revise a game
when the players get used to it, bored with it, or new social
stimuli or fads 'date' the content.

The advent of the personal computer as a medium for gaming
opens up a wide range of possibilities which might solve some,
if not all, of the above limitations of board-anchored games. In
addition, gaming with a computer also reveals the fun and
excitement of the computer itself to youthful populations who may
ordinarily resist such exposure.

Adding computers to the world of therapeutic games have provided a number of advantages, both mechanical and psychological, including faster and more accurate retrieval of information involved in games, such as points (awarded or accumulated), as well as reminders of each player's turn or even when they are penalized a turn. A second contribution is the programmed display capacity of the computer which can be used to inform players either randomly or at proscribed moments in the game about how and when to proceed, and in what way. The rich array of graphics available to portray events and processes in a way and manner which only a computer can offer is another advantage, making the game more interesting, attractive, and involving to sensation-seeking adolescents. Finally, from a psychological point of view, the computer can become to the youthful player an object of identification. Players may impute magical properties or qualities to the computer, thus increasing its power and potential impact on them. Then, for example, when the computer through its program instructs players to share interpersonal concerns with a group, they seem more willing to do so.

The first computer program aimed at on-line communication between client and computer was developed by Weizenbaum in the 1960s (Colby et al, 1966). This program, 'Eliza', simulated a patient/therapist dialogue. Keying in certain words triggered responses in the computer to clarify, focus, ask a question or rephrase the user's comment.

More recently, other computer programs allow individual clients to interact with the computer and gain self-understanding and solve problems (Das et al, 1983). Some of these programs include packaged therapies in progressive relaxation, desensitization, assertiveness training, and development of social skills. Software programs have even been developed that can be used by couples and individuals to make more rational and intelligent decisions about their relationships and by families to negotiate contracts which reward improved behavior within the family (Bleckman et al, 1986; Lehtinen and Smith, 1985).

One study examined the use of computers in the treatment of depression. Clients were given six to eight sessions over a six-week period that used the computer to administer the Beck Depression Inventory. Multiple choice items and case vignettes taught clients to identify and deal with dysfunctional thoughts. Initial findings of this research seem to show that clients who use system experience a level of improvement that is significant when compared to traditional therapies (Selmi et al, 1982).

The impartiality and anonymity of the computer may be especially attractive to adolescents. Research by Stollack and Guerny (1964) and a follow-up study by Schwitzgebel and Kolb (1964) showed that delinquents who talked into a tape recorder about their problems had a reduction in their delinquent behavior.

The attraction of fast-paced games of chance for the acting-out adolescent seems to point to the potential of computer games as a novel method of shaping antisocial behavior. Some work has already begun in this area. Clark and Schoech (1984) have developed a computer-assisted game for adolescents that presents opportunities to make choices, strive for goals, and accept consequences in a fantasy world. The game involves recovering a lost crown using the aid of a thief, a fighter, or a magic user. The characters relate to the delinquent problems of fighting, stealing, and relying on luck. The mentor in the game (therapist) offers support and encouragement for thinking before acting and making good decisions.

Allen (1984) has also adapted several computer games for therapeutic use. He describes a game called Ultima where a player can be a fighter, wizard, cleric, or thief, Again, the therapist acts as a mentor who points out how the player can get into more trouble by making evil or impulsive choices. Other such games are Crush, Crumble, and Chomp and Softalk. Allen points out that playing games gives the therapist many opportunities to draw metaphors between the actions of the game and real life.

The computer sim-game 'Smack' has been developed recently in Ireland by Londac Data to reduce drug abuse through realistic stages and conditions encountered by drug abusing youth. Students who choose drug abusing options slide into social, moral, and physical decline. The program is available for use with computers which are widely used in Irish schools.

Finally, a recent contribution is the Computer Marriage Contract Game (Bleckman and McEnroe, 1986) designed to help parents and children resolve home-type conflicts. A particular feature in this computer marriage contract game is its contingency contracting where couples: (1) select one problem to negotiate; (2) convert a specific complaint into a target behavior; (3) select a co-operative behavior; (4) sign a contract describing details of the agreement; and (5) chart responsibilities. Since it was created by behaviorally oriented therapists and scholars, this game is a purer extension of theory into the computer game world than the others described.

BUSTED

Description

The computer program which is the focus of this paper was adapted from a board game developed a number of years ago, called 'Busted' (see Resnick, Boler and Merril, 1986), and is designed to help troubled teenagers in educational or social welfare settings to increase their awareness of the consequences of their behavior. The game 'requires' them to engage in simulated situations which help them *experience* the link between their behaviors and many of the consequences which follow – addressing a deficiency often ascribed to this population. Busted, computerized when the advantages of the computer and the disadvantages of the two-dimensional board game became evident, is a recent addition to a growing computerized therapeutic game inventory in the human service profession.

Busted uses a traditional board format of 24 squares outlined around the perimeter of a board displayed on the computer screen during the game. Players, after selecting a token from a bank of tokens on the screen when the game begins, 'roll' dice (touch the 'd' key) and land on one of the 24 squares located around the board. When a player lands on a 'situation' square, the situation database is activated and presents a situation in text on the screen. The situations represent typical dilemmas for teenagers in trouble, such as:

Your friends tell you they have the answers to a big math test and ask if you want them.

The situation is followed by a list of four possible options to deal with this situation. The player is then prompted to select one of the four options (touch 1, 2, 3 or 4 key). After the option is chosen the consequence database is in turn activated and displays a realistic consequence to the player, letting the players know what their behavior led to. Such a consequence might be depending upon the option they chose:

Your teacher discovers the answers were stolen and suspects you and your friends and suspends you all. Lose ten points.

The next player is then prompted to touch the dice (d) key and the game continues. Players move around the board trying to win as many points as they can by making choices. These points can be exchanged at the end of the game (depending on whether the game is played in an educational or group home or correctional setting) into cigarettes, candy, or extra credits. As players continue, they encounter situations from four social arenas – peers, work, school, and family and select options to deal with these situations and experience realistic consequences.

Other more recently added elements of Busted are the:

Burn square. A player, upon landing on this square, is posed a challenging question about his or her relationships with family, friends, authorities, and even this particular group of players. After hearing the players' response, the group, with the help of the adult advisor, discusses and evaluates that response by awarding or taking away points from the player. The computer displays each judgement (plus 5 to minus 5), averages the group evaluation, and then adds or subtracts these points to the player's total points.

Action square. Players are given an opportunity to recommend actions to improve lives of others. Example: What do you think the police should do to help kids in trouble? The group evaluates this response as well.

Fun square. Players are exposed to different entertainment activities and asked to choose between two activities and explain why. In this square, the computer, not the group, awards the player with points for choosing any one of the two activities.

This game's primary focus is on improving the player's awareness of the link between their behaviors and consequences. Over time, the designers have added components which are intended to increase the attractiveness of the game as well as to strengthen its impact.

A major modification has been to increase the use of the playing group as a means of influence rather than as a context for influence. The Burn and Action squares now ask the player to engage with the group in order to receive points. This increases the salience of the group upon its members and strengthens both the attractiveness of the game and its impact. Of course, the game advisor's skill and effectiveness become more important.

Assumptions

Designers of Busted made the following assumptions:

A Teenagers (with problems) would be highly attracted to and willing to participate in this therapeutic intervention in school or in a group home because:

1   The events in the simulation-game are relevant to their life and close to their experience.

2   The game is fun to play but it is also challenging and helpful to think about the options they have in dealing with the situations (Serok, 1986).

3   The graphics, the winning and losing of points and turns, the selection of tokens, the rolling of the dice, fit in with the adolescent need for sensation, challenge, testing of themselves, and the like.

4   It is played with a group of people their own age, which serves as an attraction to reluctant participants. The peer group then becomes another context of influence. The facilitator encourages the group to adopt prosocial norms when it is evaluating members' choices in response to the Burn and Action squares.

5   The game provides players with feelings of power and self-confidence when they can: (a) bring graphics or text onto the screen by merely pressing a key; or (b) use a computer, very often for the first time.

B Teenagers would increase their capacity to:

(a) think about the consequences of their behavior; and as a result

(b) reduce their antisocial behaviors (Serok, 1986).

C Educational and social welfare institutions would value this electronic device as an educational therapeutic tool, and be able to integrate it into their curriculum or program.

D Repeated experiences provided by Busted of receiving realistic consequences as a result of choices they made in the game will lead to a greater awareness (cognitive change) of the link between their behaviors and the consequences they receive in the real world. It is hoped that this improvement in awareness will be followed by changed antisocial attitudes and behaviors.

Change Theories

The theories used to make the game attractive and capable of changing players' attitudes and behaviors are derived from:

A Behavioral theory – prosocial behaviors are rewarded (mostly) and antisocial behaviors are punished (mostly) (Chambless and Goldstein, 1979).

B Group process theories – prosocial norms of the group are developed by the computer, the facilitator, and group members which encouraged self-disclosure, making smart instead of foolish or impulsive choices, and thinking about helping others.

C Cognitive theory – thoughts, beliefs and cognitive capacities are increasingly recognized as targets of change of effective therapeutic work. The designers of Busted assume that repeated experiences in the safe environment of the sim-game – and in the presence of their peers – will increase the players' capacity to choose prosocial behaviors in the 'real' world. These game experiences will help them think ahead and be more aware of the consequences of their behavior and as a result of this improved awareness change their behavior (DiGuippe, 1981).

Preliminary Evaluation

The purpose of this evaluation was to study the extent to which the target population (12- to 17-year-olds, predelinquent or delinquent boys and girls) in a public educational setting were *attracted* to the game and willing to play it for a two- to three-month period, two to three times per week and one to one and a half hours per round. Without such attraction, the game would not be played frequently enough to have any impact. This obviously is the ultimate goal of the game designers – the rudimentary state of the prototype limits testing.

The Population Tested

The two senior high classes whose four teachers expressed interest in testing Busted contained 20 teenagers between the ages of 14 and 17. All of the youngsters in these classes had experienced difficulty in traditional public school settings and had been referred to this alternative program available in each of the school districts in the state of Washington. They were mostly white, working class boys and girls whose parents signed permission slips allowing their children to participate in the computerized sim-game program. Most of the students had problems of conflict with parents, police, school authorities, etc.

Teachers were interviewed at the end of the research period by the author and his research assistant. Unfortunately, many of the students who played the game for the five-week period were inadvertently scheduled for a bus trip on the day the interviews were held, and so were unavailable for the arranged interview. Only three of the 12 boys and two of the eight girls were interviewed. Further contact was not possible with the 15 students because of the end of the school term.

Setting of Research

Although the researcher was able to gain entry into this school setting (the principal, after seeing a demonstration of Busted, sent a letter to the children's parents requesting permission to use the game with their children), it was much more difficult to integrate the game into the curriculum and as a result the full, on-going commitment and support from the teachers was not always present. Teachers didn't have sufficient time or skill to facilitate the interactive moments in the game which often required: (a) on-going explanation of the rules; (b) frequent and intensive facilitation work discussion the topics which emerged in the game; or (c) occasional setting limits when the youngsters were misusing the point system. Further, Busted was sometimes used as an entertainment or control device rather than as an integral part of the curriculum supported by the faculty and the administration of the school to help them achieve their objectives. This must be achieved before a tool such as Busted can be truly evaluated.

Summary of Findings

The four teachers and five students interviewed agreed that Busted was an enjoyable and useful addition to the classroom program. They reported that girls seem to play it with greater enthusiasm and seemed to benefit more from their experience. But the boys also felt they learned some things from Busted including seeing how other kids would handle tough situations or learning how to talk in front of other kids (as in Burn or Action square).

Teachers also reported that students who normally have very short attention spans were able to play the game for up to 50 minutes at times! Both boys and girls also reported it helped them consider options when facing tough situations.

Although the game was only played one hour per week (or less) for five weeks, all teachers reported there was a great deal of interest in playing the game whenever they could. One teacher found the discussions which took place in response to the Burn or Action square situations helped the teachers know their students better, even using these discussions to refer the students to community agencies for help.

Both teachers and students felt Busted was helpful, would want to use it for next semester, and recommended that Busted be used in other schools. Students added they thought kids their age would like playing it.

SUMMARY AND CONCLUSIONS

Even though the development of computer games for therapeutic purposes is in its infancy, some statements can be made about their purpose, potential contribution, and driving forces.

Computer therapeutic games should be seen first as part of the effort begun in the 1960s to experiment with electronic technology and its possible applications in therapeutic work. The computer as surrogate therapist is one direction this experimentation can take, although there are technical and ethical problems as well as questions about effectiveness. The computer offers its flexibility, objectivity, and speed; it cannot be programmed to care. It cannot deal with manipulation, respond to the unexpected, or reach for and share insights and interpretations based on non-verbal hints. The designers of computer games are moving in another direction. Computer therapeutic games comprise an effort to use the computer as a symbol producer, not just an information processing machine, and take the therapeutic process into new and uncharted country. Games, fantasies, stories, and simulations all have therapeutic potential and have been used in therapeutic practice. Their potential integrated with the computer, could be significant and needs to be investigated.

These innovative efforts also continue the profession's attempts to use games as helping tools or agents. Purpose designed and off-the-shelf games have become part of people changing work both in social welfare and education throughout the last decade. Computerization of these games, it is hoped, will increase the games' attractiveness, sophistication, and therefore impact. Certainly the authors of Busted have had this experience. More systematic empirical research is needed to determine the extent to which and under what specific conditions the games are effective.

Although the experience in this school and with this population was positive enough to warrant another, more planned effort in the following semester, it is not possible even yet to say that playing the game will lead to the attainment of desired behavioral and attitude change. It is clear from our brief evaluation that a computerized game is an attractive element in a class curriculum, students enjoy it, have some serious discussions, and want to play more. But whether or not this intervention in this setting has the potential for effecting behavioral change remains to be seen.

REFERENCES

Allen, D. (1984). 'The Use of Computer Fantasy Games in Child Therapy'. In D. Schwartz (ed.), *Using Computers in Clinical Practice: Psychotherapy and Mental Health Applications.* Haworth Press, New York.

Axline, V. (1947). *Play Therapy.* Houghton-Mifflin, Boston.

Bettelheim, B. (1984). *A Home for the Heart.* A. Knopf, New York.

Bleckman, A., Rabin, C. and McEnroe, M. (1986). 'Family Communication and Problem Solving with Board Games and Computer Games'. In C.E. Schaefer and S. Reid (eds.), *Game Play: Therapeutic Uses of Childhood Games.* John Wiley & Sons, New York.

Clark, B. and Schoech, D. (1984). 'A Computer Assessed Therapeutic Game for Adolescents: Initial Development and Comments'. In D. Schwartz, op.cit.

Capell, M. (1968). 'Passive Mastery of Helplessness in Games'. *American Image,* **25**, 309–330.

Chambless, D.L. and Goldstein, D.J. (1979). 'Behavioral Psychotherapy'. In J. Corsini et al (eds.), *Current Psychotherapies.* Peacock Press, Illinois.

Colby, K., Watt, J.B. and Gilbert, J.P. (1966). 'A Computer Method of Psychotherapy: Preliminary Communication'. *J. Nervous Mental Diseases,* **142**, 149–152.

Corder, B.F., Whiteside, R. and Wall, S. (1981). *A Structured Social Skills Learning Program for Adolescents.* University of North Carolina Press, Chapel Hill.

Corder, B. (1986). 'Therapeutic Games in Group Therapy with Adolescents'. In C. Schaefer and S. Reid, op.cit.

Creative Therapists (1983). *The Talking, Feeling and Doing Game.* Creative Therapists, 155 Country Road, Cresskill, New Jersey.

Cressy, R.D. and Ward, A.D. (1969). *Delinquency, Crime and Social Process.* Harper & Row, New York.

Das, A., Bright, L. and Amaby, M. (1983). 'Uses and Abuses of Computers in Counseling'. *Elementary School Guidance and Counseling,* **18**(1), 51–57.

DiGuieppe, R.J. (1981). 'Cognitive Therapy with Children'. In G. Emery, S.D. Holon and R. Bedrosian (eds.), *New Directions in Cognitive Therapy.* Guildford Press, New York.

Foy, R. and McMorrare, M.J. (1984). *Stacking the Deck.* Research Press, Champaign, Illinois.

Gardner, R. (1973). *Understanding Children.* Aronson, New York.

Grotevant, H.D. and Cooper, C.R. (eds.) (1983). *Adolescent Development in the Family.* Jossey-Bass, San Francisco.

Lehtinen, M.W. and Smith, G. (1985). 'The Personal Computer as Marriage Counselor'. *Marriage and Family Review.* **8**(1–2), 137–154.

Lepper, M.R. (1985). 'Microcomputers in Education: Motivational Social Issues'. *American Psychologist,* **40**, 1–18.

Nickerson, F. and O'Laughlin, K. (1983). 'The Therapeutic Use of Games'. In C. Schaefer and K. O'Connor (eds.), *Handbook of Play Therapy.* John Wiley & Sons, New York.

Piaget, J. (1962). *Play, Dreams, and Imitation in Childhood.* Norton, New York.

Resnick, H., Boler, M. and Merril, N. (1986). 'Busted, a Therapeutic Simulation Game', in C. Schaefer and S. Reid (eds.), op.cit.

Schaefer, C. and Reid, S. (1986). *Game Play: Therapeutic Uses of Childhood Games.* John Wiley & Sons, New York.

Schwitzgebel, R. and Kolb, P. (1964). 'Inducing Behavior Change in Adolescent Delinquents'. *Behavior Residential Therapy*, 1, 297.

Selmi, P.M., Klein, M.H., Greist, J.H., Johnson, J.H. and Harris, W.G. (1982). 'An Investigation of Computer Assisted Cognitive-Behavior Therapy in the Treatment of Depression'. *Behavior Research Methods and Instrumentation*, 14, 181–185.

Serok, S. (1986). 'Therapeutic Implications of Games with Juvenile Delinquents'. In C. Schaefer and S. Reid, op.cit.

Stollack, G.E. and Guerny, B. (1964). 'Exploration of Personal Problems by Juvenile Delinquents under Conditions of Minimal Reinforcement'. *J Clinical Psychology*, 20, 279.

Ungame Company (1984). *Ungame*. Anaheim, California.

PART II

AGENCY FOCUS

CHAPTER 4

Education and Training

In North America education and training is presently an area of
rapid development of human service information technology
applications. Progress in these areas has been competitive,
expensive, and, in some cases, led by the commercial interests
of either vendors or educational institutions. Training activities
outside the formal educational institutions, when viewed as a
market place, probably represent the single largest area of
potential application development available today. Because of the
high rate of financial return possible in this area, a few
countries have experienced a gold rush in the development of
training resources. In the human services, this has meant that
many corporations and individual practitioners have begun to
offer training activities to human service organizations, thereby
increasing their opportunities to educate staff and to support
the introduction of information technologies at non-management
levels. It has also meant that educational institutions have
begun to see yet another major part of their traditional market
erode and, in many cases, have responded with a renewed
emphasis upon the development of innovative educational
programming, often built upon information technologies. It has
also had the unfortunate, though hopefully temporary consequence, of increasing competitiveness of the worst sort, with
speculation about profit taking and concerns about intellectual
property rights dominating the real need to share techniques,
tools, and products, As a result, the ability to generate an
agenda of research or to engage co-operatively in technology
transfer to other trainers or educators in this area has been
severely limited.

Europe has some of this dynamicism, and faces some of these
problems, but in most ways is a paler image of the picture
across the Atlantic. The use of some forms of information
technology, especially those which are audio-visual, are
reasonably well established, with growing commercial as well as
agency and educational activity. There are fewer examples of
applications using computer-based formats, though it is valid to
make a distinction between education and training *about* IT, and
the use of IT as a medium. The former, with its narrower
curriculum range, is firmly rooted, particularly in courses for
beginners in using computers, and short training sessions in the
using the more popular pieces of commercial software (word
processors, databases and so forth). Agency in-service programmes have played an important part in acclimatising staff to
use terminals and microcomputers to access the agency's own
information system. In contrast, the use of computers as a

medium for instruction remains under-developed, with a shortage in agencies and educational centres both of classroom equipment and software.

In this chapter two examples of training have been included. One describes the experience of a large public welfare agency in the United States and demonstrates what can be done with co-operative ventures between a human service organization with training needs and a University. In this case, a public social service agency, with seventeen hundred employees, a one billion dollar budget, and reaching nearly a quarter of a million individuals a month, has contracted with a School of Social Work to provide specialized training in order to prepare its staff for an organizational environment which supports the utilization of information technology applications in its work. The paper documents the training experience, but more importantly, demonstrates an open and co-operative approach in the conceptualization and implementation of training. The design for the training is elegant, utilizing a range of computing devices and computer-based training tools.

The second training paper describes a programme undertaken by the Israeli National Adult Probation Services. That agency has worked for over four years to attempt to develop computer-based 'Supervisory Knowledge Modules' which can relieve supervisors of routine administrative and educational duties and allow them to concentrate upon other supervisory and treatment tasks. In carrying out this project, supervisors have apparently participated in what can be considered the most thorough information technology application training course in supervision, decision-making, and knowledge representation yet described in the human service literature.

In education, the development of coursework has been rather uneven, with some faculties and departments still questioning whether or not information technology should be taught in the human services. Available coursework ranges from single self-standing courses at the North American undergraduate college level, to graduate courses covering full areas of the curriculum as well as doctoral work, such as at the University of Denver. Beyond the coursework, more exciting developments are evolving, particularly in the development of electronic workstations, distance learning, and a combination of these capabilities with elements of artificial intelligence. The term 'electronic workstation' has been used to talk about the capabilities of an advanced PC, which functions as an extremely powerful symbol processor, and which has a set of programs that make few technical demands upon the user, yet provide the user with tools to perform sophisticated tasks, such as writing, communicating with geographically distant sites, and database searching. Distance learning refers to the capability to conduct education and training over distances utilizing computer and communicating technologies. Artificial intelligence refers to a set of structured programming techniques which permit the user to establish a relationship between a computer-based symbol set and the user's knowledge of that set.

Three of the papers, those of Forgie, Bellamy, and Mielnic-zuk, describe the combined efforts of the University of Toronto Social Information Resource Centre, the Advanced Communicating Laboratory, and the Faculty of Social Work to implement an approach which includes the 'Integrated Work Station', an electronic workstation under development at the University. This work is probably the most advanced work being done in the human services which involves the notion of an electronic workstation. However, it is critical to note, as it is with the other pieces in this volume, how the philosophy and principles of the human services influence and shape the technology in use.

In a separate but related piece, MacFadden, one of the Faculty of Social Work at the University of Toronto, describes the participation of graduate social work students in an educational project to develop a computer-assisted instruction package in child sexual abuse assessment. Using a work team of child abuse specialists, students, and staff, the author describes an example of sound educational design that both transfers technical acumen to team members and produces a practical, worthwhile product. LaMendola describes the frame-work of an approach to distance learning undertaken by the University of Denver and AT & T. In his article, we are struck by the moulding of the technical approach to the requirements of the human services, both in terms of educational principles and human values.

PREPARING HUMAN SERVICE STAFF FOR THE
AUTOMATED ENVIRONMENT
THE CONNECTICUT EXPERIENCE

Judith M. Feinstein, Shelley Mills-Brinckley,
and Peter Petrella

AUTOMATION AND HUMAN SERVICES

Computer technology is a growing field which has an impact on
all facets of our lives. Its introduction into Human Services has
forced us, not to redefine our focus, but to plan for this technology in ways that support the ethical and human dynamics
which are the cornerstone of our human service delivery system,
Automation is enabling us to expand services, be more fiscally
accountable, forecast, plan, and evaluate, and improve the
quality of services without sacrificing the human interaction. In
fact, technology allows us to focus our efforts more clearly on
the client population and the human side of human services.

To maximize this great potential, it is necessary that staff
who provide and support our delivery systems be trained in
understanding, using, and evaluating the automated systems and
the variety of computer technologies that are available. Only
with a solid commitment from staff, gained through a comprehensive training program, will such technologies realize their
capabilities as viable tools.

To ensure this commitment and skill requires training that
gives all levels of staff within a stated environment an
opportunity to be involved in the conceptualization, rationale,
and hands-on use of the systems. In the State of Connecticut's
welfare department, known as The Department of Income
Maintenance, a comprehensive training program is being
implemented to prepare the 1700 staff members for the automated
environment. The purpose of this paper is twofold: (a) to
discuss the role of training in the design, development, and the
delivery of training to support the implementation of the new
automated eligibility management system; and (b) to offer
practical hands-on training strategies that can be applied in a
variety of environments to secure staff commitment to the
automated environment.

OPERATIONAL BACKGROUND

Currently in the State of Connecticut, the Department of Income
Maintenance (DIM) is investing over fifteen million dollars in a
battery of systems and hardware to support the delivery of
money payments, medical, and food stamps to the State's welfare
population. DIM, which is the State's largest agency, spends
approximately one quarter of the State budget, or about one
billion dollars, on the administration of the Aid to Families with
Dependent Children program, Medicaid, Food Stamps, State

Supplement to SSA program, Refugee Assistance, and Energy Assistance. The Department has thirteen field offices located throughout the State and employs some 1700 individuals. DIM's programs reach 225,000 individuals each month.

In order to receive federal financial participation to support these programs, the federal government requires states to provide policy and program training to all staff. To meet this requirement, the Department maintains a contractual agreement with the University of Connecticut, School of Social Work, under which the University employs specialized staff to provide a full complement of training services to the Department. Two Human Resource Development Managers are employed to supervize and direct the training program. One manager is responsible for the functional and administrative management of nine District Office training staff who deliver program policy training. The other manager is responsible for the management and co-ordination of centralized curriculum development activities and training programs for the Agency supervisors, managers, clerical and 'Central Office' staff, and for computer training programs and centralized generic skill programs. There are nine centralized Human Resources Development Specialists who design and deliver these programs and three secretaries who support the entire training unit.

THE CONNECTICUT EXPERIENCE

The United States Department of Health and Human Services Office of Family Assistance has mandated that all states develop and implement a federally certifiable family assistance management information system. In July 1984, the Connecticut Department of Income Maintenance began planning for a mainframe automated eligibility determination system. The overall goal of the project is to develop an integrated automated system which will aid staff in the determination of client eligibility for all programs administered by the Department, dispense benefits and notices to clients, and provide management support to all levels of program administration.

To support this massive effort the Department is committed to a three-pronged automated approach.

EMS

Eligibility Management System,
a mainframe based automated
integrated eligibility determination
system for all welfare programs

CBT

Computer Based Training
using Phoenix, a mainframe
based authoring and
delivery system

PCs

The introduction of microcomputers to act as
sensitizing and transitional
tools to EMS, and to back up
current mainframe system efforts

These three systems are not stand alone efforts, but three tools dependent on each other to create an environment which maximizes its technological and human resources.

EMS - Eligibility Management System Description

The Eligibility Management System (EMS) will provide integrated automated support for all aspects of initial client screening, intake interviewing, eligibility determination, and ongoing case maintenance activities. EMS will also provide an integrated approach to financial and management information reporting.

Over one thousand field staff administering complex welfare programs to some 225,000 individuals each month will utilize the Eligibility Management System on a daily basis to assist them in making accurate eligibility decisions. The other 700 staff will use the system in a variety of ways to support the delivery of services. The programs covered by EMS include Aid to Families with Dependent Children (AFDC), Medical Assistance (including Medicaid), Food Stamps, State Supplement, Refugee Assistance, and Energy Assistance.

EMS will automatically interface with the Department's Medicaid Management Information System as well as the Departments of Labor, Motor Vehicles, and Human Resources to update case information. The new system will take advantage of automated data matches with the Federal Social Security System, the National Food Stamp Disqualification Network, and the Internal Revenue Service Income and Eligibility Verification System (IEVS).

The Eligibility Management System will be an online information system that will be designed to support 1200+ display stations and 200+ printers located throughout the State of Connecticut. The system will process an estimated 500,000 transactions daily. A computer-based training package will be accessible to all display stations through EMS. EMS will also have electronic mail capability.

To support this dramatic change from a primarily paper-driven organization to the more automated process, the Staff Development and Training Unit is charged with: (a) identifying the most appropriate strategies and configurations for preparing staff for the automated environment; and (b) designing, developing, and delivering the overall training for EMS.

The first step taken by training management was to identify the role of training in the automation project, and then establish and secure that role. Towards this end, one of the most significant decisions made by the training unit's management was to organizationally position a staff representative on the EMS Project Team. The EMS team, which is composed of the project director, a policy consultant, a technical adviser, a field liaison, and the training unit staff person, is charged with developing and implementing EMS. This strategic positioning of a trainer on the project team allowed the training unit the opportunity to gain in-depth knowledge of what was being planned, and to develop the content for the EMS planning document.

In addition to positioning a training staff member on the project team, training management established a Training Committee to address training issues associated with the implementation of the new system. The purpose of establishing such a committee was to ensure a strong user input from all parts of the organization into training design and development. The Training Committee is composed of individuals from all levels within the Department – from management to clerical. The goal of the Training Committee is threefold: to analyze training needs, to review the design of the training plan, and to assist in the implementation of training. One of the first tasks of the Training Committee was to design, develop, and administer a training needs assessment to agency staff. The focus of the needs assessment was to determine staff's current 'comfort level' with automation and determine the support training necessary to implement EMS.

In addition to administering the needs assessment, a number of other tasks and activities were performed by the training unit. These tasks serve as the foundation to ensure that the most efficient and effective tools and methods are employed in the delivery of EMS training.

Secure from EMS project management a training/practice/test system that emulates the production system being developed.

Identify and establish training's role in the development and review of the system help screens, alert messages, and any on-line documentation. In this way the concept of embedded training is introduced as a system feature.

Participate in the development of user's manuals. This will ensure user-friendly documents that can serve as training aids.

Research and develop curriculum on the ergonomic issues associated with the use of computers. In Connecticut, the training unit developed a computer-based training course related to some ergonomic issues and relaxation.

Develop and deliver training in other areas that will change as a result of system development and implementation. For example, the Staff Development and Training Unit has provided training on changing job roles, managing computers, and enhancing keyboard skills.

Develop an organizational and informal relationship with your Data Processing department. This can be done by introducing training resources to support DP in their role, and by including DP as a member of the training plan review team.

Counteract rumors. Rumors about the system development process are bound to arise. One way to counteract these rumors is to provide information to all staff about the system development process. In Connecticut, training is responsible for the publishing of *EMS UPDATE*, a newsletter that goes out bi-monthly to all departmental staff.

Identify competencies for EMS. Staff will be tested throughout the delivery of training and then certified as 'user ready' upon reaching the competency standard.

Design, develop, and deliver curricula for EMS. Curricula will focus on conceptual sessions followed by hands-on mastery.

Design Computer Based Training (CBT) courses to support EMS. CBT will be used primarily to measure and track competencies.

CBT - Computer Based Training

The introduction of Phoenix, a mainframe authoring system, into DIM provided the Department with a sophisticated tool to assist in the design, development, delivery, and management of training. CBT is allowing staff to become familiar with automated system in a non-threatening environment.

Increasing efficiency and effectiveness is the overall goal of using Phoenix as a training tool. Furthermore, a computer-based training system assists the training function in the following areas which are crucial in the design and delivery of mass training efforts to a large population.

Increased Control

- Insurance that instructional curricula are presented uniformly.
- Opportunity for participants to practice skills until mastered.
- Control over management of the training function through access to data relative to training population.

Reduced Resource Requirements

- Allows for the training of major policy and/or system changes to bring a large population up to speed at the same time.

Individualization

- Allows each student to learn at own pace.

Reduced Training Time

- Reflection of individualization and availability; decreases amount of time participant is away from the job.

Timeliness, Availability, and Convenience

- With the EMS system in place at the work location, the convenience of expanding the terminal capability to put training on-line provides continual accessibility while eliminating site and travel arrangements.

Reduction of Development Time

- Updating of curricula becomes an automated process which can tie into the on-line policy changes.
- Time spent in the administration and scoring of testing is greatly reduced (Kearsley, 1983).

Specifically, the Staff Development and Training Unit will be seeking to accomplish two major goals beyond the general advantages of CBT.

(a) Use CBT to establish competencies for the use of EMS for each level of staff, and train those staff with CBT programs to meet and measure those competencies. In its simplest forn this translates to providing a training tool which most closely approximates to the environment in which the student will perform. The best way to teach a person to open a can is to provide a can and a can opener. The best way to learn the functions and use of EMS is through a CBT program using EMS. The hands-on use stimulates the competency level needed to perform to standard.

(b) Use of Phoenix to build in a policy training sub-system for the major entitlement programs (AFDC, Food Stamps, Medicaid, Title XIX, Energy). This will allow for the use of CBT to establish and measure knowledge competency levels for staff involved in the processing of entitlement program information.

The use of CBT allows the trainer to invest his/her energies into efforts that enhance the success of computer learning and address the unique needs of the adult learner while maximizing the participant's opportunity to gain optimal keyboard skills and comfort with automation.

PCs - Microcomputer

To support efforts of both the field offices and the central administrative office, the Department has also purchased several microcomputers. In addition, a variety of software packages have been purchased for use with the microcomputers. The microcomputers serve several functions in relation to the office automation plan of the Agency. Currently the micros are primarily used for increasing productivity through the design of applications to support the current mainframe processing system. The micros have been used as a sensitizing mechanism for the upcoming EMS system and to diminish myths and misconceptions about computers and their uses.

The training unit has formulated a strategy in conjunction with the distribution of the micros. In order to maximize the effectiveness of the micros, both micro users and micro managers must develop a specific set of competencies. The micro user must be able to conceptualize, design applications, input data, use reports, and evaluate data. To manage micros in the office environment, a manager must be able to conceptualize, relate applications to unit goals and objectives, and manage the use of equipment and software. Towards meeting these competencies, a series of courses have been developed that include an Overview of Microcomputers, Introduction to Software Packages (i.e. LOTUS 1-2-3, DBase III, Multimate Word Processing), and courses about

Management Issues and Application Potential. To further this effort, the Staff Development and Training Unit, in conjunction with Data Processing and Management Planning and Evaluation Units, organized an agency-wide user group. The user group provides services and support to managers and staff in their efforts to use the software packages in productive and creative ways to meet office and unit objectives. Training's role in the user group is to provide staff with the necessary skills to use the software in applications identified either by the user or the Management Planning and Evaluation Unit. In addition, training is charged with assessing training requests to determine if a knowledge/skill gap exists or if the micro application is appropriate for the software being utilized. Training also maintains and operates a microcomputer learning center.

Implementing this strategy will not only increase agency productivity in relation to the micros, but will also serve the overall agency strategy of moving from a manual, paper-based system to an automated one.

CONCLUSION

Staff understanding and use of the office automation technologies does not just happen. A creative, multi-faceted, and dynamic training plan must be developed to ensure that staff become well trained users. The training function must seize the opportunity, assert its role in the organization, and ensure its involvement in the developmental and implementation process. This paper has presented several ideas and activities that the Training Unit of Connecticut's Department of Income Maintenance utilized in the implementation of a major automated eligibility system.

Although organizations have unique problems and situations, these tasks and activities can serve as a boiler plate to train workers to use technology in a humane and supportive manner.

DOCUMENTS AVAILABLE

Eligibility Management Systems Needs Assessment and Report

Comprehensive needs assessment to determine staff comfort level with automation, and accompanying report of response analysis.

Personal Computer Needs Assessment for Managers and Report

Needs assessment to determine managers' level of skills and knowledge in the areas of PC hardware and software and microcomputer management.

Justification to Purchase Mainframe CBT Software

Justification paper outlining the training and organizational benefits of investing in CBT as a training tool.

Introduction to Computers (A Stand Up Training Curruculum)

An introductory curriculum overviewing computers, how they work, computer jargon, and potential.

Keyboard Skills (A CBT Curriculum)

An introduction to generic information about computer terminals, control knobs, different keys and their uses, and general care.

EMS Training Model

A four-phased training model that covers the necessary stages and topics for the design and development of a comprehensive training plan. Included is a three-tiered training delivery approach for implementation training.

EMS Training Plan

An overall blueprint for initial and ongoing EMS training detailing the curriculum design, the training plan for the specific learner groups, and training implementation/delivery plan.

Organizational Chart of CBT Staff, Functions and Tasks

This chart details all of the functions and tasks that must be assumed by training staff to develop, design, and implement Computer Based Training.

Criteria for Selecting Mainframe CBT Software

This analysis reviews the desirable attributes of a CBT mainframe software package and compares the currently available authoring systems.

REFERENCES

Kearsley, Greg (1983). *Computer Based Training: a Guide to Selection and Implementation*. Addison Wesley, Reading, MA.
US Department of Health and Human Services, Social Security Administration, Office of Family Assistance, Division of State Systems Management (1983). *Family Assistance Management Information System (FAMIS) Trainer's Guide*. Washington, DC.

APPLICATION OF COMPUTERS IN CLINICAL SUPERVISION

Ram A. Cnaan

Clinical supervision is an essential component of social work, and supervisors in human service organizations must carry out many functions. The growing literature on supervision enables us to better understand this position and its role. This study pertains to the potential roles of computers in supervision. Examples of preliminary steps taken in one agency toward computerizing supervision are presented. Finally, general developmental caveats regarding the future of clinical supervision in social work are given.

The author wishes to thank the workers, supervisors, and management of the Israeli National Adult Probation Services who encouraged and carried our most of the ideas in this paper. Special thanks are due to the Department of Computing at the Israeli Ministry of Labour and Social Affairs which programmed and provided all technical assistance. The actual writing was done when the author was a visiting professor at the School of Social Work at the University of Pennsylvania.

A PROPOSED MODEL FOR COMPUTERIZED CLINICAL SUPERVISION

Currently, important pioneering work is in progress concerning the application of expert systems to clinical social work (Carlson, 1985).

A two-stage model of utilizing data bases for clinical supervision is presented here. The first stage involves selection of relevant variables and categories to be included in the data base. The second stage involves the incorporation of supervisory comments and suggestions into the data base which can be accessed and printed out when required.

To develop such a model sounds relatively simple, but such is not the case. The agency studied for the purpose of this paper wished to use this model and is still struggling with it after nearly four years of work. This agency has a group of very experienced supervisors who meet regularly to determine which relevant clinical and administrative questions should be incorporated. Each supervisor has his/her own preferences and theoretical commitments to consider. However, supervisors must agree on which variables are the most useful and important for the database. The key criteria for inclusion/exclusion of any question in the database were:

1 Is the item of information relevant for clinical practice?

2 Is the inclusion/exclusion decision in line with the ideology, regulations and modes of service delivery of the agency?

3 Is the question clear? Is it accurately measurable? Are the items mutually exclusive?

4 Is the issue one that most supervisors would like workers to broach in a supervisory session?

5 Should an interesting issue that is seldom raised be included?

6 Can workers obtain answers to these questions in the course of regular treatment without further data collection, e.g. home visits solely for the purpose of generating data for the data base?

Other questions were also included so that collection of data for an on-going statistical series would not be jeopardized. In addition, each case file contains a section where the worker can enter free form comments. Developing and implementing took over two years (Green, 1986).

In the second stage, the supervisors are asked to reach a consensus on the meaning of possible answers (categories or their combinations). They should identify what certain case data mean for practice, i.e. how the information would be used in routine supervision. This process of using knowledge and experience to identify clinical meanings relevant to practice case data characteristics is called 'knowledge engineering'.

When agreement is reached, the clinical supervisory knowledge is summarized in a brief essay. This summary is then stored in the computer memory and can be printed out as needed. When the case data of any client are stored in the computer, clinically relevant categories indicate an issue of importance, and supervisory material printouts are generated that suggest interpretations and/or course of action. Like expert systems, the computerized supervisory summaries suggest possible actions. However, unlike expert systems, these summaries have no certainty factors, and the final decisions rest with the line workers. Furthermore, the proposed model can be programmed in any database language; it does not require LISP, Prolog or any other recursive programming language.

Creating a 'Supervisory Knowledge Module' (SKM) as described above requires much work, time, and effort but little computer expertise. For example, a group of 5-7 supervisors or competent experienced social workers may need several months of work to produce one SKM that will be accepted by their colleagues. The computerization itself takes relatively little time. Any commonly available relational database software (such as dBase III), can be used to store and activate these SKMs. A simple computer routine can be written so that when a certain category (or combination of categories) is selected, a relevant printout will be mailed to the relevant parties. (For further details, see the following examples). Thus the key to this computerized supervisory model is the iterative development of SKMs that, once agreed upon, can automatically be delivered to the relevant workers without the direct intervention of a live supervisor.

In summary, it can be said that supervisors are asked to do the following: (a) identify the most important questions and categories both therapeutically and administratively; (b) summarize the meaning of these data, i.e. how would they have conducted a supervisory session based on these data; and (c) install the SKMs in the computer and determine which categories (attribute values) will generate a given SKM printout. It may sound simple; however, the process is both long and tedious, as shown by the following examples.

EXAMPLES OF APPLYING COMPUTER TO CLINICAL SUPERVISION

The model presented in the previous section is slowly being implemented by a social service organization in Israel. Three examples from this process of adaptation will be presented. Each was chosen to emphasize a different function of supervision. The first example relates to the educational function; the second, to the administrative function. The third example relates to the incorporation of relevant case data in clinical decision-making. No example is given for the support function since prospects for computerization are less likely.

Example 1: Computerized Supervision in Diagnosis

This example of computerization supervision in diagnosis is borrowed from The Israeli National Adult Probation Services. Two highly experienced supervisors from this service reviewed the literature to determine appropriate care for people who committed acts of fraudulence.

They found that since most of these people could be categorized by personality traits and motivating factors into four groups, relevant interventions could also be proposed for each group. In arriving at this important clinical knowledge, the two supervisors had identified clinical interventions appropriate to specific case characteristics, i.e. they had carried out knowledge engineering. However, this knowledge was not disseminated.

In Israel, the courts assign those accused of fraudulent acts to probation officers at random. Thus, the likelihood that a client accused of fraud would be treated by a worker under the direction of either of these two knowledgeable supervisors is very slim, since the National Adult Probation Services has twenty teams throughout the county. As a result, clients are deprived of the best care since only a few workers have the relevant clinical knowledge to recommend the appropriate interventions. Furthermore, since the other probation officers are not aware of the four distinct personality groups identified by their co-workers, the probability of misdiagnosis is increased. Probation officers in outlying offices are even less likely than their urban counterparts to have had contact with the two supervisors who generated the knowledge.

This agglomeration of knowledge, which had been summarized into two typed pages, was stored in the computer. Thereafter, whenever a probation officer entered 'fraudulence' as a cause of referral by the court for a client, the computer would generate a SKM printout about personality types as well as suggested interventions. The worker who receives the printout is also cautioned that his/her specific client may be an exception to the basic personality types. The worker is also given the names of the two supervisors in the service who are experts in the field. She/he is advised to consult these experts if she/he finds a client is an exceptional case.

Similiar SKMs which represent the expert knowledge of the professionals in this service are being prepared. Some are relevant to other types of crimes, while others pertain to issues such as domestic background, social history, previous encounters with services, family origin history, employment history, level of denial, and locus of control. The Adult Probation Service assigned various expert committees to prepare these SKMs which will by used by all workers whenever a relevant case arises.

Example 2: Monitoring Case Dates

As noted previously, clinical supervisors spend a considerable amount of time in administrative duties. One important duty is keeping track of important case dates (Poertner and Rapp, 1983). For example, each social worker in the Israeli Adult Probation Services has at least two major case dates during the period of social investigation for the court: a date for delivery of the case-review to the court and a date for the worker to appear in court. During the probation period, there are other crucial case dates for reporting and/or court appearances. It was found that many supervisors and even regional managers spend a great deal of time in monitoring these case dates. Each supervisor developed his/her own manual monitoring system and it was generally considered an unrewarding burden. Most supervisors claimed that their supervisees who are professional social workers should keep track of these crucial dates. However, the workers' performance in this task was found to be poor. The Israeli State Comptroller's (1985) report revealed that case reviews are often submitted to court after the assigned dates which may have affected court decisions.

In the first stage of computerization, a form was designed to be used by the referring court. The form indicated the date for the submission of the case review and the date on which the social worker (probation officer conducting the social investigation) was expected to appear in court. The first screen of every new or renewed case file displayed this form. The secretary who received the form copied it verbatim to the computer. Shortly thereafter, two additional items of information were added: the name of the social worker assigned to the case and the name of the relevant supervisor. Printouts of specific dates were sent out as follows.

(a)   Weekly deadlines of case reviews for each social worker.

(b)   Weekly and monthly deadlines of case reviews per social worker and per court to supervisors and regional managers.

(c)   Weekly list of overdue case reviews per worker and per court to social workers, supervisors, and regional managers.

(d)   Weekly and monthly schedules of court appearances per social worker and per court to social workers, supervisors, and regional managers.

This computerized monitoring superseded the laborious manual systems and made this administrative function easy to handle, and most importantly, less time-consuming.

Since notifications of court dates were systematically generated and mailed to those concered, supervisors could concentrate instead on resolving problems with delays or other matters concerning an indidual worker or groups of workers. The program also gave them more time for caseload management, another administrative responsibility. For example, case loads are lightened for a worker scheduled to submit a number of written case reviews by a certain date. Alternatively, the courts are asked to grant additional time so that probation officers can complete a more thorough social investigation. Furthermore, the accurate tracking of scheduled court appearances enables supervisors and managers to plan transportation and caseload issues more effectively. In some cases, a worker was able to go to a specific court and submit case reviews made by his/her colleagues which saved them the trip. In several instances, when the program indicated that a worker was expected to appear in two courts at the same time, arrangements were made to reschedule one of the dates.

Example 3: Ensuring the Incorporation of Relevant Data into Practice

In the Adult Probation Services, the supervisors agreed that the most important and neglected clinical information is the analysis of a client's criminal record which is provided by the police. The criminal record lists court appearances, criminal accusations, verdicts, and time spent in prison or on parole. The criminal records of many adults who are referred for social investigation are long and difficult to read. Thus, in many instances, the social workers examined these records only cursorily. Most supervisors saw this superficial inspection of the criminal record as the most critical area of neglecting information in the process of clinical decision-making.

Consequently, a screen was included in the database that required information about the client's criminal record. This required workers to review the police report thoroughly. The screen has six questions: name the first, second and third most frequent crimes in the client's record: and name up to three less frequent, though of clinical value, crimes listed in the criminal record. For the last three questions, a list was compiled which included crimes such as fraudulence (see example 1), imposture, arson, shoplifting, assault, rape and murder. Each of these crimes has different prospects for rehabilitation and different implications for clinical treatment. When data relevant to any of these crimes are entered into the computer, any 'supervisory knowledge module' that is available about the clinical aspects of the crime is generated for the social worker.

DISCUSSION

The foregoing three examples reveal the tip-of-the-iceberg with regard to the potential of computerized supervision. Although it is not expected that computers will replace human beings in clinical supervision, many aspects of supervision can be transferred to computers. The computer model will relieve the supervisors of routine administrative and educational duties and allow them to concentrate on the more challenging, creative, and stimulating aspects of their work.

Eleven problems germane to supervision are now evaluated in the light of computerized supervision.

Lack of Access to Relevant Clinical Data in Supervision

Supervisors will be able to use computer models as a means of identifying those issues on which workers should concentrate. Forms can be incorporated into the database and reviewed by supervisors at their convenience. As indicated in the third example, the limited use of forms and questionnaires can enhance the quality of clinical decisions. While unexpected clinical issues will continue to arise, those most frequently occuring will be assured of gaining the attention of the supervisors.

The Incompatibility of Supervisor/Supervisee

It is possible that the requirement for supervisors to co-ordinate and share their perspectives in order to implement the computer model, may also make them more open to share supervisees or exchange team members.

Supervision in Remote Locations

With the availability of computers in distant offices, the quality of basic supervision will be more equitable. Every SKM that is stored in the computer will be immediately available for use by any worker in any office that is computerized.

Lack of Agreement among Supervisors

Supervisors must reach a consensus about each SKM to be incorporated into the computer. While this will not eliminate disagreements and contradictory viewpoints among supervisors, it will nevertheless compel the supervisors to discuss their differences and to reach consensus.

Supervision Narrows the Supervisee's Perspectives

As noted in the first example, workers will be offered a set of options from which to choose. Each SKM will be so constructed as to include as many options as possible.

The Cost of Supervision

With computerized supervision, human service organizations can either increase the ratio of workers to supervisors or delegate new roles to supervisors with no increase in cost.

Over-emphasis on Administrative Function

The second example is only one of many complex administrative functions for which computerization would be feasible and effective. In a similar manner, statistical reports, caseload management and monitoring could be efficiently performed by computers.

Problems in Leadership

Computers can do very little in this respect. However, computerization may affect the selection of supervisors (i.e. requirements for more knowledge), their attitude toward supervision (i.e. willingness to share their expertise with others), and their expectations concerning this role. This issue will require further study over time.

Perpetuating Dependency and Authoritative Relationships

As shown in the first example, the the SKM model the worker is not told what to do but rather is presented with a set of options from which to choose. She/he is also encouraged to seek additional options from outside the SKM. To reduce the possibility of worker dependence on the computer, the supervisors who prepare the SKMs must allow latitude for the worker's own initiative.

Supervision Covers only a Limited Portion of Practice

When supervisors determine that a particular category merits attention, a program computer routine is installed which automatically notifies them whenever a worker enters case data in that category. As a result, many more cases have a better chance to be discussed at a live supervisory session, even though the workers may not realize their importance. However, this advantage is limited to agreed-upon subjects.

Problems in Transition from one Agency to Another

Workers who move from one agency to another will be oriented more quickly to unfamiliar administrative procedures since these will be brought to the worker's attention on an ongoing basis as the need arises. When a worker confronts a particular situation, the computer will send a message relevant to the agency's policy.

CONCLUSIONS

The model presented here will: (a) reduce the administrative burden of supervisors; and (b) incorporate supervisory knowledge modules that will automatically be brought to the attention of the workers as necessary. The key concept in this model is to make available the expertise and knowledge of more experienced workers to less experienced line staff in as many cases as are relevant so that more systematic and knowledgeable clinical judgements can be made.

Social workers prefer the role of consultee to that of supervisee. Computers in supervision will affect this area, and the effects may be more profound than currently expected. Many administrative functions will be computerized. Educational SKMs will be computerized and will suggest, but not dictate, courses of action. Thus the new expectations placed upon supervisors may lead to an increase in consultive relationships.

Incorporation of such a model into any human service organization requires the full committment of management, supervisors and staff. Since the use of such a model will be somewhat revolutionary in social work, a two-stage preparation is required. First, the idea must be marketed - people must be persuaded that it is a worthwhile enterprise. Second, people must be taught how to use the model. It is possible that in the future, as computer technology becomes ubiquitous, such preparation will be unnecessary and the computer will be regarded as standard office equipment just as the typewriter is today.

Computerized supervision will make available methods of intervention to more workers but it will be able to assess which interventive method is superior. Such decisions are the responsibility of the agency's professional management. Once the decisions are made, the supervisors then direct the creation and incorporation of SKMs. The process of knowledge engineering is based on consensus among supervisors. Thus the model can reflect a few approaches or one preferred approach but it cannot compare their effectiveness.

The model is based on a modular, iterative and developmental professional process that can be applied to most databases in almost all hardwares; thus it may be very attractive to human service organizations. It has some built-in problems whose meaning it is too early even to assess. These problems are overflow of repetitive SKMs, updating SKMs based on new knowledge, and overcompliance with the recommendations of the SKM. It will take at least a decade to find out whether this computerized supervision model was widely adopted and what its impacts were on the profession.

REFERENCES

Carlson, R.W. (1985). 'Connecting Clinical Information Processing with Computer Support'. *Computers in Human Services*, **1**, 51-66.
Green, V. (1986). 'The Incorporation of Computers in the Israeli Adult Probation Services'. Unpublished thesis, Tel Aviv University.
The Israeli State Comptroller (1985). *Yearly Report - 1984*. Jerusalem: State of Israel.

Poertner, J. and Rapp, C.A. (1983). 'What is Social Work Supervision?'. *The Clinical Supervisor*, **1**, 53-65.

THE ROLE OF THE INTEGRATED WORK STATION
IN DEVELOPING SOCIAL INFORMATION RESOURCE SERVICES

The Theoretical Conceptual Framework
of Information Networks and
Computer Comunications Technology for Human Services

Donald J. Forgie

INTRODUCTION

The word 'communication is a contradiction' in a term. The word we all use, communication transforms a dynamic process, into a finished, time bound and static concept. The intended meanings are mangled. Communicating is an on-going, and continuous process, essential to the idea of life, thought, and development. Communication is a finished act, dead, time bound, unchanging – a static record of the past. Our use of this word may well be culturally bonded to those peoples and cultures who, for generations, transformed their living, dynamic, thought processes into the static visual language of the written and printed word, organized in letters and communications and books that are read in sequence from a beginning to an end.

In establishing the Advanced Communicating Laboratory at the Faculty of Library and Information Science at the University of Toronto, Canada, I had considerable difficulty using the term 'communicating' in the title. When Media Services who had always been highly supportive of my work presented me with a sign for the door it read, unbelievably 'The Advanced Communications Lab'. I have left this sign unchanged for the past seven years as a tribute to the cultural legacy and mind set we all wear as a part of our 19th century intellectual clothing.

In the heat of change, we must today shed some of the vestments of our passing culture, if our discussion of integrated work stations and human services are to have meaning. In this paper ideas and relationships may well be developed that do not fit comfortably in our present common conceptual patterns. But the purpose here is to reach beyond normal conceptual space to grasp new understandings required to function in a world rapidly changing in fundamental ways. Is it not of some significance that this first international conference on human service information technology applications is taking place in Britain, and at a Polytechnic? Poly, meaning many, is particularly appropriate to the many technologies, forms, facets, and theories that are the functional units of our integrated work station prototype.

Theoretical concepts have had practical importance to the work of the Advanced Communicating Laboratory, with its emphasis on research and development of human applications of new interactive   communicating   technologies,   focusing   on   people, rather   than   equipment.   Theory   has   also   been   significant   in   the development   of   the   ACL   Integrated   Work   Station   and   to   the   Social Information   Resource   Centre   project   in   which   we   are   currently engaged.   These   are   examples   that   link   theory   with   practice,   and theory   with   changing   social   contexts   and   environments.   Nothing is   more   powerful,   important,   or   practical   than   a   theory   that works   in   practice.   These   projects   are   providing   some   evidence   to support   the   hypothesis   that   poly-technical   innovations   have   an identifiable   relationship   with   social   change,   and   that   the provision   of   information   services   using   primary   records   in electronic   form   is   of   extreme   importance   to   all   concerned   with human   service   information   technology   applications.

ASSUMPTIONS (OFTEN HIDDEN) MADE IN DESIGN
AND DEVELOPMENT OF INFORMATION SERVICES

In   this   section   of   the   paper   we   wish   to   deal   with   some   of   the theoretical   and   conceptual   approaches   commonly   used   in   study-ing,   reporting   or   developing   information   and   communications systems   and   networks.   We   will   wish   to   think   about   these critically,   and   to   discuss   the   effect   these   concepts   may   have upon   the   way   we   think   about   information   resource   services   and networks   in   general,   and   in   particular   those   concerned   with social   policies   and   practices.   To   assist   us,   I   have   developed   for this   paper   a   two   dimensional   static   model   of   communicating processes.   I   have   also   transformed   this   into   a   several dimensional   interactive   dynamic   model   (not   shown   here   in   print), using   the   capabilities   of   the   Integrated   Work   Station   and television   recording   to   provide   some   limited   comparisons   between these   two   conceptual   forms: (a)   two   dimensional   static   models; and   (b)   multi-dimensional,   interactive   models   involving   inter-action   with   more   than   one   person.

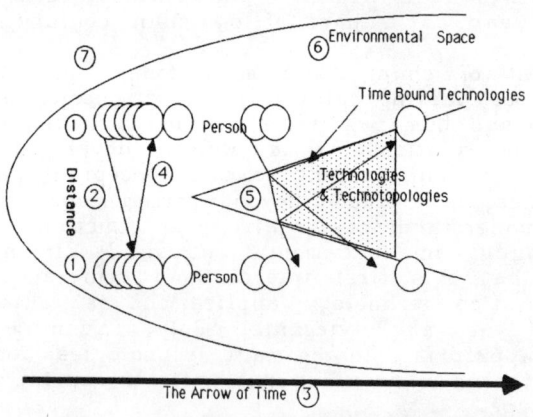

Figure 4.1

General Model for Communicating Processes

The above model is intended to have all the components of any communicating system, namely: (1) two or more persons; (2) distance; (3) the concept of time; (4) signals (records); (5) the concept of technologies or tools (human discoveries); (6) environments; (7) the system functioning as a whole transmitting signals directly or through technologies across distance, over time, and in an environmental context of spaces.

In Figure 4.1 each circle represents a person at a new position in time. At each time frame we are a different person from even a few seconds earlier, physically, and in our mind/memory continuum. We are continuously exposed to interactions with our environments. We are not a closed system. We are continuously developing, changing, aging. Throughout this entire process we are also sending sets of simultaneous signals using a variety of sensory stimuli – visually while speaking, or when we both talk at once. We share the same physical environments, and sometimes share the same visual space as well as the same acoustic space. Our interactions are dynamic, spontaneous, filled with considerable uncertainty, and responsive. They represent interaction between living human beings using a minimum of technology. In this diagram you must locate the 'information' in the mind of the person, and not assume it is in the record or signal transmitted, Understanding this difference is critical in the design and development of information networks.

People use technologies to transmit records across physical distances and over time, but always in a direction to the future. Thus all records are records of past attempts to communicate through technology. They require not only a medium of record, but the technology required to create and display the records, and the human ability to perceive the record and transform it into some patterns of meaning or uncertainty. The process of perception and comprehension creates the information in the mind. The information exists in a dynamic context, usually within the mind/body of a living being, although the informing process is currently being stimulated in electronic contexts.

In Figure 4.1 the arrows represent transmission of records with or without technology across a distance (elements 2 and 4). When transmitted, one can understand the information they represent in terms of levels of uncertainty or likelihood that the record sent would be the same as the record received after the record had been transmitted (transported), transformed and reformed at the destination. This concept is extremely important to all forms of distance communicating processes. The advanced systems we will be discussing will not necessarily reform the signal at the destination, but transform it, say from a print form to a sound form. Many theories concerned with distance transmission do not concern themselves with changed taking place in the minds of people, except with respect to the changes that may occur as a result of the form in which the record is displayed, or the effects caused by the received record differing from the sent record or the expected-to-be-received record.

Another group of theories and concepts are largely concerned with selection of words, and appropriate technologies, to alter human concepts and actions. These theories are important to development of support for politicians and parties, for advertisers and marketing strategists, for establishing stereotypes, images, and for propaganda. Education, to a considerable degree, is intended to identify these practices and methods and help educate literate persons to understand how they may be manipulated and how to defend themselves against manipulation. Illiterates may be culturally immune to the process, lacking the apperceptive background necessary for any response. Both literates and illiterates are often reached through music and/or dance, sculptures and icons rather than through words and rhetoric. The 'effects' changes in behaviour following transmission of a record to a person or a group are concerned with the human element in Figure 4.1, and tends to assume casual relationships that may not be either stable or even true in many environments, and for many people.

Other theorists are concerned with the manner in which technology affects the way social, economic, and political groups organize and function. The key dependent variables of concern are the institutional and political structures and their span of control over geographic areas (distance) which he referred to as space, and their ability to function as command control centres over time. Thus empires, religious and other institutions were considered to be responsive to the communications technologies which they used and learned to master. This suggests that the kind of technology and the way it retains records over time or transmits records across space will affect institutions and the way they evolve and survive. In Figure 4.1 this would be seen as organizational structures composed of people linked by technologies capable of recording and transmitting records of human thought patterns, but also creating a common conceptual cultural envelope defined by the capabilities and biases of available communication technologies. The name 'technotology' is suggested to describe such a cultural envelope. This particular theoretical framework is concerned with the impact on organizational structures or environments associated with diffusion of new technological discoveries in the context of previously internalized technologies which they reinforce or with which they compete.

Marshall McLuhan (1962) was concerned with all effects of a technology. Among these were the creation of new environments through use of a technology. The automobile creates an invisible environment - roads, multi-lane highways, cloverleafs, shopping malls, the way we view the world, the ways we date and make love, our sense of distance, our sense of time and so on. Thus a new technology appeared to McLuhan to be capable of altering human perception, our sense of time and space, and our culture. New tools and technologies were identified as extending or altering basic human capabilities and sense ratios. McLuhan identified new technology not as neutral, but by its intrinsic nature tending to emphasize certain aspects of culture and human actions while altering others. The process of frequently using any technology is believed to alter the human sensorium and the environment in which we live, the way we work and the games we play. In Figure 4.1 this concerns element 7 – the way the system functions and changes over time.

There is considerable evidence to support the hypothesis that new communications technologies have multiple effects upon all elements of the communicating process. An awareness of possible inter-relationships may assist us in introducing new capabilities in ways intended to minimize adverse effects in critical areas of concern, and possibly more important, to avoid development strategies that disregard the forces of change, on the one hand, and human needs on the other. Ideally one wishes to participate in shaping the technologies and the development process to meet human needs, rather than adapting people to fit technological requirements.

OLD AND EMERGING TECHNOLOGIES: WHAT ARE THE EFFECTS?

Let us now turn to two specific technologies: (1) the communicating (micro) computer, a relatively old technology; and (2) the ACL Integrated Work Station (IWS), as an example of an emerging technology. Both these technologies are being used in the development of information systems. We are concerned with observing the effects of each on all aspects of communicating processes during the devlopmental process. Further, we wish to alter our development strategies based on the observations made as the development process proceeds. The purpose is to identify and respond to human needs at all levels as the technologies are internalized and diffused.

The communicating computer is old. The first digital computers required the operators to interact with the memory locations, and this led to the development of early time sharing systems by System Development Corporation and also Dartmouth College. Remote access began by using teletype networks, and then modems that permitted remote access through terminals and telephone lines to mainframes. The advent of the microcomputer led quickly to communicating microcomputers using modems and voice lines, and then to digital networks permitting direct communication without use of modems. The Integrated Work Station synthesized the poly-technologies being developed independently to harness combinations of capabilities to meet changing human needs.

Individuals sitting at an IWS have numerous capabilities at hand, including:

(a)   The capability to call up groups of software programs and move from one screen to another in developing a report. This report has been developed on a MacIntosh Lisa, provided by MacIntosh Canada, and adapted to function as a MacXL. I have chosen three pieces of software – MacWrite, MacDraw, and More – to create this article, using Switcher to move between these and to transfer graphics, when completed into the text. The outline capabilities of More permit me to check my outline or add to it as I go.

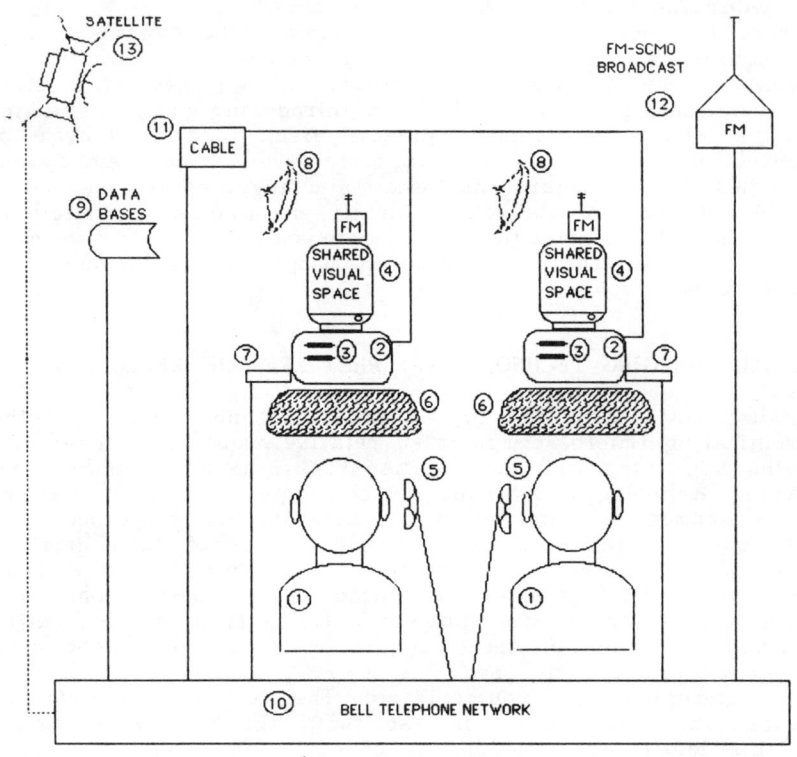

NODE		NETWORK
1. PERSON	6. INTERACTIVE ACCESS (VISION) THE KEYBOARD	10. TELEPHONE NETWORK
2. THE MICROPROCESSOR		11. CABLE
3. THE SOFTWARE	7. THE TWO-WAY COMMUNICATING NETWORK THE MODEM	12. FM-SCMO BROADCAST
4. VISUAL DISPLAY, THE CRT		13. SATELLITE
5. INTERACTIVE ACCESS (SOUND) THE TELEPHONE	8. THE RADIO RECEIVER AND/OR DISH	
	9. PUBLIC AND COMMERCIAL DATA BASES	

Figure 4.2

*ACL Integrated Workstation
(developed at the Advanced Communicating Lab
Faculty of Library and Information Science,
University of Toronto)*

(b)   The ability to select from both internal and external databases to obtain information necessary for the paper. The paper has been largely produced on my work station in my country home 75 miles from Toronto. Due to line charges and lack of direct access in a rural area to datapac I do not usually make use of the modem and remote communication capabilities available. It would be possible, however, to work in shared space with the Social Information Resource Centre, downloading files, and doing shared development of text and graphics, or having the results of bibliographic database searches edited for the Bibliography.

In the Advanced Communicating Lab we have access to both voice and data lines permitting us not only to work in shared visual space through linked terminals but also to discuss the results via telephone in shared acoustic space. In Canada it is still difficult and expensive to have two telephone lines for each station. In fact, culturally, we still think of the telephone as voice communication without the computer. Telephones are located in homes and offices, television sets in bedrooms, living rooms, recreation rooms and hotel rooms, and are not associated with the telephone. Microcomputers are located in office space at home or in the office, but are still seldom voice/data combinations with simultaneous access. The integrated work station concept requires access to these integrated voice/data communications networks, as well as access to broadcast data distribution systems where appropriate.

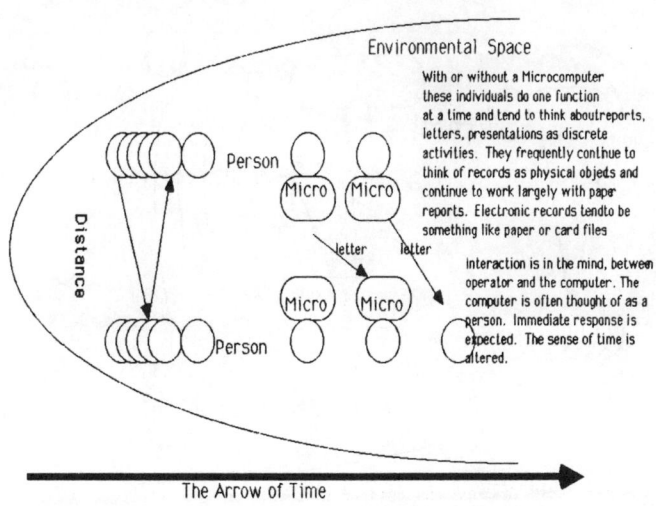

Figure 4.3

Microcomputer Technology operated using
Specialized Independent Capabilities

In Figure 4.3, we have introduced the old communicating microcomputer technology into our communicating process model. The act of using this technology will introduce some changes in a number of areas. For example, it will raise questions for telecommunications engineers concerning network interconection, channel capacity, simultaneity or delay in transmission, effect or change in records trasmitted, differences in form of record (electronic vs physical paper record), amount of paper used and transported – electronic vs regular mail. The use of these capabilities will impact the way people work and think. These questions are more closely related to questions raised by McLuhan (1964), and those concerned with psychological responses. Their use may also begin to affect institutional concepts and the way institutions function and the way different groups of people relate to each other, as suggested by Innis (1950).

Basically this old form of computer communication did not alter greatly the way people thought about communications. Interactions and relationships were largely those, on a personal scale, already experienced by those involved in operating mainframe computers, or using time sharing systems. Development of learner centred information centres did not become common, but remote access to databases by specialists became more common. The specialist approach remained fundamentally unchanged.

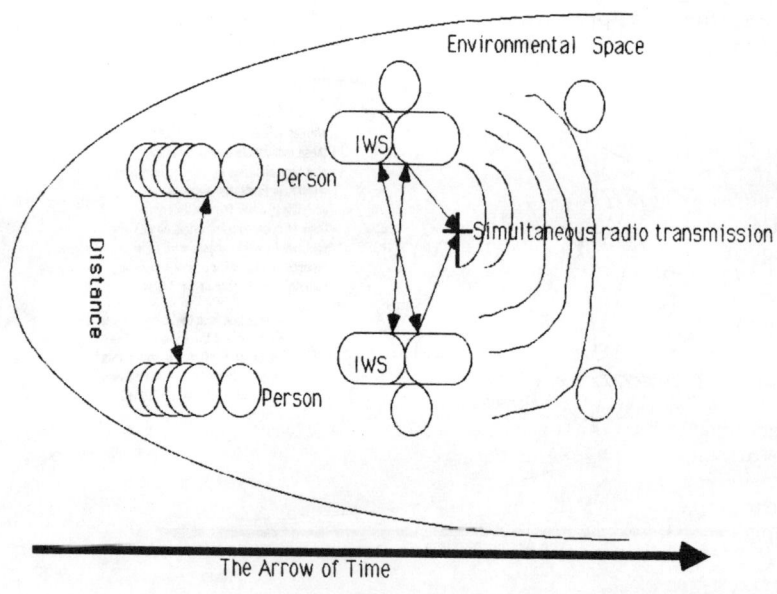

Figure 4.4

The Emerging Integrated Workstation Technology

The technology introduced in Figure 4.4 pictures in combination existent technologies, both electronic and traditional, synthesizing and integrating the combinations of capabilities in the context of a single work space. This permits the operator of the system to move easily and comfortably from print to graphics, with or without sound. A dynamic interaction occurs not only with the records and the electronic technologies but also with people using shared voice and shared visual capabilities.

This integrated capability will also be expected to introduce changes in all areas discussed. It will bridge the gap between those who function as individual specialists and those who function as team members. Persons will be capable of functioning at various levels of abstraction, and be at home with a variety of presentation levels such as print, visual moving icons, illustrations, graphs or statistical and mathematical formulae. The user will have the ability to transform the same electronic record into a variety of forms, or to have several on the screens simultaneously and select the most appropriate. The operator can enter remote databases alone, or with a team, and share the comprehensive understandings of several persons. This introduces new extensions of human memory and intellect, and even permits access to new logical algorithms described as expert systems of intelligent front ends.

The above is a simple description of some of the increased complexity associated with operation of an integrated work station in a communicating networking environment. It is this combined capability that we have been testing and developing in the Advanced Communicating Laboratory for the past six or seven years with the interest and support of colleagues in the University, in the field of social service, and with large and small Canadian companies. Our research methodology becomes somewhat more difficult in complex inter-related systems that have not previously existed in the desired prototype form. It also requires training and bringing together complex specialist capabilities to be operated, not by a generalist, but by an intelligent person able to function simultaneously as a multi-specialist. Those who can learn to think and work in these new ways may become quite different people.

A challenge of the Social Information Resource Project at the Faculty of Social Work, University of Toronto, is to provide the integrated technologies of the work station within a University/ Practitioner environment that functions within the changing socio-economic and cultural environment of Ontario, Canada, with its unique background and developmental history. Within these environments we have introduced a technological intervention, the Integrated Workstation and are involved in carrying out developmental research while operating a functioning information centre. Finding and training an operator for the system who has synthesized special knowledge and operational practice in the fields of computer applications, library and information science and service, social work and social services as well as having ability and experience in teaching, training and managing is in and of itself difficult. We have been fortunate in finding one

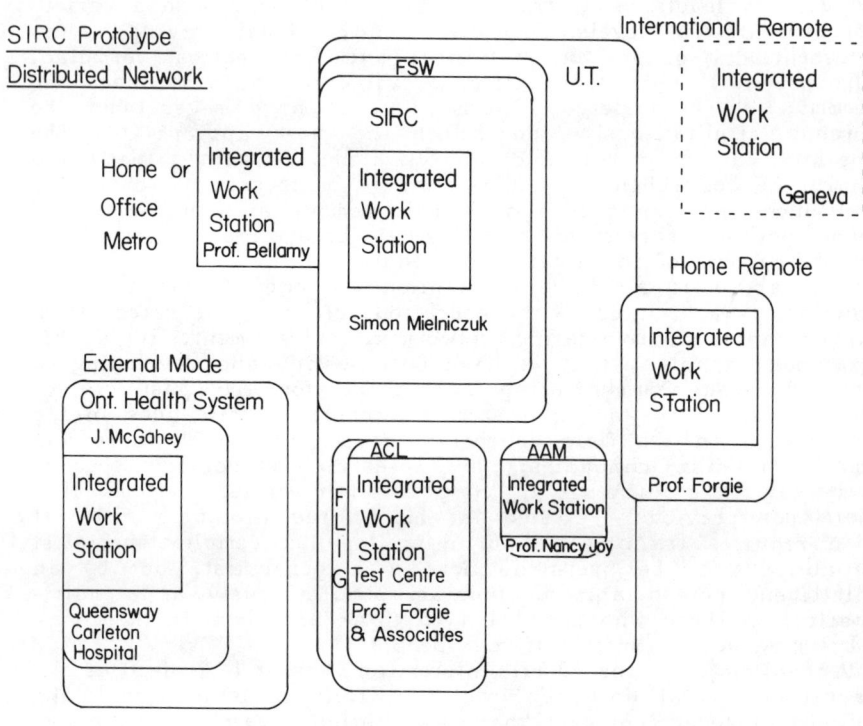

Figure 4.5

A Prototype Network of Integrated Work Stations

person with some expertise in all areas, backed by a team of specialists who have worked with the ACLab in doing early experimental work in developing the integrated work station concept.

Figure 4.5 identifies the operational components of the project that are now being tested. In the Summer of 1986 it was decided to begin field testing our newly acquired MacLisa XLs converted to function as integrated work stations. A fairly full range of capabilities had been tested in the Advanced Communicating Laboratory in the development stages and these were synthesized in a particular hardware/software configuration. While the tests have not been hardware or software dependent, and IBM PC, Radio Shack, Apple 11 and MacIntosh hardware/software con-figurations have been used, it was decided that Apple MacIntosh provided the widest variety of test capabilities in one existing machine. Independently we learned that telecommunications groups in Canada and the USA also felt it held important communications opportunities with a human oriented object language approach. Work still continues with other competitive equipment, however.

Our areas of concern were welfare, health, education, and management of resources and records. We decided initial tests should include a community based social service centre, a hospital, a university library/reading room/information centre, and individuals of various backgrounds and ages. We brought these individuals together and trained them in the ACLab to operate the basic work station. One work station was then transported to the Queensway Carleton Hospital in Ottawa where a comprehensive report on all hospital operations and services had just been completed. The Assistant Director of Nursing, one of two authors of the report, trained on the equipment, but was not provided initially with either printing facilities or communication equipment. Part of the test was to see how the introduction of such a technological capability (an intervention) might be internalized in the system, how it would be used, what problems might arise. A second work station was provided to Flemingdon Neighbourhood Services, a community multi-service centre, again without printer or modem, for use by the manager of the centre. A third workstation was available to be moved to other locations such as a professor's home. A fourth workstation was located in the ACLab for a variety of tests and for training of the Senior Research Assistant of the Lab who was involved in conducting a development analysis of existing information services at the Faculty of Social Work. Following training and development a unit with printer and modem was provided to the SIRC Project at the Faculty of Social Work and units were moved as required for test and development purposes. During the 1986/87 term Professor Bellamy and I team taught a course in Research Methods introducing students to the capabilities of the Integrated Work Station. Simon Mielniczuk then left Flemingdon Park to manage the SIRC Research and Development Project and operate the existing reading room facilities.

Our main concern was to carry out a variety of operational tests to determine operational feasibility, training feasibility, and develop the applications programs necessary to meet anticipated user needs. In this development context we were actively observing effects of the technology on us as individuals and on the institutions into which the technology was introduced. We also needed to collect the preliminary knowledge and experience needed to proceed with more rigorous testing, and operational development. While results of tests to date must be considered tentative, we have gained what we believe are important insights in all areas of the communicating process, and identified some of the existing boundaries for effective implementation and development.

CONCLUSION

There is a clear connection between theories of interactive communicating processes, and the practical and effective introduction of new technologies in operating information systems and their associated networks. As Figure 4.1 illustrates, in developing theories of communicating processes we focus on only part of the process, leaving out other important components and relationships. When we leave out people, we leave out the most important element. The most critical element in the SIRC system is the training and development of the information manager – the person who helps others create, store, obtain access to, and make use of electronic record and messaging systems. Those engaged in development and operation of information service centres must understand clearly the telecommunication theories, concepts, practices, and systems – one way, two way, and fully interactive systems. They must understand the theories concerning the effects of records and technologies on people and the environments in which they work. The differences between primary oral records, primary written records, primary printed records, primary electronic records, and electronic records capable of sensory transformation. They must know how the new combinations of technologies are affecting themselves and the organization structures in which they are working. Their sense of time, their sense of space, human relationships, span of control, extent of decentralization, sense of well being, all these can be affected. Knowing any one of these areas is not enough.

Those concerned with the development of policies, and the organization and management of institutions, such as governments, universities, colleges and schools, hospitals and medical centres, welfare agencies and social information services need to understand all these relationships even more intimately if they are to be able to provided guidance, direction, and stability and effectiveness of operation during the transforming process in which we are all now engaged, whether we like it, or not.

The Human Service Environment: Present and Future

Donald F. Bellamy

An ecological approach is useful for examining environmental issues in the human services. The perspective which has been explored in depth by Germain and Gitterman (1980) and which they associated with a life model of social work away from a medical model. The significance of the approach for this paper lies in the centrality of transactions through which people, service systems, and governments experience and express needs and problems and achieve adaptation and change. Our interest in communicating equipment and media in the constructed or built physical world leads us to sense the essential linkage role of communicating in such a model, but we believe it is underplayed in social work practice. The essential linkages are not given the emphasis required to move the human services into the kind of advanced communicating world which is now falling into place.

Making use of the ecological framework, this presentation identifies three issues that concern social work and social welfare in Ontario provincial and Canadian contexts which are those most familiar to the author. The issues are followed by three examples of the use of the workstation as a stand-alone system. The conclusions discuss some challenges facing the human services.

ISSUES

The Tension of Centralization and Decentralization

New technology has the capability to create its own environment through the way people respond to the technology. While there is evidence of the increased centralization of power which carries with it the functions of holding, withholding, and distributing information, the counterbailing forces are also powerful. Factors leading toward a world in which central regulation is breaking down are the vastness of the record systems and the complexity of interpersonal relations in central organizations, together with the redistribution of power resulting in part from the introduction of advanced systems. Evidence of such systemic failure is found in policies in many 'advanced' countries to deregulate (including deprofessionalize), deinstitutionalize and privatize public services. This type of movement is taking place across many policy fields. It seems to be happening despite the notion of 'one world', which still has important philosophical and moral connotations, but as an economic or political objective cannot be realized. This is so because of the difficulty of controlling the working parts of the complex systems involved, many of them at an international level.

Advanced communicating technology can make it possible to integrate large and quite different systems where needed to ensure access and equity. But effective application in human service is far from straightforward and predictable. We are concerned that the social applications and impacts of developments be assigned a higher priority than is now the case in Canada.

In the digital world we now live in, the phrase "no centres and no margins" (Kroker, 1984, p.129) conjures an image of a world with no major centres of power, only small, manageable ones. Widespread access to the microprocessor together with encouragement of the decentralizing policy directions will enable private individuals and groups to create and operate their own organizations. There is evidence that:

(a) Mutual aid and self-help groups are struggling with some success to compete with traditional 'welfare state' services, despite funding restrictions. This is an important trend as the Canadian welfare state undergoes a major transformation like that in the western world generally.

(b) Population subgroups, separated according to language, ethnicity, religion, gender, or human problems, in their search for commonality and strength, turn inward and close their boundaries to assert their territorial purposes. Their aim is to retain old traditions in danger of disappearing, or to frustate and fight back at an alien environment. They connect with each other. They meet many of their own needs; they bypass bureaucratic systems and in doing so, threaten the existence of large and unresponsive systems

Our human service problems are only in small part economic (cost) problems; a major factor is the inability of planners and designers to develop integrated systems that function effectively. Problems of this type arise particularly when human-made systems use obsolete models, and theories that cannot predict. Humane advanced communicating technology might hold the key to planned change which united the best of the incremental and the comprehensive.

Solving problems in our world, now and increasingly in the future, is hindered by the compression of time and space. This is so because advanced communicating systems require people to learn new ways of relating to their external environments - both physiologically and mentally. The human effects seem analogous to 'jet lag', but much stronger, more persistent, and with more serious consequences. The problem of relearning is accentuated by the unequal rates of change of people, organizations, and advanced technology.

The Illusion of Access

The development of open systems and increasing awareness of just claims has paralleled the legislated right of people to gain access to information and services. Theoretically, without centres and margins every person and idea has access. With reference to Ontario's social welfare systems, which are residual and not created within a coherent framework, the rights are illusory.

Despite promises to do so, it is impossible to assure the clients of consistency of access to service delivery. A concrete example of the way access services (I&R) are affected by a residual approach yet must cope with underlying pressure to adapt to the realities of technological change is available in Ontario. In this huge province of ten million people a multiplicity of specialized social information resources which come and go with frequency, adhere to one set standard of quality of information, and often have tenuous public accountability.

Although often treated as marginal these services clearly carry an important integrating function; they invariably lack the support of advanced communicating technology - unfamiliar and therefore likely unwelcome. Approximately 70 other small 'generic' community information (I&R) centres throughout the province do operate under a shared set of standards. These organizations are sharing in a more orderly development and delivery of information through electronically based networks now being built and field-tested. Extension of this concept with linkages to integrated workstations will occur as their organization leadership becomes concerned about the problem, knowledgeable about what can be possible using advanced technology, and inquisitive about the human effects of such systems. This is a major challenge for the small, scattered, and underfunded networks of community information centres.

Knowledge-Based Practice Innovation

Much professional practice is wedded to theories of human behaviour and helping processes that fail to incorporate the accelerating changes in communicating technology taking place.

(a)   Practitioners in social work and social welfare in Ontario are frequently passive, if not antagonistic, toward computer technology generally. They are rarely prepared to deal with other than traditional modes of communicating technology.

(b)   Social work and social welfare curricula offer little or nothing to prepare students for a practice that is impacted by new modes of communicating, and that prepares the students to have an effect on the technology based on understanding of social impacts.

(c)   In many workplaces, in business, industry, and human services, technology is often installed from the executive suite down without adequate planning, involvement, and training of personnel.

(d)   Primary attention is given to equipment, and little or no attention to social effects of the technology.

We need practitioners who are willing to learn about and to use advanced communicating systems. Two particular tasks are involved for human service practitioners. The first is to participate in investigating the human aspects of the technology.

The second is to use the systems in order to improve practice knowledge and skill. Examples of the latter include developing and accessing specialized collections of research findings, bibliographic references, and professional resources. (A sample study in the field of child sexual abuse is presented below.) Joining electronic conferences and networking with experts in the field are other options.

Workers associated with ACLab at the University of Toronto have begun to search for answers to some of the questions. The results allow us informed speculation about future developments. They encourage us to promote this area of inquiry as important and fruitful for social work educators and practitioners. In the remainder of this paper are presented some observations from studies undertaken on human aspects of advanced communicating technology. The illustrations are limited to use of the stand-alone workstation, that is without using its integrated features. Much research activity with graduate students and associates of the ACLab has been concerned with testing the utility of communicating on the workstation outside an integrated mode. Three examples will illustrate the potency and general applicability of this communicating technology in the human services.

The first illustration is one of a series of studies which employed simulations relevant to social work practice. Each of them used the concept of common and shared space referred to previously by Professor Forgie. The series explored applications in information and referral service (I&R), conflict mediation between individuals, and case management/supervision of a service provider in a remote location. Only the first of these will be presented here. The second example concerns the need for a specialized collection of information to assist professionals in the province of Ontario who are called upon to treat child sexual offenders. The third illustration reports on a test of transferring a document (Ph.D. thesis) from one type of computer equipment used by the student to the equipment in the integrated workstation. The experience is relevant to desk-top publishing capability in the Faculty.

Project One: Reflexive Communicating

One of the capabilities which has interested members of the ACLab originated at the Bell-Northern Laboratory in Ottawa; it has now had limited application in some special fields. It is an important component of the workstation described by Professor Forgie, using concepts developed by Gordon Thompson, with the preferred terminology, "shared visual and acoustic space" (Thompson 1984). It has also been referred to as "shared workspace conferencing" (Tapscott et al, 1985).

Two or more persons linked by communicating software from their keyboards view the same 'live' information on their monitors; both can alter the information (scroll, edit, etc.) in shared visual space from their own workstations. If the participants are out of earshot, they may achieve shared acoustic space by means of the common telephone. The combination allows them to discuss the text, graphics, or numbers they see on the screen, in its original form, in its evolving state as it is being edited, and in its final form for storage, printing, possible future work at another time, for transfer to someone else. This reflexive communicating capability allows interruptions that normally occur in face-to-face communication and over the telephone in shared acoustic space. The participants can talk their way through the review or preparation of a document in 'shared editorial' space in a way that is quite different from commonly used and important, but conceptually less sophisticated, asynchronous computer-mediated conferencing referred to above. Fitted together, the visual and auditory communicating modes in shared space unite the senses of each participant, but much more than that, enable the participants to feel, think, and communicate as one. Reflexive communication thus confers on its users a powerful new means of achieving synergy.

Why Shared Space? Most social work practitioners and undoubtedly many professionals in other 'talking' disciplines would agree with the assertion that "face to face is better" (Johansen, Vallee, and Spengler, 1979, p.5). The interpersonal dynamics of being face-to-face are important when dealing with conflict, when using persuasion, or when exchanging a high volume of information. In negotiating, the stress placed on affect is invaluable; our training and experience condition us to be tuned in to interpersonal cues and aberrations, and to deal with them as the face-to-face process moves along. On the other hand, we have accommodated some of the disadvantages inherent in face-to-face communication, such as the potential for one person to dominate the communicating, to limit ideas and quality of decisions reached, and to be distracted by the visual cues. Research indicates that face-to-face is not the single 'best' way to communicate any more than are other modes. Rather, we have to make choices between the different modes available to us. In research, teaching, and other forms of practice, we select communicating modes based on the perceived demands of the task together with our understanding as to the efficacy of particular modes of communication. The chief stumbling block is that successful communicating demands a major effort to master the knowledge and skills of other modes, to experiment and evaluate them, and a collective willingness to undergo the inevitable shifts in individual perceptions and organizational structures, and not the least, to be prepared to experience changes in our professional subculture. Herein may lie important reasons for resisting these innovations.

Our various studies in reflexive communicating dealt with the potential for applying technological developments to personal problem-solving in social work practice. The results suggested that a logical next step might be iteration - repeating problem definition and design - and eventually progression to field trials and the development of a prototype interventive system. This would require further testing of human impacts, benefit/cost studies, etc., before establishing an operating system.

The rigor of methodology in the series of studies, of which only one is reported here, was governed by a number of factors. It was clear at the outset that control of variables was not possible because of the early exploratory stage in our studies of communicating in shared space, the constraints of space and student time, and the rapidity of development of communicating technology. The work was carried out with the reports of face-to-face communication and teleconferencing modes as a backdrop. A number of studies reported by Johansen et al (1979), were instrumental in developing a series of observational trials to compare face-to-face communication of students with shared space computer communication. This was an extremely important step given the complete absence of reports of previous research on communicating in shared space. Control of extra-neous variables was not sought, and had it been, would have been difficult to achieve under the circumstances. Despite the limitations, careful design was not overlooked.

The method employed in these tests appropriately was quasi-experimental lab testing in which the researchers were able within limits to control the parameters of the test – time, place, equipment, the intervention – but naturally found that their data collection was affected by the equipment used and their own skill level in using it. (For example, computer conferencing is reported not to require much competence at a keyboard; however, in the case of shared space, where the communicating is 'live' on the screen, we found that good typing skills prevent frustation and in other ways facilitate the communicating.) Other salient factors affecting the quality of the data were the experimental nature of the communicating software used and the difficulty the participants had in trying to sharpen their keyboard skills.

The student team made general use of the simulations (tasks and roles) to test the workability and possible future application of the shared space concept. Together, several data collection techniques yielded important impressions and pointed the way to potential applications and further study.

Specific Example: Shared Space in Information and Referral. The starting point in the research was an initial belief that the shared visual and acoustic space concept had potential utility in disseminating social information between human service information centres and between the centres and their user/ clients. Using rudimentary and 'unfriendly' experimental hard-ware and software, aided by Research Council (SSHRC) seed money, we had previously submitted our hypothesis of utility of the concept to a demonstration and hands-on laboratory experience with a group of information centre personnel most of whom were not computer literate (Bellamy, 1984). An important finding was their enthusiasm and success using the equipment in shared space after an exposure of a few minutes.

This particular development research continued through the efforts of four graduate social work students in a research course. They had varied undergraduate preparation; in general they were shy of computers. A high proportion of the full classes of research students believed that computers were dehumanizing. But because they were interested in finding out more about the technology, largely a side benefit of the project, they became interested in testing the applicability of the shared space concept to social work practice roles. The aim of the I&R project was to explore computer-mediated, telephone, and face-to-face referral interviews between a simulated referral source and a community resource.

The student sub-group compared the strengths and weaknesses "on a psychosocial level" with referral using communicating computers in shared space (Cappuccio et al, 1986, p.13).

1 The setting: a two-room furnished space, each room equipped with a telephone jack. Other equipment included:

    1.1 Two telephone handsets
    1.2 Two Apple 2+ computers with modems linked by phone line
    1.3 Two monitors
    1.4 One printer.

2 The Procedures developed:

    2.1 Students wrote simulated exercises in which information was exchanged for the referral of a psychiatric in-patient to a centre for psychiatrically disabled adults. Using the same particulars for each case, a measure of standardization was achieved.

    2.2 The modes of communication were face-to-face, telephone (shared acoustic space), and shared visual space with the computer. Shared visual and acoustic space were not used together in the tests.

    2.3 Six simulations were held during a series of weekly meetings: one face-to-face, one by telephone, and four by computer. The last included practice sessions on the equipment.

    2.4 Data were collected immediately after each session. The analysis emphasized comparisons.

    2.5 Ten observational criteria were developed for data collection. They were: time; cost; referral result; non-verbal communication; affective component; hierarchy, status, and power; quality of relationship; confidentiality; conflict management; and satisfaction of participants.

3 Their conclusions (based on this study of shared visual and acoustic space used separately) suggest the following tentative notions with regard to shared visual and acoustic space when used together for I&R:

    3.1 Because shared space conferencing is much less dependent on time and space than is face-to-face communication it is fast and inexpensive. The effect in shared space of focusing the interaction is a contributing factor. On the other hand, face-to-face communication enhances small talk and other extraneous conversation.

3.2 The use of the new technology produces more satisfactory results in terms of what was intended of the referral interview.

3.3 The satisfaction of high non-verbal communication content face-to-face can be equalled by the retention of para-verbal cues via telephone discussion alongside the computer.

3.4 Positive affect communicated face-to-face and by telephone is facilitative. Negative affect is dampened in the relative intimacy of these modes. When computer communication is used alone some negative affect is communicated because of the more impersonal quality (see 3.5); the basis for the negative affect is in part unfamiliarity with the technology and resulting frustration.

3.5 Face-to-face and telephone (shared acoustic space) communication encourage warmth and tolerance in a referral relationship and inhibit open confrontation. The depersonalizing effect and sterile atmosphere in shared visual space has the potential to free up the expression of conflict and offset the inhibition of irritation and intolerance in face-to-face and telephone communication.

3.6 In the referral context, none of the modes studied appears to present any realistic concern about confidentiality.

3.7 The combination of shared visual and acoustic space has the potential for satisfaction and rich interaction because of the characteristics of the auditory mode. Together they compare favourably with face-to-face interaction.

Project Two: Compiling Information for Practitioners

An integrated workstation as a major network node has a key place in a social information resource centre - one that is concerned with collecting information and creating data bases for ready user access. In the case of the Social Information Resource Centre project of the ACLab located in the Faculty of Social Work, the purposes of databases it creates are to support scholarship (research and teaching) and/or professional practice of user groups.

A project initiated by graduate social work students in 1986 began with the knowledge they had gained previously in their practice concerning the prevalence of child sexual abuse and the "disturbing concern to those involved in its treatment" (Grant, James and Maloney, 1987).

As in previous projects, the students were assured it was not a 'computer course' and were given complete freedom to use or not use the equipment in the workstation. Although none of them had prior computer experience, they learned the basic operations after a few minutes of hands-on instruction. As we had found in earlier work, these students progressed to the point of using the workstation throughout the project. The ease with which they gained the skill was again a useful finding.

Without a previous reference point to indicate the type of inquiry involved, the early inclination of the researchers was to pursue a somewhat traditional approach – to examine the accessibility of professional information available in the field of child sexual abuse in the province. Rethinking yielded a somewhat different focus, namely the absence of an organized service delivery system in the province for dealing with the particular group offenders. The inquiry became transformed into a multi-stage project now expected to be government funded for completion: phase one was a province-wide survey of treatment needs perceived by practitioners in the field; phase two examined the extent of interest in a service directory of resources to assist in treatment of the regressed adult male sexual offender. A synthesis of information known to clinical practitioners and researchers located provincially, nationally, and internationally has the potential to become an important central resource for sharing essential information among professionals and policy-planners practicing in Ontario.

Following their exploratory surveys among known practitioners the student project under the Social Information Resource Centre moved to the stage of developing a model of information dissemination, feedback and re-integration. Future stages of the R&D needed to complete the project will raise a host of operational questions to be addressed, such as:

(a) Will the directory be useful to communities in Ontario?
(b) Under whose auspices should the directory be located?
(c) Who should have accesss to it? By what means? How facilitated?
(d) What procedures are needed for sifting and updating material?
(e) Who is to determine which professionals should be listed/delisted, and using what criteria?
(f) What will be the role of the integrated workstation? How will it be affected by the collection project? Will it provide a model for others to come?

With regard to social aspects, in particular the outcomes of the project, the research questions are far-reaching:

(a) How will the professions and their participating members be affected by a usable system?
(b) How will the system affect: (i) teaching; and (ii) research on the problem?
(c) What will be its organizational consequences, structurally and functionally?
(d) What will be the effects on apprehension of offenders, sentencing patterns, and treatment of perpetrators?

(e)   What   impact   will   a   successful   system   have   on   the
integrated workstation?

Project Three: Transferring Documents

Authors frequently use basic equipment with limited capabilities
that does not permit the integration of text and graphics, as is
possible on the integrated workstation. The original presentation
may   be   qualitatively   inadequate.   The   preparation   of   this
conference paper is an illustration; word processing was done
using a five year old Apple//e.

The preparation of a doctoral dissertation using an early
Apple//+ and dot matrix printer is another example of the
workstation's utility. In order to improve the quality of the text
and facilitate the inclusion of charts and graphs, the Ph.D.
student made use of a telephone hookup between the Apple and
the MacLisa workstation. Sections of the text transferred were
easily reformatted on the workstation to produce a final copy for
the laser printer.

This rather simple process is an important adjunct in the
operation of a workstation with publishing capability. It allows
the equipment workload to be widely distributed among less
sophisticated stand-alone units or incompatible equipment.

CONCLUSIONS

The question arises, will advanced communicating technology
achieve its promise to improve human services? We know that in
some of the human services, among which social work is a prime
example, there is a serious lag. To make possible the necessary
developments, human service practitioners must achieve knowledge   and   understanding   of   the   technology   and   use   its
capabilities well. This can enable us to respond proactively, so
that   the   technology   creates   an   environment   we   want – an
environment that the technology happens to create in its own
deterministic fashion because we are fearful or unimaginative
will not serve well.

Knowledge of human effects of the technology must emerge from
research and not untested assumption or practice wisdom. The
illustrative projects in this paper suggest two main entry points
in the initation, the pre-search, of applied study. The first is
to   examine   the   technological   capability   to   determine   its
relevance for practice. The starting place is to appraise the
attributes, limits, and possibilities of the technology. 'How
might it be used?' and 'will it work?' are among the important
questions to follow. The I&R series of studies began in this
way. The second entry begins with a search of the environment
for practice problems that might be prevented or alleviated by
an intervention like the Social Information Resource Centre. The
deficiencies of the service system in child sexual abuse are in
this category. Any one of these constitutes an initiation stage in
an R&D process in which the successive stages are redefinition
of the problem and purpose of application, design and model
building for testing, and diffusion by actively 'growing' the

intervention system. The important work of Rothman and Thomas at the University of Michigan (Rothman 1980; Thomas 1984) is basic reference material on methodology that will advance research for practice.

The impact on the human services of powerful environmental forces in the next decade, some old and familiar but most in new and unpredictable forms, can either enhance or destroy our prospects of creating a humane social environment. The improvement of human service practice through advanced communicating systems is an exciting challenge. The transformations that must occur in the helping professions will require commitment, creativity, and knowledge of the problems and possibilities. They will require great skill to bring out the best collaborative efforts of people in all the relevant basic and applied disciplines. Our studies lead us to believe that the synergy which is inherent in communicating networks of integrated workstations is one of our strongest allies.

Practical and Operational Concerns
in the Application of an Emerging Technology
in a Changing Environment

Simon Mielniczuk

Designing and operating an Integrated Work Station (IWS) (Forgie, 1984) as part of the Social Information Resource Centre (SIRC) project within the Faculty of Social Work at the University of Toronto brings into sharp focus the contrasts and tensions between the 'hard' and 'soft' sciences. In the IWS the person, hardware, and software come together to demonstrate these tensions and their underlying values in a tangible operating system and also to suggest some effective approaches which optimize each of these components.

It has been my experience as both a worker and supervisor of social workers that many social service agencies spend limited resources on the supports necessary to ensure accurate, up to date records for either client services or management efficiency. Potential for new funding or an upcoming program evaluation is likely to trigger the greatest efforts at records collection and analysis. That experience concurs with the opening comments in a recent article on the use of information for advocacy (Garner, 1987).

Information seeking behaviours likely to be most familiar to us are the endless telephone tags chasing the correct resource and searches through piles of personal or institutional records. Frequently, the valued resource is the available expertise of the skilled worker who points us to the right record or gives it to us orally/aurally. When microcomputer technology is introduced into this process, it forces a re-examination of our record keeping systems, and the people responsible for them. Although this re-examination is initially necessary largely to meet the technical requirements of system design and coding, it precipitates an evaluation of the importance of the people and records involved. Although the implementation and use of this technology requires significant analytic skills, little exposure is given in current curricula. In practice settings social workers and their agencies experience significant human and organizational factors limiting the utilization of ageing and rapidly changing technology assisted systems (Gandy and Djao, 1987; Turem, 1986).

Human skills required for the integration of these systems into personal and professional application are in the process of identification. Their lack among social workers is not simply attributable to technophobia. Knowing where and how to find records becomes even more critical as their sources and numbers grow. Graduate social work students are given a variety of curriculum opportunities to learn specific theoretical foundations and analyzing techniques, yet I have seen many experience for the first time the wonderous possibilities of the microfiche catalog and the community services directory, two of the most basic information tools of social work education and practice.

Both require some introduction for effective use, yet such introduction is simply assumed. Our project is beginning to analyze the role of information resources and their attendant technologies in the teaching and practice of social work.

At the start of the project, utilization was circumscribed to a few essential services - professor's boxes of assigned readings, a collection of faculty publications, and a limited reference collection of journals and books. Students remarked that 'it was a place to sit and write' with little use being made of the available materials.

Under such conditions, any improvements in available materials or services receive instant support. These improvements, in turn, generate a variety of requests which assist the definition of both the information centre and the application of the IWS. Operating under prototype conditions allows for the limitation of certain repetitious requests which help confirm the need for a particular service, but which have been sufficiently explored for the purposes of designing the operating system.

On the other hand, dangers exist that certain potentials are not developed or explored because the users have insufficient experience with the capabilities of information technology, in general, or of our particular system. For example, computer simulations are a growing area of interest across several disciplines. Yet, in the forseeable future, it is unlikely that there will be any interest in this applications area. Illustrations appear almost constantly in the physical sciences. Social scientists, however, generally lack the ability to turn descriptions of phenomena into clear graphics. Several people have asked for assistance with graphics for personal presentations; however, no-one outside our project advisory committee makes regular use of graphics embedded in text as illustration.

R & D AND PROTOTYPING

The initial system must pay constant attention to which skills and capabilities are used or needed to set up and test the prototype system with sufficient thoroughness so that the detailed specifications for both human and technical components emerge for a fully operating social information resource centre. The concepts of research and development and prototyping are beginning to move into the areas of social research. Jack Rothman's (1980) work on social R & D provides a most lucid explanation of the rigorous application of engineering R & D approaches to human concerns. Our project uses a method which Forgie (1980) calls Presearch and Development. In my estimation, it may be more practically suited to our daily realities. Rather than try to address a large scale problem with an armada of people and research resources, it devotes considerable effort to analysing all the components of the system in question, isolating them at a workable level of abstraction, identifying their relationships, and watching their dynamics over time. Specific components are targeted for research and development. Tests are carried out; the results analyzed and fed back into the dynamic system. If it works better, we use it; if it doesn't, we find out why, make changes and try it again or set it aside.

Throughout this iterative process the personal phenomena of the people involved and their purposes are the primary focus. Other references to this human orientation to R & D are found, interestingly enough, in the work at Xerox's Palo Alto Center and summarized by Daniel Ingalls (1981). The article on their design criteria for Smalltalk (a computer language which is the precursor of Apple's Macintosh visual interface and now apparently emulated in the coming OS/2 from IBM and Microsoft) states: "Just to get warmed up, I'll start with a principle that is more social than technical . . . Personal Mastery: if a system is to serve the creative spirit, it must be entirely comprehensible to a single individual." And further on: "A system should be built with a minimum set of unchangeable parts; those parts should be as general as possible; and all parts of the system should be held in a uniform framework" (p.286). That outlook has guided our operations from their inception and, to date, it appears to be working. One of the primary difficulties of this method is assuring that all components are, in fact, present in the prototype system and that the framework remains uniform over time.

In our research and development environment the manager has to develop and maintain a creative and controlled set of multiple personalities. Role shifts are fast and frequent between librarian and adviser, computer technician and program designer, manager, and research assistant. These parallel the system's multiple and simultaneous capabilities. Prior to the introduction of these capabilities, record processing roles were handled by various individuals in a more or less linear fashion over time. Using the multiple and simultaneous capabilities of the Integrated Work Station requires foremost a reasonably integrated person – or at least one who can control his or her fragmentation.

OPERATIONAL MODEL

The initial conceptualization of the SIRC is a simple, logical model of the SIRC interacting with people and records. People in the diagram are defined as faculty, students, practitioners and others. Records include print, electronic and human resources.

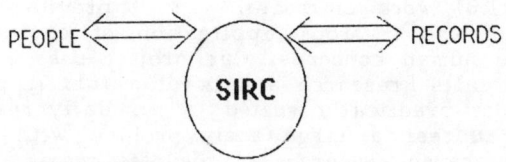

Figure 4.6

The Fundamental Conceptualization
of the Social Information Resource Centre Project

Data collection is a combination of techniques. A daily log records significant events similar to the critical incident recording technique mentioned by Bloom and Fischer (1982). Complex requests which require use of multiple resources are detailed. Those which have the potential of testing the limits of the IWS or adding to its capabilities are carried out and evaluated as systems tests. Using the pre-search and development process described earlier, the results are fed back into the system and a more specific model begins to take shape. Seven primary components are identified for the emerging system: marketing, management, services, collection, communications, research and development, and other.

Component details are further identified through the application of knowledge about information centre operations, user demands, and technical developments, in our prototype, marketing consists of: funding (university, government, agency, foundation, corporate); public relations (university, faculty, practice); and intelligence. Management includes staffing, reporting, prioritization, evaluation, activities, and accounting/budget. Our services component includes: internal databases; external databases; reference; training; computer lab; and reading room. Collection consists of: journals; reserve; general; special; bibliographies; periodicals; government; software; manuals; databases; electronic links; CAI materials; and social work applications. The R & D component consists of: IWS (a focal point) publishing; conferences; external networks; research aids; collection project; emerging technologies; research class projects; and the graphics project. The communications component includes: phone; Usenet; Netnorth/Bitnet; BBS; FSW Remote; and FM-SCMO. In our model we also always leave room for the empty set, other, to take advantage of new insights and experiences.

INITIAL FINDINGS

Each of the project components mentioned above operationalize the capabilities of the Integrated Work Station (Forgie, 1984). Our initial prototype is based on Apple's LISA/Macintosh utilizing word processing, graphics, spreadsheet, communications, presentation, and database software. Various software sets can be combined to remain resident in the machine at one time thereby permitting rapid shifting from one capability to another and easy transfer of data across applications.

Figure 4.7 is a partial screen print showing some of the software capabilities found on our electronic desktop.

Compared to the IWS model, our prototype has only limited shared space capability and only test access to the FM-SCMO communication channel. Consequently, these two capabilities have been tested, but are not in full utilization. Other limitations are imposed by the available software and skills. For example, our internal database application is limited to several sets of flat files which at present cannot be relationally connected.

Even with these limitations, a complex set of applications has emerged to date. And it is interesting to note the relationship

164

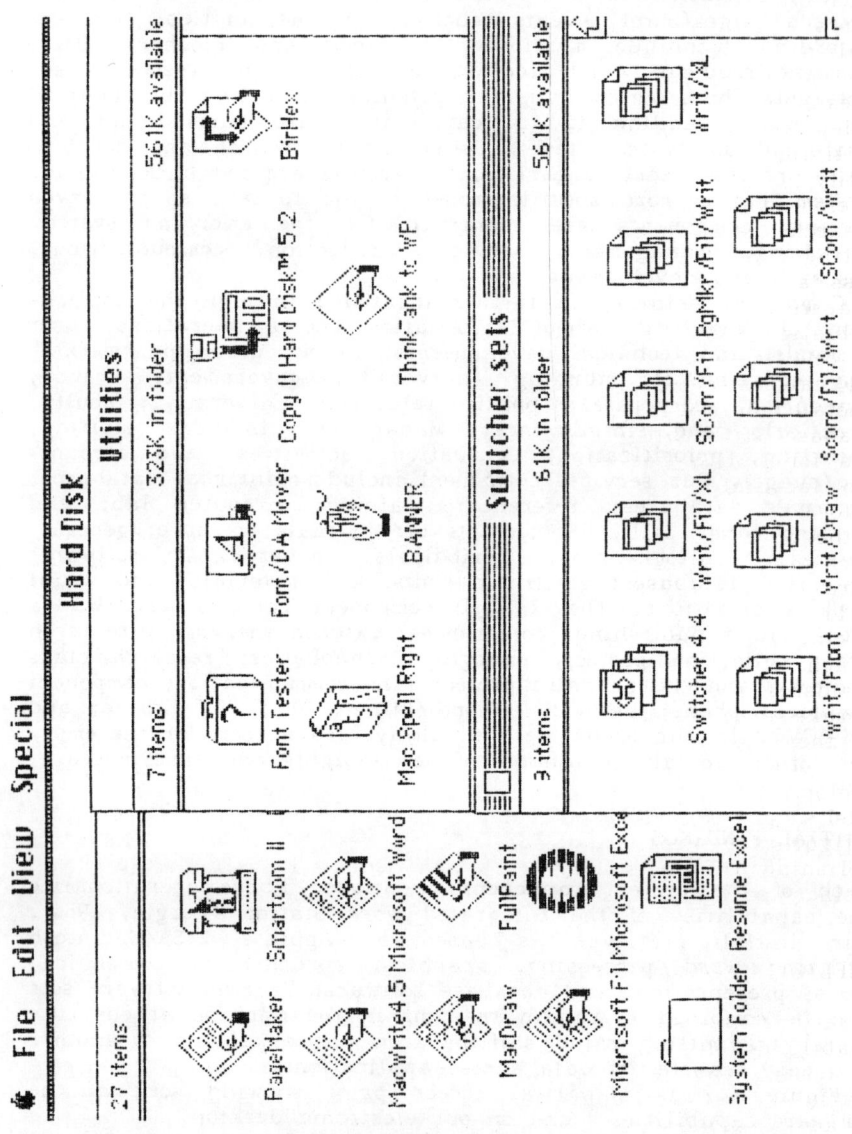

Figure 4.7

A Print of a Portion of the Screen
from the SIRC IWS showing some of the
Software Capabilities

which the operation of the IWS brings to seemingly unrelated events. Professor Nancy Joy, recently retired Head of Arts as Applied to Medicine, came with a report preparation problem. Solving that problem led to the utilization of the Excel spreadsheet program to create a project management, planning, review and reporting system. The association with Professor Joy facilitated the development of the Graphics Project to test the utility of the IWS and computer assisted graphics for the development of prevention education materials. Demands of a research class prompted the development of a Research Proposal Writing Guide which in turn was circulated in another research class and prompted a policy analysis guide. The search for a cheaper and easier alternative to the previous method of course evaluation analysis led to design of a macro which can be used for countless other statistical problems requiring the extraction and calculation of multiple variables from a set of data. An annotated bibliography project led to the development of a database of Faculty of Social Work publications. One project's need for mail merge capabilities to contact various practitioners also facilitated the Alumni Association's fundraising drive. A doctoral student's desire to have her thesis printed by laser led to the development of a standard configuration for data transfer which has been re-used for three other data transfer problems. There is a synergistic element to the application of the IWS that would be familiar to anyone who has enjoyed the feeling of working within a dynamic, supporting team.

Each of the above, files and code embedded processes, are considered products of the project and the IWS. Our practice is to make them available on request. We are currently investigating the feasibility of compiling some of them on a public domain disk for general release. The above process shapes the development of the fully operational system. We have used this model and method to develop the specifications for several configurations including: a field IWS; a faculty IWS; a publishing IWS; a student IWS; and a network for linking them together locally and remotely.

CONFLICTING DEMANDS

Operating an information centre together with the enabling capabilities of the IWS also surfaces some interesting conflicts. For testing purposes, it is necessary to limit the variety of any particular software application. Yet, in the first nine months, we added three new ones and dropped two used previously because their limitations were too severe to meet the immediate operating needs. The pressure to change components is likely to escalate in a fully operating system as software and hardware improvements leap ahead.

Staffing, training and funding implications follow. We have all read the news reports that indicate various jobs which are threatened with elimination through technology. What about the skills we teach? A class on single case design invited me to do a presentation on computer applications. I asked for samples of the work they were doing. In three hours I was able to create a template which calculated observation data, made a preliminary check for validity, and proceeded to graph the results on the screen. The template can be used repeatedly and a laborious hand calculation and graphing task of an hour or so is reduced to a 20 second data entry task. I suspect that, if the computer capability and the template were introduced at the beginning, some students might even consider using them in practice rather than resigning this analytic technique to research or academic requirement.

There are obvious management and resource allocation issues associated with the above, but let me raise two immediate ones. Who pays for all these capabilities, and who owns them? At the University of Toronto we have site licenses for several programs, but they hardly cover the full range of software required. It is as easy to control the unauthorized distribution of software as it is to control the copyright violations on the photocopier. It is not simply a matter of theft; one hard disk in our laboratory is constantly receiving unauthorized 'donations'. Is is sufficient to post warnings? Piracy of commercial software is at least easy to define if not enforce sanctions against. What about the encoded processes which are developed with legitimate software? Does anyone own them? How do we recognize the intellectual legitimacy of these processes and ascertain their originality when changes and improvements are made faster than they can be documented?

We are also experiencing a growing number of external demands. How do we respond? These demands are for working systems which will withstand the test of practice. Our own prototype IWS keeps some files on individual diskettes because it cannot handle the demands of even a very small collection. Operating a prototype IWS also brings with it the conflicting demands normally associated with practice based research. The demands of service have to take precedence over the demands of research. As I become engrossed in developing a particular capability, I have to remind myself that the person in front of me is more important. On our prototype work station sits a little sign. It says 'Please interrupt'. Additionally, under service strain, the demands of recording sometimes slip. When explaining system features to others jargon inevitably creeps in and belies attempts at establishing communication and user friendliness. The ACLab model of the IWS (Forgie, 1984) puts the person at the centre of the system. Focusing on the human dimension is absolutely essential for the effective operation of any communicating technology. In doing so we apply the best traditions of Social Work and help ensure that these systems stay within our understandings.

REFERENCES

Bellamy, D.F. (1984). 'Shared Visual and Acoustic Space in Community Information Centres: a Report on a Test of Applicability of the Concept'. University of Toronto, Faculty of Library and Information Science, ACLab.

Bloom, M. and Fischer, J. (1982). *Evaluating Practice: Guidelines for the Accountable Professional.* Prentice-Hall, Englewood Cliffs, New Jersey.

Cappuccio, P., Carinelli, M., Gliksman, J., and Ponzo, N. (1986). 'Explorations in Shared Space'. Unpublished course paper, Faculty of Social Work, University of Toronto.

Forgie, D.J. (1980). 'Presearch in Library and Information Science. The Library in Electronic Space – Three Explorations'. *J Canadian Library Science Society*, no.4.

Forgie, D.J. (1984). 'Technological Development and the Integrated Work Station'. *Canadian J Information Science*, **9**.

Gandy, J.M. and Djao, A. (1987). *Staff Resistance to Computerization of Information Systems in Social Welfare.*

Garner, L.H. (1987). 'Using Information to Define Problems: a New Perspective on the Administrator's Role'. *Administration in Social Work*, **11**(1), 6980.

Germain, C.B. and Gitterman, A. (1980). *The Life Model of Social Work Practice.* Columbia University Press, New York.

Grant, N., James, M. and Maloney, J. (1987). 'Child Sexual Abuse Project'. Student research in progress, Faculty of Social Work, University of Toronto.

Ingalls, D.H.H. (1981). 'Design Principles Behind Smalltalk'. *Byte*, August, 286–298.

Innis, H.A. (1950). *Empire and Communications.* Clarendon Press, Oxford. Revised 1975 by Mary Q. Innis, University of Toronto Press.

Johansen, R., Vallee, J. and Spangler, K. (1979). *Electronic Meetings: Technological Alternatives and Social Choices.* Addison-Wesley, Reading, Massachusetts.

Kroker, A. (1984). 'Technology and the Canadian Mind: Innis, McLuhan, Grant'. *New World Perspectives*, Montreal.

McLuhan, M. (1962). *The Gutenberg Galaxy: the Making of Typographic Man.* University of Toronto Press, Canada.

McLuhan, M. (1964). *Understanding Media.* (Signet Edition), New American Library, Toronto.

Rothman, J. (1980). *Social R & D: Research and Development in the Human Services.* Prentice-Hall, Englewood Cliffs, New Jersey.

Tapscott, D., Henderson, D. and Greenberg, M. (1985). *Planning for Integrated Office Systems: a Strategic Approach.* Holt, Rhinehart and Winston, Toronto.

Thomas, E.J. (1984). *Designing Interventions for the Helping Professions.* Sage Publications, Beverley Hills, California.

Thompson, G.B. (1984). 'Challenge of Choice'. *Intermedia*, July/September, **12**:4/5, 60–63.

Turem, J.S. (1986). 'Social Work Administration and Modern Management Technology'. *Administration in Social Work*, **10**(3), 15–24.

THE ELECTRONIC ARISTOTLE:
COMPUTER-ASSISTED INSTRUCTION IN HUMAN SERVICES

Robert J. MacFadden

Early writers envisaged computer-assisted instruction as herald-ing a revolutionary new era where the computer would function like an electronic Aristotle (McDougall, 1975), infinitely patient and dedicated to meeting each learner's needs. While these glorious promises have not yet been realized, considerable advances have been made. This paper presents a definition of CAI, describes related terms and explores some applications in industry and human services. A program created by the author, graduate social work students and a content specialist to instruct in child sexual abuse assessment is highlighted and developmental issues discussed. The presentation concludes with an examination of the effectiveness of CAI and the promise for the future.

DEFINITION

Computer-assisted instruction or CAI refers to the direct use of computers to provide primary instructional service (Burke, 1982). The term CAI can be used narrowly to refer to an emphasis on the computer as one type of instructional medium similar to slides, video or textbooks. A related term, computer-assisted learning (CAL) emphasizes the computer as a powerful and versatile tool to maximize student learning in many different ways. While the CAL perspective has become dominant in North America, the terms CAI and CAL are frequently used inter-changeably (Kearsley, 1983). Computer-managed instruction (CMI) describes the ability of some programs to include a variety of instructional management functions like scheduling of student activities, calculating test scores and resource utilization (Flynn, 1982). Computer-based training (CBT) is another broad term that incorporates CAI, CAL, CMI and other related functions (Kearsley, 1983). In this presentation the term CAI will be employed in this broad sense to incorporate both CAI and CAL philosophies.

Background, Advantages and Limitations of CAI

CAI originated in the era when behavioral psychology was predominant in North America. Early development was based on stimulus-response theory and programmed instruction. The student was presented with a stimulus or question and then responded. A correct response was rewarded immediately. B F Skinner's teaching machine concept in 1954 incorporated pro-grammed instruction, was based on operant conditioning and utilized hinting, prompting and suggesting. Other pioneers like Norman Crowder in the 1960s added features like branching to promote more individualized learner direction and responses

(Collagon, 1976). The evolution has continued towards increasing complexity and more recognition of the unique cognitive elements in learning and incorporation of this into CAI development (Burke, 1982).

Advantages

Based on programmed instruction, CAI provides small learning steps, active responding and immediate feedback. It engages the learner, requiring constant attention and participation, and provides rapid feedback, enabling progress to be evaluated. Well-designed CAI progresses at the learner's pace, starting and stopping at user selected points and allowing maximum flexibility. The learner can review material, make up for work missed at a time and location that can be varied and individualized to meet the learner's needs.

CAI can store large amounts of information including past learner performance, if desired, and be combined with other media such as films, slides and video. For some people, using novel, popular technology with graphics, colour and sound enhances the learning experience and encourages a sense of technological competency and control over one's learning environment. The computer provides a confidential and impartial tutor that responds quickly, fairly and patiently. Slow learners are not embarrassed and gifted learners can move rapidly.

CAI systems can be centralized, utilizing a large mainframe computer and many remote terminals or stand-alone microcomputers. Using microcomputer technology, CAI lesson disks can be copied inexpensively and sent via regular mail to remote locations. Standardization of training, if desired, can be accomplished through a CAI approach to learning.

Disadvantages

Computer-assisted instruction can be very time-consuming and expensive to develop. Estimates vary between 100–300 hours of time to create one hour of courseware (Ragsdale, 1982; Burke, 1982: Hebenstreit, 1980). Development requires expertise in at least three technologies: computer hardware and software, educational and content familiarity. This background is difficult to find in one individual and frequently teams are created which can both add to and detract from the process and outcome.

The lack of standardization of hardware and software may make sharing of CAI materials difficult, impossible and/or expensive. Even within the same brand of hardware, incompatibility may exist across new versions of computers. Cost of hardware, although decreasing, can be expensive, especially for human services agencies where funds for training are typically nominal.

The quality of content of the CAI program is critical. A famous computer expression is: 'Garbage In, Garbage Out' or GIGO. A system may be technically superior but contain irrelevant or weak content, limiting its credibility and utility. In human services training, content relevancy may vary widely among trainers and make the creation of broad appeal courseware difficult.

Some learners may not like a machine approach to learning, especially within human services. CAI depends heavily upon reading ability and comprehension which may be a problem for some learners. In addition, learners are typically able to question an instructor. In CAI, students are usually unable to question the computer or learn more than is programmed (Flynn and Kerczeruk, 1984).

Applications within Human Services

Much of the writing, research and development of CAI in North America has occurred within traditional educational settings. A review of CAI literature characterized it as extremely technical, esoteric and highly abstract with many articles within the educational technology field and minimal material in the human services training area (see Flynn, 1982, or Kearsley, 1983).

Human service organizations are now beginning to recognize the merit of CAI. Flynn (1982) describes a project designed to train 29 social service workers who license homes for child welfare placement. Expecting some resistance, the researchers were surprised that the participants overwhelmingly rated the CAI experience as positive and that CAI would be a useful supplement to training. A large majority of participants indicated they felt in control of their progress and gained significant knowledge. Lynett (1984) describes a major pre-service program developed for the Florida Department of Health and Rehabilitation Service for use with more than 1000 public assistance eligibility specialists. The program teaches workers how to determine client eligibility for financial assistance through the Aid for Dependent Children (AFDC) program. The program incorporates computers and videodisc technology. It is competency-based and utilized for evaluating trainee performance at eight testing points.

CAATS - A COMPUTER-ASSISTED ABUSE
ASSESSMENT TRAINING SYSTEM

A CAI program to instruct new protection workers in child sexual abuse assessment was developed over two academic terms by the author, fourteen graduate social work students and a specialist in child abuse. Although the author had some beginning experience in programming CAI material, none of the other team members had any significant experience with computers. Some students had worked previously in child protection. A specialist in child abuse training assisted the team to ensure the system was anchored in practice realities and contained critical content. The work was divided between three teams with the author as co-ordinator: the instructional, the content and the programming teams.

Instructional Team

The instructional team developed the basic learning objectives, identified important educational principles and selected the instructional design. They also wrote the documentation which describes and accompanies the courseware.

In CAI, several strategies are available for lesson design ranging from drill and practice, tutorial and socratic approaches to simulation and games (Kearsley, 1983). The needs of the learners, objectives of the system and resource availability are factors which affect choice of a particular strategy. A tutorial strategy was selected since it offered the presentation of new material in a controlled context with rapid testing of comprehension. One or several frames of information are provided with an optional review followed by one or more questions. Successful completion moves the learner to new content within the module or back to the basic menu. This fundamental design was premised on several principles of adult learning or andragogy (Knowles, 1980) and assumes a motivated adult learner with at least a high school level of education and attempts to maximize learner choice.

A modular menu design allows easy entrance and exits and individualizes the learning through the multiple and unique paths that may be chosen. Considerable effort was expended on developing the screen layout, condensing and presenting information for impact and clarity (Landa, 1984). Computer responses to learner responses were designed to be personalized, encouraging and informative. Questions were developed that were clear and unequivocal. Ambiguity in the questions or responses could greatly undermine the credibility of the system and frustrate the learner. No permanent record of names or performance was to be maintained in order to encourage the learner to risk, make mistakes and experiment at an individualized pace.

A printed, accompanying manual was developed to orient the new learner to the system, including CAI, specific foci, hardware and software requirements, an outline of content, a glossary of basic computer terms, and index and child sexual abuse bibliography. The manual contains a 'Quick Start' section for simplicity and the learner need only place the program disk in the computer and turn it on. The system starts automatically and prompts for previous experience and first name.

This system is viewed as a supplement to existing training. Work in the child sexual abuse area is demanding emotionally the learners should have regular interpersonal contact through supervision and training. The cognitive orientation of CAATS was planned to be balanced with the social support available through standard approaches to training. The CAATS system was designed to support instruction in a familiar clinical model, to reduce resistance and to promote acceptance.

Content Team

The child sexual abuse area was chosen because of its importance and general consensus related to concepts, indicators and processes. The focus was further narrowed to 'child sexual abuse assessment' to ensure better coverage of the content. A well-accepted clinical model was used (Sgroi, 1982). It provided credibility and promoted a sense of familiarity among learners and trainers. The model was modified somewhat to incorporate dimensions relevant to local issues such as protocols and government regulations.

The content of the system was designed by the team to include: (a) an **introduction** welcoming the learner, identifying system objectives, biases (e.g. intrafamilial, child-centered) and other caveats; (b) a **protocol** module that reviewed the appropriate standards, guidelines and procedures; (c) an **investigation** module which described procedures involved in investigation; (d) a **validation** module that outlined significant validation principles; (e) a **child protection assessment** module that identified procedures involved when an incident of abuse is confirmed, Sgroi's primary protection factors, and initial case management issues; and (f) a **bibliography** that contained relevant readings for child sexual abuse assessment and treatment.

Programming Team

Without funding for the project, existing resources within the Faculty were employed on the programming team. Authoring software programs to create CAI programs were reviewed prior to the project. This involved examining authoring languages and systems. An authoring language is a specialized type of program designed specifically to create educational courseware. It contains a limited number of commands designed to maximize the ease of writing questions, handling responses and displaying graphics, as examples. A typical authoring system is menu driven, prompts the author about various options and content, and does not require sophistication in programming. An authoring system writes the computer CAI program based upon design sessions with the author. Authoring systems the team reviewed were easier to use but considerably more expensive and not as flexible as authoring languages (Burke, 1982). A recent version of the PC PILOT (Programmed Inquiry, Learning or Teaching) language was selected for its economy and versatility. Beginning facility with the language was attained quickly through exercises, but advanced expertise was more difficult given the time parameters of the project.

Effectiveness of CAI

A preliminary version of CAATS was developed and pilot tested at a local child protection agency and reviewed by an independent government trainer in child abuse. Some minor revisions were made and funding is being sought to test the system with new protection workers using control groups and a

combined formative and summative approach to evaluation (Signer, 1983; Kearsley, 1983; Kidd & Holmes, 1984).
Few well designed and controlled studies examining the effectiveness of CAI exist (see Thomas, 1979; Chambers & Sprecher, 1980; Bagley & Klasson, 1979; Nelson, 1978; Misselt et al, 1980; and Orlansky and String, 1979). In a review of two decades of use, Kearsley, Hunter and Seidel (1983) conclude that CAI makes instruction more effective and efficient. The complexity of CAI needs further exploration. What learning strategies are most appropriate in which situations with what type of learners and content? What learners benefit most from CAI? How can CAI best utilize video, graphics, sound and other enhancements? What approaches to CAI development are possible to reduce the extensive costs and yet maintain quality?

SUMMARY

Many human service agencies in North America are reaching a level of maturity with computers where they are looking for expanded uses of this technology. A wide range of applications currently exist for large and small agencies (MacFadden, 1986). Falling hardware prices, increasing sophistication of authoring systems, and the development skill and interest of human service providers are likely to affect the rate of development and use of CAI in human services. The promise is substantial. For example, CAI is being used to create programs that have a clinical focus such as restructuring faulty cognitions to improve adjustment in various areas (Reitman, 1984; Meier, 1986).
The CAI system described within this paper was developed largely without funds or computer specialists by social work professionals and students. While it may not be technically elegant, it functions well and instructs within an important area. Gaining expertise in developing CAI programs is one significant way social service professionals can respond to the challenge of computer technology and begin to make an impact for themselves and clients consistent with professional values and objectives.

REFERENCES

Bagley, C.A. and Klasson, D. (1979). 'Instructional Computing in Correctional Institutions'. *Educational Technology*, **19**(4), 37-40.
Burke, R.L. (1982). *CAI Sourcebook*. Prentice-Hall, Englewood Cliffs, New Jersey.
Chambers, J.A. and Sprecher, J.W. (1980). 'Computer-assisted Instruction: Current Trends and Critical Issues'. *Association for Computing Machinery, Communications*, **23**, 332-342.
Collagon, R.B. (1976). 'A Programming Primer'. *School Science & Mathematics*, **76**(5), 381-391.

Flynn, J.P. (1982). *Computer-assisted Instruction as a Training Methodology for Child Placement Licensing Staff.* School of Social Work, Western Michigan University.

Flynn, J.P. and Kerczeruk, T. (1984). 'Computer-assisted Instruction for the Private Practitioner'. In M.D. Schwartz (ed.) *Using Computers in Clinical Practice.* Haworth Press, New York, 395-416.

Hebenstreit, J. (1980). '10,000 Microcomputers for French Secondary Schools'. *Computer,* **13**(7), 17-21.

Kearsley, G. (1983). *Computer-based Training.* Addison-Wesley, Reading, Mass.

Kearsley, G., Hunter, B. and Seidel, R.J. (1983). 'Two Decades of Computer-based Instruction Projects: What have we Learned?' (Part two). *Technological Horizons in Education J,* February, 8896.

Kidd, M. and Holmes, G. (1984). 'CAI Evaluation: a Cautionary Word'. *Computing Education,* **8**(1), 77-84.

Knowles, M. (1980). *Modern Practice of Adult Education: From Pedagogy to Andragogy.* Association Press, Wilton, CT.

Landa, R. (1984). *Creating Courseware.* Harper & Row, New York.

Lynett, P. (1984). 'Interactive Videodisc for AFDC Eligibility Specialists'. *Computer Use in Social Services Network,* Summer, 14.

MacFadden, R.J. (1986). 'The Microcomputer Millenium: Transforming the Small Social Agency'. *Social Casework.* **67**(3), 160-165.

McDougall, A. (1975). 'The Computer as Part of the Educational Environment: a Review of the Research'. *Australian Journal of Education,* **19**(2), 178-190.

Meier, S. (1986). *If You Drink* (Computer Program). Multi-Health Systems Inc., Toronto.

Misselt, A., Frances, L., Call-Himwich, H. and Avner, R.A. (1980). 'Implementation and Operation of Computer-based Instruction'. MTC Report 25, August. CERL, University of Illinois.

Nelson, E.G. (1978). 'Individualized Instruction: Another Point of View'. *Balance Sheet,* **60**(3), 122-125.

Orlansky, J. and String, J. (1979). *Cost-effectiveness of Computer-based Instruction in Military Training.* (IDA P-1375), April. Institute for Defense Analyses, Arlington, VA.

Ragsdale, R.C. (1982). *Computers in the Schools: a Guide for Planning.* OISE Press, Toronto.

Reitman, R. (1984). 'The Use of Small Computers in Self-help Sex Therapy'. In M.D. Schwartz, (ed.) op.cit., 363-380.

Sgroi, S. (1982). *Handbook of Clinical Intervention in Sexual Abuse.* D.C. Heath & Co., Lexington, MA.

Signer, B. (1983). 'The Need for Sequential Formative and Summative Evaluations made Evident from Practice'. *J Educational Technology,* **12**(1), 67-73.

Thomas, D.B. (1979). 'The Effectiveness of Computer-assisted Instruction in Secondary Schools'. *AEDS Journal.* **12**(3), 103-116.

DISTANCE LEARNING

Walter LaMendola

One of the problems faced by people interested in education and training is that often the population they wish to serve is some distance from them. Geographic distances have limited the options available to the educator. One option was to send materials to the student. This meant that there was little or no interaction between student and instructor that could be immediate or face-to-face. Another option was to send the instructor to the student. This option relied upon the gathering of enough students to justify the expense of sending the instructor. It also meant that instructors had to be willing to travel, often with very little compensation for the time involved. A third option required that the student come to the site of the educational institution. This option is the one most widely used.

The development of computer and communication technologies has led to the use of other options. These options have, in most part, assumed that the use of the technologies could only be effective when they mirrored the present situation, that is, if they could be used to recreate the classroom setting at the receiving end. They would require full frame interactive video, in other words, to allow the instructor to parade before the students in a manner representing as much as possible a one-to-one recreation of the classroom situation. For example, it is possible to send coursework to a remote site using satellites or microwave transmitters. This delivery mechanism has the limit of being extremely expensive at both the sending and receiving ends, and often requires a considerable expense in a system that cannot be used for other purposes.

Another option has been to develop coursework which utilizes computer and/or communication technologies. For example, many instructors have worked to translate their coursework into a computer-assisted format. This has meant learning authoring systems, most of which demand quite a lot from the user, but one real problem has been that, in this format, the instructor has had to think very carefully through the structure of the material and rehearse materials and flow. It is difficult to anticipate all of the reactions of the student, even with material that is straightforward, without dealing with subjects that require conceptual understanding and, presumably, the benefit of discussion and thoughtfulness. Still, there has been some success, particularly with straightforward material, and a great deal of activity in this area. Community and cable television have also been used for educational purposes. Such applications are relatively straightforward, with the instructor appearing on the TV screen, delivering the material. Often such courses are accompanied by written requirements, either in the form of papers or competency testing. The use of video has also gathered some following. Video training tapes are available through large publishing companies and some training institutes.

Their format is often the same as television based learning. Another use of video in training has been to film the event around which educational efforts will take place. For example, an instructor interested in the homeless may use as a class assignment the filming of a video of the homeless problem in their locality, or a class teaching personnel skills may film student interviews. The videos are then used as a part of the training or educational effort, often with remarkably good results.

Although all of these techniques have been used in the education and training of human service professionals, the limits of the various approaches have meant that, other than video and television, most other options have only sparingly been used. One cannot, however, blame the sparing use completely upon the limits of each particular approach except, of course, to point out any untoward expense, whether of time, materials, or equipment, which would be inhibiting in any case. There are, in fact, other requirements for the use of information technologies in educating and training human service professionals which must be taken into account.

Perhaps the most important requirement in such training is that there be an active interaction between the instructor and the student and between the student and other students. For a number of human service professions, the use of the self as a professional tool in interacting with others requires a good deal of sensory interaction, with factors such as smell, movement, positioning, and verbal responsiveness being elements of training, but they are there nonetheless. The students may also feel this requirement themselves, and for different reasons. Often students will express the belief that the most important element of their training was their interaction with other students.

Another requirement of much human service training is that the material covered is often conceptual and abstract. This type of material requires a certain amount of active learning to go on, in which students are directly challenged by others and where the instructor must often move by intuition to assist students in their learning process.

There are also ethical and value dimensions which must be resolved in undertaking educational efforts utilizing information technologies. For example, if television is used, it may give a message to students that learning is a consumptive process, not unlike viewing a situation comedy, that television watching is an educational process, that isolation in front of the TV is valued in their chosen profession, that they need not discuss issues with anyone, or that interaction with other students and instructors is not really valuable.

In our particular situation at the Graduate School of Social Work, we encountered a number of other problems in our attempts to provide education and training to rural areas, minority groups, and American Indians. In the case of rural areas, all of the problems already mentioned were important. They were overcome, in part, by the design of educational delivery systems conducted by regular faculty on weekends at the Denver site, or the delivery of programs in the geographic

area of the students during evening hours on four or five
intensive days a month. In this case again, an attempt was
made to use regular faculty to conduct the program. The
weekend program has fared well, probably because it allows
working persons to participate and discomforts regular faculty
not at all. In fact, it provides them with supplementary income
at the cost of a Saturday and/or Sunday teaching assignment.
However, over the past three years, all programs delivered to
rural sites by moving faculty to those sites periodically have
stopped. This leaves rural persons in Colorado with no
opportunity for the advanced professional training that we can
offer. In part, one can blame faculty for not wanting to travel,
but the distances are large, roads difficult whether plains or
mountains, the compensation slight, and the time demands
heavy.

Minority groups have experienced similar difficulties, but
their situation is more complicated. Rather than use the example
of the rural minorities, whose difficulties include those of any
rural population group, it is more instructive to examine the
case of the urban minorities. The Hispanic population in Denver
will soon be the majority population. Their percentage of the
student population is well below their percentage in the
population at large. The problems of recruiting minority students
and providing them with a meaningful experience have nothing
at all to do with the availability and use of computer and
communication technologies at this time. Instead, there is, for
example, great competition for qualified applicants who are
minority students. This usually means that those programs who
have resources to offer the students in the form of financial or
other incentives, or future employment potential, are often
successful in recruiting them. For the minority community this
constitutes a 'brain drain' of unprecedented magnitude. For as
many of the talented students in all areas leave the community,
few return to lived in that community after their training is
completed. Another problem is that as trained people do not
return to the community, educational programs which rely upon
internship or field experience often have limited opportunities to
place students with talented field-based instructors who are also
minority persons. It is also the purpose of field-based training,
in part, to help the student, learn to practice their skills
within a certain cultural context. In many cases, minority
students are placed in a white middle class context. This may
cause them to experience a number of difficulties in learning,
not the least of which is the added encumbrance of learning an
entirely different culture. Many of these students are dissatis-
fied with their field placements and perceive many of the
activities of the educational system to be racist in character.

The problem of delivering an educational program to the
American Indian involves all of the factors mentioned so far
plus a few more. The American Indian populations, in general,
have very few resources. They are located in areas that are
often far from cities. Their cultures are not clearly specified
nor have they been completely documented. Their language may
be unknown outside the tribe. They are small in number. Their

health statistics are poor, with infant mortality, alcoholism, hypertension, and diabetes often of epidemic proportions. For an educational program to be effective, there is much that the educators must learn from the Indians. They must learn something of their culture, lifestyle, needs, and customs. Since outsiders are rarely welcome, the University must involve the tribal councils in a meaningful manner in the design and carrying out of the educational program. A goal of the program must be that a large proportion of trained persons must stay with the tribe after training is completed. Any technologies used to carry out the training should be effectively transferred to the participating tribe so that they can use such technologies on their own should they desire to do so.

With this brief background on the available delivery systems, some problems which influence their use, and the special needs of some human service training programs when dealing with different populations, the use of computer and communication technologies may seem to be unlikely candidates to resolve these issues. In fact, that case is not to be advanced here. Instead, the argument to be made is that computer and communication technologies may allow us to approach the problem in a different manner than it could ever be approached before they were available; and that their use may be an effective supplement to the provision of an educational program to both usual and special student populations. One use of these technologies with which I have decided to experiment in the hopes that just such a resolution may be examined is called Distance Learning.

It may be useful to begin to discuss the notion of distance learning as developed by AT&T by describing the equipment necessary to implement the approach at the broadcasting and receiving ends. At both ends, one needs to have a PC with a hard disk, an available telephone line, a notch modem, a Targa board, writing tablet, speaker 'phone, and software. At our broadcast facility, we have also added a separate graphics terminal, specialized microphone system, and video capture facility through the use of video camera. Our total expenses including soundproofing the room, carpeting, draperies, oak cabinet for the equipment, bookcases, and conference table and chairs, has been about $30,000. The cost of the receiving end will, of course, vary by what is available already. If there were no available PC, telephone line, speaker 'phone, etc., the total cost at the low end would be about $12,000. This cost varies by vendor, of course, and it can be expected that price for various items will fall if the approach gains wide use and competition more severe. In almost all cases, rural communities, urban minority population centers, and Indian reservations will have a facility which owns a PC, telephone line, and speaker 'phone. In Colorado, often the hospital or library not only has the equipment, but also has a community room which can be used by groups of persons in the community for events such as classroom training.

The distance learning event begins with all participating sites being connected together by the broadcast facility. In the United States, the person at the broadcast facility simply gives the 'phone numbers to the conference operator. Through the alliance bridge, 56 sites can be simultaneously connected before adding another bridge; however, my initial judgement is that an instructor, and probably the students, cannot relate to more than a few sites at a time.

After all sites are connected, each site has full audio and tablet graphic capability; in other words, everyone can talk to everyone else and be heard, and anyone can initiate written comments by writing on the tablet which, again, is simultaneously available at each site. The instructor, prior to the class, will load a set of graphic images into the hard disk of each PC. During the instruction, the instructor will page through the graphic images in any sequence, make notes on the images by using the tablet, invite comments, and converse freely with the participants. The instructor may also have supplementary material, such as a database table, which can be shown on the terminal. The instructor could also decide to send new material during the class period. This is usually not done because, at least at present, the time it would take to send the image would hold up the class.

It is perhaps important to note what this level of training is not. It does not use full movement video. In other words, the students do not see the instructor as the instructor teaches. As one person said: "No talking heads!" Full movement video is possible, but it is much more expensive: distance learning as we have envisioned it here can be conducted at a cost as low as $12 per hour.

While it is presumably not difficult to envision how in fact this technology may be used to some great advantage with rural populations, it is probably not as clear what advantage the training may have for other special populations. There are some common advantages which should not be overlooked. The development of coursework is not as difficult and time-consuming as other approaches. A two-hour training episode may take only two hours to prepare. Two problems seem critical. One is the teaching style of the instructor. Those instructors who do not work in a structured manner, that is, who walk in the classroom with no notion of what they want to say or accomplish that day, will have trouble in structuring their approach and, presumably, will take more time than the instructor who has a structured approach, knowing what concepts and ideas are to be covered and the order in which they are to be discussed. Another is the availability of graphic images. In many cases, charts, graphs, and tables are used by the instructor, and this is no problem. Any image which can be photographed can be captured and used. The problem arises when the instructor does not know what graphic image they want to use in their presentation, or, when they know what image they want but it must be created. Personally, I found that the use of graphics gave me much more power in supplementing my lecture material and I willingly pushed at my time limits to get the right image to go with the structure of my dialogue.

Another common advantage is that regular faculty do not have to travel to deliver coursework, yet can be used to deliver that coursework. It is also true that the educational program can contract with the best person available to teach a course. The person will require very little training to master the technology, and they do not have to be at the university broadcast facility to deliver the coursework. In fact, any remote site with the equipment characteristics I outlined above can broadcast coursework. AT&T has a number of facilities available in major urban centers in the United States where their staff deliver and receive training.

A third common advantage is that once a course is prepared each site will have the course materials, including the graphics and the instructor's script, in a coursebook. The materials can be reviewed and studied at any time. Notes made during the actual training session can be saved on their PC, retrieved later, and also studied and reviewed.

For special populations, the remote site can become a community resource. It is our intention that coursework will be delivered with a facilitator present at the receiving site. After the instruction is completed, we then expect the facilitators to continue the educational process with discussions and student interaction. The facilitators are planned to be trained if need be at the educational site, and are to be recruited from within the community at which the training will take place. We also plan to train persons, again if that is a need, to use the equipment and maintain it for the community. This at least begins to deal with the issues of having a training cadre of persons in the community who are to be used in some instructional capacity with the students. It will be difficult for the facilitators to avoid being a resource to the learners! Students will not be asked to leave their cultural context in order to receive training, begin professional practice, and train others. It may be that there will be some period of residence required at the educational institution, but that can be minimized in favor of community-based training.

Developing such a resource can fulfill the needs of the community to provide or receive training of any type. It is our wish, for example, in the case of the training of American Indians, that they be encouraged to develop coursework to teach us and others about their culture, customs, and lifestyle. For people in rural areas, we have also thought that they may be able to use the resource to receive training for their school teachers, or for certification and continuing education of rural based human service practitioners.

Mastery of the technology by the participating groups can also allow them to do networking of various types, from library-based to special interest-based bulletin boards, to participating in electronic networking in all of its variety and diversity. For example, the Mountain Ute Indian communities may network with the Zunis to receive training to carry out their highly effective diabetes prevention program. Hispanic groups may exchange cultural training with other urban groups around problems such as teenage pregnancy. The rural group may participate in AA meetings via electronic networks. State government may provide leadership training. Human service agencies could train personnel. Legislative advocacy groups could educate isolated populations about issues facing larger groups in the State. In one project, just about to get underway, we are working with the United Way of America to use distance learning as one of the educational approaches used by their National Center on Voluntarism. We expect, over the next few years, to train United Way professionals, board members, and agency personnel, who have never been able to participate in such coursework before because of the expense of leaving their home to travel to Washington for such training. For these people, it has not been reasonable to undergo such expense and time commitment despite the undeniable value of the coursework.

In summary, the distance learning approach seems to hold some promise as an appropriate technology. Our experience with it will be shared with the larger community of persons utilizing similar technologies, but it is our intent to place our fullest efforts into sharing the technology with those populations who use it with the purpose of empowering them in as many ways as we are able to do so. It is an unfortunate fact with most other approaches that their reliance upon devices which cannot be easily mastered or used for other purposes that they often have the effect of alienating those who can benefit, who must benefit from their use. It is also true that we are skeptical about the use of these devices and will guide our future plans by the results of the experiments we conduct over the next few years.

Information Technology and the Human Services
Edited by B. Glastonbury, W. LaMendola and S. Toole
© 1988 John Wiley & Sons Ltd

CHAPTER 5

Policy Development and Administration

One aspect of this topic, the development of management information systems (MIS), generated a great many papers for HUSITA. However, in selecting material for the chapter the editors have tried to encompass a wider range of concerns. The availability of MIS in the human services has been an invaluable tool in the development of more realistic policies and better informed administrative actions. At the same time, to view the 'information revolution' solely in these terms is unnecessarily narrow. As well as being a tool of policy making, IT is of such importance that it must also be a subject of policy. The development of the technology has forced the issue of whether agencies can function properly without information policies, and placed considerable emphasis on their nature and content. In a similar way, IT can be seen as an aid to administrative convenience and great efficiency, or it can be viewed more widely in the context of its impact on patterns of work, communications and authority structure of agencies. In short, several of the papers chosen for this chapter seek to broaden the discussion to encompass the developing concept of information strategy.

The first paper, from Bryan Glastonbury, seeks to put IT policy in the broader context of Social Policy. Some fundamental questions are posed – do we need IT policies? If so, what should go into them? The paper discusses the problems of rational policy-making at a time when there is so little stability on the technological front, and suggests that the pace of technology change will make some elements of a comprehensive policy obsolete before they can approach implementation. The paper also challenges the economic viability of IT expenditure in terms of its productivity, and queries whether IT value systems can be aligned with those of service professionals.

The paper from Harris looks at the role of information and its impact on the way agencies function. From a community work base in London, he starts from the premise that in social work and social service agencies information is seriously undervalued, and in consequence information units are underresourced. This is a view which might be challenged as a generalisation about all human services agencies, but which does point up the disparity between larger organisations, with substantial budgets, and smaller groups, who are hard pressed to find the necessary investment to take advantage of IT opportunities. The author argues that information is not only important in itself, but needs to be used constructively. He suggests that a poor use of information leads to 'reactive' decision-making rather than careful strategic planning.

Fiene looks in detail at specific types of information systems, and the contexts in which they are most useful. He sees system structure as needing to vary in response to the type of interrogations which will be put to it, and the ways in which it will be used. Administrators and professionals may well require information to be handled in different ways, to be of most value. Whereas Fiene argues that the development of MIS is a response to a crisis of accountability within agencies, Grove and Frakes are more concerned with effective financial planning and control. Their paper advances a computer model that can be used by human service organisations of any size for handling budgetary planning. The model is based on sound accountancy principles, and the authors stress its suitability for micro-computer users – that is for agencies with relatively small scale, low cost equipment.

Williams and Forrest take on another aspect of technological development, that of automated office systems for human services agencies, primarily to handle communications. The question they pose is how far can these advances benefit the 'sharp end' workers in the social services, those staff who have face-to-face contact with clients. The paper, drawing on a research project which the authors undertook, examines a range of issues which will affect the extent to which IT is central to the proposals for improving the exchange of practice and development information. A challenge is set out for all those senior staff responsible for ensuring that investment in technology is relevant to the day-to-day tasks of practitioners.

The final paper in the chapter, from Imbrogno, draws attention to a development which would have been unthinkable before the advent of computers – modelling administrative and managerial systems, as opposed to the traditional 'trial and error' approach. He describes a computer model based on 'informational components' (such as problems, goals, outcomes, etc.) and 'analytical methods' (structuring, forecasting and so forth). His work supports the view that IT facilitates improvements in human service agency functioning which have a strong and well constructed theoretical framework.

POLICY DEVELOPMENT AND ADMINISTRATION

Bryan Glastonbury

The author began his working life as a social worker, but for the last two decades has been teaching social policy to social workers. Though personally committed to the use of IT in the personal social services, he remains surrounded by social workers and social policy teachers who are generally sceptical about the potential of new technology. This paper puts forward and comments on some of this scepticism.

INTRODUCTION

The paper begins with discussion of policy development, and then moves on to matters more connected with the implementation or adminstration of those policies. Howevever, there is no clear distinction. Policy-making and its implementation may be separate activities, carried out by different groups of people, in many subject areas, but with IT a relatively small number of staff handle everything. They are primarily IT specialists, who are rarely involved in policy-making other than for IT. Thus the first, and perhaps one of the most important points about IT policy is that it is made 'on the run' by staff who are generally inexperienced policy-makers, and have extensive IT administrative roles. Indeed, the pace of technical change is such that it is open to question whether we can afford the luxury of a carefully worked out policy, a point which will be taken up later.

A second of what might be called the 'parameters' of IT policy is the acknowledgement that it must be related to the reality of IT resources and skills. Some agencies have a log; some very little; none have enough to form the basis of a comprehensive policy. IT policies are made up of several fragmented bits, blending into and held together by aspirations and fantasies for the future.

LIMITS TO POLICY-MAKING

It is pertinent to ask whether there is any need for a policy. This is not a silly question: after all, most of the UK's personal social services have grown in response to needs, localised initiatives, and a host of other factors, with occasional injections or overlays of policy. Social policy often emerges in response to the way services have developed, rationalising after the event, rather than as a plan for future provision. So what is the position regarding IT?

Leaving that question aside for a moment, there is a preliminary question which needs posing. How far are human service agencies able to make their own policies, even if they want to? In the UK the major agencies are social services departments. They are run by local authorities, and in addition to the usual impediments of resource shortages, there are two further ways in which they are limited in their scope to create policies:

1 The context of corporate management with other local authority departments, which may result in policies and decisions (such as those covering hardware and software purchasing) unsuited to the specific circumstances of human services.

2 The tendency of many local authorities to concentrate their IT resources and policy-making activities in separate computer services or data processing departments, and explicitly or implicitly prevent developments in front line servicing agencies.

The position of many social services departments, therefore, is that they may have some scope for policy-making, but much of it rests with the local authority as a whole, or its Computer Services Department, or higher up the political hierarchy in central government.

Returning now to the earlier question – do we need IT policies? If so, what for? Some sorts of policies are probably not worth making, except in the most tentative fashion. Three types stand out:

1 Long-term development policies, other than those framed in the most general of terms. The pace of technology change makes detailed long-term policies meaningless, because they become obsolete so quickly.

2 Policies based on 'promised' rather than 'proven' hardware and software, except of course in the narrow context of hardware and software development. We have a poor record of predicting just what new developments will come into operation, as for example with some long-standing policies based on the assumption that by the late 1980s most human-to-computer communication would be spoken.

3 Technology-led policies, which ignore the scope of agencies and their staff to make proper use of the technical capabilities of advanced systems. Often, nevertheless, such policies do exist – for example in the area of microcomputer purchasing.

In contrast, some aspects of policy development are vitally important:

1 Policies to integrate IT into the value system of society. This is being tackled in many papers to the HUSITA Convention, so will not be pursued here.

2 Policies to integrate IT into existing patterns, priorities and values for human service provision and agency administration. The next section will take up this theme.

INTEGRATING IT WITH HUMAN SERVICE AGENCIES

The very notion of 'integration' needs careful attention. If there is any sort of marriage of IT to professional social work it is an arranged one, reluctantly entered into. In the UK, and probably elsewhere, IT came into service agencies as an aid to managers, and most early developments served managerial purposes (see Glastonbury, 1985, for a detailed discussion). There were few signs in the early days of a burning passion for IT amongst managers or social workers. Indeed it was often the case of other local authority departments saying: "There's a lot of unused computer capacity around: how about trying some?"

It would be safe to assert that as a group social workers have not been in the vanguard of demands for computer applications. There is no substantial data on how social workers perceive computers, but the circumstantial evidence is that they are seen as office equipment rather than aids to professional practice. There are many nuances to this perception, but the overall position is one in which UK social workers see much to commend in the view that computers have minimal professional value. This is not wholly a 'head in the sand' attitude. Computers may be essential for basic client indexing, or paying salaries, but professional practice has a well-established basis in theory, values and methods which is not only independent of IT, but in the eyes of many could be damaged by the introduction of IT. There is undoubtedly a clash between the way social workers think their job should be done, and the way computers have functioned so far.

It is outside the span of this paper to enlarge this debate about the interaction of technology and professional values, but there are some policy aspects to be derived from the attitudes of social workers:

1 As a 'tool of management' IT has an impact on the delicate relationship between manager and professional, in that it increases the potential for managerial control. The notion of IT as a source of power will be taken up later.

2 As something which, in the eyes of social workers, is not endowed with a privileged standing, IT has to take its place in the general scheme of agency priorities. Spending on IT is at the expense of spending on other aspects of human servicing. Is it justified?

IT COSTS AND BENEFITS

This issue of the comparative value of IT in relation to other resources is, of course, much more than a matter of social worker attitudes. It is vital to the future role of IT. There is little accurate information on the total spending of human service agencies on IT, but local authorities in the UK are estimated to have spent about £300 million in 1986, with plans for a 50% expansion in 1987. This takes it above the total salary bill for all field social workers. Whatever the true IT spending on human services, it is now clearly at a substantial level, and its productivity needs to be established. Several HUSITA papers suggest that expectations of IT are not always being met, and hence productivity may be low.

Despite the complexities of a particular situation, the broad claim of IT advocates is that it improves agency efficiency both in quantitative and qualitative senses. Such a view has to mean that IT will enable more clients to be helped (or to help themselves), while work with specific individuals will be based on such factors as more accurate assessments, a better knowledge of likely outcomes, and a more effective fit of resources to needs.

Many professionals will argue that the same objectives could be gained, and the whole issue of efficiency/productivity moulded more carefully into human service value systems, if IT investment was kept to word processing and client indexing, and the rest of the money spent on employing more social workers, psychologists, or other service staff. As things stand at present it is difficult to make a serious dent in this argument. IT today and yesterday has only shown flashes of its real capability: it flourishes in the human services on the promise of tomorrow. There are limits to the credibility of a technology which seems perpetually unable to deliver the goods today.

IT AND POWER

One more point before beginning to delve further into the administration of IT policies within service agencies. Several HUSITA papers appear to be challenging the idea of IT as an agency controlled and operated resource, preferring to see it as a community resource (Epstein, Scandinavian 'telehouses', etc.). In part this is a functional argument - if IT is to be of direct benefit to members of society, why not maintain a policy of locating it where it can be directly accessed? But there are also strong overtones of a more authoritarian kind - IT, as the name implies, deals in information, and control of information is power.

Time prevents getting into the broader sociological or international aspects of this issue, beyond noting that it is vitally important to the debate about poor countries and technology transfer, tackled in other HUSITA papers (Tan, etc.). But there are some internalised concerns, about IT and power within human service agencies.

Organisational theorists (e.g. J.H. Smith at Fulbright Colloquium) now appear to take it almost for granted that the authority structure of an agency can be gauged from its IT networking. At its crudest, a mainframe computer at HQ, with terminals to sub-offices, reflects centralised control and the dominance of vertical communications. In contrast a micro-computer-based system with extensive networking between offices and individuals represents strong lateral as well as vertical communications, and points to devolved power, or a weakening of central management.

Hence policy relating to the structure of the IT system is much more than a matter of technology. It is a policy for authority, accountability and communication within the agency, and probably also a policy for external relations. As a result it is vitally important for managers and practitioners, requiring careful balancing. Broadly speaking early IT developments in UK agencies (based on HQ mainframes) left two distinct power bases within an agency, in terms of information control. One rested, as it always has done, with front line staff who gather client information; the other emerged at HQ on the mainframe client record system. One is control of the raw data: the other is control over processed information.

Exactly how effective policy should handle this situation would involve too much discussion of the nature of the human servicing task to tackle here. Suffice to reassert that it is a balancing act, and note what can occur if a balance is not achieved. Until relatively recently hardware configurations favoured closed centralisation. In California, nearly a decade ago, Dery (1981) noted that the resentment caused by such centralisation, and the way HQ used computerised information, provoked field workers to distort the raw data put into the system, and so convert HQ data from fact to fiction. In the UK it is arguable that similar centralising tendencies have been an important factor in stirring up the resentment of many social workers towards IT.

Current possibilities for hardware configurations, networking and software show much more flexibility than earlier systems, and hence open up many more policy options for agency structuring. It is difficult to generalise about how this will eventually impact on agency organisation, but we can at least be aware of some of the scope being offered. The ability to improve, dramatically, the quality and quantity of communications permits us to challenge some of the existing dogmas of organisational policies. Take, for instance, the notion of 'small is beautiful' and the contrasting assertion of the benefits of large-scale organisation. Both concepts are based in part on assumptions about the nature, effectiveness and capacity of communication systems; both therefore need to be reviewed in the light of new technologies.

IT AND SOCIAL WORK VALUES

Decisions about IT will affect another broad area of agency activity - that concerned with processes of service provision. In the UK there is a long-standing separation of social security from social work services. The former have developed into a largely mechanistic calculation of eligibility and entitlement.

The latter have procedures which are substantially derived from social work values – of each client being different, tailoring services to individuals rather than looking for standardisation, and so forth. Computerisation has provoked a radical reassessment of such agency processes, and challenged the viability of procedures based on social work values. Some of the impact may have been negative – the dehumanisation, for example, which social workers sometimes claim. Other aspects have undoubtedly been beneficial – like the growth of systematic case reviews.

IT AND AGENCY SELF-SUFFICIENCY

This paper has already discussed limitations placed on agencies in the formulation of their IT policies. Several papers at HUSITA (e.g. Graaf) suggest comparable inhibitions on policy administration. In particular there have been points made about hardware and software incompatibilities, and the way these have forced agencies to become dependent on one outside firm as both supplier and back-up, and on one operating system. There are various ways of approaching this problem. One is to promote policies of internal self-sufficiency. Another, and this appears to have widespread support, is for agencies to join together to negotiate deals for supply and support from a position of strength. There is a quicker return from this latter policy, but in the long term it is important for agencies to be able to depend on their own internal expertise for policy decision and system evaluations.

CONCLUSION

This paper has attempted to put forward three central points about policy-making and administration.

1 Policy development in IT is not an easy matter for human service agencies. The pace of change is too rapid, and policy drafts quickly become obsolete. In some senses IT developments at present are out of control, not responsive to careful policy-making.

2 Where policy-making and thorough implementation is vitally important is in trying to establish the infrastructural context for IT, whether we are thinking of ethical or organisational infrastructures, or the protection of cherished and needed professional value systems.

3 Much policy-making and implementation must necessarily be concerned with providing means for balancing competing aspects of human servicing – balancing the good from the past with the potential of technology; gaining an accord in professional and managerial priorities; or balancing the overall picture of resource development. In essence this is a

process of trying to keep IT under some sort of control, and harnessing it productively to the servicing task.

This paper began by mentioning some scepticism about IT in the human services, and will finish with a word of warning. One of the central themes of HUSITA 87 is IT in Decision Support, and the picture emerges of future social workers each having a desktop or 'attaché case' computer as an essential companion. So instead of the traditional idea of working with a client as twosome we introduce the computer and become a threesome. While we tread that path it would be wise to keep in mind that to us, the committed, the computer is a friend. To our clients it may undergo a personality conversion, into the nasty machine which turned down a request for a welfare benefit, or the player of aggressive games, zapping everything in sight, including social workers!

REFERENCES

Dery, D. (1981). *Computers in Welfare*. John Wiley and Sons, New York.
Glastonbury, B. (1985). *Computers in Social Work*. Macmillan, London.

STRATEGIC THINKING IN INFORMATION SERVICES:
AN EXAMPLE FROM COMMUNITY DEVELOPMENT

Kevin A. Harris

INTRODUCTION

From an information services viewpoint, most kinds of non-scientific and non-financial organisation are characterised by the low status accorded to information as a resource or commodity. More specifically, it is true to say that formally published information is comparatively not as significant, nor as predominant in, say, social work or social services, as it is in certain other fields. As a result, information units tend to be under-capitalised, and in the human services this is typically the case. Information workers in this sector are often on their own and isolated from other services; bibliographic and reference tools are not always adequate; networks of contacts in related services are often undeveloped; and, crucially, users' expectations of the service tend to be low – an unappealing scenario, particularly as the flow of paper continues to increase.

In many fields it is virtually impossible to keep track of the births, deaths and marriages of journals, newsletters and bulletins – many of them irregular, some of them illegible, each of them a telling drop in the ocean with something to say. It seems to me that attempting to confront such problems as these with traditional manual systems can give rise to disadvantages which may well compound the problems.

One disadvantage is that we are often obliged to process documents more than once in providing for more than one kind of information need at a time. We get bogged down in the business of 'collecting and storing', and by the time we look up to attend to the user's needs, his or her expectations of the service have dropped. Low expectations will result in low demand; low demand results in low status. Low status accorded to information in any organisation will almost inevitably stifle growth. Clearly, information technology can be the catalyst here, providing that its introduction is carefully planned and matched to the organisation's needs; and providing also that it is not used merely to replicate established manual procedures.

In this respect, the issue I wish to discuss here is our reluctance to pay attention to information service strategies. 'Strategy' has been defined as 'the art of conducting a campaign', and it is usefully distinguished from 'tactics'. A strategy is worked out in advance and brought to a given arena: tactical decisions are decisions taken at the time of application, within their own context – 'real-time' decisions, if you like.

My point is this: partly because of the low status of information services, and partly because they tend to be under-capitalised anyway, we are invariably inclined to take tactical decisions which might have been better confronted in a strategic plan - we are reluctant to spend ostensibly profitless time preparing a strategy.

Obviously I am not suggesting that tactical decision-making has no place in a modern service. I *am* suggesting that to persist in running day-to-day, reactive support services without some kind of strategic thinking is irresponsible in that it helps to perpetuate the image of information as an incidental extra. There is a mould of established and expected patterns of behaviour in information provision, which is ready to be broken: it is the more easily broken because it is characterised by clerical procedures which are directly challenged by information technology.

CPF INFORMATION SERVICE

At Community Projects Foundation (CPF) in London, we began developing a strategy in the Summer of 1986 and started implementing it in February 1987. The first stage in the development was an analysis of information needs and the characteristics of the literature in the field of community development.

CPF is the national agency in the UK for community development. As such it runs a number of innovative projects and has an important obligation to disseminate the learning gained in its experience. The information service is oriented to the needs both of project staff and headquarters, and has to provide for three distinct kinds of need.

Currency - the need for current awareness, an overview of developments and knowledge in the field.

User-orientation - the need for mechanisms which filter an appropriate selection of information according to an individually tailored search profile, thus reducing the risk of paralysing people with what one of my colleagues describes as 'info-clog'.

Comprehensiveness - the need to be confident that no important items in a given period and/or subject area have been missed.

It is important to recognise that these criteria tend to be mutually exclusive, so that with any manual system one would be obliged to establish three distinct services with distinct procedures.

Information in the field of community development is characterised by the broad range of sources - unpublished reports, expensively published books, project desriptions, newsletters, funding announcements, campaign leaflets, annual reports, newspaper articles, videos, etc.; by the lack of structure of the literature (citation practice is haphazard); and by the low level of awareness, among users, of the sheer volume of material which is available and potentially of use to them.

The information services strategy drawn up to cater for these needs and characteristics begins with recognition of the need for a flexible partial-text database – that is, a database comprising bibliographic records with abstracts, in this case, generally very brief abstracts. The community development database, known as 'CDbase' is used to cater for the needs I have described – current awareness service, selective alert services for individual subject specialists, a comprehensive bi-monthly digest, and retrospective searches.

At CPF we spent some time researching suitable software, since this is obviously the crucial element in the service. We chose 'Inmagic', marketed in the UK by Head Computers. Inmagic is a middle-of-the-range text retrieval program, which is increasingly popular among organisations in the community and voluntary sector. It is relatively easy to use for database design; very easy to search; and particularly advantageous in the flexibility of report formating. Inmagic is supported by Head Computers' special software: 'Headset' for batch entry to Inmagic; 'Headline' for online communications; and 'Headform' for reformating records retrieved online, to match the structure of the home database.

Quite a lot of effort at CPF has gone into building our database of community development information. This is done by batch input using Headset, which offers particular advantages in screen editing, incremental numbers for the records, and automatic carrying of data from one record to the next. Periodically, the file created in Headset is copied into CDbase, thus becoming available for searching and report generation using Inmagic.

Apart from a standard individual search report, we have two report formats which we use regularly. The first is used to create our current awareness sheet, *Communique*; the second to produce our bi-monthly digest, *Community Currents*.

The procedures for producing these services are as follows. Documents are recorded at the keyboard, with subject terms and an annotation included. A unique number distinguishes each record. Information relating to forthcoming conferences and courses can be accommodated within the database structure. When we wish to produce an issue of our current awareness sheet, *Communique*, we search the database to create a subset of those items which are to be included. The report format established for *Communique* screens out unwanted fields and adds punctuation: we have chosen not to include authors, subject headings or annotations in *Communique*, although we include fields for title augmentation, events (courses and conferences), and the availability of copies.

When we come to prepare *Community Currents* for publication, every two months, again we create a subset of pre-selected items, but the report format generates a completely different result: in this case, with authors, subject terms, and annotation, but without certain other fields. I should add that the range of options which Inmagic allows for arranging the record on the page is invaluable.

There are two factors in this system to which I wish to draw your attention. The first, at which I have been hinting, is that both of these quite distinct products – *Communique* and *Community Currents*, are provided from a single input: there is no duplication or multiplication of effort, no hand writing or re-keying involved. In addition, of course, Inmagic sorts the output according to a range of criteria, if required, and will even screen out the field which has been chosen for the sort.

The second point is that indexing for our database has been deliberately limited. We have made a conscious decision to expend less effort at the input end of the spectrum and accept the trade-off of being required on occasion to spend more time and be more inventive at the retrieval stage than we might otherwise. Partly we were influenced by the comparatively short half-life of material in our field; partly also by Inmagic's virtues as a retrieval tool, for although full-record searching is possible only by combining all fields, the range of searching options and the speed of retrieval are very impressive. Furthermore, it has always been the case that a machine-readable system, properly set up, will reach the parts of a document collection that a manual system cannot reach.

STRATEGIC THINKING AND INFORMATION MANAGEMENT

Both these points – the eradication of repetitive inputting tasks to generate more than one service, and the deliberately limited indexing policy – are examples of strategic decisions taken well in advance of implementation. And as such they draw attention to a final point which I wish to stress: this relates closely to our inheritance from librarianship of the characteristics of insularism and over-indulgence in detail, and to the emergence of a contrasting tradition in information management. The point is this: decisions taken as part of a strategy are informed by the entire context of the system or systems to which they apply. Librarians and information workers have not distinguished themselves for this kind of thinking in the past. However, the concept is fundamental to information management. By information management I mean the design, implementation and supervision of a number of related information systems and sub-systems, in order to maximise the benefits which they offer together and independently. The relationship between information management, information technology, and planning should be made clear. Information technology radically transforms the power to systematise: proper use of the technology demands that context of related systems: it is clearly irresponsible to have the power to systematise and yet not to plan.

And in case any of us is preparing the argument, against planning, that decreasing availability of resources leaves us without the chance to develop any strategy, Vernon Palmour, an American library management consultant, makes this particular point: "A period of retrenchment strikes me as the time when systematic thinking is most needed about actions to be taken."

Figure 5.1

Hierarchical Structure: Levels of Responsibility, Degrees of Programmed Decisions, Kinds of Information and Logical Components of Information Systems

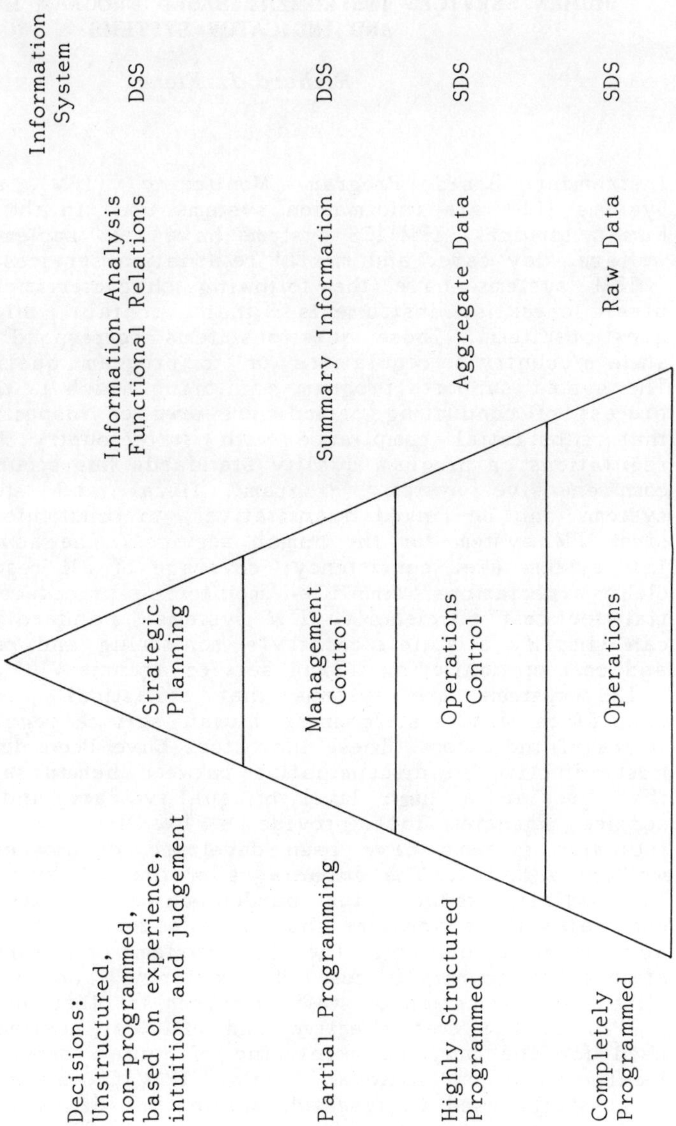

Information System	Information Analysis Functional Relations	DSS
Strategic Planning	Decisions: Unstructured, non-programmed, based on experience, intuition and judgement	
DSS	Summary Information	Management Control
	Partial Programming	
SDS	Aggregate Data	Operations Control
	Highly Structured Programmed	
SDS	Raw Data	Operations
	Completely Programmed	

REFERENCE

Palmour, Vernon E. (1985). 'Some Reflections on Strategic Planning in Public Libraries'. *Drexel Library Quarterly*, 21(4), Fall, 58.

HUMAN SERVICES INSTRUMENT BASED PROGRAM MONITORING AND INDICATOR SYSTEMS

Richard J. Fiene

Instrument Based Program Monitoring (IPM) and Indicator Systems (CS) are information systems used in the assessment of human services. IPM/ICS systems have been implemented in child welfare, day care, and mental retardation services.

IPM systems have the following characteristics: the system uses checklists/instruments that contain highly specific questions/items. These questions/items correspond directly to a state's/country's regulations or to program quality standards. The system supports program monitoring which is the management process of conducting periodic reviews or inspections to ensure that substantial compliance with state/country human service regulations or program quality standards has occurred. IPM is a comprehensive system. Program, fiscal and statistical sub-systems can be linked quantitatively to constitute a comprehensive IPM system for the human services. The advantages of an IPM system are: consistency; coverage of all regulatory areas; clear expectations; simplified monitoring procedures; and potential for cost efficiencies. IPM systems' standardized procedures can simplify a state's/country's monitoring and reduce the time and cost of monitoring human service agencies.

ICS systems are systems that statistically predict overall compliance with state/country human service regulations from a series of indicators. These indicators have been determined to be most effective in discriminating between human service agencies that provide a high level of quality care and those human service agencies that provide a low level of care. Generic indicator systems have been developed in day care and child welfare services. The advantages of the ICS system are that it substantially reduces the burden on human service agencies, especially those agencies that have a record of high compliance and program quality. The ICS system can further reduce a state's or country's cost of monitoring and permit the more efficient reallocation of staff resources to other activities.

IPM/ICS are cost effective and efficient systems that can be used for the program monitoring of human service agencies at local, state or national levels. IPM/ICS systems have been successfully used in research studies in identifying key process indicators of program quality and compliance that have a positive impact on client outcomes. IPM/ICS systems have been used in fiscal studies to determine the most cost efficient means for delivering human services. And lastly, reliability and validity studies have been completed on the IPM/ICS system.

During the late 1970s and into the 1980s an accountability crisis developed in the human services field that has not abated and appears to be a constant concern that will continue well into the 1990s. Because of the reductions in the dollars provided to human service programs due to sagging economies in the highly industrialized nations of the world, these programs have had to be very cost effective and efficient in the delivery of services.

The maturing of information system technologies has provided some relief for human service programs as they attempt to become more effective and efficient. However, researchers (Stevens and LaPlante, 1986) have pointed out the obstacles to the successful implementation of effective and efficient information systems for making resource allocation decisions. It has only been recently that an information technology described extensively (Fiene, 1985; Fiene, 1986b; Fiene and Nixon, 1985; LaPlante and Fiene, 1987) in the human service research literature shows great promise in developing effective and efficient information systems for making resource allocation decisions that is itself cost effective and efficient.

This innovative information technology utilizes instrument-based program monitoring and indicators (IPM/ICS) for developing effective and efficient information systems.

IPM/ICS systems can be used at a local, state or national level. They have been successfully used in several human services, for example day care, family day care homes, mental retardation services, child welfare services, and group residential services. IPM/ICS information technology has been used extensively in the United States and in Canada. Within the United States the following states have experimented with this new information technology: Pennsylvania (day care, family day care, group home day care, child welfare, group residential services, mental retardation services); California (child development programs, infant toddler programs, child welfare); West Virginia (day care programs, family day care homes, plans for residential programs); Michigan (day care programs); Texas (day care programs); New York City (day care programs); Massachusetts (family day care homes); and North Carolina (day care programs). The provinces of Alberta and Ontario in child care services have or are experimenting with IPM/ICS systems. IPM/ICS research literature has been distributed in Europe and Australia.

The IPM/ICS information technology has been extensively field tested to the point that generic indicators have been developed in day care and child welfare services based on reliability and validity testing in the United States and Canada (Fiene, 1984a and 1984b). Child development and child welfare outcome studies have been completed utilizing the IPM/ICS information technology in the United States (Fiene, 1985; Kontos and Fiene, 1986).

IPM/ICS utilizes data from local, statewide and national data bases. Data are integrated from programmatic, statistical and fiscal systems and are reduced to a series of programmatic indicators. The result from the data integration and reduction of information systems is a human service statistical model that can be used for resource allocation decision-making (LaPlante and Fiene, 1987).

The remainder of this paper will describe the IPM/ICS information technology. The most critical feature of the IPM/ICS information technology is that the system is based on a clearly

articulated   measurable   set   of   standards.   These   standards
generally   measure   the   components   of   a   human   service   delivery
system.   These   standards   can   be   very   minimal   in   nature   of
specific   goals   of   a   human   service   delivery   model,   such   as   day
care,   child   welfare,   etc.   Based   on   these   clearly   articulated
standards,   specific   items/questions   are   developed   that   measure   if
a   particular   standard   is   in   compliance   or   not.

These   items/questions   are   organized   into   instruments   that   are
used   by   program   monitoring   personnel   in   assessing   human
service   programs.   These   instruments   can   be   used   in   a
self-evaluative   fashion   but   generally   they   have   been   used   in   a
third   party   assessment   model.   A   key   element   regarding   the   items
is   that   each   item   is   assigned   a   relative   weight   based   upon   the
risk   that   a   client   is   placed   in   when   the   item   is   out   of
compliance.   The   instruments   are   administered   periodically   when
key   dates   occur,   such   as: licensing   reviews;   or   contract
compliance   reviews   (Fiene   and   Nixon,   1981).

When   the   data   regarding   human   service   programs   are
organized   into   a   quantifiable   fashion   as   occurs   in   an   IPM/ICS
system,   these   data   can   be   compared   with   data   from   fiscal   and
statistical   systems   in   order   to   determine   cost   benefit,   cost
effectiveness,   and   cost   efficiency.   Prior   to   IPM   systems,   informed
policy   and   resource   allocation   decisions   were   difficult   to   make
because   a   major   information   source   was   missing.   IPM   systems
help   to   fill   that   gap.

In   the   United   States,   several   states   have   conducted   studies
utilizing   their   IPM   systems.   The   results   have   tremendous   policy
implications.   In   one   study   in   which   data   from   an   IPM   system
and   data   on   client   outcomes   were   correlated,   the   result   was   a
curvilinear   rather   than   a   linear   relationship.   It   appears   that
compliance   with   human   service   regulations   is   in   the   best
interests   of   the   client,   but   only   compliance   with   selected
regulations   and   not   full   compliance   with   all   human   service
regulations.   This   compliance   outcome   curve   appears   to   suggest
that   a   substantial   (relative)   compliance   level   rather   than   a   full
(absolute)   compliance   level   is   a   more   appropriate   policy
decision.   This   decision,   if   implemented,   could   have   a   major
impact   on   how   staff   resources   are   used   for   monitoring   (Fiene,
1985).

In   a   second   study   in   which   data   from   an   IPM   system   and
data   on   unit   costs   were   correlated,   the   result   was   again   a
curvilinear   rather   than   a   linear   relationship.   It   appears   that
the   most   costly   human   service   agencies   were   not   the   highest
quality   programs.   This   compliance   cost   curve   could   have   a   major
impact   on   resource   allocation   decisions.   If   implemented,   it   would
suggest   establishing   a   ceiling   on   unit   costs   where   the
compliance   cost   curve   begins   to   flatten   out   (Fiene   and   Nixon,
1981).

The   above   studies   are   just   two   examples   of   studies   that   can
be   completed   with   the   IPM/ICS   information   technology   and   its
potential   impact   in   resource   allocation   decisions.

Let   us   now   turn   our   attention   to   the   indicator   systems   (ICS)
of   the   IPM/ICS   information   technology.

ICS systems are systems that statistically predict overall compliance with human service regulations from a series of indicators or predictor items. These indicators have been determined to be most effective in discriminating between human service programs that provide a high level of quality care and those human service programs that provide a low level of care.

ICS systems are a further improvement of IPM systems through data reduction techniques that allow program monitoring of human service programs with a series of process indicators. It was discovered through the use of IPM systems that the curvilinear relationship between outcomes and compliance had several indicators of compliance. These process indicators were having a disproportionately greater effect on outcomes than the majority of regulatory items (Fiene, 1986b). The methodology for determining these indicators has been described in detail in several publications (e.g. Fiene and Nixon, 1985).

The beneficial effect of ICS systems is that it substantially reduces the amount of time required to monitor human services programs because it centers in on key indicator/predictor items of regulatory compliance. Rather than monitoring for full compliance with all regulations, ICS allows a program monitor to selectively focus on these key indicators that predict overall compliance. This information technology substantially reduces the burden on human service programs who have a history of high substantial compliance. It also further reduces the cost of monitoring and permits the more efficient reallocation of staff resources to other technical assistance activities.

Briefly, there are four steps in the construction of an ICS system.

1 Begin with an existing, comprehensive IPM system that has a sufficiently large number of items so as to make greater efficiency desirable.

2 The IPM system should have been used long enough so that it is considered reliable for monitoring purposes. The IPM system should have generated sufficient data that can be used to distinguish among human service agencies in substantial compliance and low complaint agencies.

3 With the IPM system in place and some historical score information, use the phi coefficient (Fiene and Nixon, 1983) to select those indicators from the IPM that are most useful in distinguishing between good and inadequate programs. These distinguishing/predictor indicators form the basis of the ICS system.

4 The final step is to include in the ICS system particular items for the IPM system that are of critical importance to the health and safety of children.

As has been indicated earlier, IPM/ICS systems have been extensively field tested and experimented with in the United States and Canada. This information technology has repeatedly

Table 5.1

Generic Human Service Regulatory Administration Indicators*
General Theory of Compliance

Indicator	Component Area	Average	Range
Staff child ratio/ supervision	child development staffing administration	.33	.19–.46
Age appropriate equipment and materials	child development environmental safety	.35	.34–.42
Inaccessible hazardous materials	environmental safety	.34	.28–.39
Fire safety procedures	environmental safety	.41	.30–.49
Exits are unobstructed	environmental safety	.35	.28–.39
Staff physicals	health staffing	.57	.38–.82
Child immunizations/ health history	health	.56	.48–.64
Records reviewed/ assessment of program	child development	.51	.30–.71
Staff evaluations	staffing	.34	.31–.37
Inaccessible heat sources	environmental safety	.32	.30–.34
Emergency phone numbers	administration environmental safety	.28	.27–.29
Parents participate in program plans	child development social services	.28	.20–.35
Abuse and neglect reporting procedures	social services	.31	.25–.36
Acquiring skills/ completing service	child development social services	.46	.20–.71
Windows are screened when opened	environmental safety	.30	.25–.35

* Data compiled from Indicator Systems (ICS) for day care centers, family day care homes, child welfare services, and mental retardation services. Pennsylvania, New York City, Massachusetts, Michigan, West Virginia ICSs used. Five ICSs were analysed in all. All results are phi coefficients significant at the p<.05 level.

demonstrated its usefulness as a cost effective and efficient monitoring information system for the human services. Generic indicator systems have been developed in day care by the Children's Services Monitoring Consortium (1985), and in child welfare by the National Child Welfare Resource Center (Fiene and McDonald, 1987). IPM/ICS information technology has been proposed as a national model for the program monitoring of human services, in particular in child care services (Fiene, 1986a).

Very recently a series of research studies have been completed to develop a generic series of indicators for human service regulatory administration systems. These indicators hold promise as a national set of indicators for the regulatory administration field. They were taken from several different human service delivery systems in five different states' indicator systems.

The following indicators of compliance were consistently identified in these respective indicator systems: staff to client ratios; fire safety procedures; emergency phone numbers and information; child immunizations/health history; age appropriate equipment and material being safe and clean and inaccessible hazardous materials; records reviewed and progress/assessments/service objectives completed; parents participate in service plans; staff physicals/evaluations, inaccessible heat sources; and exits are unobstructed. States could use these indicators as their core regulations for human services.

In conclusion, IPM/ICS information technology has been demonstrated to be a viable systems model for the program monitoring of human service programs. IPM/ICS systems are effective and efficient information systems that can be used for making resource allocation decisions at local, state or national levels which leads to cost effective and efficient delivery of human services.

REFERENCES

Children's Services Monitoring Consortium (1985). 'Generic Checklist for Day Care Monitoring'. CSMC, Washington DC.
Fiene (1984a). 'Child Development Program Evaluation Scale and Indicator Checklist'. Pennsylvania Office of Children, Youth and Families, Harrisburg.
Fiene (1984b). 'Child Welfare Indicator Checklist'. Pennsylvania Office of Children, Youth and Families, Harrisburg.
Fiene (1985). 'Measuring the Effectiveness of Regulations: Compliance Theory'. *New England J Human Services*, **5**(2), 38–39.
Fiene (1986a). 'National Child Care Regulatory, Monitoring and Evaluation Systems Model'. National Association for the Education of Youth Children, Washington DC.
Fiene (1986b). 'State Child Care Regulatory, Monitoring and Evaluation System as a Means for Ensuring Quality Child Development Programs'. Virginia Commonwealth University Licensing Institute School of Social Work, Richmond.

Fiene and McDonald (1987). 'Child Welfare Instrument Based Program Monitoring and Indicator Systems'. National Child Welfare Resource Center, Portland.

Fiene and Nixon (1981). 'Instrument Based Program Monitoring Information System: a New Tool for Day Care Monitoring'. Children's Services Monitoring Consortium, Washington DC.

Fiene and Nixon (1983). 'Indicator Checklist Statistical Methodology'. National Children's Services Monitoring Consortium, Washington DC.

Fiene and Nixon (1985). 'Instrument Based Program Monitoring Information System and Indicator Checklist for Child Care', *Child Care Quarterly*, **14**(3), 198–214.

Kontos and Fiene (1986). 'Predictors of Quality and Children's Development in Day Care'. Virgina Commonwealth University Licensing Institute School of Social Work, Richmond.

LaPlante and Fiene (1987). 'Using an Integrated Fiscal System to Support Human Services Resource Allocation Decision Making'. Paper presented at the American Society for Public Administration's Annual Conference, Boston, Massachusetts, March 27 – April 1.

Stevens and LaPlante (1986). 'Factors Associated with Financial-Decision Support Systems in State Government: an Empirical Exploration', *Public Administration Review*, **46**, 522–531.

A PLANNING AND CONTROL COMPUTER MODEL
FOR HUMAN SERVICE ORGANIZATIONS

Hugh Grove and Joyce E. Frakes

Once people in human service and other fields have become familiar with computers, they frequently develop into rather sophisticated users and tend to forget the anxiety and frustration they might have experienced when they were making their first tentative efforts to become more computer literate. The first objective of this paper is to provide a starting point for those who have not yet discovered the power of personal computing.

The starting point chosen is the budgeting process. Few other tasks are both as familiar to human service managers and as adaptable to computer modelling. Although there will usually be hours of start-up time involved in learning basic computer skills and developing the initial budgeting model, subsequent reiterations of the budgeting process will more than compensate for this time commitment in the form of future time savings and improved quality of the budgets produced.

Furthermore, the basic budgeting model, if properly developed, can be used as a flexible management tool for basic cost control and other purposes. Another relevant alternative use of the model in today's environment is that of cut-back or retrenchment management. Such flexible models, however, require the implementation of some basic concepts of managerial accounting such as cost behavior and separable costs. The second objective of this paper is to demonstrate these managerial accounting concepts in a human services rather than a manufacturing context. To meet these two objectives, this paper will address the development and use of the basic budgeting model as well as its potential for cost control and minimization of the negative effects of an unforeseen cutback in funding. In doing so it will introduce or reinforce some of the very fundamental concepts of managerial accounting and introduce the reader to a very basic application of computer software.

MODEL DEVELOPMENT

A simplified example of a state (non-profit) mental health center with two programs can be used to illustrate the procedure for developing a budgeting model. Table 5.2 illustrates typical revenue and expense line items from a proposed budget for a state mental health center (SMHC).

The budget as presented below is not very useful as a planning or decision-making tool. The lack of essential detail is deliberate in order to simplify the example. However, even a detailed budget prepared in the above format fails to make explicit the assumptions underlying the numbers. Hence, it is difficult to determine what would happen if any of these assumptions changed. One of the primary advantages of using a computerized budgeting model is the capacity for determining almost instantaneously how various changes in assumptions (e.g. fees charged, hours of inpatient care provided, salary rates, inflation rates, etc.) could affect the budget. Thus, the computer model can be constructed with this kind of maximum flexibility in mind.

Table 5.2

Projected Statement of Activity
for Fiscal Year, June 30, 1987

Revenues:		
	First and Third Party Billings	$ 300,000
	State Appropriations	700,000
	Total Revenues	$1,000,000
Expenses:		
	Staff	$ 660,000
	Operating	340,000
	Total Expenses	$1,000,000
Excess (Deficit)		$ - 0 -

REVENUE AND COST BEHAVIOR

The mere identification of revenue and expense line items is not sufficient for our budgeting model. Rather, it is necessary to determine revenue and cost behavior. Is it fixed or variable? These terms are used to refer to the behavior of revenues or expenses when there is a change in some activity level such as hours of service or patient care days provided. If the revenue or cost item appears to vary consistently with the change in activity level, it is considered variable. If it tends to remain constant regardless of rather major changes in activity level, it is considered to be fixed.

Revenues in particular tend to fit one or the other of these two categories. For example, fees for psychotherapy would tend to vary directly with hours of psychotherapy provided. On the other hand, state appropriations or grants would frequently not be affected by actual activity level, at least within some rather broad ranges, unless the appropriation was explicitly made on an activity basis.

Cost behavior is often not quite so obviously variable or fixed. Perhaps the majority of expense items in a not-for-profit organization would be neither exclusively variable nor fixed. Some expenses such as telephone have both fixed and variable components (mixed costs) - a standard monthly fee plus a charge which varies with actual usage. Also, some expenses might be fixed within a given range of activity, but will change or vary when the activity level crosses certain thresholds (semi-fixed or step variable costs). To cite an example of a semi-fixed cost, depending upon management policy, an additional counsellor might be hired if patient hours exceed a certain maximum per staff member - or laid off if patient hours decrease below a certain minimum. The major problem, of course, is to have managers specifically express their policies so that the corresponding costs can be modelled quantitatively.

The behavior of many costs is a function of management policy. The semi-fixed personnel cost mentioned above is a good example. Also, decisions to spend a fixed dollar amount on public relations and to dedicate a certain percentage of state appropriations to an indigent service fund would be examples of managerially determined fixed and variable costs respectively. Careful examination and consideration of all expense items should usually enable the manager to identify and quantify those expenses whose behavior is determined by management policy.

A close analysis of expenses and activity within the accounts may also lead to a reasonable quantification of other expenses which are not totally managerially determined. For example, the telephone costs cited above might be susceptible to this kind of analysis. Frequently, however, it will prove necessary to use a more technical approach to define cost behavior. Graphic analysis, high-low analysis and regression techniques might all prove helpful and can be computerized using widely available and easy to use software as discussed below (for example, the new version of Lotus 123 has regression analysis capabilities).

PROGRAM REVENUES AND COSTS

Once all revenues and expenses have been analysed into their fixed and variable components, the incorporation of one additional concept is especially useful. The concept is that of separability. The manager should attempt to classify revenue and expense items according to the particular program or activity to which they are directly traceable. At least in theory, these revenues and costs would disappear if the program to which they are directly traceable were to be discontinued, e.g. revenues or funding for a specific program. Revenues and expenses which cannot be directly associated with a particular program, i.e. which would not disappear if the program were discontinued, should be considered collectively as common revenues and expenses which are distinct from the program revenues and costs.

Common expenses in particular are typically allocated to programs or departments based on some measure of activity or

Table 5.3

SMHC
Budget Model
Fiscal Year Ending June 30, 1987

Type of Revenue/Cost	Outpatient	Partial Care
Program Revenues:		
First & Third Party Billings		
(Billing rate x hours)	$8.33 x 12,000	
(Billing rate x days)		$25.00 x 8,000
Staff Wages (Part–Time):		
(Wages x hours)	$5.00 x 12,000	
(Wages x days)		$20.00 x 8,000
Staff Salaries:		
Number required:		
$\dfrac{\text{Current activity level}}{\text{Hours (days) per staff member}}$	12,000 ÷ 1,000	8,000 ÷ 2,000
Salaries:		
Number required x salary	12 x $25,000	4 x $25,000
Drugs:		
(Drug cost x hours)	$2.00 x 12,000	
(Drug cost x days)		$16.25 x 8,000
EDP Cost:		
(Fixed + EDP cost x hours	$10,000 + ($1.33 x 12,000)	
(Fixed + EDP cost x days)		$5,000 + ($1.25 x 8,000)
Administrative:		
(Fixed)	$30,000	$30,000

usage in order to determine the 'total' program costs for various purposes, e.g. a funding requirement. Even although common expenses may benefit individual programs, they would nevertheless continue to exist independently of any particular program. Of course, a very significant reduction in activity may lead to an overall reduction of the center's operations and hence affect these common costs. For example, the rental expense typically allocated to an individual program for the use of a portion of a rented facility will not disappear because the program is discontinued. If the need for space is sufficiently reduced, however, the center might move to a smaller facility at a lower rental.

By including only the separable revenues and expenses in the model for each individual program or department, the manager can readily determine which units contribute the most toward covering the common (and relatively stable) center-wide expenses and can also assess the immediate impact of changing aspects of various programs.

As a final step before turning to the computer, it is probably wise to build an abstract model manually, identifying each line item by program or department, and expressing variable and semi-variable costs or budget line items as a function of the relevant activity level in the form:

Total Cost = Fixed Cost + (Variable Cost per Unit x Units)

Although it is very easy to modify and rearrange a computerized model as it is being developed, it is nevertheless helpful to have at the outset a clear idea of what the final model should be.

A simplified version of the separable program portion of a manually produced model might appear as illustrated in Table 5.3. Note that in this model the formulae have been expressed both verbally and quantitatively to clarify and identify the underlying assumptions. In this example the model is built on the somewhat unrealistic assumption that Outpatient variable costs are a function of outpatient hours, whereas Partial Care variable costs are a function of patient care days. In an actual budgeting process, of course, one would attempt to determine the measure of activity with which changes in expenses are most closely correlated. Another point to notice is the formula for determining the semi-fixed costs of staff salaries. It is assumed in this model that one permanent staff member is needed for every 1,000 outpatient hours or every 2,000 patient care days.

COMPUTERIZATION OF THE MODEL

The software chosen for the development of the computer model is Ashton Tate's Lotus 123 because of its widespread availability and familiarity.

As noted above, one of the main advantages of a computerized model is the ability to change the underlying assumptions. The development of a separate table of assumptions will facilitate both the identification and change of the assumptions on which the budget is built. Hence, the first step is to gather all of the assumptions from the manual model into a table as illustrated in Table 5.4.

The next step is to build the budget model itself, usually below the table of assumptions. It is easiest to type in the heading and names of the various line items before attempting to

Table 5.4

	A	B	C	D	E	F
1						
2		SMHC				
3		Table of Assumptions				
4		Assumption			Outpatient	Partial Care	Common
5							
6		Billing Rate			$8.33	$25.00	
7		Outpatient Hours			12,000	8,000	
8		Patient Care Days				8,000	
9		Staff Wage/Hour			$5.00		
10		Staff Wage/Day				$20.00	
11		Staff Annual Salary			$25,000	$25,000	
12		Hours Per Staff			1,000		
13		Partial Days Per Staff				2,000	
14		Drug Cost/Hour			$2.00		
15		Drug Cost/Day				$16.25	
16		EDP Cost/Hour			$1.33		
17		EDP Cost/Day				$1.25	
18		EDP Fixed Costs			$10,000	$5,000	
19		Administrative Fixed Costs			$30,000	$30,000	$40,000
20		Consulting & Education					$25,000
21		Contract Inpatient Services					$25,000
22		Rent					$35,000
23		State Appropriations					$700,000
24							

Table 5.5

	A	B	C	D	E	F
28			SMHC			
29			Budget Model			
30		Fiscal Year Ending June 30, 1987				
31						
32	Type of Revenue/Cost			Outpatient		
33	--------------------			-----------		
34	Program Revenues:					
35						
36	First & Third Party Billings			+D6*D7		
37						
38	Program Expenses:					
39						
40	Staff Wages (Part-time)			+D9*D7		
41	Staff Salaries			@ROUND(+D7/D12-0.5,0)*D11		
42	Drugs			+D14*D7		
43	EDP			+D18+D16*D7		
44	Administrative			+D19		
45				'--------- -----		
46	Total Program Expenses			@SUM(D38..D44)		
47				'---------------		
48	Excess (Deficit) by Program			+D36-D46		
49				'===============		

fill out the numerical aspects of the model. The formulae used in the manually developed complex model will be preserved, but no actual values will be used in order to facilitate subsequent changes and analyses. Rather, the address of the cell containing the numerical value of an assumption or variable will replace the variable in the formula. For example, instead of expressing Outpatient First and Third Party Billings as: $8.33 x 12,000, the equation will reference the cells containing the values for Outpatient Billing Rate and Outpatient Hours and be entered as: +D6*D7.

Table 5.5 shows how the formulae would be entered for the Outpatient program portion of the budget. Note that the explanatory lines have been omitted to avoid the cluttered appearance of the manual model and produce a budget more familiar in appearance. Anyone using the model can always determine the precise computation for any given budget number by examining the contents of the cell with Lotus.

Note, too, that the electronic spreadsheet can deal readily with the kind of semi-fixed cost presented by permanent staff and typical of so many other expenses in a service organiza-tion. In this example it is assumed that a new staff person will not be added until he/she can be fully utilized. This policy is reflected in the formula which divides the anticipated number of outpatient hours by the number of hours considered a full load for one staff and then rounds the answer down before multiplying by the annual salary. The formula could easily be

Table 5.6

SMHC
Budget Model
Fiscal Year Ending June 30, 1987

A B C	D	E	F
Type of Revenue/Cost	Outpatient	Partial Care	Total/Common
Program Revenues:			
First & Third Party Billings	$99,960	$200,000	$299,960
Program Expenses:			
Staff Wages (Part-time)	$60,000	$160,000	$220,000
Staff Salaries	300,000	100,000	400,000
Drugs	24,000	130,000	154,000
EDP	25,960	15,000	40,960
Administrative	30,000	30,000	60,000
Total Program Expenses	439,960	435,000	874,960
Excess (Deficit) by Program	($340,000)	($235,000)	($575,000)
Common Expenses:			
Consulting and Education			25,000
Administration	40,000		
Contract Inpatient Services			25,000
Rent			35,000
Total Common Expenses			125,000
Total Center Excess of Expenses over Revenues			(700,000)
State Appropriations			700,000
Final Excess/Deficit			$0

adapted to accommodate a different management policy. Table 5.6 presents the finished model utilizing the values shown in Table 5.4.

COST BENEFIT ANALYSIS: COMPUTER MODEL

Although considerable costs of time and effort will go into the development of an actual budget model for a real organization, the benefits are potentially significant. Even the process of preparing the first manual model will force management to focus more carefully on the exact nature and behavior of various expense items. Having developed the computer model, management can then eaisly experiment with changes in the underlying assumptions, i.e. 'what-if' analyses. What would happen, for example, if the estimate of outpatient hours should prove to be incorrect and the center delivers only 9,000 hours? Or what if the actual hours were to exceed the original estimate by 3,000 hours? By changing only one number, the estimate of outpatient hours in the table of assumptions, the manager can immediately see the potential impact of this difference on the center's finances.

This same feature can be of critical importance if an organization is confronted with a cutback in state funding or is forced to retrench for any reason. One can readily determine the effects on the organization of eliminating a particular program, increasing fees in a given area, eliminating staff, or any other proposal made to deal with the retrenchment. By experimenting with the various proposals, a manager can identify the alternative most likely to fall within budget constraints with the least negative impact on the organization's functioning.

Also, ongoing benefits include the potential for evaluating current operations, identifying potential problems on a timely basis, and taking corrective action while it is still possible. The model developed in this paper was for an entire year. However, using the 'copy' command of the spreadsheet software, it would have been almost as fast to develop a budget by months or even by weeks. That is, the entire budget can be copied in its entirety and duplicated as many times as desired. Any annual estimates such as activity level and salaries would, of course, have to be restated to a monthly or weekly basis. If desired, a fourth column reflecting year to date accumulations could easily be added to the budget format.

Monthly or weekly computerized budgets could help the manager to detect problems in the early stages of development while corrective action can still be taken. The computerized model could be designed in such a way that when the actual data are entered the model would automatically compute variances from budget both in absolute and percentage terms on a weekly, monthly, and year to date basis. Table 5.7 illustrates what a monthly budget for one program might look like with columns for dollar and percentage variances between budgeted and actual results.

Table 5.7

	A	B	C	D	E	F	G
		SMHC			Outpatient		
		Budget Model					
		Year Ending June 30, 1987					
25							
26							
27							
28							
29	Type of Revenue/Cost			Budget	Actual	Variance	%
30							
31							
32	Program Revenues:						
33							
34							
35	First & Third Party Billings			$8,330	8,200	(130)	-2%
36							
37	Program Expenses:						
38							
39	Staff Wages (Part-time)			$5,000	5,350	350	7%
40	Staff Salaries			25,000	27,200	2,200	9%
41	Drugs			2,000	1,870	(130)	-7%
42	EDP			2,163	3,000	837	39%
43	Administrative			2,500	2,450	(50)	-2%
44							
45	Total Program Expenses			36,663	39,870	3,207	9%
46							
47	Excess (Deficit) by Program			($28,333)	($31,670)	3,337	-12%
48							

Furthermore, the actually achieved activity level (which would naturally affect both variable revenue and expense figures) could be entered into the table of assumptions for the period under review, changing the budget to reflect the actual activity. The manager could then see what revenues and expenses should have been for the level of activity actually experienced during that period (as opposed to the original estimates) and more accurately assess what revenue or expense items are problematic, i.e. 'flexible budgeting'. Furthermore, if the weekly or monthly budgets have been tied together to produce budgeted year to date figures, the ultimate effect on the entire year will be automatically computed.

Finally, the constant comparison between budgeted and actual numbers will allow for refinement of the budgeted numbers, both activity estimates and the determination of the fixed and variable components of expenses. These revisions as well as those arising from changes in circumstances, e.g. Medicaid will no longer reimburse for certain kinds of service effective February 1, can easily be incorporated into the budgets for the remaining time periods simply by changing the table of assumptions for these periods. Again, the manager can see immediately the impact of these changes on the annual results and implement strategies for achieving a balanced budget.

Once the manager has mastered the very basic techniques discussed above, the potential for extension and elaboration of the model and its applications is almost endless. Graphic or regression analysis capabilities could be used to discern the fixed and variable components of various expenses. Graphs could also be used to present various reports to non-technical audiences. Although more sophisticated budgeting and computer techniques lead to more refined and realistic budgets and useful extensions, there is value in the very basic processes outlined above, especially in specifying management's operating assumptions. Also, in developing even this relatively simple computer model, the human services manager will be developing computer and accounting skills to serve as a foundation for more advanced applications.

PART II AGENCY FOCUS

TECHNOLOGY ON TRIAL

Sandra Williams and Jan Forrest

A ROLE FOR TECHNOLOGY

Both social workers and social work managers experience difficulty in retrieving and communicating information that is important to the effective and efficient performance of their roles. For a number of reasons, paper based manual systems are not regarded as satisfactory and the telephone system is not seen as an efficient or cost effective alternative. In some cases a solution might be achieved through the revision of manual systems or through organisational changes. However, we found that office automation facilities, such as electronic mail systems and viewdata, are beginning to be considered as a new way of tackling individual, departmental and authority-wide communications problems.

The innovation underlying office automation is the linking or networking of systems to combine creation and processing of text and data, information storage and retrieval, electronic mail and, increasingly, the possibility of automatic search techniques. Exploited in this way, technology can offer social services departments the potential for faster and easier access to wider-based information for a greater number of people.

Office automation is effective for aiding communication in situations where individuals or units within the organisation need to be accessible both to each other and to headquarters but are geographically dispersed, functionally split, or simply perceive themselves to be isolated. Although relatively unexploited in the environment of social work practice, the technology would seem to be an appropriate medium for the exchange of practice and development information and thus for supporting the delivery of service to clients.

The justification for installing an automated office system lies in the benefits to be gained from its use, but in the cost-conscious culture of local government these benefits are difficult to pin down and are especially hard to quantify. In social services departments in particular, it is difficult to identify direct cost savings arising from the introduction of office automation. So far, the use of this technology has been predominantly administrative and the language of benefits has reflected this; office automation systems have been justified on their potential to streamline communications and to increase operational efficiency by reducing the administrative burden on staff. However, the case for introducing automated office facilities for use by front-line workers will have to go beyond this and demonstrate the specific benefits for professional practice as the prime justification for investment.

Ensuring that advancements in computing and telecommunications bring benefits to sharp-end workers in social services depends largely on whether information technology is deliberately and effectively exploited as a tool for professional operational information uses or whether, like previous computer systems, it is developed primarily for management purposes. Moreover, if it is to be more widely introduced into social work practice then the management of that change becomes an over-riding concern. This will determine both the impact of the technology on the job satisfaction and working procedures of social workers, and their willingness to adapt their information behaviour to the perceived limitations of computers. These issues pose challenges for the future development of information technology in social services departments. Their resolution will be determined by the actions of all those involved from social worker to data processing manager and beyond, to the politicians who ultimately control resources.

THE CHALLENGES OF CHANGE

Social Workers

For social workers, the main challenge is to get involved and to advocate their right to influence the evaluation and development of technology tools, which could boost the effectiveness of their information handling activities. Without appropriate training for using and understanding the technology, and without social workers' participation in the evaluation and development of office automation systems which might be of value to them, the use of technology will never be integrated into their normal patterns of work. Without that integration the technology itself will be seen as intrusive and will assume a disproportionate dominance.

Information technology can provide support for professional practice. In a climate where their decision-making is increasingly becoming the focus of media attention, social workers need quick access to reliable information about individual care episodes of clients, about the availability of local resources and about procedures and professional practice developments. They are not skilled information seekers and the pressures of the job leave little time to search through information which is often unco-ordinated and difficult to access in order to find an answer to an immediate problem. Moreover, there is a traditional reluctance on the part of social workers to structure their exchange of practice and development information. They tend to rely on informal personal contacts and to store information in their heads, rather than recording it on paper.

Office automation can be exploited to develop information systems or to make them more accessible. In some of the social services departments we visited we found evidence of this already happening. For example, viewdata systems were being used to provide access to a central bank of information. The databases typically contained both corporate and departmental information. Corporate entries covered items such as salary scales, car mileage, details about county councillors and financial accounting information. Departmental entries covered procedures, legislation, information about local resources provided both by the department and by outside agencies and groups, details of foster parents, establishment addresses and bibliographic information. We also found examples of interactive uses of viewdata systems which incorporated a mailbox facility. These ranged from simple administrative applications, such as the ability to place orders for supplies electronically with the central purchasing department, to more complex transactions involving, for example, transport bookings by day centres and the updating of bed vacancies in residential establishments.

Although there is evidence that information technology can be harnessed as an effective medium for information exchange, it is also apparent that the technology cannot easily be integrated into the culture and routine of social work practice. Our general impression of social workers' reactions towards the innovation of office automation was largely one of negative attitudes, among which the following were highlighted:

– fear and ignorance of the unknown

– embarrassment and indignity of making mistakes

– distrust both of the reliability of the system and the accuracy of the information

– new technology jargon is a foreign language

– maintaining confidentiality of personal client information is seen as problematic

– clients cannot be standardised and reduced to statistics.

However, these negative attitudes were largely a continuation of fears and anxieties based on previous computer experience, rather than an informed reaction to the technology. To date, computer systems in social services departments have been set up for predominantly administrative tasks and for management information purposes. As social services are currently organised and delivered, it would be unrealistic to ignore the fact that managers are increasingly subject to pressures which advance their demands for management information. Nevertheless, it is this predominant use of the technology for management information systems that underlies the hostility social workers load onto new technology, which is additional to the apprehension most people have when confronted by computers for the first time. Among the social workers we interviewed, computers were frequently held as a scapegoat for all their negative feelings about record keeping, an activity which is fundamentally a part of social work practice, whether computers are involved or not. There was also anxiety that the computer would become regarded as the new 'expert', rather than as a tool, threatening their professional identity and autonomy and becoming a barrier in their relationship with clients.

Currently, if social workers use computers they are likely to do so through clerical and administrative support staff who invariably 'stage-manage' the computer scene for them. Keyboards are associated with secretarial, clerical and administrative work, not social work. This aversion to keyboards is not a problem in isolation, but is a manifestation of the more intangible problem of their not understanding, or accepting, the logic of computer systems and how these can help them in their job. The culture of social work is predominantly oral and adjusting to working with the limitations and unsubtleties of dialogue with computers is difficult for social workers whose information behaviour is typified by person-to-person contact and informal conversations.

Using office automation does involve the challenge of adapting to new procedures and habits of working and there is no motivation for social workers to make the adjustments unless they can see a specific benefit in it for them. In the short term, the introduction of office automation applications, like other computer systems, may actually increase their workload without them seeing any immediate benefits. A challenge to management is to encourage sharp-end workers to look beyond these transitional problems and to help them appreciate and understand what the technology can do for them and how they can control it, rather than thinking of the machines as controlling them.

Management

This management challenge has to be set against the organisational and political realities of the local authority.

It is more than a truism to say that without commitment from social services management at all levels, the introduction and use of technology is unlikely to succeed. We have established that in social services the situation is made more difficult by the history of computing with its emphasis on management information systems, which are maintained by social workers but typically offer little in return. To attribute this situation to a deliberate act on the part of management would not reflect the atmosphere in our case study sites. Managers were not unconcerned about the information needs of social workers but not surprisingly they were more familiar with their own pressing requirements and how these could benefit from the application of technology. However, the underlying organisational implications of providing distributed computing to the extent that we have speculated, must be for a shift in the balance of power and control. The management of that change could have far-reaching consequences for both the organisation of social work and the traditional hierarchical relationships which exist in the local authority departments including social services.

The challenge is for managers to balance the corporate, departmental or authority need for 'facts' against the provision of technology tools which primarily benefit the social worker. A shift in this balance will depend on a co-operative, open and informed approach so that no-one retrenches into rigid and blinkered attitudes which prevent the constructive assessment of the potential for the tools to be useful. How can managers open the door to involvement and commitment from social workers?

Two factors seem to be critical. The first is acknowledgement and use of the culture in social services. The second is the adoption of best practice in planning and managing technology projects.

We have talked about practitioners adapting to using automated office systems, but if the technology is to penetrate successfully into social work practice then managers will also need to learn to use, not abuse, the values and culture of social work. On a general level other commentators have argued that imported technologies bring a value set with them. Social workers need to be reassured that commercial computer systems will not, 'by stealth', over-write the values and culture of social work practice and reduce their professional autonomy. On a practical level, managers need to accept and confront a dislocation between the organisational concepts used by the computer and the procedures, skills and requirements entrenched in social work practice. Failure in this is likely to generate hostility and rejection of the new ways of working that are implied for social workers.

The expression of that opposition may take several forms but it will not be uncommon for one central theme to be the confidentiality of information about clients. Social workers must be reassured about the confidentiality of information that enters any system. Concern about confidentiality and the possible misuse of information is more of an issue with client record systems, which contain personal details about clients, than with office automation and the exchange of resource information. However, it could arise as an issue with electronic mail if the scope of its subject matter extended to include client related messages. It is also present with resource information where the system stores the personal details of, for example, child minders and foster parents. Adequate and demonstrable security is an essential prerequisite to the acceptance of technology by social workers.

Finally, in terms of the culture, we return to the importance of integrating plans for the use of technology into social work practice so that it is the practitioners who are in control of the technology. To this end departments need to communicate computer plans to social workers and to involve them from the beginning. They must, however, avoid raising expectations about future developments and then risk frustration and disillusionment because equipment or training are not subsequently available. Planning for technology and the subsequent successful realisation of those plans has not always been easy in social services.

One mechanism for planning is to develop an information technology strategy for the department. Internally this means that managers have to learn more about the information needs and behaviour of their professional staff, as well as their administrative and clerical support staff. We found little evidence of social workers being widely consulted on this basis. It also requires that social services management has to establish a framework for the management and control of technology which determines the organisation of and staffing for technology, a training policy and details of the resource implications of any specific developments which are planned.

Among those departments who were experimenting with information technology or planning for its introduction, there was a general consensus that some form of project co-ordinator was needed to plan and timetable projects, monitor and chase their progress, co-ordinate the various activities they entail and ensure that target operational dates are met. Some had appointed or 'acquired' from the authority's central technology division, a professional IT manager. Some had a computer development officer with a background in social services and a knowledge of technology. Others were rethinking the traditional role of their information officers in the light of increased use of technology. How effective this group of workers can be depends not only on their skills in handling the cultural specifics of social services but also on their ability to operate in the wider local authority.

In some departments, the directorate management team represent the social services' requirements at a corporate level. Their role includes negotiating ways to work within the local authority IT strategy if one exists, lobbying for professional support from the central technology division or occasionally acting independently when there seems no hope of winning a useful slice of the corporate IT cake for their departments. More often, it is the social services' own 'specialists' who have to manage the relationship with the rest of the local authority. Whichever is the case, social services has to be able to speak in the language of corporate IT. This requires an understanding of the formal project management techniques typically adopted by central IT divisions together with a reliable assessment of the costs of acquisition and ownership of technology.

When implementing strategy plans it is important for departments to ensure that their targets for information technology developments are both realistic and capable of being monitored for evaluation purposes. If targets are unrealistic, then departments run the risk of failure and as a consequence, staff disaffection. If they are too general and success criteria are intangible, then it is difficult to assess when and if they have been achieved. Moreover, information technology projects are easier to justify where a strong application need can be identified and potentially satisfied. Some of the key cost factors which have to be taken into account are set out below together with the project management issues which they raise for social services.

1 **Hardware and Software** – The use of both departmental and personal computing has increased rapidly in social services departments. At a time when departmental demands for on-line computer applications have overloaded both the local authority mainframe computer and the staff in the central data processing department, microcomputers and/or departmental minicomputers offer the potential for overcoming the bottle-neck. This raises issues about compatibility and standards in the context of a corporate computer strategy. It also raises issues about the mechanisms for information flows and who controls them, and creates the potential for a conflict of power and responsibilities. In various forms, power struggles

were evident in our case study areas. They were a central feature of the situation in one county authority where there was a fundamental incompatibility between the Treasurer's interpretation of the corporate computer strategy and the social services department's approach to introducing departmental computer systems. Conversely, where the philosophy of the corporate strategy and the package of departmental proposals matched, then corporate policy could be supportive.

The challenge for social services managers is to strike a balance between adherence to corporate demands, designed to maximise future communications and developmental potential, and the requirements of the department. The challenge for the data processing people in local authorities is to recognise that benefits for social workers from the information technology revolution also depend upon imaginative support from the technocrats.

2 **Maintenance and Support** – This can be provided either by the manufacturer directly, or by central computer services acting as an intermediary. One of the Audit Commission's criticisms of the management of computing in local government was that authorities rarely had control over users' computing costs or recharged users on a realistic or reliable basis. We noted a shift in thinking about internal budgetary methods in our case study authorities, which would alert departments to the real cost of their computing activities and enable them to weigh up these solutions against other options.

Most of the directors or managers of central computer services that we interviewed were reviewing their internal budgetary methods against growing demands on them to make their services more cost-effective. Generally speaking, they favoured moving from the traditional pattern of recharging, where all of the central departments' services (including computer services) are charged out to service departments on a basis estimated at the beginning of the year, to direct charging for computer services according to actual usage. This shifts the emphasis of corporate relationships, turning social services departments into fee paying customers.

3 **Training** – The introduction of information technology creates a demand for staff who can meet the training needs of users and can provide support both during the implementation phase and when the system is in general use.

However, our interviews suggest that in social services departments, as the DTI case studies have shown to be the case in the public sector generally, the importance of training is frequently preached, but often poorly practised. There is inevitably a learning hump to be overcome before either the individual user or the organisation begins to gain real benefits. However, training is not a single task to be provided around the time of introducing a new system. It is part of a process which needs to continue after installation, in the form of user support. The design of training courses is critical. Training is not just about acquiring operational

skills but learning about the potential of information technology.

A general impression was that it was difficult to 'sell'
training courses to social workers. It is an investment for
the future and social workers under pressure are reluctant
to give up the time to train or adjust to using new technology on the promise of a possible pay-back at a later date.
As summed up by one social worker: "There is no time to consider what applications you could use new technology for.
When you are busy you can go into automatic with what is
familiar." As they found it difficult to allocate any time in
a pressured environment for training, some social workers
suggested it would be preferable to receive training offsite,
where they could avoid inevitable interruptions. Others preferred to learn less formally, on the job from colleagues, in
front of whom they felt less embarrassed about making mistakes. Several local offices had approached the problem of
familiarising users with computer systems by initially
encouraging staff to play games on the equipment. While this
had broken down the barriers to use for some, others had
dismissed it as 'nervously theatrical' and it had reinforced
their scepticism of the usual role of computer-aided communication in social work.

4 **Access and Environment** – It is important to provide sufficient
terminals which are easily accessible and reliable. None of
the possible benefits we have discussed in relation to social
workers using information technology are possible unless there
is sufficient equipment to support the system. A crucial factor
we identified was the importance of having enough terminals
located in the right places.

For the most part social workers wanted immediate access
to information and they were not enthusiastic about queuing
for access to a terminal. Reliability is equally important. The
reactions where this has not been the case are summed up in
the comment of the team leader in a local office: "You are
asking people to abandon security and put their faith in a
system which appears unreliable. A drawer full of index cards
is a comfort." In this situation they are likely to find it
more convenient to continue in their traditional ways of
communicating and retrieving information.

5 **Conversion** – Early experiences with information technology
indicate that departments should not underestimate the general
staffing and workload implications of transferring from manual
to computer systems. In particular, this means ensuring there
are enough staff to implement the new system. It also means
thinking ahead to the operational phase and to plan who will
subsequently maintain the system and, where necessary,
update the information. Some of the departments we visited
were experimenting with viewdata facilities and the creation
and maintenance of the information databases underpinning
these systems was proving to be particularly time-consuming.

Relating all of these costs to the benefits which can be expected from investment in automated office systems is notoriously difficult. We have argued that the root justification should be the benefit which improved communications and access to information can bring to practitioners in carrying out the day-to-day business of social services. A key factor in this is the attitude of councillors to new technology and their willingness to sanction investment in computer systems for use within the authority. Our case studies illustrated varying levels of commitment at Member level. They included a London Borough with a 'commercial conservative administration', where most of the Members, Labour as well as Conservative, used computers in their business and viewed new technology as 'a good thing'. In other authorities, elected members are faced with very difficult resource decisions between investment in technology and more direct increases in provision of service.

Weighing long-term benefit against pressure to resource an immediate crisis is not a challenge which many politicians confront gladly.

CONCLUSION

We have highlighted the major challenges confronting all those involved in determining whether or not the benefits of information technology will reach front-line workers. It is clear that the issues arising from introducing information technology into organisations which are usually commented upon are overlaid in social services by a complex pattern of traditional roles and values and an increased demand for service provision. This pattern is further complicated by the impact of the interplay between corporate and departmental computing strategies and ambitions. Social Services departments will have to weigh up the case for office automation in the context of their own local circumstances and information requirements. This paper sets out an agenda of issues which are central to the effective introduction of office automation systems and which provide a backcloth against which departments might profitably review their own strategies and procedures.

LAB EXPERIMENTATION IN COMPUTER POLICY MODELS IN THE HUMAN SERVICES

Salvatore Imbrogno

INTRODUCTION

Policy analytical models have been developed and used in the human services with increasing frequency as a means for structuring policy problems, forecasting alternatives, goals and objectives, monitoring policy outcomes and evaluating the impact policy has on a clientele group or community. Advancements made in social policy theory and methodology have elevated the level of inquiry to now include computer simulation technology. The use of this technology becomes imperative in the face of highly complex policy systems, the 'over-abundance' of information and the increasing practicality of computers. It is now propitious to incorporate computer simulation methodology into the epistemological foundations and methodological directives in human service policy analytical models.

Simulation of policy has qualitative and quantitative elements necessary for conducting laboratory experiments. Hence, simulation models are defined as a symbolic representation and conceptual design for a real-world policy system whose behavior is being represented over extended periods of time. This is a major innovative conception for the human services in that laboratory experimentations become an alterative for field work experientials. Computer simulation policy models confront the ambiguities, indeterminance and uncertainties of complex policy systems without direct involvement of a clientele group or community. Computer laboratory experimentations make dynamic use of time, possess the capability for synthesizing social theories, can integrate different policy system designs and select and process information from a variety of sources representing a multiplicity of values, interest and belief systems.

A computer simulation policy model is a comprehensive and unified conception of the policy-making process. This paper delineates the relationship between mainstream policy analytical models and the emerging methodology of computer simulation in the human services. A primary task is to present a description of prototype informational components and analytical methods to policy-making as a prerequisite to the understanding of computer simulation models. Though emphasis is placed on the generalized designs of computers, building-block designs is offered as an alternative value to the human services. Finally, an archetype for computer simulation of policy provides an exploratory model for applications in the human services.

PROTOTYPE INFORMATIONAL COMPONENTS AND ANALYTICAL METHODS TO POLICY-MAKING

A discussion on the design of computer simulation policy models (CSPM) is very much contingent upon the importance of understanding the epistemological foundations and methodological directives associated with mainstream informational components and analytical methods of policy-making (Dunn, 1981).

Informational Components	*Analytical Methods*
Policy problems	Structuring
Policy alternatives	Forecasting
Policy actions	Recommending
Policy outcomes	Monitoring
Policy performance	Evaluating

Different meanings are given to the interpretation of each of these components and methods of policy development. In the main, however, they represent all of the key factors in the analysis 'of and for' policy and serve as a prelude to a CSPM.

Structuring Policy Problems

Theories on policy problem structure are conceptualized and specified to result in a solution, dissolution or resolution through a number of different world views: social problems are independent; some, however, can be isolated for special classification and treatment; and, still others, the dynamics of social problems produce different solutions for a given problem as there are definitions of that problem. Problems can also be characterized by their means-end relations as characterized in the following quadrants (Mitroff and Kilman, 1982).

```
                                  Preferred Ends

                       Known and in   |  Unknown or in
                       Agreement       |  Disagreement
                                       |
                   I                   |  II
                                       |
Known and in           Well           |  Ill
Agreement              Structured      |  Structured
                                       |
Feasible Means     _____|_____
                                       |
                   III                 |  IV
                                       |
Unknown or in          Moderately      |  Unstructured
Disagreement           Structured      |
                                       |
```

Many policy problems in the human services fall in quadrant IV: unstructured in that there is no known or agreed upon means/ends relation to solution. In the face of having to act, decisions must be made regarding the policy problem. The selection of a CSPM is an indication of this complex policy decision process where the professional must solicit support in the making of decisions (i.e. conceptualization and specification of the policy problem). A DSS (decision support system) is an advanced interactive computer base system that provides a design that enables policy decision makers to utilize data and models in a pursuit of a solution.

Forecasting Alternatives, Goals and Objectives

Hypotheses are deduced from the structuring of policy problems. They are syllogized through analytical methods such as conjecturing, projections and predictions. Conjectures are speculations on future events and occurrences; projections on the extrapolation of existing data, and predictions based on theoretical assumptions on cause/effect relations. The selection of a forecasting method is determined by how the policy problem was structured (i.e. predictions on well-structured problems).

Recommending Policy Action

The implementation of policy requires a decision-making schema that can transform and activate the 'ideals' of abstract policy goals into a 'reality intrinsic to the delivery of services'. This involves a number of discretionary and interpretative decisions for implementation that when taken in aggregate play a significant role in the meaning given to policy (i.e. policy formulation). A number of highly sophisticated decision models have been advanced and will be discussed momentarily.

Monitoring Policy Outcomes

Observations and measurements are needed to assess the connections between a recommended policy action and the outcomes experienced by a clientele group. Monitoring information is empirically derived through such methods as social indicators, social auditing, social accounting and social experimentations. This information is fed back to produce corrective actions in policy formulation (i.e. alternatives, goals, and objectives). A very unique function, and least understood of monitoring, is the linkage it provides between policy formulation and implementation (Rivlin, 1971).

Evaluating Policy Performance

Monitoring information provides answers to such empirical questions as "what happened, how and why?" Evaluation responds to questions such as "What difference did the policy and its outcomes make?" Evaluation is interested in appraising the impact policy has on social changes in a clientele group in which it served. This necessitates the use of analytical methods such as Ideals Strategy, Critical Path Methods and Gantt

Charts. These analytical methods stress systematic analysis of the design, its goals and implementation with emphasis on results.

Restructuring Policy Problems

A number of inferences can be drawn from the evaluation of policy performance to indicate changes in how the original problem was structured. Policy implementation should have generated changes in both the internal (i.e. social agency) and the external environments (i.e. clientele group); hence, changes in the purpose and direction of the agency in its future activity. The policy problem is restructure and the policy cycle continues unabated (Chelinsky, 1985).

If these five policy-informational components and six analytical methods that comprise a prototype model are viewed as cyclical within a systems context, then the following observations can be made for CSPM application.

1 The top half of the framework produces information on knowing what problem to solve in a retrospective analysis and on knowing what happened that is necessary for a prospective analysis of knowing what will happen and what to do.

2 The bottom half of the model, in contrast to policy formulation, is policy implementation. Empirical data is produced subject to quantitative analysis. This model is therefore deductive and inductive; qualitative and quantitative; retrospective and prospective – a coalescence of polar opposites to produce information on a continuum of change.

3 Hence, there is no simple starting or ending point in the process of policy-making and its inquiry. One can begin as well as terminate the process at any point. This is a very necessary attribute for computer simulation applications.

4 The starting and ending points are equally applicable for those prescribing to highly linear causal and quantifiable analysis as it is for those prescribing to highly creative, innovative qualitative analysis.

5 A cyclical model integrates policy/planning, program planning and project planning into a unified conception. Each is affected and affects the other through a continuous mutual interactive exchange of information.

This prototype conceptual framework serves as a foundation for the development of CSPM. It offers a comprehensive analysis and an innovative and experimental prospectus for alternative courses of action in a continuous process of change over time. It must, however, be designed to 'fit' laboratory experiments (i.e. simulated) in which the key variables (input, output and withinput) can purposefully be controlled and manipulated.

BUILDING BLOCK DESIGNS: COMPUTER ANALYTICAL MODELS

Informational components and analytical methods in a three dimensional organizational matrix of individual and small group participation has direct applications for generalized computer simulation designs. As an alternative, building block designs represent an idiosyncratic and parochial perspective of policy based on discrete axiological commitments, epistemological foundations and methodological directives of policy. A building block design can be computerized as an analytical model (i.e. Lever; Increm; Merge).

Computer analytical models in contrast to computer simulation models are deterministic. Inputs produce a single, repeatable set of outputs (dependent variables). They are particularly effective for testing the impact of small changes to various components of the policy configuration. Or have special application to well-structured policy problems where the end/means are known and in agreement (i.e. pure rational and economic models in quadrant I: well structured). A computer simulation model is expected to produce a range of outputs for a set of inputs (i.e where either the means or ends are not known or agreed upon in incremental, satisfying, conflict and sequential). Rerunning a simulation model with the same inputs may produce slightly different values as outputs. Computer analytical models can be very significant and practical tools for policy where quening theory can be applied.

This introduces two other critical distinctions in types of simulation:

Discrete simulation: derived from quening theory in which quantifiable data (i.e. demographics on applications and termination of clientele service) is used to simulate the process of people (subjects) with the specific services or an agency (objects).

Continuous simulation: in contrast to the emphasis on process/services, is related to systems/change involved in development over time (Flynn, 1985).

Following is a brief description of mainstream and computer analytical policy models.

Amenable to Computer Analytical/Discrete Simulation Models

Pure Rational Model

One must establish a linear causal relation between the components of policy through a logical and rational analytical process. The means and ends to policy must be known and agreed upon (well-structured problems); intervening and non-controllable variables are accounted for through probabilistic and stochastic processes. Policy action decisions are quantified and therefore result in efficiency and effectiveness.

Economic Model

In addition to developing a mathematical or probabilistic pay-off measure for a decision made on policy actions, there is the matter of economic resources and constraints that have to be included in the calculation of utility. An economic decision model would have us compare and advocate policy actions by quantifying their total monetary costs and total monetary benefits or in monetary units of particular human services or programs.

Potential for Continuous CSPM

Satisfying Model

Social workers are seldom in positions to maximize their actions in pure rationality nor can they always measure the utility of the actions in a cost-benefit ratio. Instead, social work policy-makers do define the limits and ranges of possible outcomes that can be delivered so as to satisfy – a good enough decision based on bounded rationality.

Sequential Decisions

Rationality for policy actions need not be pure or bounded. It can be calculated through a quasi-experimental method. These decisions are predicated on the position that a policy problem is unstructured (original); the goals are known and in agreement but the means in policy actions are unknown. Decisions are therefore made in sequential development. As policy evolves in practice, participants acquire a great deal of knowledge, information, technology and experience to increase their problem-solving capabilities and abilities. Given, therefore, learning from experience in a trial and error process, policy actions can be calculated and the most parsimonious decisions made.

Conflict Model

It is expected that all policy actions will precipitate tension, stress and strains upon those affected by it. Policy goals, no matter how well formulated, will confront a multiplicity of values and a diversity of interest to create diametrically opposing positions. Conflict policy decisions, when taken to their extremes, can only be reconciled by raising the policy goals to a higher level of complexity so as to 'sweep in' parochial perspectives.

Incremental Model

If the others view rationality as pure, bounded and to be calculated, this model for policy action views the participants' rationality as limited. Given the plurality of values and interests, policy problems are always ill-structured in that the ends are unknown or in disagreement. Policy actions are recommended only if they are marginal to and dependent upon the prevailing values, interests and norms of the social milieu. Policy actions are for adjustments leading to mitigation, remediation or restoration. Consequently, the policy problem as originally perceived undergoes restructuring in a process of fitting in different policy actions.

There are a number of variations on these models as, for example, mixed-scanning, that argues for the coalescence of a pure rational model with that of incrementalism to create a new strategy for policy actions specifically based on how the policy-maker structures the policy problem. Structuring is directly related to how the goals were formulated. Significantly, too, the nature of this inter-relationship (the structuring of the policy problem, forecasting of policy goals and recommending policy actions) is a revelation on the direction social work policy practice will take. For example, policy advocacy in the human services can be expressed as a process of mediation (incrementalism), of policy agitation for social action (conflict), of social research (rationality) and for social development experimentations in development (sequential).

Each analytical model represents a parochial perspective (i.e. a three-dimensional model [LEVER] for the identification of leverage points in the power structure and processes of policy formation) or from a disciplinary perspective (i.e. problem definition models in sociology [PRODEF] and/or INCREM in political science). Given the scope and magnitude of professional activity in the human services an eclectic model has been adopted and/or merged where these discrete analytical models representing different theoretical perspectives are utilized (Warren, 1977). Each use the EXPER SIM source files adapted for their particular theoretical use (i.e. ACTION) (Flynn, 1985).

SCOPE OF COMPUTER SIMULATION POLICY MODELS

The aforementioned mainstream components and analytical methods to policy-making can be developed and applied in a social agency without reference to simulation (i.e. gaming) or computer simulation. Computer simulation is not a prerequisite or an absolute requirement in scientific policy analysis or development. For example, systems tools and methods can be used in a variety of ways to document the decision-making processes of models presented earlier (i.e. conflict, sequential, satisfying). In fact, where there exists a known and generally accepted empirical data base to structuring policy problems it is preferable to apply standard analytical models.

Limitations of computer simulation policy models in the human services are as follows:

1 Data derived from the human services necessary for modelling and/or test are not always available or agreed upon in the face of a multiplicity of values and a diversity of interest that permeates the field.

2 Computer simulation models require at a minimum a solid foundation in the analysis 'of a for' policy as a prerequisite

to understanding the complexity underlying the values and assumptions of modelling as a research activity. The human services are just beginning to view policy as a professional activity.

3 Computer simulation models are laboratory experiments and as such eliminate the 'human factor' (i.e. constituency, clientele group) in trial runs. It places demands on the professional expected to program the system to respond to new or different values and norms that it is expected will impact upon a clientele group.

4 Findings in computer simulation models are only as reliable as the model they symbolically represented necessitating a very close involvement of all affected constituents of a program. This is no small achievement.

The explicit role of computer simulation in human services is that it can determine instantaneously the results of many different sets of circumstances rather than only one. For example, decisions affecting a policy can be explored through a compromising/incremental process while simultaneously in another run decisions can be determined by their conflictual quality and antagonistic nature policy that generates inevitably. Four major concepts emerge for consideration in computer simulation models of policy.

1 Computer simulation is a method of analyzing the behavior of a policy system (i.e. social agency) by computing its time path for given initial conditions and given parameters determined by the programmer.

2 Simulation in computer technology moves a policy system forward in time step by step with the movement of the system under study.

3 Computer simulation models are based on mathematical and logical relationships that are explicitly contingent upon a conceptual understanding of the behavior of a policy system under study.

4 A symbolic or conceptual analogue provides a clearly specified structure of how reality ought to be organized and managed by the designer.

By providing a clearly specified world view of reality, it allows for the application of mathematical and probabilistic methods. CSPM are designed to conduct experiments over extended periods of time and under dynamic conditions with the methods of the system represented. Mainstream statistics and mathematics models which have analytical solutions are inapplicable to social agency policy problems. Problems in the human services are non-linear and involve a multiplicity of values and a diversity of interest. All policies, particularly in the human services, are inherently ambiguous and indeterminant eluding the scientific conditions that govern causal and quantifiable analysis. Lastly, computer simulation models are tied together by connective logical and mathematical relations to achieve a symbolic representation of the policy system under study. The primary purpose is to achieve verification and not reliability or predictability.

The advantages of computer simulation to the human services are:

1 system performance can be observed under all conceivable conditions

2 results of field work performance can be extrapolated with a simulation model for prediction purposes

3 policy decisions concerning future systems presently in a conceptual stage can be examined

4 trials of systems under test can be accomplished in a much-reduced period of time

5 simulation results can be obtained at lower cost than real experientials

6 study of hypothetical situations can be achieved even when the hypothetical situation would be unrealisable in actual life at the present time

7 computer modelling and simulation is often the only feasible or safe technique to analyse and evaluate a system in human services.

Given the balance between the limitations and advantages of computer simulation policy models to the human services, it is imperative that professionals be very clear as to the value and purpose made for the use of this complex technology.

SUMMARY

The foregoing discussion demonstrated that computer simulation is used in and is potentially applicable to a wide range of policy problems in the human services ranging from parochially-oriented questions to more complex comprehensive-oriented problems. Each perspective encompasses a different world view. Social problems in the human services are board-based and are almost always unstructured. The focus in this paper, therefore, was on generalized designs. In any case, the key to computer simulation was lodged in conceptions on modelling – a highly complex scientific process by which computer simulation can symbolically represent reality. Modelling in this context is an emerging professional activity and for that matter so is policy formulation and implementation. Computer simulation models and policy-making (CSPM) require the integration of scientific knowledge 'in and about' modelling, policy and computers.

REFERENCES

Chelinsky, E. (1985). 'Program Evaluation: Patterns and Directions'. American Society for Public Administration, Washington DC.

Dunn, W. (1981). *Introduction to Public Policy Analysis*. Prentice-Hall, Englewood Cliffs, N.J.

Flynn, J. (1985). 'Merge: Computer Simulations of Social Policy Process'. *Computers in Human Services*, **1**, 2, Summer, 33-53.

Mitroff, I. and Kilmann, Ralph (1978). *Methodological Approaches to Social Sciences*. Jossey-Bass, San Francisco, CA.

Rivlin, A. (1971). *Systematic Thinking for Social Action*. The Brooking Institute, Washington DC.

Warren, R.L. (1977). *Social Change and Human Purpose*. Rand Mcnally, Chicago.

PART III

TECHNOLOGY FOCUS

Information Technology and the Human Services
Edited by B. Glastonbury, W. LaMendola and S. Toole
© 1988 John Wiley & Sons Ltd

CHAPTER 6

Networks and Electronic Communication

One of the bases of society is the way people care for each
other, help each other, and share with each other. In most of
the world, the human service worker is part of a formal
framework of resources available to people to ensure that the
caring, helping, and sharing is more effectively spread
throughout the society. In most cases, this means that human
service workers are part of a formalized human network which
in some way fits with or supports the informal networks of
altruism, community social life, and social support which
already exist in their community. The types of networks referred
to in this section are not formal or informal in a human sense.
Instead they are the electronic means of allowing people who
are, for example, geographically separated or limited by a
physical handicap, to interact. These networks can also be
understood as devices or means of supporting human communicating much like the telephone. However, electronic networks often
do not include the capability of the telephone in the sense that
voice transmission is not their primary purpose. Their primary
purpose may be to store, access, or manipulate a specialized
file of data. For example, a human service worker using a
personal computer and other electronic equipment may access a
library of resources for an unemployed disabled person,
reviewing listings of job possibilities which fit that person's
situation, or perhaps even schedule an interview for the
unemployed person at a local agency. The use of the computer
in this manner is an example of electronic networking. Another
primary purpose may be electronic communicating. Electronic
communication is a term commonly used to describe a particular
type of electronic networking by which people talk to each
other, usually by leaving electronically stored messages or
notes, exchanging ideas, discussing ongoing topics, expressing
opinions, feelings, or other emotions, or carrying out a specific
task. In this case, the electronic network may not have a
public purpose, such as the previous example of the job system,
but it may, for example, serve to allow cerebral palsied persons
to discuss their experiences with the job system, expressing
disappointment, offering social support, or sharing notes about
employment possibilities among themselves without ever accessing
the publicly supported system. In turn, electronic networks are
increasingly used by employers so that, in the example of the
cerebral palsied person, a person may do work at home on their
computer, work that does not always require their physical
presence at the office. In that case, the use of the electronics
supports what may be one of the goals of the human service

worker, namely, employment of an unemployed disabled person. The human service worker may then also electronically communicate with the newly employed person, and that person may share experiences with the worker or with other disabled persons electronically.

The papers in this section trace, by example, the ethical, value, and practical implications of the use of networks and electronic communication in support of human service work. In the topic paper, LaMendola briefly overviews the area and proposes a taxonomy of such systems as they are presently being used in human service work. Examples of these systems are presented, one or more of which most of us have had some contact with in the conduct of our work. Marlett's paper describes a joint project conducted by the Canadian government and the University of Calgary called the Disability Information Services of Canada. The implication of the project for the empowerment of the disabled person is an example which can be extended to every disadvantaged population group with whom we work in the human services. Marlett includes examples of the content of electronic communicating so that the reader can appreciate the diversity of the conversations taking place via electronic means in the disability information network. As she points out, electronic communicating redefines our patterns of communicating. In her example, disabled persons are able to shift from groupings based on the concept of impairment or disability to natural groupings based upon interests, ideas, work, or handicap. In a significant note on empowerment, the electronic network is perceived as a means to influence the balance of power: disabled people communicate with others without stigma or the barriers associated with being seen as disabled.

In an unusual but compelling example of the impact of networks upon human service work, Lars Qvortrup describes an initiative in Sweden, Norway, Finland, and Denmark in which data processing and network services are being provided to isolated rural communities through the development of information and community service centres, or 'telehouses'. Telehouses combine communal access to electronic equipment and electronic networks with access to all personal social services, including training, employment services, and counselling. The persons who work in the telehouses must combine their human service skills with the ability to train people in the use of information technology. The human service worker must have the skills to use the technology effectively, but must also be able to help community members to use the technology to meet their own needs.

Finally, William O'Connor, an Ombudsman for elderly people in Alaska, presents a different view of the application of the technology, one that relies upon the professional using the technology to access centralised databanks in order to advocate for clients. In this case, the professional is able to provide benefits to clients which were not possible prior to the introduction of the technology.

NETWORK AND ELECTRONIC COMMUNICATIONS

Walter LaMendola

Fantasies concerning the ability of humans to communicate electronically were tempered by a surge in the development of real abilities to do so which began about half a century ago. As telephone capabilities, television, electronic mail, satellite, document facsimile, and shared database access spreads, so does our experience with the differential effects of human communicating via electronic networks. In what manner will the nature, form, and values of human services be affected? That question cannot be answered now, but we do have a basis for outlining at least the categories of electronic networks in use, and the areas of possible inquiry to which we must turn.

Early work by Harold Sackman suggested that electronic networks would begin to take over the work of government recordkeeping, access, and security, and that postal services, conduct of democratic debate, and participatory decision-making would take place largely through public access, at the individual level, to electronic networks (Sackman, 1967). He felt that electronic networks were public utilities and that most of these capabilities should be regulated by and for the public interest (Sackman, 1971). In fact, the public interest in the various countries has taken different approaches to the implementation of activities around and diffusion of devices used to support electronically the act of human communicating (Nora and Minc, 1981). In the United States, electronic networking is subject to government regulation only through its use of telephone lines even though new legislation has been considered, and has developed largly as a commercial enterprise (Information Age Commission Act, 1985). However, the impact of electronic networks upon home based work has spawned a number of lawsuits, surprisingly decided largely in favour of the workers and supported by the unions (Pros and Cons of Home Based Clerical Work, 1986). A recent battle is now in progress between those members of the United States federal telephone line regulatory commission who would tax electronic network users differently than other line users for their use of the lines, and a number of professional and consumer groups. Taxes and other costs may inhibit the growth of non-commercial electronic networks operating to switch messages across the United States. In England, the government, through the post office and broadcasting system, offers a variety of cost plus services to the individual in their home. In France, the official government goal has been to provide every citizen with a microcomputer, and, via a government-supported electronic network, to provide every citizen access to every other citizen.

Other published work foresaw a new millenium, one which would lead inevitably to a global village or electronic cottage. This new age has both a negative and positive side (Dertouzos, 1984; Illich, 1984; Wicklein, 1981). One author pointed out the potential development of either an inhuman, technical, digital society or a democratic, humanistic grapevine society (Vallee, 1982). There have been signs of both potentials, but major technical and popular writings have expressed a growing disappointment with the development of networks in support of democratic principles in the United States (Brunnell, 1987). The warnings of Masuda (1981) about the importance of issues of privacy in this stage of cultural development need to be heeded, but his agenda includes a number of other social problems, such as unemployment, which will certainly appear and will need to be addressed (Huddleston, 1987). Still, there is a great deal of idealism and practical insight about the use of electronic networks. As Dr Soedjatmoko, Rector of the United Nations University, has pointed out, network technologies are the hub of the development of world systems to liberate the poor, transfer knowledge to the third world, and provide the basis for the development of social units that cross nationalistic boundaries (Kidder, 1987).

A few of these arguments have been joined by governments and public interest groups, by professionals and others. In fact, the use of electronic devices has accelerated continuously regardless of the debate or forum. In most of today's Western world, electronic devices already perform sophisticated communications switching, postal service jobs, facsimile transmission, manufacturing assistance, security and defence jobs, as well as having complemented and altered the transaction and presentation modes of commerce, merchandising, publishing, telephone and television, and government. They are useful and used everywhere.

Most of the futurist and science fiction writers anticipated and wrote about the social and cultural changes which would accompany the continued development of information technologies. These writings express serious concerns about unemployment, gender based differences, political philosophy, institutional racism, poverty, violence, humanistic and religious values, and privacy. Despite the wide proliferation of these writings and the accessibility to experiments or experiences which lay behind them, the human services and human service practitioners have not embraced their study. Few human service professionals have spent time studying the topics of electronic networking and communication even when they refer to human communicating. On the other hand, persons working in the disciplines related to electronic communication are generally uninterested in any specialized knowledge of human communication. Both fields have suffered from this mutual exclusiveness. At times, the exclusiveness has seemed to be both linguistic and psychological. The linguistic differences relate to the jargon involved, but the psychological differences are rooted in value perceptions. Human service professionals have been reluctant to accept machines and technical capacity as a part of their work. They see the values of the technical community as largely antihumanistic, and reject not only that community but its products. This stance has been compromised by the severe shortage of resources currently being allocated to human service work, the work of individuals in the human service fields who have pioneered in electronic networking and communicating, and the overwhelming use, applicability, availability, and declining costs of information technologies in the developed countries.

In North America, the United Kingdom, and parts of Europe, human service organizations have moved to a cautious but open stance toward networks and electronic communication. Some conjunctions of the two fields now exist, and there is some documentation available that discusses electronic networks that may be of interest to human service professionals. The first widely distributed work that included electronic networks of interest to human service workers was published as a report and directory by Jessica Lipnack and Jeffrey Stamps in 1982 (Lipnack and Stamps, 1982). The variety of networks encouraged them to construct a taxonomy. The taxonomy included healing (health and the life cycle), sharing (communities and co-operatives), using (ecology and energy), valuing (politics and economics), learning (education and communications), growing (personal and spiritual growth), and evolving (global and futures) types of networks. Well over one thousand networks were identified, some of which were conducted electronically. Since their work, the growth of these types of networks, specifically as electronic networks, has been undocumented, but typical North American metropolitan areas support hundreds of them. In the Denver area alone, there are well over three hundred separate electronic network sites (A Listing, 1987). Such documentation does not, however, inform the reader about the number, type, and variety of networks in which persons who use electronic networking participate.

The Computer Users in Social Services Network (CUSSN) began to establish electronic networking capabilities in 1984. At that time, Richard Schoech and Walter LaMendola set up computers as network nodes using a public software program called FIDO. FIDO had a communications program distributed with it called FIDONET. Today there are twelve nodes in North America which participate in the CUSSN electronic network. There are also English and European nodes of the network. The experience of CUSSN as an electronic network continues to be bittersweet. The time commitment of the persons who act as system operators to maintain the software, electronic messaging and correspondence, and the computer files can be overwhelming. The elegance of the software is not such that it conducts its work with a minimum of attention except in the most minimal of circumstances. Changes are often made in application of the software, upgrades appear, agreements must be made to handle the networking, and daily checkups must be carried out. The actual content of the daily traffic between, among and on the network computers varies (CUSSN, 1987). At times, there is little which is sent between boards; at other times, traffice is high. The CUSSN experience is possibly the sole human service exemplar of an attempt to conduct electronic networking following principles of non-subscription based, open exchange, democratic participation computing, specifically run by and committed to the use of human service workers.

Most other human service activity in electronic networks can be classified into six categories: public service networks; community networks; human service organization networks; administrative networks; professional networks; and client centered networks.

Public service networks are networks which have been initiated to perform an international, national, federal, or state function. The academic networks, such as BITNET, are truly international in terms of participation and the free flow of ideas. FIDONET and its affiliates, such as CUSSN, are international in scope and, unlike the academic networks, can involve the participation of anyone with access to a computer and modem. In the United States examples of national network might include the national library system or legislative reference systems. An example of a federal network would be the social security system. State networks include job and employment systems and a variety of benefit networks. Many of the public networks have no public access and may have strict limits on use. Some of the public service networks, such as United Way of America's Human Care Network, charge a fee for use and regulate use and access. Some public service networks have specialized advocacy goals, such as Peacenet; others are commercial, such as Compuserve, but contain groups of human service practitioners who use that service to discuss practice issues.

Community networks are those which have been initiated to serve a community function. These include information and referral, library, health service, self-support, social interest, and topical conversation networks. Some American communities now have computer accessible information and referral services. In a typical American urban area, there are thousands of agencies which serve the human service needs of their population. This is now an area of great interest and electronic network development in the United States. Also, in American urban communities, it is not unusual to be able to use computer and modem to access the library and search for a book. Communities often have networks of pharmacies. Self-support groups such as Alcoholics Anonymous, Cancer Care, or the Association of Retarded Citizens, may have electronic networks which supplement their face-to-face work. Social interest groups are the most significant networks in terms of numbers. Social interest groups vary, from hobbies and crafts to cooking and flying. Topical conversation networks might have no organizing theme. For example, one network, founded by David Hughes and Louis Jaffee, runs an electronic network called Roy's Bar from Colorado Springs, Colorado. David Hughes calls himself the electronic bartender. All topics, with few exceptions, are legitimate, and the discussion, at turns, gets heated, poetic, penetrating, or pedantic. A number of the community networks have ties to national networks, such as the disabled persons network, but their goal is to support community functions.

Human service organization networks are networks which link human service organizations together. These types of networks have corollaries in the commercial world where geographically distant field offices are often linked together. Usually, these networks are administrative in nature, such as the linking together of case management systems or accounting systems. Some are linked together to share resource information. For example, some women's shelters in the United States use electronic networks to optimize their use of bed space. Human service organization networks also include those networks which are not geographically disparate, but represent activities conducted at the same organizational site. These networks are called local area networks. A number of these networks have been developed to handle treatment systems.

Professional networks are networks whose intent is to link together professionals who have different or similar interests. They often have a task or goal that is being addressed. For example, Daniel Ben-Horin has initiated a project in San Francisco which links together information technologists with human service practitioners who are experiencing problems or have questions about information technology on a national network called the Whole Earth Electronic Network (the WELL). A project at the Information Technology Center, Graduate School of Social Work, University of Denver, called HUSITANET, sponsored by the Colorado Trust, will experiment with not only problem discussion and matching persons with problems with resource persons, but also with offering co-ordinated assistance in problem solving in a forum which will include both urban and rural human service practitioners and information technology experts. Walter Hudson's informal group on BITNET is presently sharing ideas about the exploration of artificial intelligence in the human services and direct service software.

Client networks are those which exist to link together and advocate for people who share a common problem and need support in coping or developing shared meaning in their lives. Probably the most successful example of this is the variety of electronic networks becoming available to the disabled. Through mastery of electronic networks it is possible to conceive of a time when the disabled will become a dominant political force. Physical disabilities need not be an impediment to electronic communicating. And electronic communicating can certainly be used as a tool of influence, a gateway to participatory decision-making.

Each of these categories of networks is thriving to some degree in the developed countries. The problem of involving the third world in the progress in this area demands the highest priority of the United Nations, the World Health Organization, other international organizations, international commercial interests, the various industrialized countries, and the leadership of the third world. The ultimate goal of electronic network visionaries, to influence the social form of human society with electronic communicating, seems distant. The most visible of the networks, those in the public interest, are particularly susceptible to invasions of privacy, poor guardianship of public data, and misuse. It is here that the human service professional, with many others, must spend time and resources to protect privacy, confidentiality, and choice. Public service networks must be carefully shepherded, for it is their impact which will overshadow any gains made by the other categories of electronic networks. Presently, the other categories of electronic networks can be a source of delight as well as a source of personal and organizational irritation. There are certainly signs in these categories that participatory decision-making is possible using electronic media. The idea that groups of people can form voluntary communities circumscribed by areas of intellectual, emotional, social, sexual, or political interest is both compelling and real to those who use electronic networks. For the most part, in electronic networking the transformative powers of the technology are usually more vivid and clear than in other implementations of information technology: it is people connecting to people, sharing knowledge, suffering, ideas, joy, interests, laughter, skills, sarcasm, work – sharing each other.

REFERENCES

Brunell, D. (1987). Editorial, *PC World Magazine*, December, 1987.

CUSS Electronic Network (1987). *Computer Users in Social Services Network Newsletter*. University of Texas at Arlington, PO Box 19129, Arlington, Texas, 76019–0129, USA.

Dertouzos, M. (1984). 'The Information Revolution', in H. Pagels (ed.), *Computer Culture*. New York Academy of Sciences, New York.

Huddleston, L. (1987). 'A Proposal to Study the Displaced Worker in the Information Society'. Doctoral Dissertation Proposal, Graduate School of Social Work, University of Denver, Colorado.

Illich, I. (1984). *Gender*. Harper & Row, New York.

Information Age Commission Act (1985). Senate Bill 786, March 28, 1985. U.S. Government Printing Office, Washington DC.

Kidder, R. (1987). 'How to Educate the World's Poor'. The *Christian Science Monitor*, July 10, 1987.

Lipnack, J. and Stamps, J. (1982). *Networking*. Doubleday and Company, New York.

Listing of Denver Computer Network Nodes (1987). Boardwatch, Denver, Colorado.

Masuda, Y. (1981). *The Information Society*. World Future Society, Washington DC.

Nora, S. and Minc, A. (1981). *The Computerization of Society*. MIT Press, Cambridge, Massachusetts.

Pros and Cons of Home Based Clerical Work (1986). A Hearing before a Subcommittee of the Committee on Government Relations, February 26, 1987. U.S. House of Representatives, U.S. Government Printing Office, Washington DC.

Sackman, H. (1967). *Computers, Systems Science, and Evolving Society*. John Wiley and Sons, New York.

Sackman, H. (1971). *Mass Information Utilities and Social Excellence*. Auerbach, Princeton, New Jersey.

Vallee, J. (1982). *The Network Revolution*. And/Or Press, Berkeley, California.

Wicklein, J. (1981). *The Electronic Nightmare*. Viking Press, New York.

EMPOWERMENT THROUGH COMPUTER TELECOMMUNICATIONS

Nancy Marlett

OVERVIEW

Disability Information Services of Canada (DISC) is a Canadian telecommunications network which facilitates the exchange of information among disabled persons and those who work to improve their status. It uses the advances of computer technology, information science and networking to increase consumer control and choice, to empower persons with disabilities to achieve respect within their communities as partners and citizens. It works to facilitate the development of information resources at all levels on specialized topics of interest to persons with disabilities, e.g. technical aids, employment, research, and local information related to supports and services for independent living and integration.

DISC emerges from a Canadian context which has provided significant telecommunications advances, notably in satellite communications, Telidon, and telecommunications hardware and software. Many Canadians have had considerable experience in distance telecommunications and the establishment of relatively inexpensive lines such as BITNET and DATAPAC make multiple user systems possible for even larger groups of users. The major advance related to network capabilities has been the break-through in interface capacity which makes it possible for computers to speak to each other despite differences in machine language.

DISC SERVICES

DISC provides services, technical support, training and consultation for:

The Network

'Putting people in need of information in touch with people who have it'. DISC is a low cost and open computer telecommunication network that will eventually include local drop-in centres, regional phone-in lines, and computer links. DISC is presently funded to establish the computer network to ensure that it is accessible to any person with a disability and to all makes of computers and Technical Devices for the Deaf (TDD) that are ASCII compatible. Associations, agencies, libraries and colleges/universities are being encouraged to provide computer access to those who do not have their own equipment. Users of the DISC network can send mail to specific people or groups of people, hold electronic phone conversations, find someone who shares a common interest, locate information sources, join an open discussion on a bulletin board or take part in a computer conference.

Special Interest Groups

The driving force behind DISC is the energy of persons who share common concerns but various perspectives. These special interest groups provide active exchange between consumers, service providers, funders, and policy makers. DISC attempts to provide the resources for special interest groups (e.g. employ-ment equity, technical aids, etc.) to use electronic bulletin boards and conferences and to make contact with existing international bulletin boards and databases in their area of interest.

Resource Centres

While there are well developed international databases, there is a need for Canadian Resource Centres to develop Canadian materials and to provide our own perspective on literature and research. Resource centres that wish to make their resources widely available are encouraged to computerize their holdings and work with other centres and library consultants to develop a co-ordinated approach to database development and manage-ment, on-line searching, and user services.

Local Disability Information Services

Regional and central staff assist local consumer groups to collect, manage and disseminate the information that consumers need to live independently. DISC, in conjunction with other relevant organizations, will provide training in computer networks, computer information systems, community development of information networks, peer-based information services, and needs surveys.

EQUIPMENT

The host computer, a 'VAX', currently has 32 ports available, meaning that 32 people can interact with the host at any one time. The 'VAX' system is comprised of an 11/750 Central Processing Unit with 6 megabytes of memory and one 120 megabyte system drive and a 450 megabyte drive.

The network software on the VAX includes VAX mail and phone, VMS notes (bulletin boards and conference), Kermit (file transfer) and basic database software. Persons can use: microcomputers – almost all recent computer makes can be used as long as they can support a modem; mainframes – any mainframe with either Kermit software or terminal emulation capability, preferably a VT family emulator; or Telephone Devices for the Deaf (TDD) that are ASCII compatible. DISC operates on DATAPAC (owned by the Telecom Canada) as they have close to 1000 entry stations across Canada. Users dial into their local datapac number and then connect to the University of Calgary's VAX 11/750.

POTENTIAL USERS

There are numerous hardware and software adaptations designed to facilitate disabled Canadians with special needs. Groups such as the Neil Squire Foundation, VITA (Visually Impaired for Technological Advancement), and Deafnet, advocate computers as important communication aids. DISC allows individual consumers (regardless of their disability) across Canada to share common interests and concerns and work together on projects. Some groups, for example the Canadian Coordinating Council on Deafness, already use computer telecommunications to make their national links more effective. While each group may wish a closed or private bulletin board to encourage debate among their members regarding management, policy, funding and/or projects, we hope that each will contribute to, and manage, open bulletin boards as well.

DISC allows Canadian academics and students to work on joint projects, opening new opportunities for research partnerships with consumers and service providers. Universities and colleges are being asked to provide support to disabled persons in using DISC and to assist emerging local information centres and resource centres. To date, St Mary's University in Halifax and the Ontario Institute of Studies in Education at the University of Toronto have become DISC affiliates. Links between outreach projects, rehabilitation centres, employment centres or early intervention programs will promote the sharing of demonstration projects, training ideas, new technology, etc. to improve the services to persons with disabilities. Interaction with consumers by policy makers and researchers will make the services more responsive to changing needs. Canadian companies offering innovations in technical and teaching aids and service alternatives are encouraged to join DISC. If people in need of assistance can be put in touch with people with ideas and the people able to turn those ideas into products, DISC will be able to assist in forging a Canadian technological, industrial, and service industry built on consumer ideas.

Because libraries are our main source of existing information and resource sharing, they are logical places to approach for providing computer access to that specialized information. Libraries on DISC will be able to communicate more effectively with each other, download information and connect directly to resource centres across the country. Professionals with a commitment to disabled persons, e.g. lawyers, counsellors, physicians, engineers, etc. will be encouraged to form their own networks within DISC – between colleagues and with consumers e.g. sharing legal precedents and strategies for constitutional reform, establishing research forums for bioengineers. A Canadian network of the various government departments (at all three levels) related to disability with input from consumers and service providers could help find creative solutions to increasing the status of disabled citizens.

BACKGROUND

Whereas professional models within human services hold information and dispense it to those within their closed systems, citizenship development and self-help movements rely on full and meaningful access to information. The International Year of Disabled Persons Document of the Federal Government, recognized the need for specialized information in Recommendation 61.

"That the federal government, in cooperation with the Provinces and the private sector, assist in the establishment of a Canadian Information Resource Centre on Disability to link up and coordinate information resources and to assist regional showrooms of technical aids.

"That, pending the establishment of such a Centre, the Federal Government prepare and publish a directory of federal programs and activities of interest to disabled persons, as well as a catalogue of relevant research projects and studies." (Federal Government, 1981).

In 1983, an Information Referral Services fund was set up under the Secretariat to implement Recommendation 61. As a first step funds were granted to each of seven national disability specific groups (National Institute on Mental Retardation [NIMR], Canadian Rehabilitation Council for the Disabled [CRCD], Canadian National Institute for the Blind [CNIB], Canadian Association for Children with Learning Disabilities [CACLD], Canadian Federation of the Blind [CFB], Canadian Mental Health Association [CAMH], and the Coalition of Provincial Organizations of the Handicapped [COPOH]) to investigate the use of computers in improving their information flow. All parties felt increased comfort levels with computers and felt computerization was an important step in preparing to move communications to the provincial and local level. However, the project did not address the practical needs of the consumer and direct service providers and there needed to be a way to share information between groups in addition to providing a mechanism for vertical flow of information between national and local levels within the same organization.

In the Summer of 1985, Professor Marlett was invited by the Secretary of State to propose a conceptual model for information development and dissemination. The University of Calgary Rehabilitation Studies program has a strong commitment to research and professional training related to improving service options and lifestyle of disabled persons and their families. The program had been involved extensively in developing Canadian information resources. The overview was presented at a meeting of National Associations involved with the 1981 federal recommendations to increase access to information related to disabilities. During the Fall of 1985, a University of Calgary project team developed a proposal related to a decentralized network of Resource Centres and Local Information Centres.

The DISC project coalesced around a number of values; namely

1 Computers have the potential to be a tool to change the context within which people live – a way around the barriers of disability – mobility, communication, attitude, learning, sensory – a way around the barrier of location.

2 Computer communication reduces the stigmas associated with disability by allowing people to communicate on equal status – the barriers to open communication are minimized by the adaptive interfaces and the apparent aspects of the disabling condition are reduced.

3 A network which strives to improve the status of disabled persons should be based on consumer control.

4 Information in a network is a dynamic process not a static product. In a consumer driven approach, information emerges from many sources and the juxtaposition of information creates debate, discussion and new needs for information.

5 The network should expand the information horizon to include other networks and information resources and promote integration through networking in local community networks.

The networking goals of DISC are to have in working operation a national, bilingual, computerized information service that is accessible to all persons with disabilities and to those who work to improve their status.

1 To establish a technical and administrative structure that will facilitate and support a community of persons using computers for communication and information exchange, and which will allow the users of the system to exercise control over the development of the network.

2 To establish local ownership of the DISC network by facilitating the expression of regional characteristics in the development of computer networking, information exchange and public education/customer service for the network at the regional level.

3 To develop a network of computer access ports which will be open to disabled individuals who do not have a personal computer.

4 To assist associations of disabled persons, and other special interest groups to use the network to improve communication among their constituents.

5 To encourage partnerships of persons from different backgrounds to solve common concerns; e.g. research partnerships between consumers and academics, social change partnerships.

The information development goals of DISC are to identify information resources available in Canada and abroad and to facilitate their accessibility by members of the network, by encouraging and supporting Resource Centres and Local Information Centres to become active participants in the network.

1 To identify existing information resources of interest to the community of users and invite them to become part of the Resource Centre Bulletin Board.

2 To provide technical support to those resource centres who are interested in computerizing their holdings, to do so in a manner which will facilitate information exchange between resource centres and with network members.

3 To provide training to those who wish to become bulletin board managers and assist in identifying consumer driven information structures.

4 To provide technical assistance to National Disability Groups and other associations of the disabled to use computer/ telecommunications systems and publication processes in their public education efforts.

5 To support pilot projects working to create locally developed and user controlled information resources that will support disabled persons to achieve independence and control over their lives.

PROGRESS TO DATE

The System

The basic technical configuration is now operational. Of the original technical objectives only the bilingual interface and the interface with baudot TDDs remain to be solved. The success of the system has generated a new set of problems related to providing the service at a reasonable cost. With the rapidly expanding membership and the increased competence with the various options, e.g. phone, file transfer and using DISC as a gateway to other networks, the transmission costs are escalating beyond the ability of the university or the project to support within the existing financial arrangements.

In the coming year, attention will begin to focus on the establishment of local and regional networks that can act as distributed conference sites within the DISC system. Because this technology is so new we will be forced to enter again into primary research.

The network has grown to more than 850 users. The following is a breakdown of a sample consisting of the DISC User List. It shows the geographic distribution, the breakdown by membership type, and the interests identified by the members.

Table 6.1

Geographical Distribution of 628 of 850 DISC Members

	%
Alberta	18.6
British Columbia	14.5
Ontario	32.8
Prince Edward Island	0.5
Nova Scotia	4.0
Manitoba	4.6
Saskatchewan	8.1
Northwest Territories	0.6
Quebec	5.9
Newfoundland	1.1
New Brunswick	3.2
USA	1.0
Location of User Unknown	5.1

Table 6.2

Distribution by Membership Category
628 of 850 DISC Members

	%
Consumer	39.6
Association	19.9
Treatment Centre	1.9
Service Provider	25.3
Researcher	8.8
Social Change Agent	14.8
College/University	4.9
Government Official	3.5
Resource Centre	20.2
No Selection	25.3

Table 6.3

Identified Interests of DISC Members

	%
Independent Living	35.5
Social Change	41.6
Public Education	42.0
Human Rights	41.2
Family/Social Support	26.4
Accessibility	34.2
Funding	34.1
Housing	22.6
Transportation	26.4
Technical Aids	57.0
Skill Development	39.3
Employment	42.0
Education	47.6
Rehabilitation	30.7
Medicine	28.5
Software Development	36.8
No Selection	29.3

To date there are 43 current bulletin boards each with a member manager. The listing and description of the bulletin boards will give you an indication of the types of special interest groups and organization of the bulletin boards. The description appearing is that which appears on the screen.

Table 6.4

Bulletin Boards

TITLE	TOPICS	ENTRIES	DESCRIPTION
ANNOUNCEMENTS	18	46	ANNOUNCEMENTS ANNOUNCEMENTS ANNOUNCEMENTS Notice to the general user group of DISC for response.
ANNOUNCEMENTS OF NEW CONFERENCES	6	32	This conference is to the central place to look for new conferences. The reason for the conference and introductory text will be included in all new conferences. You can join a new conference directly from here.
BOOST	4	7	BOOST (Blind Organization of Ontario with Self-help Tactics). We are all united by our common desire to achieve the social-economic integration of people with disabilities.
CAILC	3	2	This meeting is a private meeting made for the Canadian Association of Independent Living Center's Board meetings. This is only open to members.
CCCD	2	2	This meeting is for the exchange of information with the Canadian Coordinating Committee on Deafness (CCCD). This meeting is public and open to all.
CHITCHAT	61	377	This conference is open to all for any topic that you wish to discuss.
CLUB18	32	182	It is to be read at your own risk, knowing full well that you asked to join. I will let almost anything go. Key word there is almost.

TITLE	TOPICS	ENTRIES	DESCRIPTION
CNIB	6	14	This meeting is for the exchange of information to and from the Canadian National Institute for the Blind.
COMPUTER ACCESSIBILITY	8	30	This meeting is for the discussion of concerns and strategies for computer accessibility to the disabled. This meeting is open to all.
DISCUSSION OF CP/M OPERATING SYSTEM FOR MICROS	6	32	To enable cp/m users to exchange ideas, suggestions, helpful hints.
DEAFNEWS	13	101	This conference is for the exchange of information among our hearing impaired users, as well as the rest of the community.
DIALOGUE	1	1	The purpose of this conference is to discuss the mission statement, goals and objectives and the values of DISC.
DOWNSYNDROME	1	1	This conference is for the exchange of information on all aspects of Down Syndrome.
EMPLOYMENT	10	50	This is a conference for active discussion of information and issues related to employment and disability.
EXPERTSYSTEMS	6	156	This is a closed conference to the members of the group called the 'problem solvers'. I hope that together we can solve some of the problems besetting us all.

TITLE	TOPICS	ENTRIES	DESCRIPTION
FUNDRAISING	2	2	This conference is set up for groups interested in sharing information on fundraising strategies for non-profit groups. Groups are encouraged to share information on approaches they have used and either found successful or not.
GATE	8	19	To discuss the Alberta network.
JOKES	23	97	This is the Clean Jokes Conference, with the key word being CLEAN. Any jokes that are found to be tasteless or that ANYONE protests over will be deleted ASP.
KIDSCHAT	1	1	KIDSCHAT is a special bulletin board that is being set up for the benefit of disabled children, or children who have parents or siblings that are disabled. We feel there is a need for children to be able to share their concerns with other children their own age. This bulletin board is intended for children up to and including the age of 12.
MODERATOR	8	73	This is a training conference for new moderators or those who want to discuss issues related to being a moderator.
NORTH DAKOTA NEWS	16	73	This meeting is established to display the information through the disability focus of BITNET – a North American academic and research focus.

TITLE	TOPICS	ENTRIES	DESCRIPTION
PROBLEM REPORTING	13	94	This meeting was set up as a forum to discuss and solve problems of a technical nature in regard to the DISC access and VAX system. This meeting is public and open to all.
PROFILES	15	30	Profiles is a conference where DISC users can introduce themselves to the DISC user population. The conference is listed according to the province you live in. There will also be a topic called DISC Staff. This is where you can find out about your favorite DISC personalities.
PUSHONTARIO	16	41	PUSH is a provincial consumer organization. Conference will be listing a forum around consumer issues.
RESOURCESHARING	3	32	This is a resource list that can act as an information source to all of those who are interested in social support. There is a literature review and a listing of social support groups.
RUMOR	5	3	RUMORS RUMORS RUMORS Feel free to send or pass on for verification any rumors that you would like checked out.
SOCIAL SUPPORT	5	28	This conference is being set up to give people the chance to talk to each other about what social support means to them. The topics for the conference will be: Topic #2: Self-Help Topic #3: Community Development Topic #4: Personal Support Networks Topic #5: Peer Support/Counselling

TITLE	TOPICS	ENTRIES	DESCRIPTION
STAFF CONFERENCE	33	186	This conference was opened as a central site for the DISC internal staff transactions.
SUGGEST BOX	9	88	This is the Generic SUGGESTION BOX concerning the running of DISC or suggestions for conference TOPICS.
TECHNICAL NEWS	29	71	This meeting is for the purpose of exchanging information regarding technical devices and innovations available to the disabled. If a certain subject is of special interest.
TEENCHAT	1	1	This bulletin board is set up for the benefit of disabled teenagers, or teenagers who live with a disabled parent or sibling.
TRADINGPOST	8	16	The purpose of this conference is to provide a forum to enable participants to buy and sell good quality used devices and/or accessories designed for use by the disabled.
VACATION	3	5	This conference has been set up in the hopes of providing information for the consumer regarding vacation spots which can accommodate the disabled.
VISUALLY IMPAIRED TECHNICAL AIDS	9	34	This meeting is being set up as an information source for news on Technical Aids for the Visually Impaired.

The following is a rough categorization of the emergence of Special Interest Groups to date. Note that these have, by and large, been generated by the membership.

Open-ended bulletin boards are conversations that allow people to get to know each other. CHITCHAT, Profiles, Dialogue, Club18, each have their own character and you can see by the number of topics and entries that meeting people is a major interest of our members.

System-related bulletin boards like Expert Systems, Suggestions, and Problem Reporting exist to monitor and adapt the system to the members' needs. This is an active group of experts – either because of their computer knowledge or their knowledge of the interface requirements – who are shaping the future configuration of the system.

Self-help bulletin boards will become an increasingly important component within DISC as parents, youngsters, people with specific problems, e.g. chronic pain, feel comfortable with sharing their feelings openly. At present there is a need to establish etiquette that will protect people's feelings in an open debate.

Organization bulletin boards are being implemented slowly . . . perhaps because the organizations have pre-established communication patterns and are somewhat reluctant to change their methods without experimentation. The exception to this is the deaf and hearing impaired community who find the DISC system just an extension of their existing communication patterns. Disabled members understood the concepts and the potential of DISC much more readily than do agencies, professionals and organizations. This is likely because computer networking has been most useful with newly emerging groups who are developing new concepts or ideas and have a need to find supporters and share ideas over a wide geographical area and among diverse groups. This makes the network an ideal tool for social action and self-help which tend to remain on the fringe of established organizations. It will be interesting to see if the emerging groups within an alternative organizational medium will evolve into more traditional structures over time because of the pressure of the funding mechanisms.

Issues-related or functional bulletin boards are developing a slightly different format – with more emphasis on formal information development. Examples of these are technical aids, employment and social support. It is hoped that resource centres will become active participants in this type of bulletin board structure as they are a natural source of information development and dissemination. Conferences not yet underway but envisioned include transportation, accessible housing, leisure, heritage access.

Commercial bulletin boards – a concept wherein companies and services advertise and provide information and assistance on-line, is ready for a trial run once the fee structure is worked out.

ORGANIZATIONAL STRUCTURE

DISC is a decentralized organization with the majority of member contact and service vested in the regions. The four regional representatives have established regional sites and each has a different character and mandate.

In the Atlantic Provinces the focus is on basic public education and the development of computer literacy within the user community. In many respects the support of DISC is creating a situation where the disabled users of the system are surpassing community standards of computer literacy. Direct consumer groups and emerging independent centres have also been a major focus.

Quebec is complex because the balance of service delivery and consumer organizations is in flux. All services are provided by the government and the disability associations are primarily advocates. Regional committees, made up of persons of all disabilities, are gaining strength as local planning and co-ordinating bodies and the consumer movement is still establishing a foothold in the province. Because of the political complexities, the regional representative works through a provincial co-ordinating group of all the stakeholders. There is the potential within Quebec of establishing the first distributed conference; building on both an established provincial information structure and an existing local bulletin board.

Ontario has a high level of computer literacy through the schools and in the provincial government. The regional office is focusing on assisting consumer groups to understand the potential uses of telecommunications. The Ontario representative also works with the national offices of the major disability organizations, assisting them with planning and implementing an information strategy.

The Western Provinces and Northwest Territories is a recent development with the initial focus on the establishment of links within the province of British Columbia. Alberta is advanced in computer connections and the development of resource centres with a computer data structure. (A predecessor to national DISC was a local consortium of resource centres.) Manitoba and Saskatchewan both have good coverage in the sparsely populated areas. The Northwest Territories have yet to be exposed to the system.

The technical support of DISC is located at the Walter Dinsdale Centre and consists of a Network Manager and a Systems Manager, University of Calgary network and system staff, secretarial and administrative staff.

RESOURCE CENTRES

While the development of a national resource centre consortium was one of the initial goals of DISC, the initial focus on the network and special interest groups led to a serious reconsideration of DISC's role with respect to Mandated Resource Centres. As the need for information arises in the bulletin boards, resource centres are encouraged to take part by responding to information requests, advertising their services, and generating information packages for distribution on-line. We are providing support to resource centres in computerizing their holdings with a manual for developing databases, providing informal training courses for resource centre staff and arranging for member discounts on a data management software package.

EMPOWERMENT ISSUES

The fundamental beliefs of the project now are in evidence every day as people join the network and find 850+ new peers – people who share their interests. As with any new network there was the initial embarrassment of having a party with nobody there, but once a critical mass of 200-300 persons were on-line (during March of 1987) a magic of creation occurred. Isolated people (by disability or location) broke free to meet people. Chance encounters led to friendships, small businesses emerged, disabled people became tutors and guides for the non-disabled. Members of the network assumed more control of policy and procedures, new groups and issues formed. With the trauma of a technological and organizational nightmare behind us, we are now able to look at what is being created and address the many complex issues that arise at the crossroads of new technologies and social change. This section of the paper will begin to look at:

- the emergence of a communications medium that has cultural implications

- the emergence of an electronic community and how it can affect our way of decision-making, both on an individual and a corporate level and the emergence of new partnership models

- the challenges to our original concepts of information data, and how a consumer-driven information structure is beginning to emerge.

That the computer has the potential to minimize the barriers encountered by disabled people has been accepted for some time. The computer has become a standard adaptive aid for those with visual impairments, hearing impairments, physical disabilities and, of course, multiple disabilities. The computer is also being used extensively with persons with emotional problems and learning disabilities to provide augmentative problem solving for these groups.

Computers open the Communication Door

The potential impact of the computer becomes most dramatic when we look at the communication process. In a basic communication dyad one person sends a message and another person receives and understands the message so long as the message is in a common language code across an open channel. Communication disabilities (noise, disruptions) potentially exist at each point. Persons with severe physical disabilities often experience difficulty transmitting information, either through voice or through a written medium. With adaptive keyboards and devices such as morse code the physically disabled are able to transmit information. The deaf community, although unhampered within their own culture, experience similar problems in trying to transmit information to a non-signing individual because of the lack of speech, and the inability of the receiver to understand the language being used. Similarly, in receiving information, individuals with severe hearing impairment can often not understand oral information, although they have no trouble with written communication, whereas the visually impaired community have trouble understanding the written components of communications but have no problem with the oral component. The major problem inhibiting communication between disabled groups has been the lack of a common language system. The use of braille by visually impaired, sign language by the hearing impaired, and augmentative communications systems such as Bliss and PIC among the physically disabled and mentally retarded, haa left a 'Tower of Babel' barrier that has been – to this point – insurmountable. The common use of computers by all disability groups has meant that not only are individuals able to send and receive messages, it has encouraged a common communication channel and a common language. This means that groups who have been restricted to intra-group communication are now able to communicate inter-group.

Cross-disability communication opens the way to sharing experiences and frustrations that are common to all disabled persons in a way that has been difficult in the past. With the collegiality among persons with different handicaps that is possible when people share a common language and bonds of a shared history comes a strength to face the ongoing obstacles confronting all disabled persons. The culture of a DISC network is also built on the excitement of development – working together to build something unique and admired by society. In the early stages when the many obstacles were still apparent, users expressed anger that the promise of the network seemed thwarted. The initial response was to demand that the system be fixed by 'THE EXPERTS' paid to run the system. As a few expert users became involved in solving the problems they became the model to turn the energy of thwarted hope into positive group action. The resulting partnership between users and staff continues to grow as members assume more and more of the responsibilities of running and modifying the system. Hopefully, this common bond will continue to empower the community of DISC as we face the obstacles of the next stage – ongoing funding and developing local and regional conferences.

Computer Telecommunication as Cultural Medium

Once a communication foundation is established persons with disabilities become part of the creation of a new information culture. By overcoming the barriers of time and space we can choose when and how to interact with people because one does not have to have a receiver at the other end of the channel in order to send a message. Computer telecommunication provides an opportunity for an individual to move from a situation of being a single, isolated user sitting alone in front of a terminal, to a person with unlimited ability to interact with others through this new window on the world. The impact of telecommunications is seen in the fact that sales of modems are growing at 15% per year. One of the early pioneers in telecommunications indicated that computer telecommunications had the potential to decentralize knowledge and put it with its concomitant power into the hands of people in ways that we haven't even begun to think about yet. With the establishment of telemetry - using radio waves rather than telephone lines, the electronic community can become a part of everyone's life, not just those that have access to telephone modems.

The impact of the new technology is widespread. Business has achieved sophisticated inventory control through direct telecommunications. The field of research is being dramatically altered by direct networks of researchers around the world. The establishment of the academic and research networks through BITNET not only spells the beginning of collaborative research and ongoing interactive communication about research findings, but spells the death of our concept of journals and control of information through publication. Telecommunications are changing even our thinking patterns: our western tradition of linear thought expands and diverges through the juxtaposition of ideas and the ever broadening array of alternate information sources.

Electronic Community

Our concepts of organizations are also being challenged by the development of computer networking which has extended the sharing access of information. People in various parts of the country and at different times can collaboratively analyze and synthesize information to make decisions. This has become the basis of networking as an emerging social phenomena. Networks exist to foster self-help, to exchange information, to change society, to improve productivity in worklife and to share resources.

Groups that have the most to gain from information technology advancement are those just developing new concepts or ideas and which have the need to network across a variety of people or over great distances. One such group are disabled Canadians who are taking a much more active role in their attempt to lead independent and fulfilling lives. The consumer movement, the independent living movement, and a number of self-help alternatives can hopefully use the emerging technology of computer conferencing to focus their development on empowerment of the members rather than the creation of artificial hierarchical structures to serve organization needs. For example, the Canadian Down Syndrome Society is being set up to facilitate information exchange among parents, persons with symptoms associated with Down Syndrome, professionals, researchers and government officials. Rather than create a tiered hierarchical system, the association is investigating the potential use of a network to achieve its ends. This will rechannel energy on development and dissemination of information, and the establishment of collaborative partnerships among the various groups.

The existence of support for self-help, social action and public education within the same communication medium means that DISC could be the tool to forge a new generation of organizations. Special interest groups will emerge as the need arises, and will expand and diversify and may eventually blend with other groups. As the initiatives and the individuals change, the structures within the network can respond to the changing needs.

Political action with DISC exists because of the potential collaboration of groups which have traditionally been isolated and protected. The stakeholders are consumers (be they disabled persons or their families), service providers, professionals, researchers and academics, government officials and policy-makers and business. One of the major problems in creating policies responsive to social change has rested in the inability of the various stakeholders to communicate effectively and comfortably with each other. In fact, much energy has gone into the development of professional and bureaucratic languages which diminish the ability to communicate freely across groups. Separate language systems and isolated channels of communication protects groups from challenges. Computer telecommunications, on the other hand, allow for natural communication to occur between these various stakeholders, around functions which will hopefully diminish the need for isolated language systems and allow for more comfort in the communication process.

DISC is a means of broadening social contacts. Many new members wish to contact peers who share the same problems. Soon, they venture into meeting people who share common interests. As the individuals gain strength through sharing experiences with those who have been through similar situations with similar disabilities, they have a number of alternatives open to them. They can engage in open conversations within conferences around specific issues, meeting others from all backgrounds. They can assist new users to come on-line as a DISC buddy. They can provide information to other individuals. Individuals can also generate their own discussions and become a moderator and a facilitator of information for other individuals. The competence in a communication will broaden from DISC into a number of other local, regional and indeed international networks. The communications options become almost limitless. DISC is encouraging the development of local bulletin boards and encourages members of local information networks to meet people in their communities. Indeed, this will become a strong force for integration - become part of a community through shared culture - albeit a local computer culture. One can see how networking becomes an addiction to many – much like ham radio – computer telecommunications is a way to be part of a number of groups – local to international – a way to be connected and part of social networks – when and how the person chooses.

SUMMARY

DISC encourages a redefinition of our communication patterns. First, DISC encourages a cross-disability focus and a partnership between disabled persons, parents, advocates, professionals and policy planners. Inherent in this is a shift from groupings built on the concept of impairment or disability (the underlying etiology and functional loss) to natural groups based on interests and handicaps (the breakdown at the interface between the individual and society in transportation, employment, etc.). Involved in this is a paradigmatic shift from providing services to devalued persons to one of partnership in the creation of a new communications medium. The computer network is fast becoming the wedge to redefine the roles of communicators and the balance of power. Computer telecommunications eliminates the stigmas associated with disability by allowing people to communicate without the barriers associated with visible or apparent aspects of the disabling condition. DISC members have begun a brave Canadian experiment in empowerment at the grass roots.

The developmental project has demonstrated that a network such as DISC is technically viable and capable of positive impact on the lives of persons with disabilities. Our focus in the next phase will shift to members taking responsibility as stewards of the limited resources. Decisions regarding management of the system – e.g. on-line time, CPU time, storage space – must be made quickly and this will require self-restraint and control.

While most bulletin boards for the handicapped do not have initiation fees all require users to cover on-line charges. However, Canada is a very sparsely populated country and the differences in on-line fees are considerable – e.g. a packet sent from Ontario could cost $1.00, whereas the same information sent from a rural Quebec town only 20 miles from the border could be $7.00. In addition, the very persons we are trying to reach – those using computers as a communication device – are often very slow in sending messages. Many persons with disabilities are on fixed incomes with little leeway to cover any but essential costs. Many have had their computers donated to them by service clubs, etc. It appears that a modest fixed yearly rate would be all that most users could afford to stay involved. Those using the system for private or commercial use will likely be charged for their use above a standard amount. DISC has opened doors for persons previously isolated, given voice to many more. It is difficult to imagine what will happen if these contacts are removed and the doors closed again. Our funding strategy will indeed need to be creative and effective to meet the on-line charges.

Two new directions are anticipated in the network – broadening our international links and building at least two distributed conferences (Quebec and Ontario). One interesting possibility is the introduction of the French minitel system of low cost, in home terminals. These may overcome the cost barrier and make network membership possible for all disabled persons who wish it.

As the first phase – the NETWORK – becomes secure, attention will focus on attracting research and projects to work in conjunction with the network, e.g. employment matches, social impact studies, constitutional reform conferences.

We look ahead now to phase 2 – research and teaching as a University of Calgary Research Centre. We anticipate major collaboration among professors both at the University of Calgary, and other universities, students from a variety of academic disciplines, and of course, the people who own the system – the DISC users.

REFERENCES

Federal Government (1981). International Year of Disabled Persons Document, *stacles*, February, p.69.

ELECTRONIC VILLAGE HALLS -
IT AND IT-ASSISTED SERVICES
FOR RURAL VILLAGE COMMUNITIES

Lars Qvortrup

INTRODUCTION

In Sweden, Norway, Finland and Denmark a number of so-called 'Information and Community Service Centres' (ICSCs) have been established. Their popular names are 'Electronic Village Halls' or just 'Telehouses'. Their main aim is to provide isolated village communities with access to data processing and tele-communications services, and to computer-assisted services. Instead of linking individual households onto a network, the working-parties on these projects have chosen to concentrate IT facilities within specially designed telehouses, containing video and EDP equipment which are thus at the disposal of the entire local communities involved. The facilities are intended as much for private as for commercial use, with satellite TV reception, teleshopping, and interactive Citizens Advice services.

The first telehouse was established in Sweden in September 1985, and today 18 telehouses have been or are being established in Sweden, Norway, Finland and Denmark. The success of the idea, that is, to offer communal access to telecommunications facilities, and to combine access with training services, with EDP working facilities, and with social services, has been obvious.

TELEHOUSES: THE SOCIAL CONTEXT

A general tendency towards the centralisation and the concentra-tion of capital is the economic background against which the ICSC initiatives in Denmark, Norway, Sweden and Finland have emerged. In the rural district of Lemvig, for example, this economic problem is especially felt by the agricultural sector, reflecting the general trend in Denmark. In 1950, 465,900 people were employed in the agricultural sector in the whole of Denmark, but in 1980 the figure was only 162,880. And if the existing trends continue unmodified, there will only be some 30,000 full-time farms left in 1990. With so few farms spread over the total rural area in Denmark, many traditional but vitally necessary services in the small villages (local shops, craftsmen, schools, public libraries, post offices) will disappear.

A similar tendency may be detected in Sweden. Here the dominant economic sector in rural areas has been forestry. But structural changes and increases in productivity in the forestry business generally have caused unemployment figures to rise far beyond the national average. A further consequence is the loss of the small village's cultural identity, since the tourist industry has now become the most important source of income for a number of mid-Swedish rural districts. The social network, with its households, and with its formal and informal commercial, social and cultural institutions, is falling apart.

Thus the professed aims of the ICSCs in the Nordic countries are to counteract, or at any rate mitigate, some of the negative consequences of these seemingly irreversible socio-economic tendencies. Through the provision of services intended to support local businesses – consultant, information services, and improved telecommunications – and through the provision of distance-working facilities, it is hoped that the ICSCs will be able to alleviate some of the economic and employment problems facing geographically marginal and increasingly depopulated regions within the Nordic nations. Through the provision of improved educational facilities, both by means of NIT, and with regard to the study of NIT itself, and by rendering more immediately accessible information of public interest from centres of regional and national government, the ICSCs are intended to redress some of the educational and political disadvantages faced by socio-geographically marginal populations. By supplying library services and satellite television reception – and by providing meeting and conference facilities – the ICSCs are intended to mitigate some of the cultural disadvantages attendant on remote habitation.

TELEHOUSES IN THE NORDIC COUNTRIES

An ICSC may be defined as a centre where NIT apparatus is placed at the disposal of the citizens of a specific local community with a characteristically marginal geographical location, so that communal use may be made of the facilities available. The purpose of the ICSC is to counteract some geographically determined disadvantages under which the local community involved has been forced to suffer, whether they have been of an economic, educational or cultural nature, or have concerned employment, services, or other infrastructural facilities.

Within the limits of a definition of this kind the various ICSCs are of course organised very differently. But it is generally the case that all or most of the following basic services are provided in the telehouses:

1 **An information service is available** to the local population, with access to municipal information, business information, library catalogues, and other national and international databases.

2 The day-to-day management of the ICSC is undertaken by an NIT consultant, the so-called **telehouse caretaker.** He or she helps local businesses and organisations to get the most out of the equipment available.

3 Facilities are provided for **distance working,** where the ICSC's provision of a number of work stations in close proximity to

each other enables workers to retain a sense of work-place fellowship.

4 **Educational courses** are offered in IT, introductory computer courses, for example, and educational courses are provided by means of IT, such as CAL, CAT, and Open University-type on-line tutorials.

5 **Telecommunications facilities** are provided, enabling local citizens to communicate with the rest of the world within or beyond their national borders, using teletex or telefax terminals.

6 The ICSC plays a role in the **political and cultural life** of its community, primarily by providing rooms and facilities for meetings, but also by supplying municipal and county information, and, for example, by permitting local citizens to watch national and international TV programmes together.

Finally, local authorities in the rural district are improving the public services to citizens in the more outlying areas by using the telehouses as 'decentralized municipal offices', and, with the help of the ICSCs, they also hope to be able to provide more efficient educational facilities for adults and children alike. Amongst other things, extension and retraining courses have been planned, together with open computer workshops. Some of the telehouses also provide frameworks for preventive, and improved on-the-spot health care projects by facilitating close collaboration between doctors, district nurses, home helps and social workers, who have immediate access to hospitals, medical consultants' surgeries, and welfare offices.

At the time of writing, ICSCs have been planned and are being established in three rural districts in Denmark: in Lemvig three have been established; in Egvad five are being constructed; and on the small island of Fejø in the rural district of Ravnsborg one ICSC was established in early 1987. In the summer of 1986, the Danish Government authorised a grant of 11 million Dkr towards the cost of these experiments. In Norway ICSCs have been started in Vardø and Hamarøy, in the northern part of Norway, and in Gjesdal and Forsand, near Stavanger. In Sweden the first fully equipped ICSC to open was the one in Vemdalen, a small village in the rural district of Härjedalen, and two more ICSCs in the same municipality are being established in the small villages of Stugun and Strömsund. The Swedish government has just decided on an ambitious 'telehouse project', according to which more than ten telehouses will open all over Sweden in 1987 and 1988. Finally, in Finalnd six ICSCs have recently been planned in Pello, Kauhajoki, Vääksy, Porvoo, Järvenpää and at the Technical High School in Helsinki.

'Härjedalens Telestuga'

The first fully equipped ICSC to open in Scandinavia was the one in Vemdalen: 'Härjedalens Telestuga'. Not far from the mountainous Norwegian border, Vemdalen is a small rural village with

800 inhabitants. It is 125 kilometers away from the nearest large town, Östersund, with 50,000 inhabitants, and 400 kilometers north west of Stockholm, Sweden's capital.

'Härjedalens Telestuga' is equipped with teleprinting and facsimile transceiving devices, with interactive videotex, and with 15 personal computers. It has also been planned to install satellite TV reception equipment and video communication equipment as well, with two-way micro-link video access to the local university in Östersund and to the municipal administration in Sveg, 60 kilometers from Vemdalen. In all, the telehouse at Härjedalen is supposed to provide the village community with six basic services.

1 **Information retrieval.** The local population can retrieve information from the municipal administration, from the local library, and from national and international data bases.

2 **A consultancy service.** One full-time consultant is employed. He provides a consultancy service for the small firms in the community, custom-designing and/or tailoring computer programs, etc. The consultant is also the manager of the ICSC, and he gives in-service training and adult extension courses in EDP and IT.

3 **Distance working.** The ICSC in Vemdalen will provide local employees with distance working facilities. Living in Vemdalen you often have to travel 50–100 kilometers to your place of work (and unemployment figures are far above the average). But in the future a number of administrative work stations will be installed at the telehouse. It is, however, a precondition that distance working isn't 'home working', but is a communal activity supporting a working fellowship. It is also a precondition that working conditions, wages, etc. are accepted by the unions. Eight places of work have been established in the ICSC.

4 **Training and education.** Even before the official opening of the ICSC in Vemdalen, ten percent of the 800 inhabitants in Vemdalen had finished an introductory computer course at their telehouse. At a later stage the ICSC will offer educational packages for study groups, combining computer-aided training and video communication facilities with access to the university in Östersund.

5 **National and international communications.** All the local inhabitants in Vemdalen may use the teleprinting and facsimile transceiving devices at the ICSC for national and international communications. This is considered to be important for the small local firms which cannot afford to buy individual devices. They can use their telehouse as an electronic post office – sending messages, or using it as a communal mailbox.

6 **An electronic village hall.** 'Härjedalens Telestuga' is not devoted only to business and educational activities. It is also

intended to become a centre for the local community's cultural
and political life. In the first phase, there is interactive
videotex access to information from the local municipality and
from the municipal library. But at a later stage, the Swedish
PTT, 'Televerket', has planned to install receiving equipment
for international satellite television. People will then be able
to meet in the Telestuga's lounge to watch television, discuss
local politics, with on-line access to relevant information, and
arrange long distance video meetings with interest groups in
the entire rural community of Härjedalen, or elsewhere in
Sweden. 'Härjedalens Telestuga' is thus intended to function
as a real electronic village hall for the community in
Vemdalen.

Finally, it is important to reconsider the traditional public
welfare model. In Denmark – and in the other Scandinavian
countries – traditional welfare programmes are in a crisis: an
economic crisis because they are considered to be too expensive,
and in an ideological crisis because they are considered to be
too centralised and inflexible. I think that the telehouses
provide us with important experience regarding a new computer-
assisted, decentralised, integrated, and participatory public
advice and service model.

I am convinced that the Nordic telehouse model can be utilised
in the rest of Europe and in other parts of the world as well.
In Western Europe alone 300,000 villages face social and cultural
problems similar to those of the Scandinavian villages. And, in
third world countries, access to information and communication
facilities on a cheap co-operative basis and in close integration
with computer training seems to be even more important.

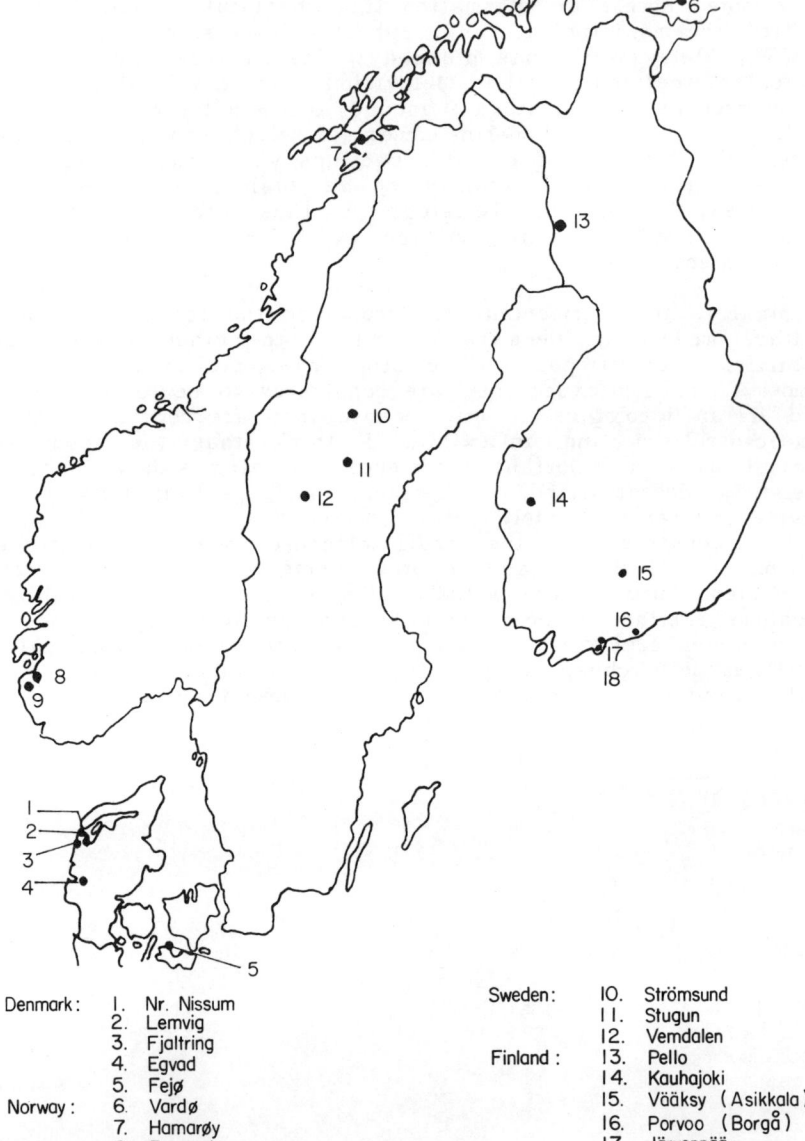

Denmark:	1.	Nr. Nissum
	2.	Lemvig
	3.	Fjaltring
	4.	Egvad
	5.	Fejø
Norway:	6.	Vardø
	7.	Hamarøy
	8.	Forsand
	9.	Gjesdal

Sweden:	10.	Strömsund
	11.	Stugun
	12.	Verndalen
Finland:	13.	Pello
	14.	Kauhajoki
	15.	Vääksy (Asikkala)
	16.	Porvoo (Borgå)
	17.	Järvenpää
	18.	Helsinki Technical
		Highschool

Figure 6.1

Information and Community Service Centres
in the Nordic Countries

TELECOMMUNICATIONS:
THE ACQUISITION OF INFORMATION TO ASSIST
CLIENTS RESIDING IN REMOTE LOCATIONS

William O'Connor

INTRODUCTION

Telecommunications, the practice of acquiring or disseminating information over long distances, is a recent phenomenon in the social sciences. Science, business, and the military have been involved in telecommunications for the past 10 to 20 years, mainly in the transmission of data to and from central offices and remote sites. Business executives have come to rely on information databases for various applications, from charting stock market activities to researching credit ratings (Stillman, 1984). Medical applications of data transmissions, such as remote electrocardiograms, electroencephalograms, and blood chemistry analysis have been used in emergency medical service applications for some ten years (Athanasiou, 1982). The military has been involved in remote data transmissions for a longer period. Most prior applications have been in the area of transmission of data from one point to another, usually involving a large database. However, it has been just recently, within the past two or three years, that social scientists have come to rely on telecommunications to acquire and disseminate information useful in assisting consumer clients.

The purpose of this paper is to document the use of telecommunications by a social and health service agency, the Office of the Older Alaskans Ombudsman under the Alaska Department of Administration. Many applications from this experience can be tailored to a given agency, and concepts from this application can be developed by other human services agencies providing needed services to consumer clients who reside in the remote regions of the world.

REVIEW OF THE LITERATURE

The application of telecommunications to human services is a new and dynamically changing field. Much of the conceptual applications literature is to be found in user-oriented publications, such as *Byte*, *PC Magazine*, or in trade and professional publications such as *Administrative Management* or *Data Management*. Many applications for the human services have to be borrowed from business or medical applications, either through the use of templates (for Lotus, 1,2, 3, dBase III, etc.) or through the process of adaptation of design components.

There are a number of new products for the educational market, especially higher education (Tate and Kressel, 1983). Elementary education has significantly benefited from the explosion in educational software through application designs promoted by the introduction of microcomputers into the schools.

However, much of the human services software has been
devoted to case management, fiscal and program accountability,
and client tracking schemes. Few applications have been
provided for human service agencies utilizing telecommunications
in the acquisition and management of information (Schwartz,
1984). Exceptions to this have been in the field of law. Many of
the available software packages, and the databases that are
currently on-line, are for the legal community.

A recent phenomenon which poses great potential for human
service agencies is the proliferation of electronic bulletin boards
operated by dedicated, often private individuals, to promote the
exchange of ideas and concepts between various human service
disciplines, such as medicine, gerontology, social work, legal
services, and agencies providing services to the handicapped and
disabled client. Electronic bulletin boards allow for messages to
be left for individuals, or for all who use the system (Krasnoff,
1987). On-going dialogue between professionals or across
disciplines can be easily accomplished. The sharing of information to enhance the work place and the work product is
increasing an agency's ability to provide quality services for
clients. It is imagined that in a few years many agencies will
be electronically linked together in order to share ideas and
concepts, as well as best practices concepts (Groff). The benefit
to the individual client is readily apparent and all of us will
benefit from the experience.

THE ALASKA PROBLEM

The State of Alaska, 'The Last Frontier', is one fifth the size of
the United States, and the distance from the Canadian border to
the Aleutian Islands is the distance from Miami, Florida to San
Diego, California. About one third of the State is located in the
high latitudes above the Arctic Circle. Many clients who utilize
social and health services reside in villages, inaccessible by
roads or rail transport. In some cases the villages must be
reached by snow machine or dog sled in weather that is the
harshest on earth – temperatures reaching $-50°$ Fahrenheit and
winds with velocities of up to 100 miles per hour. Darkness is
measured in weeks, rather than hours in the Polar Arctic. Travel
to a remote village may entail expenditures of up to $1,200 and
two days of travel to reach the village. Once in the village,
information resources may be out-dated or non-existent.
Libraries, serving as depositories of governmental regulations,
policies and procedures, and state-of-the-art information regarding complex social and health problems, do not exist. Isolated
clinics or government agencies may not have the most timely
information on hand to allow an investigator the ability to
research a problem and seek a resolution.

An ombudsman serving in the Polar Arctic faces many
difficulties, since (s)he must rely on information as a tool for
resolving problems for clients. Was medical treatment afforded
the client in accord with existing practice? Did a government
agent, relying on information at hand in the village, make a
decision to withhold a benefit or entitlement in keeping with

government regulations? Was the chemical used to line a potable water tank non-toxic? Did the government agent interpret state or federal laws or regulations in accordance with the latest legal codification? Which agency has jurisdiction over a given matter? Each of these questions requires the ombudsman to perform research to determine the answer. Access to information becomes a key in resolving problems and providing assistance to a client.

ACCESS TO INFORMATION

Social and health sciences practitioners depend on information as a tool to the delivery of services. The ability to gain access to information upon which to make an informed decision is critical to many occupations if services are to be delivered in accordance with state-of-the-art techniques. In many instances, the information necessary to make an informed decision may reside in a regional library, hundreds or thousands of miles from the point where the information is needed. An ombudsman must also have access to experts in many different disciplines. Perhaps a chemist is needed to answer questions relative to an investigation, or a geologist, or a medical doctor, or a government agent. The ombudsman must have an accessible repertoire of collateral contacts who can provide expert opinions on many different subject areas so as to determine the questions to research or translate the data acquired into something meaningful to the ombudsman.

In Alaska, the ombudsman utilizes telecommunications to maintain contact with the home office, to access the State Legislative Affairs computerized information system (ALECSYS), to access Dialog Information Services, Inc. in Palo Alto, California with over 300 databases on subjects from Anthropology to Zoology, to access the federal regional office located in Washington State to make inquiries regarding federal programs, and with the Source Telecommunications Services, Inc. in McClean, Virginia, to access collateral contacts in other disciplines, such as law, medicine, and others in the social and health sciences, as well as to access news services such as United Press International, Washington Post, and the Associated Press. The University of Alaska computer network (UACN) which links Anchorage, Fairbanks, and Juneau campus libraries can be accessed so that any publication in the library system can be researched and the status of publication availability can be determined. In addition, medical, social work and specialized publications, journals, and trade association publications can be requested by modem, eliminating the waiting time inherent in ordering such articles by mail. From any village in the State, the ombudsman can reach sources of information on nearly any subject which is needed to be researched in order to resolve a client's problem.

Alaska has a modern telecommunications network, with land-based up and down links and a satellite, the *Aurora*, in geosynchronous orbit. Teleconferences between the elected and the electorate are held in many villages by satellite. Villages are connected to the telecommunications system by high frequency radio, satellite earth stations or microwave link, or by longline telephone cables. Access to the worldwide telecommunications system can be managed from any village in Alaska by one of the above methods. Thus, the ombudsman in Alaska, although resolving complaints in an isolated village, still has access to the world of information.

SYSTEM CHARACTERISTICS

The ombudsman office, located in Alaska's largest city, Anchorage, maintains a computer for word processing, case management, desktop publications, and telecommunications. The networked system has three terminals which are utilized by staff. The system has a storage capacity of 80 megabytes, with tape backup. A spooled laser printer is network accessed, as is a dot matrix high speed printer. A modem is connected on each of two terminals for data transmissions. A dedicated telephone line is reserved for telecommunications. Software includes Framework II, dBase III, Wordstar 2000-Plus, and several public domain programs for telecommunications.

Field access to the ombudsman network can be accomplished by use of a portable laptop computer, which is software compatible with the main system, and a Scanset terminal with portable printer. A portable computer allows the ombudsman to access the home office, write reports from the field, and to maintain contact with the home office for messages and new investigations which must be initiated.

Training in search protocols, with Dialog Information Services and other information services is a part of the training that the ombudsman receives in order to fully utilize the tools of information. Through proficiency, a search can be limited to a few dollars of computer access time making the system cost effective.

CLIENT BENEFITS

The value of any telecommunications system can be measured by the degree that client problems are resolved in an efficient and cost effective manner. In many instances, clients facing problems could only be assisted by use of the ombudsman network. The time and cost in terms of travel without the system in place would be exorbitant. One trip into the remote regions of Alaska could be nearly equal in dollars to the initial purchase price of the field computer. Clients, regardless of where they reside in Alaska, have an equivalent access to information in the resolution of their complaints. No longer does the ombudsman have to rely on outdated information in investigating cases. Two examples of how the management of information can assist clients are provided.

In one case investigated by the ombudsman, a firm in Anchorage was contracted by an older Alaskan to have a potable water tank lined with a non-toxic chemical to prevent corrosion. A check of the chemical to be used through ChemSearch, a chemical industries database, revealed that the company producing the chemical had two products with very similar names. One chemical was used to line potable water tanks and was non-toxic; the other chemical was toxic and was used to line gasoline and fuel oil storage tanks. In discussing the chemicals with the firm which was applying them to the tank, it was learned that, although they only had the literature for the 'safe' chemical, they actually had in stock the toxic chemical which they were mistakenly going to apply to the water tank. The cost of the database search was only a few dollars and the real possibility of a life being saved cannot be ruled out.

A major housing program was being built in a seismically active area of the state. A collateral contact was made through the Source Telecommunications System, Inc. with a civil engineer in New Jersey, a geologist in a major university in California, and a contractor experienced in seismic construction in Hawaii, who agreed that the area was highly active and that certain precautions should be built into the design of the housing complex for the safety of residents. A local civil engineer who reviewed the data from the collateral contacts agreed that the area required safeguards to prevent a catastrophe.

Many similar cases could be cited in which the ombudsman was able to accomplish his task to better the client's life through the use of telecommunications.

A federal mandate of the ombudsman program is to monitor local, state and federal legislation, policies and procedures which affect older persons. New regulations involving the Social Security Administration were reviewed through access to the Washington Post news service acquired through the Source.

The National Association of State Units on Aging's 'AgeNet', operated through Wayne State University in Detroit, has been accessed to share new case management ideas, software, and best-use ideas between various ombudsman programs nationwide. This type of collaboration has been vital in maintaining a cohesiveness between ombudsman programs and a sharing of information which ultimately benefits a client.

Modern technology becomes a tool for the benefit of the client, in allowing more clients to be better served in less time, and cost efficiency which had not been accomplished in the past prior to the advent of telecommunications.

SUMMARY AND CONCLUSION

The geographic vastness of the State of Alaska requires a telecommunications system that allows the ombudsman instantaneous access to vital information in order to operate a cost effective system of complaint investigation and resolution for clients. Transportation between the main office and the villages scattered throughout the State is extremely costly and would impair the effectiveness of the office if return trips had to be made after research was accomplished. Modern telecommunications techniques are a tool of the ombudsman which allows him to accomplish the varied work that must be done to benefit clients.

As the snow machine slowly replaces the dog team as a mode of transportation in the Polar Arctic, technology in the management of information is evolving. A small, portable computer can be a cost effective means of acquiring information from around the world so that a client, regardless of how isolated their residence, has the same opportunity to have their complaint investigated and resolved.

Alaska is a land of dichotomy: a place on this planet where people from a culture whose ancestors crossed the Bering Land Bridge share the wind with the emerging technology of tomorrow. It is a land where a high technology earth station silently stands amid a herd of wandering caribou. A land where state-of-the-art technology serves to equalize those factors which have in the past made life on the 'Last Frontier' a pioneer effort of heroic proportions.

REFERENCES

Athanasiou, R. (1982). 'Micros in the Emergency Department'. *Interface Age*, **7**(9), 84. McPheters, Wolfe, and Jones, Cerritos, CA.

Groff, Warren H. Personal discussion of the networking being accomplished in Memphis, TN, between social services agencies, colleges and universities, and medical facilities. Shelby State Community College, Memphis, TN.

Krasnoff, Barbara (1987). 'Wired to the World'. *PC Magazine*, **6**(9). Ziff-Davis Publishing Co., New York.

Schwartz, Marc D. (1984). *Using Computers in Clinical Practice: Psychotherapy and Mental Health Applications*. Haworth Press, New York.

Stillman, Stanley (1984). 'On-line Databases: The Facts You Want Are At Your Fingertips'. *Management Technology*, **12**(7), 58. International Thompson Technology Information, Inc., New York.

Tate, Pamela and Kressel, Marilyn (1983). 'The Expanding Role of Telecommunications in Higher Education'. *New Directions for Higher Education*, Winter. Josey-Bass Inc., San Francisco, CA.

CHAPTER 7

Systems Design and Development

The challenges of information technology system design and development in the human services is probably the most critical of the many difficulties experienced in the transfer of these technologies. Presumably many of the difficulties lie in the fact that human service professionals are not typically competent in technical areas of system design and development and, in fact, may have chosen the human services as a profession precisely because of their proclivities towards human process and its problems, rather than interests in electronics, flowcharting, or machines. However, a singular truth of the matter is that one of the significant powers of information technologies is unlocked when it can be used to support human process and the resolution of human problems. That use of information technologies is properly the concern of human service workers.

There are a variety of types of system which are under design and development in the human services today. These range from devices utilized by handicapped persons, to educational learning devices, to large organizational systems in use by public welfare agencies in the various countries. In this chapter, we have chosen to focus upon examples of the design and development of systems useful for supporting changes in human service practice, particularly those which may be valuable across cultures. For example, Homer and Schoech's presentation forwards a theoretical view from an English perspective, and it is one that has been tested and found successful in training social workers at the University of Denver's Graduate School of Social Work in the United States for four years. Homer argues that human service professionals can be trained in system design and development by using a prototyping methodology and fourth generation languages. The benefits are many. Among them is that human service professionals can experience true technology transfer, rather than totally relying upon mysterious, scarce, and ultimately inadequate technical support. In short, it is a practical strategy that empowers the human service worker. At the University of Denver, students learning the prototyping methodologies have often changed the manner in which local agencies do their work by undertaking the construction of small, manageable prototypes. In general, human service workers may not immediately use their technical knowledge in their positions, but they will understand the application of it, can control and lead the building of information resources in their organization, and can promote the meaningful application of information technologies in their profession. Since system design and development skills demand systematic, critical thinking, the mastery of them can also contribute to the learner's overall human service practice skills.

Miller and Cordingley pursue the relationship between technical 'know-how' and professional skills in one area where a creative working partnership is vital - the development of expert systems for application in the human services. Their paper, called 'Structuring Initial Conversations on Expert Systems between Social Work Staff and Software Engineers', reports a very down-to-earth experiment in opening up meaningful contact between the two groups. The strength of the paper lies in its tactical depth. The theory of expert system design, through the interaction of experts in the professional topic and program writing, is not complex. The practical task of getting them together, overcoming mutual suspicions, establishing an effective medium of communication, and structuring the timetable for joint working, needs the detailed and careful handling Miller and Cordingley give it.

Witkin suggests that effective software can be designed to address treatment and facilitation needs. He stresses the compatibility between human factor approaches in software design and the knowledge base of the social and behavioral sciences. Witkin's is an encouraging review of the general nature of software design. In a more specialized approach Schoech comments on the role of expert systems in the human services. His paper on expert system development and design (in the linked presentation with Homer), though focusing upon expert systems, lists problems and issues which can be generally applied to most system development and design areas, and across all cultures, in the human services today. There are problems and issues around funding, engineering, tools, reliability, value, liability, and use. There are problems with whether or not the advances in one country can be usefully transferred to another, primarily because of the cultural constraints of human service work.

A tentative but potentially robust experiment which tests both cultural constraints and cross cultural transferability is presented by Schoech and Toole in their work on cross cultural knowledge engineering in the field of child welfare. The desperate need of technologies to support decisions in the area of child welfare exists in many cultures. Are there aspects of this knowledge base which may allow the generation of decision-making rules which are culture free? The knowledge engineering experiment presented here offers no conclusions, but provides an example for meaningful exploration of the cross-cultural problem.

Yet, from a cross-cultural, international perspective, the materials presented in this chapter will provide little relief or encouragement. Many of the human services in the industrialized countries, as well as in the third world, have few if any computing devices, let alone training programs which emphasize the understanding and use of information technologies to such an extent that sophisticated system development and design is considered. The problem of system design and development under those conditions and in those terms is one which none of the work presented in this chapter takes up, but which becomes one of the main themes of our concerns in Chapter 11.

SYSTEMS DESIGN AND DEVELOPMENT

Garry Homer and *Dick Schoech*

This paper is intended to introduce the theme of systems design and development by summarising theory and practice in two key areas, the theory of systems design (by Garry Homer) and expert systems (by Dick Schoech).

THEORETICAL VIEW OF SYSTEM DESIGN AND DEVELOPMENT

Introduction

There is currently a tremendous awakening of interest in computing and information technology amongst the Human Service professions. Nurses, doctors, social workers, etc. are beginning to realise what computer systems have to offer as management, clinical, teaching and research tools. In several sectors within the Human Service professions, there are attempts to evolve strategies for training and education to provide the computer skills and knowledge that are increasingly required. One result of this improved computing education is almost certain to be an eruption in the demand for good quality computer software, designed to meet the precise needs of these professionals. The floodgates will be opened and the computer profession will be unable to match up to the demand placed upon it. Whilst the cost of computer hardware has continued to fall in real terms, the cost of developing bespoke software has escalated dramatically.

Coupled with this mushrooming of demand for information systems, there is the vexed question of the suitability of systems designed and developed by computer professionals for use in the specialised context of the Human Service professions.

The most common reason for computer systems failing to live up to the expectations of the end user is that the requirements and facilities to be included in the system as perceived by the professional computer analyst are often far removed from the real requirements and facilities of the ultimate user of that system. There is a tremendous communications and comprehension barrier. In part this barrier is cultivated by the computer professional (for self-preservation) and in part it results from the complex nature of the technology surrounding the development of new computer systems and the high level of skill involved in designing such systems and from the equally complex processes and procedures involved in the Human Service professions.

The solution may be for the Human Service professionals to be trained to design and develop their own information systems. Nevertheless, service staff cannot be expected to attain the design and programming expertise of the specialist, so a working relationship between professional and specialist must be forged. The solution may be found in the use of prototyping as a design methodology.

Prototyping

Prototyping is a technique that can be used to support conventional approaches to systems analysis and design, or it can be used as an alternative approach, complete in its own right. It must be stressed that only in the case of fairly small, self-contained information processing problems does prototyping replace the need for thorough data and requirements analysis.

Prototyping as a means of developing computer software is directly analogous to prototyping as a means of developing a physical model of, say, a new motor car. The new system is developed progressively. The systems designer can adopt a 'suck-it-and-see' approach, trying out screen layouts and other design features and demonstrating them to fellow Human Service professionals who are to use that system. In this way, the comments and criticisms of the staff who are to use the system can be obtained from very early on in the design of the system (unlike the conventional approach to systems development, which presents the user with a fait accompli). Several different versions of, say, the layout and design of a specific data entry screen can be developed quickly and shown to the user for discussion.

Writing computer programs (in whatever language) is a time consuming, expensive, and skillful task. In traditional circumstances, when prototype software has served its purpose, all or substantial portions of that software would have to be discarded, to be replaced by other portions as the new system evolves and develops. The time, effort and money that this discarded code represents prohibits the use of any conventional programming methodology for the building of prototype software systems. For prototyping to be a viable design methodology, powerful prototyping development tools are required. These tools must enable a systems designer to design and build successive generations of prototype system quickly, easily and with little scope for the introduction of errors or 'bugs'.

The term 'Fourth Generation Language' (4GL) has been coined by James Martin to embrace a new breed of systems development software tools that offer these and other facilities. However, prototyping is not wholly dependent upon the use of true 4GLs (assuming the computer profession ever agrees upon the definition of a 4GL!). Other software tools and techniques are similarly effective in supporting prototyping as a systems design and development methodology. These tools include screen design tools, relational data base systems, pull down windowing facilities, etc.

If we examine computer programs in a typical computer system, we find that the four common activities are:

Accepting and validating data from the keyboard
Displaying information on the screen
Displaying (printing) information on reports
Handling files (i.e. reading from, writing to, deleting, searching, etc.).

These probably account for 80 to 90 percent of the total program. The remaining 10 to 20 percent is that part of the program that is truly unique to the application in question, the part that defines how the various screens and reports and files inter-relate together in that application. It follows that if a prototyping tool is able to allow the designer to quickly and effortlessly handle all creation and processing of screens, files, keyboard input and printed output, then the process of building the remaining ten or so percent becomes a much simpler task.

EXPERT SYSTEMS

Introduction

Expert systems mimic human expert processes to make decisions at skill levels comparable with the human experts they mimic. Expert systems are software programs that arrive at decisions by applying knowledge stored in computer memory to the user-supplied facts of a specific case. Expert system can be viewed as a set of system design tools and as an approach to decision support.

From the viewpoint of system design tools, expert systems consist of three basic modules which are usually written in PROLOG or LISP.

1 A **knowledge base** for storing descriptions and relationships such as IF-THEN rules, frames, or semantic nets

2 An **inference engine** containing search procedures and control mechanisms

3 The **user interface** consisting of development tools, windows, etc.

Generic expert system software packages, called shells, require the developer to load the relevant knowledge, instruct the inference engine how to work effectively and efficiently with the knowledge, and design the user interface. The user is prompted for the appropriate facts and presented with decisions and rationales in a usable format.

From the viewpoint of a decision support aproach, expert systems have the following characteristics:

1 Work with uncertainty, e.g. information containing measures of information completeness and user confidence

2 Selective search rather than linear programming, statistical inference, or algorithmic solutions. Selective search processes bypass fruitless activities by avoiding searches down blind alleys and quickly spotting useful data and promising methods for exploiting the data

3 Explanation about the operations and inference paths used to reach a conclusion

4 Increased learning from use by incorporating new knowledge generated during use into the knowledge base.

In operation, a user or database is queried by the expert system for facts about a case. The inference engine evaluates the facts using the knowledge base and reaches conclusions. At any point in the user/expert system interaction, the system can explain *why* a fact was requested or *how* a conclusion was reached. When one considers that some medical expert systems have the ability to evaluate rapidly the applicability of over 100,000 rules to a problem, the power of an expert system becomes apparent. In addition to reaching a decision, an expert system can exchange information with a computerised client record, present agency guidelines and research associated with each rule used, and print out the total logic leading up to a decision.

The Short and Long Term Future

While current efforts are experimental, human service expert systems seem promising because of the following:

1 They can possibly handle the complexity necessary to support many complex practitioner decisions

2 They can be used where human service expertise is scarce, e.g. rural and inner city poverty areas with high staff turnover

3 They are more intuitively understandable to users than algorithms, and statistical approaches

4 They can map a logic trail which is important for documenting practice

5 They seem to make an excellent training tool.

Emerging Problems and Issues

The following are some of the most important problems and issues regarding expert systems in the human services.

Funding – Expert systems take 2–3 years and substantial money to develop. A standard cost is 1–2 person hours of effort to develop each rule. Additional costs involve hardware, software, testing, validation, implementation, and maintenance. The necessary hardware and software are beyond the capacity of many funding sources. Due to the expense, time and risk, most funding sources have viewed basic information systems as more cost-beneficial than expert systems at this point in time.

Knowledge Engineering – We know little about how human service workers make complex decisions. Experts have difficulty explaining their decision-making processes and often the experts do not agree with each other on what is a good decision. Knowledge engineering is a new science. In some cases, the expertise that is most difficult to represent in a knowledge base may be the most crucial to making a correct decision.

Inadequate Tools – Micro shells are attractive, but too limited for most serious efforts. They often only allow the use of rules when, in addition, frames and semantic nets would be very helpful. Many tools require extensive programming, but LISP or PROLOG programmers who can develop expert systems are expensive and hard to find. Ways to combine uncertainty are still highly debatable.

Unreliability – Expert systems tend to be rigid and brittle. They know nothing outside their narrow speciality, cannot make jumps in reasoning, and make inferior decisions in areas where their knowledge base is limited. In essence, they lack 'common sense'. Testing and validation techniques are still in their infancy.

Overselling – We do not have enough experience to know how valuable expert systems can be. The human parallel to an expert system, a consultation session with an expert, may involve things much more important than expert decision-making and explanation; for example, emotional support, the exchange of sentiments, and an affirmation of self.

Liability – Human services often involve life or death decisions, e.g. child abuse, substance abuse, suicides, mental illness. Developers may be liable if their software gives faulty advice due to inadequate knowledge engineering or a flaw in the programming. Until the courts have decided liability issues, developers must be prepared for the expense of defending their systems in court.

Use – Experience with the use of expert systems in other fields and the use of other types of human service software suggests that practitioners will not readily use expert systems, even if they are easy to use and are performing a worthwhile task.

CONCLUSIONS

The potential of expert systems in the human services has not been fully explored, but as system development progresses, it becomes apparent that expert systems should be seen as one tool among many that can be used in developing systems to support human service decision-making. Other important tools are databases, mathematical models, three-dimensional spreadsheets, and natural language processing. What is needed at present is support to build some of the prototype efforts into usable systems.

STRUCTURING INITIAL CONVERSATIONS ON EXPERT SYSTEMS BETWEEN SOCIAL WORK STAFF AND SOFTWARE ENGINEERS

Clive Miller and *Elizabeth S. Cordingley*

INTRODUCTION

Human services are under increasing pressure. It is a pressure felt across the field, but recent events in the UK have focused attention on social services. Where they had primarily provided care and support, they are now seen as guardians of the public safety. Staff are expected to protect potential victims and undertake preventative monitoring. This paper reports initial work exploring the potential for using expert systems to support staff working with child abuse cases. It focuses on how best to structure initial conversations on expert systems between social work staff and software engineers.

The Context - Non-Accidental Injury

The difficulties experienced by social workers are particularly acute in the non-accidental injury (NAI) aspect of child abuse work. The widely publicised deaths of abused young children and recently reported statistics indicating the large numbers of children reporting abuse through facilities such as CHILDLINE has created enormous pressure to provide extra support and increased vigilance. The equally widely publicised number of children taken in to care in Cleveland following medical examinations and diagnosis of sexual abuse, has increased public concern over protection of parental rights. Social workers are among the professionals in the middle, making difficult decisions in situations which are far from clear cut.

Support of the right kind and at the right time for social workers would be welcome. The possibility that new technology could provide that help has been seen by some practitioners as worth exploring. This willingness is significant in the social services world where the new technology debate is as often about whether computer systems are appropriate at all in their professional work as it is about how computers can best be used.

The Tool - Expert Systems

Parallel and equally fundamental debates are taking place in the computer world which is under pressure and has had its public failures in the past. The public has mixed expectations of the work of computer professionals. For example, computers are seen as both all powerful and severely limited. They are seen as being incredibly quick and accurate, yet they are blamed for most delays and mistakes in the human-computer systems. Software engineers must understand what a new system will be expected to do and how it will fit in with the work of the humans who use or are supported by it before they can build or adopt an appropriate system. This fundamental requirement is nowhere more important than in the development of expert systems, but a number of basic questions about expert systems have yet to be resolved. There is no consensus about what expert systems should be like, where they should be used, or for whom they should be designed. There have been widely publicised diagnostic expert systems in the field of medicine, but few expert systems in UK social services agencies. The prototype developments at Powys Social Services Department (SSD) of expert systems for allocating Home Helps and Extra Care Housing is an interesting exception. The possiblity that there are aspects of social work for which an expert system is appropriate is worth exploring and some software engineers are willing to do so. This willingness is significant in the computer world where tractable problems are usually seen to be ones with a clear solution path and certain answers - hardly the best description of the problems faced in social work practice.

The Method - Initial Conversations

Even though software engineers and social work practitioners are ready to talk together, they come from such different worlds that it is difficult for them to engage in fruitful dialogue. To discover whether expert systems could be of use and would be acceptable to social workers dealing with cases of suspected NAI, software engineers need to learn about the problems of dealing with NAI and social workers need to appreciate the limitations and potential benefits of expert systems. To this end, a series of three half-day meetings was arranged. These meetings provided the opportunity and the structure for initial conversations, so that professionals in both worlds could make informed judgements and recommendations about whether to proceed and, if so, in what direction to do so.

CONVENTIONAL WIDSOM

The conversations were not held in a vacuum. The public debates generated a body of conventional wisdom which served as the backdrop to the conversations and could not be ignored. It is important to be aware of some of the conventional arguments for and against using expert systems in this context. The conventional wisdom served both to support and to undermine the case for using expert systems in the NAI work. On the up side was the recognised value of expert support and awareness that some features of NAI work lent themselves to this kind of support. On the down side were the perceived inability and inappropriateness of computer systems to support such critical and sensitive human-oriented work.

The Up Side of Expert Support for NAI

What Experts Have to Offer

Support from human experts can be invaluable and quite different from the pre-set offering of textbooks or conventional computer systems. Human experts can make creative leaps, explain their reasoning and handle uncertainty. If computer systems could get close to this kind of help they could make a major contribution.

Creative Leaps – Experts will often vary the questions they ask when giving advice depending on the initial information they are given. They adapt to the situation they are addressing and the person to whom they are speaking. From accumulated experience comes the flexibility and ability to make creative leaps from few pieces of seemingly unrelated information to a conclusion which might give an appropriate outcome. The ability to recognise a pattern that suggests a justifiable and safe shortcut is a hallmark of the expert.

Explaining reasoning behind conclusions – Experts not only know the safe shortcuts through problems, but they can also explain the way they come to their conclusions. People they advise and other experts can scrutinise the reasoning and, to the extent that they understand what is involved, are able to decide how well it suits their problem. In human discourse we often ask: 'Why do you want to know that?', or 'How did you reach this conclusion?'. Experts can answer both those questions, and if they are good they will do it in terms we can understand.

Handling uncertainty – Real problems rarely come in well defined packages with clear evidence for and against various possible solutions. Solutions are often far from obvious. A major feature of expertise is the ability to handle uncertain and/or unclear information in coming to useful conclusions.

Aspects of NAI Work that Lend Themselves to Such Support

A part of the child abuse work, suspected non-accidental injury (NAI), is an area of social work practice with characteristics which suggest that computer systems, especially expert systems, may be of some use. There is a need to sift uncertain information; to stand back from emotionally charged settings; and a need to keep track of the action.

Sifting uncertain information – At any one stage in an NAI investigation some of the information required for action or plans is either missing or incomplete. The seriousness of the problem and the gravity of the decisions means great care must be taken in weighing the available evidence. This, in itself, is a skilled task. Often skilled help is not readily available to help workers make effective decisions. Help in the form of an expert system might go some way towards filling this gap.

Standing back in emotionally charged settings – The experience of discovering a suspected abused child rightly produces strong emotional reactions. Staying calm and carefully producing well thought out plans requires some support. Being talked through a case by a computer may be one way of providing that support. Knowing the computer is remembering answers to its questions, is checking out the logic of decisions, and can produce an outline report at the end of the consultation is often a great relief. It does not take away the worker's decision-making powers and responsibility. It does provide an emotionally immune sounding board for testing out or thinking through plans.

Keeping track of the action – Even the best supervisor faced with a number of tricky cases finds it difficult to keep track of the action. Time has to be spent in supervision getting back up to date and remembering how the thinking on the case has changed over time and why. This is inevitably error-prone. The ability of an expert system to store the results of past consultations and to allow users to test out alternative plans is a useful support to supervision.

The Down Side of Expert Systems

Although expert systems may have potential as aids to child abuse practice, it is also possible to argue that they will be of no use. They are mechanistic, might not be used and there are major ethical objections to be considered.

Mechanisation of Caring

Anything that gets in the way of workers working directly with the main actors in a child abuse case is likely to be seen as an obstacle. Sitting down talking to an impersonal computer rather than a supervisor is one such obstacle. It denies the emotional impact of the case and deludes the worker into believing that 'understanding the facts' is all.

It Won't be Used

It could be that even if expert systems are seen to be useful they won't be used. Good practice dictates that workers must make space to plan and expert systems can help formulate those plans. Without this space it is easy to misjudge one's actions. Making space for planning is a sign of an experienced and skilled worker. However, it is the inexperienced and less skilled worker who may be the target user of the expert system. It is exactly these workers who find it most difficult to sit down and plan. It is even less likely they will use a computer terminal as an aid. So it is not a matter of whether of not the system could be useful. The danger is that it will not be used by those whom it could help the most.

Major Ethical Objections

The gravity of suspected child abuse means that ethical considerations must weigh heavy. Anything that could mislead a worker or lead the worker to opt out of ethical responsibility is to be avoided. Expert systems are only as good as the experts who create them, but they convey an authoritativeness that may be unwarranted. No-one is infallible in the area of child abuse. Any system is bound, sooner or later, either to omit to ask vital questions or to draw a wrong conclusion. Where a practitioner might challenge the decision of a human expert, they might not challenge the decision of a computer system. Ethical considera-

tions would therefore suggest that expert systems are too
dangerous to be used. A similar argument can be made about
workers becoming so dependent on the system's advice that they
cease to feel accountable for their actions and fall back on the
excuse: 'Well the system told me . . .'. This opting out of
ethical responsibility, even if the system is providing good
advice, is to be avoided at all costs.

Towards Resolution of the Issue

The conventional widsom underpinned arguments for and against
the use of expert systems in NAI aspect of child abuse work.
Arguments on both sides seemed strong. One way forward was to
ask practitioners their opinions. If, on being given an
opportunity to explore the potential of expert systems, they
advised against development, it would have the merit of being a
potential user's verdict. Against such a verdict theoretical
benefits would seem very weak. If they identified possibilities
worth further exploration, subsequent effort could be more wisely
focused. Systems developed in the light of such advice would be
more likely to be of real value to practitioners and to gain their
acceptance. The idea of holding initial conversations evolved out
of the need for finding a way for practitioners to help resolve
the issue, and a recognition that dialogue between computer
people and social workers would benefit from being structured.

THE 'CONVERSATIONS'

The conversations were held between representatives of two work
sectors. These were people with experience of designing expert
systems and leaders of social work teams with high child abuse
caseloads. For simplicity the groups will be referred to as the
'designers' and the 'practitioners'. Three half-day meetings were
held. Designers and practitioners were present at all meetings.
Two others participated in all the meetings: Clive Miller from the
National Institute of Social Work (NISW), who had provided the
impetus for the exercise and was the facilitator; and Betsy
Cordingley from the University of Surrey, with research
experience in both fields, participated as part of her study of
cross-boundary communication.

The overall programme for the exercise was to include:

- getting to know one another and one another's perspective
- building a working relationship
- discovering potential uses for expert systems in NAI work
- discussing the strengths and weaknesses of expert systems
- developing criteria for screening potential uses
- application of the criteria to the identified potential uses
- deciding whether and how to proceed.

Initially participants were asked to commit themselves to attend a half-day session and were also told that if the exercise seemed to warrant it up to two more might be planned. Participants were to decide at the end of each session whether there was any point in scheduling the next. In the event three sessions were held, one each in July, September and November 1986.

The First Meeting

The first meeting was organised to promote knowledge sharing, the understanding of unfamiliar vocabulary and concerns, and an appreciation of the value of the other in early explorations such as these. There was before the participants the whole programme for the exercise, but no pressure to complete it in the one afternoon.

Getting Started

The participants gathered together just before lunch. They were asked to introduce themselves under the headings: my job; how it relates to NAI or expert systems; how I come to be here; other connections I have with others here. The suggested plan for the afternoon was presented and agreed. Then the next task began.

Working Lunch - Informal Tutorials

Participants were put into mixed (designers and practitioners) groups of two to four people. Over a 45 minute lunch in the local pub the small groups chose tables as far apart as possible, and designers in each group briefly explained to 'their' practitioners what expert systems were all about. Similarly and also over lunch, practitioners reciprocated, telling 'their' designers what NAI work was all about. The idea was that the informal atmosphere and the limited time would encourage participants to present the bare bones of their specialities without getting bogged down in detail and make even the most reticent speaker speak. It worked.

Surprise - Naive Presentations

After lunch participants returned to the NISW and separated into their work sector groups. Fifteen minutes was allowed for practitioners to prepare a presentation all about expert systems and for designers to prepare a presentation all about NAI. These naive presentations, put together as they were with hardly time to think, allowed the newcomers to each work sector to put on record their post-lunch understandings without fear of being ridiculed. Needless to say, the presentations were full of gaps and misconceptions; but the richness of the presentations and the amount that did ring true to the presentors' lunch-time tutors built confidence that others had been listening and trying to understand. After the NAI presentation by designers, practitioners tenderly clarified points that seemed to have been misunderstood and filled in some gaps. After the expert systems presentation by practitioners, designers did the same. During the clarification stage, practitioners from different social services departments had a chance for the first time in the day to hear one another's professional view of NAI work. They began to explore areas of consensus and of difference.

Generate List of Potential Uses of Expert Systems in NAI

The task began with silent and individual contemplation. Each participant was given slips of paper and asked to write down the possibilities that came to mind. This technique gives participants an equal 'hearing' and allows them to follow different lines of thought. Ideas can later be sorted in different ways, generating different systems of categories, when that is wanted, or a communal set of categories when that is best.

On this occasion, practitioners had expressed some of their contributions in the form of questions and did so even more when the slips were read out and ideas were written on a wall chart for all to see and discuss. The discussion turned into a brainstorming session which allowed people to feed directly off one another's ideas in identifying potential uses. Team leaders brainstormed the questions with the computer personnel asking some clarifying questions on the back of the brainstorm information. The reformulated method for this part of the programme consumed the bulk of the rest of the first meeting.

What emerged was that although cases differ, it is possible to identify the stages through which a team may go in handling a suspected NAI case. At each stage there are specific things to consider, questions to answer and decisions to make. The stages have quite different characteristics and require different support tools. It was also noticeable that the stages were not a simple linear sequence through which every case progressed. They seemed to make up a more complex network. Although some stages needed to follow one another in a certain order, other stages were not so strictly ordered, and the route a particular case took was dependent on decisions taken along the way.

In some cases, the first stage is responding to a crisis. The child's safety is paramount. Even if there is no element of crisis, the team must decide whether to treat the case as potential NAI, and whether to intervene themselves. If not, the issue is who to pass the referral on to, what kind of watching brief is appropriate, or how to otherwise bring the referral to a conclusion. If intervention is appropriate they must decide how, when, in what strength, and with what support from other agencies their intervention should be made.

When a case is treated as potential child abuse, a complex collection of arrangements has to be made so as to cover numerous eventualities.

1   whether to send a worker out

2   how many people to send

3   whispering in the ear

4   decision-making in the client's home

5 further/taking immediate action

6 debriefing (back at the office).

Summing It Up

The first meeting had opened up the understanding of both Expert Systems and NAI. Some progress had been made in outlining the stages through which a suspected/actual NAI case would pass and the questions that are raised at each stage. This work was useful both in briefing the IKBS people but as importantly it helped establish common ground and identify divergencies between the team leaders.

The Second Meeting

The work of the second meeting was to decide if and how knowledge-based computer systems might be of help in the stages of NAI work identified in the first meeting. The programme for the afternoon was divided into two parts. The first provided participants with additional shared knowledge through demonstrations and an introductory account of prototype development being undertaken at the time in Powys SSD. The second part of the meeting was designed to allow the joint application of the group's divergent professional experience in identifying criteria for evaluating expert systems applications in the NAI setting.

Seeing and Hearing about Similar Expert Systems

Two prototype expert systems built using ICL's ADVISOR, an expert system shell, were demonstrated to the group. One system was to support staff who make decisions about when to open or close sluice gates to control reservoir water levels; the other was for use by advisors in assessing clients' eligibility for welfare benefits. The systems demonstrated the availability of help facilities, the ability of the system to provide the reasoning behind its answers, and its ability to provide a number of ways of extracting answers to the same question.

These demonstrations were followed by a briefing on expert system prototype developments in Powys SSD. The demonstrations successfully provided a source of shared knowledge. Points made later in the afternoon were illustrated meaningfully in terms of the systems all had just seen.

Identification and Description of Possible Uses

A second part of the afternoon was devoted to identifying an adequate framework for describing possible uses of expert systems in NAI work. It started with a discussion of what was then understood about knowledge-based systems (a term the meeting had begun to use in preference to the term expert systems) and how their use might facilitate or hinder NAI work.

Team leaders began to put flesh on the bones of potential applications. Ideas raised at the first meeting recurred. However, other kinds of uses were identified: "Use it for checking back - have we done as well as the machine recommended?" "For prompts when using the 'phone, for reflecting when you get back to the office, for long-term planning of the case." A number of questions were raised about the difficulty of providing an enduring and reliable knowledge base even for basic practice: "If you know your (sources of information) are dillies, you don't (build a system which recommends your) social workers to check with them"; "How dynamic should the system be - last for six months - incorporate new experience each quarter/six months". "(Practice) is evolving. It is the same with relations with (other agencies)". These remarks and others suggested a growing awareness of the limits to potential; highlighted the need for carefully choosing which areas of practice to support; and emphasised the need for a continuing systems-building effort to parallel practice development. The discussion produced a useful counter-balance to the expanded view of the possible usefulness of expert systems.

The meeting addressed the problem of boundaries on possible applications. In spite of realising that it might be useful in other settings and for supporting staff in agencies other than SSDs, especially those who referred cases to SSDs, the group decided to concentrate on possible applications for social workers in area offices.

They found that potential uses could not be considered out of context. "There are (links) between what you want the system to do and the language you use and response times". "Newly qualified social workers and locums on duty (both have little experience of child abuse work) - they need the here and now plain English back-up of the water engineer". "Fifty percent of NAI cases are new referrals. Need to be able to relate differently to 'known' and 'unknown' cases."

The group decided that each possible use had at least four aspects to consider:

The WHAT   The event, situation or context in which it would be used (e.g. preparation for a first case conference)

The WHO   The particular kind of person it would be used by (e.g. a social worker who was acting as Duty Officer when a NAI case first arose)

The WHEN   The timing of its use

The WHY   The objective the system would have to meet to be seen as successful (e.g. clarification of issues of the case).

Timing was not simple. There were three periods that seemed relevant: the 'whiz bang' period when the staff was under pressure to decide whether to treat the case as NAI, and, if so, to see to the safety of the child; later when the first critical period had passed, the child was known to be safe, the case 'secured' and short term plans were being made; or even later when long term plans were being made or there was time for experienced staff to refresh themselves on NAI guidelines and for less experienced staff to receive training. Timing also had a different but related meaning. The second meaning referred to how speedy the system was and how long a member of staff would need to spend using it for a particular kind of support.

The four dimensions of an application could not easily be brainstormed independently. The group found they could not generate all the WHATs separately from, say, all the WHOs. The WHO depended on the WHAT and the WHEN and so on. So an attempt was made to describe potential uses in terms of the first three aspects – the event, the user and the timing – and then to decide which objectives it would have to meet for it to be worth investing SSD resources in its development. This objective setting exercise which was intended as a step toward identifying a set of selection/evaluation criteria, not untypically, proved very difficult.

At the End of the Meeting

In spite of the difficulty, useful progress had been made. Practitioners were becoming clearer about the key software engineering issues. Designers were becoming aware of the range of contexts in the single setting of a social work team in an area office. Team leaders wanted to digest the ideas that had emerged during the afternoon, to discuss insights from the meeting with their staff, canvass their views on possible uses, and see if staff thought they would have used a system at a particular time on a particular case. There was a realisation that the group had not been able to get down to specifics in the course of the afternoon and there was more work to be done. Participants felt the meeting had been productive enough and the possibilities of progress sufficiently promising to commit themselves to a third afternoon together.

The Third Meeting

The third meeting was made up of three parts. One part consisted of a demonstration of the Powys SSD prototypes which had been the subject of the briefing of the previous meeting. A second part was to identification and initial trial of a set of criteria for evaluating possible knowledge-based systems developments. The last task was to look forward, deciding what further work, if any, to recommend, and how to publicise the work we had done so far.

Development of Prototypes for Powys SSD

The Extra Care Housing prototype system was demonstrated. It had been developed using approximately two days of the time of a Chief Administration Officer from the SSD and several hours of the time of the Assistant Director in charge of Fieldwork Services in the Department. The software engineer had been able to create the demonstration using about four person weeks of software engineering resource, which had been successful enough for social work managers to accept it in principle and be prepared to consider investing further resources in its development.

The prototyping exercise had been of value to both staff of the SSD and to the software engineers involved. The demonstration also provided valuable experience for both practitioners and designers. Designers facilitated 'hands on' experience for practitioners and indicated what changes would be possible to 'tune' the system to fit the setting of a different SSD. Various members of the group provided useful feedback on the prototype indicating, for example, where research findings such as the validity of simple but effective indicators of 'confusion' in the elderly could have informed the dialogue of the prototype and how it mirrored the model of practice of its designers.

It became apparent that there was a wider range of case types than had been taken into account in the initial prototype and unanticipated variations in the way questions could be interpreted. The case one of the practitioners had in mind when running the system for the demonstration was at the medical assessment stage. It was difficult, therefore, to answer questions about the likelihood that the client needed medical attention in the night as that would be determined by the assessment which had yet to be performed. It was also difficult for the practitioner to respond to a question about whether the client was likely to be dangerous to himself or others. The client she had in mind was not likely to go off the deep end, but if he did he would do a great deal of damage. The dual aspects of his dangerousness were not catered for in the question. It became clear that the structure, weighting and phrasing of the questions would need careful consideration and would need to be determined in consultation with experienced practitioners.

Criteria for Evaluating the Potential of Proposed Developments

Attempts were made to identify criteria which would be appropriate for particular applications taking into account the WHO, the WHAT and the WHEN identified earlier – features one must keep in mind when discussing any application. But even that proved extremely difficult. Criteria such as "the system does not get in the way" overlapped with other criteria such as "the system provides a timely response" which in turn overlapped with "allows staff to do things that could not be done before or to do things better".

Attempts to use tentative criteria which did emerge led the group to consider issues of scaling. Criteria seemed to be of the threshold variety rather than the additive variety. That is to say, it seemed necessary that an application score at least to some threshold level on every criteria for it to be worth developing. It was not acceptable for a poor performance on one criteria to be 'made up' by doing well on another. A great deal more work needs to be done on criteria setting and use.

What to do Next

The group felt there was potential to develop. Systems might not only be useful in their own right but the process of developing one to a prototype stage would be useful in increasing awareness of what was possible.

Several paths forward were agreed. Work done in the group would be shared with colleagues within the departments.

Discussions within the departments would be initiated to see if there was interest in building on the start the group had made. There was a realistic assessment that the lack of a new technology agreement within one authority made it unlikely that the department could take a full part in further developments in the immediate future. Timing was critical for there to be active support in another. Reality had thus crept into the discussions, but the tenor of the group was still positive.

It was agreed that an account of the conversations would be prepared for presentation and publication to let others know the outcome of the discussions which had begun in an atmosphere of uncertainty and reserve and ended on a note of realistic continuing interest. The group felt it important to describe the methods which had been used to facilitate and structure the conversations. There was a hope that this experience might encourage others to attempt similar exercises to explore the potential of new technology for their own work. This paper represents one effort to fulfill that commitment.

But conversations are never enough if they point the way to interesting developments. The group felt that work on a prototype would be justified, but this would require commitment of the departments both from colleagues and senior management. It would also require allocation of resources to carry the work through. It was agreed that a proposal would be prepared outlining a project for developing both a NAI expert system prototype and a methodology for participative development of computer systems for use in human service organisations. This has been completed, but funds to support it have not yet been agreed.

CONCLUSIONS

Three brief conversations do not yield firm conclusions. They do provide suggestive insights. Many of these are about the process of practitioners and designers working together rather than the formal methodology of expert system design.

Seeing it My Way

The methods used to structure the conversations deliberately allowed the two parties to have their say. The use of a third party released the designers from their normal management role. The role reversal technique in the first meeting allowed participants to safely show their ignorance of one another's worlds.

Team Building

The participative methods used deliberately attempted to equalise power. The simple nature of the techniques made both practitioners and designers experts in their use. This allowed a greater sharing and a development of a 'we' feeling rather than a computer expert/supplicant practitioner relationship.

Constituency Building

The conversations were for real. If the participants thought the project worthwhile they would sell it to their organisations. Confidence in the other party and a clear understanding of the benefits and pitfalls of the work are essential. These contribute to both the wish and the ability to explain the project in the 'lay terminology' which can be understood in one's own organisation.

Staying with the Difficulties

The methods used raised conflicts. Some were resolved, others were not. Recognition that unresolved conflicts existed and would need active management is important. It moves away from the perfection model underlying formal method system design to the 'good enough for now' stance of daily management.

These insights suggest a reframing of the normal split between 'process' and 'task'. The work of the conversations was task oriented. The task was not only investigation of the work system and its information requirements but also the negotiation of a working relationship fundamental to the design process. Both are important. Both are amenable to the use of structured methodologies.

GUIDELINES FOR THE DEVELOPMENT AND ASSESSMENT OF HUMAN FACTORS IN SOFTWARE PROGRAMS

Stanley L. Witkin

The influx of computer technology into human service settings and its influence on practice is growing rapidly. In response, educators have become increasingly interested in providing relevant training to students who will work in these settings (Brower and Nurius, 1985; Smith, 1984) while others have sought to determine the current, potential and appropriate uses of computers in the human services (Alaszewski, 1985; Mutschler, 1983; Nurius, Hooyman and Nicoll, 1987; Schoech and Arangio, 1979).

Concomitant with the general increase in the use of computers has been the development of specialized software for human service functions (e.g. clinical assessment) and the adaptation of existing applications to the generic needs of human service organizations (e.g. database management). Thus human service professionals are increasingly confronted with decisions concerning the acquisition and development of software programs for their agencies. Professional involvement in these decisions is important for several reasons. First, the tasks to be addressed by proposed programs are best understood by agency personnel. Second, agency personnel have the greatest knowledge of potential users of the program. Third, agency personnel are closest to the organizational context in which a program will function. They are in a position to predict and observe both specific and overall impact of programs. Fourth, remaining outside such decision-making relinquishes control over the implementation of this technology to those outside the human services.

Assessing the overall fit between organizational needs and the software programs best able to meet those needs is a complex task. While technological assessments are likely to remain beyond the expertise of most human service professionals (cf. Greist, 1982; Nurius, Hooyman and Nicoll, 1987), assessment of non-technological (or human) factors is not. However, despite the importance of human factors to the acceptance and utilization of computer technology, their assessment has received scant attention in the human services literature. It is the objective of this paper to discuss the importance and characteristics of human factors in software development and to suggest assessment guidelines for human service professionals.

HUMAN FACTORS

Human factors refer to the non-technological factors of computer systems (Burch, 1984). It is a part of ergonomics which is the study of the functional relationships between humans and technology. Ergonomic engineering is concerned with how to make safer, more productive and easier-to-use equipment and work environments (Rubenstein and Hersh, 1984). Applied research in human factors is a more recent development within ergonomics brought about by the proliferation of personal computers and interactive computer systems. A major focus of this research is on how users learn and use different types of software programs. This research tends to be inter-disciplinary involving contributions from computer science, learning theory, communication theory and cognitive science.

Traditionally, software development has emphasized technical proficiency rather than ease of learning and use. Over the past five years, however, the growing population of inexperienced and non-technologically sophisticated users has increased awareness of and the need for sound human factors design. Poorly designed programs, regardless of their technical virtuosity, exact a high organizational cost in terms of staff training, low productivity, and negative emotional attitudes among staff.

Most interactive software claims to be 'user friendly'. But what exactly does this mean? Some developers appear to believe it means a program that spouts human-like phrases ('Hi. What's your name?') or a program that offers users a multitude of application options, even if most of these will never be used. Unfortunately neither of these embellishments makes a program easy to learn or use. Friendliness, while an admirable *human* quality, does not exist in computers. The casual use of terms like user-friendly and the simplistic attempts to achieve it have led most human factors researchers to abandon such terms in favour of more functional ones such as 'usable' and 'useful' (Dillon, 1983; Rutkowski, 1982). As an applied scientific discipline, the field of human factors attempts to investigate in a systematic way the variables and characteristics of computer systems, computer users, and environments which affect the learning and use of those systems.

The primary concern of this paper will be with already developed programs or with those to be modified or adapted to agency use. However, in those situations where software development is initiated by the agency's request, these suggestions can serve as guidelines for that development. For purposes of clarity, human factors evaluation will be divided into three phases: assessment of end users and organizational tasks, assessment of program development; and assessment of program use.

Assessment of End Users and Organizational Tasks

Human factors can only be assessed in relation to a particular group of users and particular tasks. Thus, prior to the evaluation of a software program, it is necessary to ascertain who will be using the program to accomplish what organizational tasks. Answering these questions helps narrow the field of potential programs and provides criteria for program assessment. If potential users and tasks defy specification, it is probably premature to be considering software acquisition or development.

User Profiles

The agency should attempt to obtain a general profile of a typical user of the proposed program. Factors to consider include past computer experience, knowledge of similar programs, general attitudes towards computer systems as well as the proposed program, education and job classification.

Ideally, software programs should be geared to the needs and experience of the intended users. Understanding the targeted user group will assist in evaluating how closely a program matches the requirements of that particular group. For example, if the targeted group consists primarily of novice users who are ambivalent about their ability to master computer-based tasks, then it becomes paramount to consider factors related to ease of learning. A clear, intuitive interface and a high degree of robustness (i.e. error tolerance) would be of central importance. Conversely, experienced users can be expected to expend more effort in figuring out the logic of a program and are less apt to be undermined in their efforts by occasional errors or obstacles. For such users variables such as flexibility and speed may be most salient.

Task Analysis

While the opportunity to 'computerize' may be highly appealing to agency administrators, it can be counter-productive if specific tasks to be affected by this technology have not been identified and analyzed. Thus a task analysis can begin with the specification of current and new organizational activities addressed by a program. Word processing is a common example of the former, while telecommunication may be an example of a new activity the agency may wish to initiate. In some cases tasks will combine both old and new elements. Database management, for instance, may include both everyday filing activities as well as novel information retrieval operations.

Once a general enumeration of tasks has been completed, a more detailed analysis of task dimensions is useful. Rubenstein and Hersh (1984, pp.25-28) raise several questions relevant to these dimensions. Although directed at program designers, answering these questions can generate useful information for assessing the fit between task needs and program design.

1   'What tasks does the user now perform?' Answering this question involves a component analysis of current tasks, understanding the effects of each component on the entire activity, and a description of how personnel go about fulfilling these tasks. The best way to obtain this information is through direct observation of people doing their job. This method not only provides data about formal task activities, but informal aspects such as the opportunity to converse with peers. Failure to understand a program's impact on these informal activities can result in the rejection of an otherwise useful program.

2   'How is the task learned?' This question involves identifying
    what information has to be known to perform the task and
    whether formal trainding or special skills are necessary.

3   'Where is the task performed?' Some human services activities
    are performed in an office while others are best carried out
    in the field. Tasks are performed under different environmen-
    tal conditions such as the amount of space, light and noise
    as well as psychological conditions such as the degree of
    stress and the need for confidentiality. These conditions
    interact with the use of the program in ways that need to be
    identified and accommodated as much as possible.

4   'What is the relationship between users and data?' This
    question refers primarily to considerations of data access.
    Information about access locations, procedures and restrictive-
    ness may be useful in program assessment.

5   'What other tools does the user have?' Office environments
    may contain a variety of tools such as typewriters, file
    cabinets, and data collection instruments. Knowing the effect
    of a computer program on these tools will help planners
    understand the potential impact of a program.

6   'How do users communicate with each other?' Inter-personal
    relationships tend to be characterized by particular kinds of
    information and communication channels. Computer technology
    has the potential for altering these relationships. For
    example, in an experimental study, Kiesler et al (1985) found
    that people who communicated by computer tended to relate
    more impersonally and with less inhibitions than those
    communicating face-to-face. It may be important to know in
    advance the organizational implications of these changes.

7   'How often do users perform these tasks?' Frequency of use is
    an important human factors consideration because of its
    relation to retention. For example, infrequent users will
    require programs that allow them to be productive without the
    need to remember large amounts of information. In addition,
    preferred program response time tends to be less among
    frequent users (Shneiderman, 1984).

8   'What are the time constraints on the tasks?' Organizational
    tasks differ in relation to how quickly they must be
    accomplished. Financial aid applications may have to be
    processed immediately while filing tasks can often be delayed
    until a convenient time. Furthermore, several tasks may be
    related in time such that a task that must be performed
    quickly follows a task that can be accomplished at time of
    one's choosing. How the substitution of a software program
    affects this sequencing can be an important consideration.

9   'What happens when things go wrong?' All tasks are subject
    to errors. It is important to know what these errors are and

what people do about them when they occur. Similarly, identification of obstacles to task completion and how these are avoided or overcome can help direct development and assessment.

The development of user profiles and task analyses is important both for evaluating how well programs address agency task needs and for determining their compatibility with and potential effects on users and the organization. These assessment activities are prerequisite for the evaluation of particular programs.

Phase 2 – Assessment of Program Development

Application software programs are developed to assist people accomplish certain tasks. However, in order to be most effective, these programs must be designed to take into account not only the mechanics of the tasks, but the context in which these tasks occur and the people who will engage in them. The activities undertaken during the program development analysis are directed at assessing the extent to which relevant human factor considerations were addressed during the development of the program. Attention to these issues suggests sound human factors design and a program worthy of serious consideration.

Reliability

A program's ease of learning and use will be affected by its reliability – the degree to which it is free from errors and inefficient procedures. Complex programs with many thousands of lines of code have a high potential for errors. Sound development programs will have extensive testing programs for discovering major errors (e.g. errors that 'hang-up' the program or cause the user to lose data) prior to its public release. This testing information is a useful indicator (although not a guarantee) of the program's reliability as well as the general thoroughness of the development process. Thus, at a minimum, it is important to learn what type of testing was done during development.

Second, a program that has had long term and broad usage may have the advantage of being more reliable than a new, relatively untested, program. Thus, it is important to ask how long has the program been in use and in what settings. If the program has a previous history of use, is this the initial or a more mature version of the program?

Third, even the best programs have occasional errors. When these occur, it is important for users to know what to do about them. Standard, clearly documented error reporting procedures are helpful in these situations. Sometimes program errors can be circumvented, but often actual changes to the program code are required. Since it is impractical for developers to implement a change each time an error is discovered, it is useful to know how decisions are made to change the program. For example, some developers may wait until a scheduled update in which new program features are incorporated before correcting errors.

Fourth, a related more technical consideration concerns whether a program has been written in such a way that errors or modifications to the code can be made easily. For example, developing the program interface as a self-contained module may allow for easier modification in response to user feedback (Saja, 1985).

Fifth, in addition to learning about the scope of testing, it is important to ascertain with whom the testing has occurred. That is, to what extent was testing conducted with projected users? Moreover, the validity of testing is enhanced to the extent it simulates actual conditions of use.

Sixth, a sound testing program is not only concerned with program errors, but with how users interact with the program. For instance, what is the typical time it takes for users to become proficient in the use of the program? This information should include a profile of the users tested, how experience level was determined, and what benchmarks were used to determine program mastery.

In many respects the testing process is similar to the assessment of a new human services program. For example, few agencies would implement a job counselling program without first assessing the way it was developed, how it was tested, and its relevance to the agency's target client group. Like human factors research, this assessment process attempts to evaluate, not only whether the program does what it claims, but whether clients can actually learn and use the program.

Conceptual Model of the Program

The human factors design of software should be validated through interaction with potential users at various phases of the development process (Gould and Lewis, 1985; Schneiderman, 1983). This is necessary because the developer's conceptual model, i.e. his or her view of how the program works, may not be congruent with the conceptual model of the user. This situation was particularly evident during the early years of microcomputer software development when programs appeared to be written primarily for other programmers. Not only was the programmer's view of the system highly discrepant with the view of the typical user, but there were few attempts to construct an interface which would bridge this discrepancy.

The job of the program interface is to guide end users to adopt a conceptual model which is congruent with the system (cf. Norman, 1983). It is now understood that this cannot be done simply by conjecturing how users will conceptualize a system. User feedback is necessary. Neglecting this aspect of development often results in a program that is confusing, frustrating and of low productivity. Assessment of the conceptual model can be undertaken directly through actual use of the program. This is discussed in more detail in the next section.

Phase 3 - Assessment of Program Use

Once essential information has been gathered about intended users, tasks and the development of the program, an experiential assessment is indicated. This 'hands on' evaluation focuses on human factors issues as they actually appear in the program and are experienced by users. For best results, this phase should simulate as closely as possible the actual situation in which the program would be used.

Human service agencies can carry out their own testing regimens to assess the human factors aspects of a program as it functions within their particular organizational environment. Once again, knowledge of research methods is useful for generating relevant information from such testing.

Shneiderman (1983) describes five measurable human factors issues which can be evaluated during this phase. These issues are:

1 Time to learn – how long does it take for intended users to learn how to use the program to accomplish relevant tasks?

2 Speed of performance – how long does it take to carry out a benchmark set of tasks? These tasks should be standardized across users tested.

3 Rate of errors – what are the nature and frequency of errors when accomplishing the benchmark set of tasks

4 Subjective satisfaction – what are users' subjective impressions and feelings about using the program?

5 Retention over time – to what extent is knowledge of the program and ability to use it retained over time?

In addition to the above issues, it is possible to evaluate how well the developer's conceptual model, as expressed through the program interface, and the user's conceptual model coincide. For instance, does experience with the program allow users to predict accurately how the system will respond to their actions? Since the program interface is relatively fixed, the user must understand the program's user model (Oberquelle, Kupka, and Maass, 1983). A well designed interface leads users to form an appropriate model of the program (Carey, 1982; Saja, 1985).

The user interface has been described in terms of an 'external myth' (Rubenstein and Hersh, 1984, p.42) to emphasize that what users see may be relatively independent of the internal aspects of the system. Since the users' conceptual model (their understanding of how the program works) develops in interaction with this external myth, its presentation is important. Rubenstein and Hersh (1984) suggest several design principles for influencing the users' conceptual model:

1 The external myth should be consistently maintained.

2 The program should present clear system boundaries of limited scope. No program can do everything and what a particular program can or cannot do should be clear to the user.

3 Program modes should be limited and highly visible. For example, a word processing program may have an 'edit' mode and a 'print' mode in which different functions are performed. Particularly confusing to novice users are 'multiplexing operations' (Rubenstein and Hersh, 1984, p.47) in which keys take on different functions depending on the state of the system, e.g. a control key which prints a letter in one mode and an ASCII character in another. In such cases the program should provide users with a simple general rule which associates key functions with program modes.

4 The amount of information needed to use the program should be kept to a minimum. Overly complex command structures and system operations lead to confusion and inaccurate conceptual models.

Others, such as Carey (1982), highlight the importance of other system dimensions like: providing clear and comprehensive documentation and user training; encouraging system browsing and experimentation; informing users of ongoing processes as well as their current status within the program; permitting users to observe the results of their actions on the model; and providing consistency between the conceptual model and the users' model of existing activities (e.g. if problem solving, the conceptual model should be based on the way people solve problems). Many of these suggestions are based on extrapolations from research in other fields or the author's experience and have not been subject to systematic research.

Human-Computer Communication

Development of an easily understood and positive program model consistent with users' models is dependent, in part, on the nature of human-computer communication. As Shneiderman (1983) observes: "Novice users are unimpressed with CPU speeds, disk storage capabilities, or elegant file structures. For them, the system appears only in the form of messages on their screens or printers." (p.240). In particular, the language and syntax a program uses to describe its current state and respond to user inputs can have a substantial impact on a user's conceptual model.

Generally, people attempting to communicate with a computer expect their interaction to follow the rules and conventions of interpersonal interaction (Rubenstein and Hersh, 1984). Thus a person making a request or statement expects some type of response or acknowledgement from the program. People also expect that information will be provided relative to the current context and that the language used will be appropriate to the activity (context) and interactants. A user who types:

    Get file ajax.txt

expects either compliance with this request or an explanation of what the system did and why. In contrast, a response such as:

    syntax error, abort sequence?

not only does not provide the desired information, but may leave
the user feeling confused and inadequate. The above message
violates the rules of effective discourse: it ignores the
expectations of the user, does not explain the relationship
between messages, is not easily understood, and leaves the user
feeling inadequate, frustrated or defensive. Dean (1982) provides
several examples of how these problems are manifest. For
instance, the command:

    copy fromfile, tofile, truncate,

elicits the following message:

    missing operand in the copy command

Although this message may seem entirely reasonable from the
system's perspective, it makes little sense from the user's point
of view; it violates the user's expectations. Furthermore, the
user is not given clear direction about how to respond. However,
since computers tend to be active rather than passive learners
(cf. Carroll and Mack, 1984), their tendency will be to try and
do something. In this case the logical action would be to attempt
to find what is 'missing' which might lead to further confusion.
Dean (1982, p.432) suggests a better message might be:

    "copy fromfile, tofile, truncate," is interpreted as

    "copy fromfile, tofile, truncate."

    Proceed or modify? Type 'p' or 'm', then press ENTER

This message takes the initial problem – the use of a comma at
the end of a statement – and reinterprets it in the proper form.
In doing so the message lets the user know that his or her input
is reasonable and provides clear response options (Dean, 1982).
    Program messages should follow standard rules of grammar
and meaning. Effective communication is difficult when programs
use arbitrary syntax (e.g. requiring a semicolon at the end of a
command sequence), idiosyncratic meanings, hybrid terminology
such as words formed by combining suffixes with word roots
(e.g. 'ROMable'), and 'dead metaphors' like 'boot' and 'dump'
which originated in analogies that can no longer be inferred by
users not aware of their source (Rubenstein and Hersh, 1984,
p.75).

Error Messages

An important aspect of human–computer communication is the way
the program deals with user errors. The best design strategy in
this case is not finding a gentle way of telling users they
goofed, but to make it difficult for an error to occur. An
example of the latter approach is not accepting 'illegal'

characters in file names coupled with a simple statement of which characters, when used in file names, cannot be understood by the program. Thus, rather than receiving an error message because of an * in a file name (e.g. 'illegal file name'), the user is simply prevented from making this error.

Providing the user with information on a program's current status and its response to inputs helps make the program more predictable and comprehensible and hence reduces errors. In fact, Dean (1982, p.445) argues that error messages should be the last resort. Instead he recommends: (a) "go-ahead requests" (Processing your command will result in the deletion of this file. Proceed? Yes/No); (b) "requests to choose among alternatives" (Send output to the Printer or File? Type p or f to indicate choice); and (c) "requests for missing information" (Printing mailing labels requires that their size be specified. Press G for specification guidelines). In contrast to an error orientation, this approach tends to view all user actions as goal-oriented behavior (cf. Norman, 1983) and attempts to facilitate progress towards the user's objective. Even in prevention-oriented programs errors will occur. When they do it is important that they be reported clearly, in a timely manner and be related to the context in which they occur (Morland, 1983; Shneiderman, 1982). An error message that could refer to any of several activities or system dimensions has minimal information value to the user.

Three other aspects of error messages are consistent with good human factors design. First, error messages should be stated from the perspective of the user rather than the program (Rubenstein and Hersh, 1984; Saja, 1985). This means making the message consistent with the external myth as illustrated in the following messages (Rubenstein and Hersh, 1984, p.141):

1 Unable to open file DSK3: (SYSTEM.FONTS) TIMES-ROMAN.FONT

2 The Times Roman Typeface is not available.

Message 1 is stated from the perspective of the system, while message 2 takes the user's perspective into account. Furthermore, whereas the first message suggests the user is at fault, the second message implies that the problem stems from a limitation of the program (cf. Houghton, 1984).

Second, error messages should provide sufficient information to users so that they can take appropriate action (Shneiderman, 1982). For example, contrast 'illegal file name' with 'file names cannot exceed 8 characters'. The first message tells the user only that something is wrong. The second message, by informing the user of the source of the problem, directs corrective action.

Third, error messages should not be personified. A computer program is not a person and its anthropomorphic representation only serves to have users infer other person-like and unrealistic qualities to it. Making a program 'chatty' in an attempt to have it appear 'friendly' is usually counter-productive. The cuteness of a program that communicates in the first person and uses phrases like 'may I help you?' quickly wears off and, once true limits are discovered, can become a source of irritation.

Help Messages

Closely associated with error messages are 'help messages', designed to explain to the user the meaning of terms, the function of program commands as well as general information about the program. Help messages answer questions like: 'What do I do if I want to merge a document?', and 'What is the meaning of that menu item?'. It is a supplement to written documentation.

On-line help facilities can be very useful if they are designed in a way that makes them easy to use and understand. Help scripts need to be easily accessible. A user should not need help to access the help function! Similarly, help messages that cover or obscure current work (e.g. by temporarily overwriting the screen) often make it difficult for the user to refer the information provided to their current need. Help messages must also be accurate and consistent with the program's written documentation. The structure and logic of help messages should be consistent and the information provided complete (Houghton, 1984).

Effective help systems give users control over the amount of information they receive (Dean, 1982). Users of varying experience levels often find this an important consideration. For example, the author was involved in the design of a file management program which used a three tiered help system. Users had the option of receiving up to three levels of messages explaining possible determinants of the program's current status. Novice users could seek in-depth information while experienced users could bypass these messages and not be delayed unnecessarily. In addition to improving efficiency, the perception of control tends to be reinforcing and contributes to positive feelings about the program (cf. Heckel, 1982).

CONCLUSION

This paper has attempted to delineate several features of human factors design. Human service agencies, confronted with a myriad of software programs, need ways of assessing those programs best able to fulfill organizational requirements and the needs of intended users. Human factors are a crucial dimension of the assessment process. Irrespective of technical differences, a sound human factors design can mean the difference between user endorsement and increased task efficiency on the one hand, and lower productivity and organizational discord on the other.

This paper has argued that an understanding of human factors is highly compatible with the social and behavioral science knowledge base of human service professionals. Acquisition of this understanding will allow more informed and active participation in the assessment of software programs. This involvement can have a positive impact on the acceptance and effective utilization of computer-based technology in human service settings.

REFERENCES

Alaszewski, A. (1985). 'Literature Review: New Technology and Social Work'. *British Journal of Social Work*, **15**, 409–415.

Brower, A.M. and Nurius, P.S. (1985). 'A Teaching Model for the Use of Computers in Direct Practice'. *Computers in Human Services*, **1**, 125–131.

Burch, J.L. (ed.) (1984). *Computers: The Non-Technological (Human) Factors*. The Report Store, Lawrence, Kansas.

Carey, T. (1982). 'User Differences in Interface Design'. *Computer*, November, 14–20).

Carroll, J.M. and Mack, R.L. (1984). 'Learning to Use a Word Processor: By doing, by thinking, by knowing'. In J.C. Thomas and M.L. Schneider (eds.), *Human Factors in Computer Systems*, Ablex Publishing Corp., Norwood, NJ.

Dean, M. (1982). 'How a Computer should Talk to People'. *IBM Systems Journal*, **21**, 424–453.

Dillon, R.F. (1983). 'Human Factors in Human–Computer Interaction: An Introduction'. *Behavior Research Methods and Instrumentation*, **15**, 195–199.

Gould, J.D. and Lewis, C. (1985). 'Designing for Usability: Key principles and what designers think'. *Communications of the ACM*, **28**, 300–311.

Greist, J.H. (1982). 'Conservative Radicalism'. *Computers in Psychiatry/Psychology*, **4**, 1–3.

Heckel, P. (1982). *The Elements of Friendly Software Design*. Warner Books, New York.

Houghton, R.C. (1984). 'Online Help Systems: A conspectus'. *Communications of the ACM*, **27**, 126–133.

Kiesler, S., Zubrow, D., Moses, A.M., and Geller, V. (1985). 'Affect in Computer-mediated Communication: An experiment in synchronous terminal-to-terminal discussion'. *Human-Computer Interaction*, **1**, 77–104.

Morland, D.V. (1983). 'Human Factors Guidelines for Terminal Interface Design'. *Communications of the ACM*, **26**, 484–494.

Mutschler, E. (1983). 'Design Principles for Human–Computer Interfaces'. In A. Janda (ed.) *Human Factors in Computing Systems*. Association for Computing Machinery, New York.

Norman, D.A. (1983). 'Design Principles for Human–Computer Interfaces'. In A. Janda (ed.), op.cit.

Nurius, P., Hooyman, N., and Nicoll, A. (1987). 'A Study of Current and Future Computer Utilization in Social Work Settings'. Paper presented at the Annual Program Meeting of the Council on Social Work Education. March. St Louis, Missouri.

Oberquelle, H., Kupka, I., and Maass, S. (1983). 'A View of Human–Machine Communication and Co-operation'. *International Journal of Man-Machine Studies*, **19**, 309–333.

Rubenstein, R. and Hersh, H.M. (1984). *The Human Factor: Designing Computer Systems for People*. Digital Press, Burlington, Mass.

Rutkowski, C. (1982). 'An Introduction to the Human Applications Standard Computer Interface'. *Byte*, (October), 291–310.

Saja, A.D. (1985). 'The Cognitive Model: An approach to designing the human–computer interface'. *SIGGHI Bulletin*, **16**, 36–40.

Schoech, D.J. and Arangio, T. (1979). 'Computers in the Human Services'. *Social Work*, **24**, 96–102.

Shneiderman, B. (1982). 'The Future of Interactive Systems and the Emergence of Direct Manipulation'. *Behaviour and Information Technology*, **1**, 237–256.

Shneiderman, B. (1983). 'Human Factors of Interactive Software'. In A. Blaser and M. Zoeppritz (eds.), *Enduser Systems and their Human Factors*. Springer-Verlag, New York.

Shneiderman, B. (1984). 'Response Time and Display Rates in Human Performance with Computers'. *Computing Surveys*, **16**, 265–285.

Smith, N.J. (1984). 'Teaching Social Work Students about Computers: Outline of a course'. *Journal of Education for Social Work*, **20**, 65–70.

PART III   TECHNOLOGY FOCUS

AN APPROACH TO CROSS-CULTURAL KNOWLEDGE ENGINEERING IN THE DOMAIN OF CHILD WELFARE

Dick Schoech and *Stuart Toole*

INTRODUCTION

Professional decision-making in the child welfare area is in desperate need of any technologies which can provide decision support. The decisions made by child welfare workers impact a child/family's future and occasionally the life or death of the child. Yet, the guidance for making these decisions is minimal. While child abuse/neglect is increasing worldwide, the resources to hire trained child welfare workers are dwindling.

While extensive research has been done over the years regarding the predictors of child abuse/neglect and the decision-making process protective services staff go through at intake, no research has attempted to connect the predicting information with the decision-making process. Predicting information on the dynamics of child abuse was considered too complex and vast to codify and structure in a way that it could be integrated into a decision-making process. The advent of expert system technologies offers a new hope of using vast amounts of relevant information to provide support to the decision-making of a child welfare worker.

Resources to invest in new technology, such as expert systems, are almost non-existent in child welfare. Since child abuse occurs in all modern cultures, a cross-cultural approach to expert system development seems a logical way to maximize scarce resources. This paper describes the cross-cultural knowledge engineering approach which the authors are using in their work to develop a child welfare intake expert system.

THE DOMAIN

The child welfare process begins upon initial notification of the agency and ends in the termination of activities described in the case plan. During the child welfare process, reports of child abuse/neglect are received and screened, investigations are done, assessments are made and case plans are developed and implemented. The decisions by child welfare professionals are characterized by incomplete information, rules of thumb, judgement, and expertise derived from experience. Successful decisions are expected in spite of the limited time and resources available to the decision-maker.

Child welfare decision-making is illustrated by the case of a child protective service worker in a public welfare department who must quickly decide whether to intervene on a neighbour's reports of neglected children, and subsequently must decide whether to leave the children at home or get permanent state custody through the courts, and place them in a substitute care facility, such as a foster home or state institution. Although this series of decisions involves a very complex interaction of factors, agency decision-making guidelines are minimal. The risk involved in making a wrong decision is great, because each decision impacts the survival of the family as a social unit and possibly the physical survival of the children. Ideally, workers should have access to the following resources and expertise.

1 An expert in Federal, State and local laws and legal practice which impact child welfare decisions.

2 An expert in child protective services to apply knowledge derived from literature, research, and experience to the present case.

3 An expert in child protective services who knows the local community, culture, and the agency, and who can advise on future risk/harm from years of experience with similar cases.

4 An expert in foster and institutional care who can advise about the prospects for children who are removed from their homes and placed in state custody.

Many reasons exist for wanting to capture much of the above protective services expertise in a computer. The American Humane Association (1981) pointed out that between 1976 and 1981, the total number of abuse/neglect reports documented in the United States more than doubled and child protective services agencies are seeing more serious cases than ever before. The high rate of turnover in child protective services workers results in a continual loss of valuable expertise. For example, 24 months of experience is required for a new child protective services worker to become proficient, yet the average tenure in this position in Texas is 18 months (Arthur Young & Company, 1983). Training new staff is a large drain on agency resources.

Child protective services are becoming more legal in nature. All biological grandparents and, in some cases, foster parents, are now awarded legal status in many child custody law suits. Given the legal nature of the process, it is imperative that workers not only make accurate and consistent decisions but that they are able to defend their decisions in a court of law. An expert system could provide documentation of the logic leading up to a decision and this logic can be available to courts and other entities at the touch of a computer key.

The initial decisions seem to be the most important, as Alter (1985) points out.

"Probably the most important decision point occurs early in the process - usually within 24 to 48 hours of the initial report. A child protection worker must investigate the report and decide whether to 'substantiate' or 'not substantiate' the allegations contained in the report. This quick decision based necessarily on incomplete information, often determines the future course of action of the agency and court."

Future consequences of a bad initial decision can be costly in terms of a child's future well being as well as in terms of future expenditures. The cost of maintaining children in foster care can be twice the cost of maintaining children in their own homes even utilizing the most expensive domiciliary services, such as day care and homemakers (DiLeonardi, 1979, 1980). UK studies (City of Birmingham CCRG, 1981) have shown that once children have been removed from their home for whatever reason, they have a high chance of remaining in care for the rest of their childhood. Also, intervention and care by the state brings its own dangers and problems for a child. Unnecessary intervention can cause additional family stress, abuse/neglect, and state care can be as destructive as minor abuse and neglect.

From the above analysis, it can be seen that child welfare satisfies the requirements of a good expert system domain as follows:

- there are recognized experts
- the experts are probably better than amateurs
- the task takes an expert a few minutes to a few hours
- the task is primarily cognitive
- the skill is (routinely) taught to neophytes
- the task domain has a high payoff
- the task requires no common sense (Davis and Rich, 1983).

PREVIOUS WORK ON THE PROBLEM

In the United States

Several periods can be identified in the US history of child welfare decision-making research. During the exhortive period of the 1950s, calls for research were first made. The following investigative period saw child welfare decision-making behaviour thoroughly studied; however, it remained elusive. Many findings were contradictory and no guiding principles or predictive dynamics could be found. The third period was practice oriented in that it attempted to guide worker decision-making based on goals such as permanency planning. A fourth period focused on the definition of the decision-making process with the assumption that a good process would result in good decisions. While an acceptable structured decision-making process has been developed which saves time and results in better information collection, change in decision outcomes as a result of using the process was not substantiated (Stein and Rzepnicki, 1984).

A change in tactics may now be underway with researchers using computing technologies to analyze and synthesize the massive amount of information used in child welfare decision-making and to make this synthesized information rapidly available to the worker during actual decision-making. In 1983 the Texas Department of Human Resources began developing a computer-based prompting sequence to decide how to prioritize complaints of child abuse and neglect and whether or not to investigate the reports. This approach resulted in a model which identified the key case characteristics that most conclusively led to a determination and the value those characteristics could take. In use, decision-makers would assign scores to the various characteristics, sum the scores, multiply the sum by a constant factor, and compare the results with a numerical range associated with several dispositions. The department is presently developing a standardized intake system which can collect the information necessary to validate the model (Decision Techtronics Group, 1983).

A different approach involves using expert system technologies. Expert systems research can be distinguished from statistical modeling not only in the structure of the model, but also in the type of information gathered. With statistical models, it is difficult to use a large number of variables and add and subtract variables, so variables that are the best predictors are used. With expert system models, the number of variables is of less importance and variables can be more easily added and subtracted from the model. While major predictive information is included, other information which shows little predictive validity is also included. The goal is to be able to include the information that experts use, regardless of whether it has been proven to be a valid predictor. Some information may have psychological importance to the decision-maker, not predictive validity.

Research which moves from a statistical decision model to an expert system model is being conducted by John Schuerman in Chicago and Dick Schoech in Texas (Schuerman and Vogel, 1986; Schoech et al, 1985). Dr Schuerman has developed PLACON, a 44 rule LISP program which is the beginning of a child welfare expert system, and Dr Schoech has been testing microcomputer expert system shells for their suitability for supporting intake decisions. Both efforts have progressed very slowly due to lack of funding. Dr Schoech's efforts have resulted in the testing of various microcomputer shells and a 50 rule test system using Expert Edge. The Expert Edge system was used in recent knowledge engineering research to determine the information needs and the consistency of the information needs of a group of experts (Figure 7.1) (Wick, 1986). The effort described in this paper is an extension of Dr Schoech's research while on leave in the UK. To help in this research, MDBS has donated GURU, one of the most powerful microcomputer expert systems presently available.

In the United Kingdom

There has not been a great deal of development of decision support systems in the UK human services. For the purpose of giving a complete picture this section includes DSS as well as expert system developments.

Stuart Toole and Mike Winfield started working on the question: 'Could expert systems technology assist social workers?' in 1984. They first of all built a prototype system in the domain of enuresis management using the shell Micro Expert.

Enuresis was chosen as it was domain specific, a common problem, a problem for which there were few experts, and because the researchers had access to experts in the domain. The shell was chosen as it was the best one available to the researchers at the time (Winfield and Toole, 1985).

Further work by this group resulted in an investigation of four different shells (Toole and Winfield, 1986) and the conclusions at that time were that none of the shells evaluated were of sufficient sophistication to develop a workable expert system in the human services domain.

As a result of the above pilot work the team has been given a grant from the City of Birmingham Polytechnic, Wolverhampton Social Services Department and UniSys Limited to develop an Expert System in the Domain of Child Placement. This project has just completed its feasibility study stage and work is underway incorporating the first 100 rules into the prototype system using the KES2 software.

No other UK work has been published on expert systems in the domain of child welfare, but we are aware of the Alvey demonstrator project being developed by ICL at the University of Lancaster and the University of Surrey. They are investigating the use of expert systems in the domains of Social Security legislation and service delivery.

There has been considerable development in the field of advisory systems for Social Security claimants by organizations such as Citizens Advice Bureaux. These systems have been developed using algorithmic methods and are moving into an expert system approach.

A Brunel University team led by Jimmie Algie has developed software which assists managers to model their decision-making. This has been used in the child care field involving child abuse cases. The system structures and prioritizes influences in the decision-making process, and a mathematical module which uses decision predictors is now under development.

CROSS-CULTURAL APPROACHES TO THE PROBLEM

Combining US and UK research into an expert system requires a cross-cultural approach to developing the knowledge base. This cross-cultural approach adds a new perspective to expert system design, because it involves combining the knowledge of the domain, the restraints imposed by the expert system shell, and ways to make the system culturally free or easily modifiable to a culture.

Cross-cultural design is particularly difficult when many of the decisions have no objective guidance or objective success measures and professional discretion is so important, as indicated in the following review of the child welfare literature: "That workers exercise a great deal of personal discretion and the fact that personal values and idiosyncratic judgments exert a strong influence on decision making has been a consistent finding from studies of decision making in child welfare as well as from reports of judicial decision making." (Stein and Rzepnicki, 1984).

To begin the development work using this approach we chose a decision (Figure 7.1) common to all cultures, that is, can the child be safeguarded at home or is protective custody necessary. It was felt that this decision was meaningful to workers, yet less complex than the other common decisions, such as: is there credible evidence of abuse or neglect?

The approach chosen to make the knowledge base culturally free involved the following steps:

1 establish knowledge which is consistent across cultures
2 develop a test knowledge base which is culturally free
3 test this knowledge base in several cultures
4 establish knowledge which changes across cultures
5 establish ways to add any cultural perspective with minimum knowledge base changes and system reorganizations
6 develop and test the culturally specific knowledge base
7 customize the culturally specific knowledge to several cultures
8 test and refine the total expert system in several cultures.

Several of these steps are discussed below.

Culturally Consistent Knowledge

After considerable discussion, it was determined that the most culturally consistent knowledge was that which established demonstrable facts about abuse and neglect. Examples of these facts are whether a specific injury or illness existed, whether there was a known history of previous abuse, or whether the child was attending school. Thus, a culturally free set of rules would determine the facts of the case with a certain level of confidence. This test knowledge base is currently being constructed.

To handle any discrepancies across cultures when using the facts, the certainty levels of the rules to obtain the facts could be adjusted. For example, consider the rules in Figure 7.2) to establish whether problematic drinking exists in the child abuse/neglect situation. By adjusting the certainty levels of each rule in Figure 7.2, we can quickly add the cultural relevance of drinking to the knowledge base. This can be done without corrupting the knowledge base organization or the workings of the inference engine. If an agency did not value the police arrest records, then the certainty given rules D2 and D4 could be multiplied by a smaller factor. For example, rather than .20 in rule 2, .05 could be used. If local custom was that large amounts of alcohol were usually kept in a home, the certainty level of rule D9 could be changed from .20 to .05. While this method may not work in all cases, we assume it will work in the vast majority of rule sets which establish facts. Additional rules may need to be added in some cases, but since these rules simply establish independent facts, the impact on the workings of the overall expert system should be minimal.

Culturally Changing Information

Many of the decisions made at intake are common across cultures (see Figure 7.1), but how they are made varies by culture. For example, the decision of whether an emergency response is necessary is made in all cultures. However, in urban areas where abuse cases are high and resources low, the decision may be made using a prioritization process, while in rural areas all reports of abuse/neglect may be given the same emergency response.

To allow for these cultural differences, rule sets for the most common decisions (those in Figure 7.1) will be developed. These rule sets will connect relevant facts for each decision. An agency would customize the system by deactivating unneeded rule sets and adjusting the certainty levels on rule sets associated with the decision that they wanted to make. For example, some agencies may go out when the system suggests emergency action is needed with only a 10% certainly level while others would go out only if the system recommended emergency action with a 70% certainty level. Agencies which always go out could deactivate this rule set. If that was not satisfactory, then new rule sets may have to be developed.

For decisions not common across cultures, a different strategy would need to be used. If an agency in Dallas, Texas, needed the system to help make the decision of whether two workers should go out on a case, they may find that the system does not adequately address the decision. They could try to support this decision by customizing the rule set connected with a similar decision the system contains (e.g. Figure 7.1, #1) by adjusting the certainty levels. If this adjustment did not encompass all local cultural norms surrounding this decision, then additional rules could be added. However, these rule additions and changes would be made with the understanding that they could corrupt the structure and operation of the system. The approach is pictorially outlined in Figure 7.3).

ASSUMPTIONS AND VALUES OF THIS APPROACH

Many authors are concerned with the cultural assumptions and values inherent in expert systems (Mitter, 1986; Negrotti and Bertasio, 1986). Rather than taking space discussing this more global controversy, a few of the more practical assumptions and values of our approach will be discussed.

Decision-Making can be Modelled by Establishing Facts and their Relationships

This assumption presupposes that a large proportion of what child welfare workers do mentally when making decisions can be modelled by establishing facts and connecting the facts in some logical fashion. An opposing view would be that decision-making is substantially more than the establishment of facts and logically connecting these facts; for example, it involves intuitive mental processing that cannot be modelled.

Culturally Free Facts can be Established

This assumption presupposes that information relevant to abuse and neglect can be objectively established in modern cultures and child welfare experts across cultures use similar facts when making decisions. In other words, while different cultures may not handle abuse/neglect in the same way, abuse and neglect decisions can be supported by relating a large number of facts common to modern cultures. The contrasting view is that facts about child abuse/neglect are subjective and culturally determined, and the definition of facts would not be agreed upon in different cultures. This non-agreement would not be in how strongly these facts impact decisions, but in the facts themselves. Previous research related to this assumption is contradictory even within one culture (Stein and Rzepnicki, 1984).

Adjusting the Certainty Levels of Rules will not Corrupt the System

The assumption is made that changing certainty levels on rules may cause only minor corruption to overall operation of the expert system. Thus, certainty levels can be adjusted and the validity and reliability of the system would remain essentially unchanged.

Cultural Values can be included without Extensive Restructuring

The assumption is that adding a few culturally specific rules or rule sets will not require the total knowledge base to be restructured and that any restructuring necessary can easily be done in a short period of time.

Values in Expert Systems are Consistent with Child Welfare Values

This assumption questions the values inherent in expert system technologies (LaChat, 1986); for example, the values associated with the logic involved in Boolean connectors, goal-directed search, backward and forward chaining, and knowledge structuring techniques of rules and frames. The assumption is that the values inherent in expert system shells are similar to those in any structured decision-making process and that these values are compatible with child welfare goals. While structured decision-making via expert systems may not be liked by child welfare workers, these systems will not conflict with agency and worker values.

The values inherent in this approach are based on the consequentialist (or utilitarianist) tradition of answering the practical ethical question 'what to do?' This tradition states that an ethical position is valid if the consequences of an action are good. An opposing view is the deontological position held by Kant and his followers that an action is valid ethically if the rules are followed. Kant's view would negate our position that we can account for differences in values by varying certainty levels. Some expert system developers, such as Hartcamp (1986) propose the Kantian view. While this Kantian view has its attractions, it is difficult to operationalize in the child welfare domain.

CONCLUSION

Child welfare decision-making is in need of the support that expert systems may be able to offer. Researchers in different cultures must co-operate and share the scarce resources available to develop these systems. However, cross-cultural development requires that designs be considered to make an expert system as culturally free as possible and that mechanisms be established to customize the system to local norms without corrupting the system's validity and reliability. This paper represents a beginning attempt in cross-cultural knowledge engineering.

Figure 7.1

Child Welfare Decisions, Decision Points and Outcomes

CHILD WELFARE

A process that begins with an initial request for servies or a report of abuse or neglect and continues through the development, implementation, and termination of a service plan.

The Key Decisions to be Answered at Intake:

1   Is an emergency response necessary?
2   Is the child in immediate danger?
3   Is there credible evidence of abuse or neglect?
4   Can the child be safeguarded at home or is protective custody necessary?
5   Is assistance required with the investigation or assessment process?
6   Is it necessary to petition the court?
7   Will the child be left at home or placed in foster care?
8   What are the specific problems for which services are necessary?
9   What is the most appropriate case plan? (Stein and Rzepnicki, 1984, p.42).

Decision Point #1: At the time of initial notification

Outcomes of the decision:

(a)   Referral is not appropriate and is not written up
(b)   Referral is not appropriate for child protective services but is for other services and referral is passed on
(c)   Referral is an emergency and investigated immediately
(d)   Referral is a priority I and investigated within 24 hours
(e)   Referral is a priority II and investigated within ten days
(f)   Referral is a priority III and may or may not be investigated.

Decision Point #2: During the investigation/assessment when determining if the child is in need of protective custody

Outcomes of the decision:

(a)   Child requires protective custody and is removed
(b)   Child is currently safe and investigation/assessment can continue.

Decision Point #3: Disposition of intake

Outcomes of the decision:

(a) No need for continuing services/case closed at intake
(b) Services likely to be needed in the future/case closed at intake pending further referrals
(c) Case opened for continuing services with family unit intact
(d) Case opened for continuing services with child in relative placement
(e) Case opened for continuing services with child in substitute care
(f) Case referred elsewhere for continuing services. (Wick, 1986).

Figure 7.2

Rule Set to Verify the Fact: Problematic Drinking

This rule set can be used by the user (child welfare worker) to establish the relevance of problematic drinking in the case.

Question to fire this rule set: Is there reason to suspect problematic drinking in this case?

RULE D1:   If alcoholism is medically diagnosed,
THEN problematic drinking exists

Certainty given by user = certainty added by this rule

RULE D2:   If abuser or guardian has been arrested for an alcohol related offence,
THEN problematic drinking exists

Certainty given by user *.20 = certainty added by this rule

RULE D3:   If abuser or guardian has been arrested and convicted for an alcohol related offence,
THEN problematic drinking exists

Certainty given by user *.50 = certainty added by this rule

RULE D4:   If abuser or guardian has been arrested for three or more alcohol related offences,
THEN problematic drinking exists

Certainty given by user *.50 = certainty added by this rule

RULE D5:   If abuser or guardian has been arrested and convicted for three or more alcohol related offences,
THEN problematic drinking exists

Certainty given by user *.75 = certainty added by this rule

RULE D6:   IF problematic drinking has been verified by a non-family source which is positive towards the case
THEN problematic drinking exists

Certainty given by user *.35 = certainty added by this rule

RULE D7:   IF problematic drinking has been verified by a non-family source negative towards the case
THEN problematic drinking exists

Certainty given by user *.10 = certainty added by this rule

RULE D8:   IF problematic drinking has been verified by a person involved in the abuse, e.g. child or abuser
THEN problematic drinking exists

Certainty given by user *.25 = certainty added by this rule

RULE D9:   IF large amounts of alcohol are seen in/around the home
THEN problematic drinking exists
(Note: 'large amounts' is defined as: 20 bottles of beer, and 3 pints of the same liquor, e.g. whisky, wine)

Certainty given by user *.20 = certainty added by this rule

Figure 7.3

Knowledge Base Design

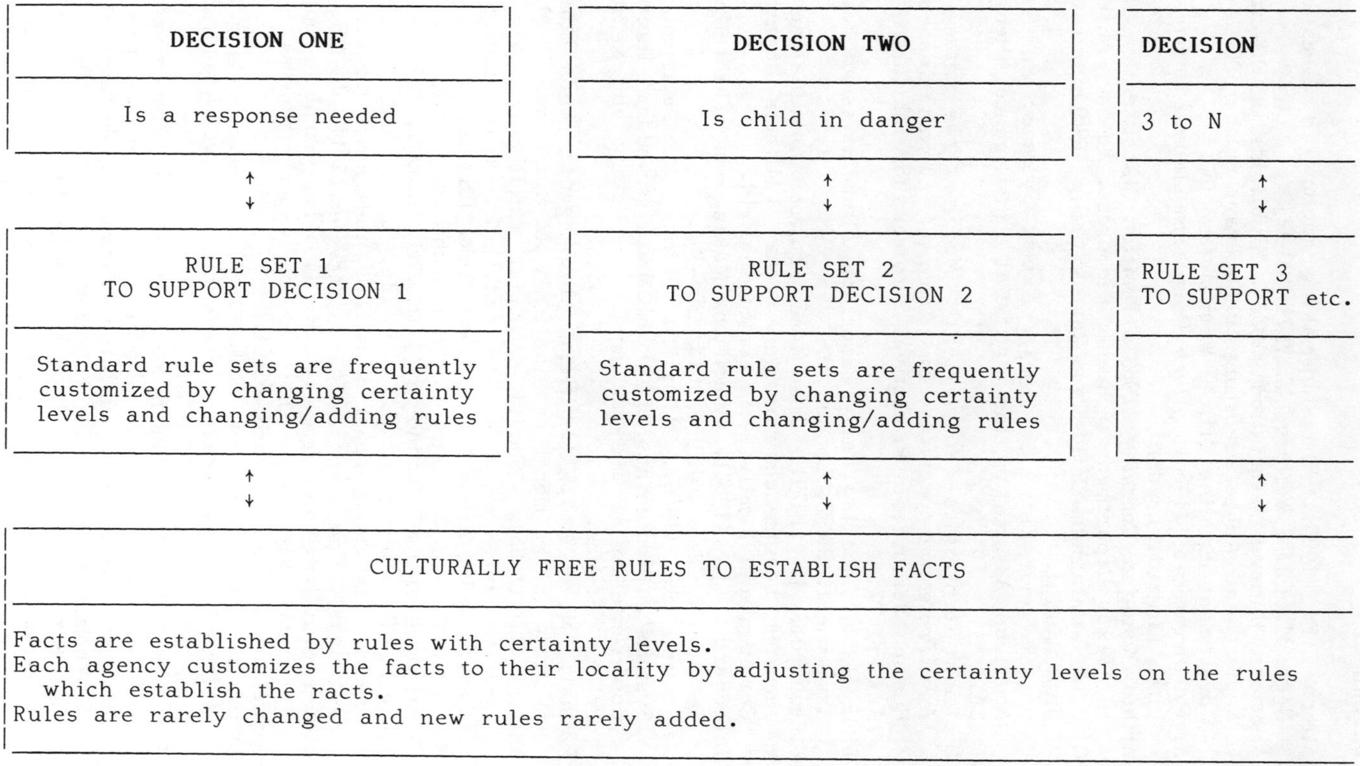

DECISION ONE	DECISION TWO	DECISION
Is a response needed	Is child in danger	3 to N
← →	← →	← →
RULE SET 1 TO SUPPORT DECISION 1	RULE SET 2 TO SUPPORT DECISION 2	RULE SET 3 TO SUPPORT etc.
Standard rule sets are frequently customized by changing certainty levels and changing/adding rules	Standard rule sets are frequently customized by changing certainty levels and changing/adding rules	
← →	← →	← →

CULTURALLY FREE RULES TO ESTABLISH FACTS

Facts are established by rules with certainty levels.
Each agency customizes the facts to their locality by adjusting the certainty levels on the rules which establish the facts.
Rules are rarely changed and new rules rarely added.

REFERENCES

Alter, C.F. (1985). 'Decision-making Factors in Cases of Child Neglect'. *Child Welfare*, **LXIV**(2), 00–111.

American Humane Association (1981). Highlights of Official Child Neglect and Abuse Reporting. DHSS Grant number 90–CA–862. US Government Printing Office, Washington, DC.

Alvey Directorate (1986). *Alvey Programme Annual Report.* G & B Litho Limited, London.

Arthur Young & Company (1983). Position Classification Study for the Texas Department of Human Resources. Author, Austin, TX.

City of Birmingham Child Care Review Group (1981). First report. Unpublished.

Davis, R. and Rich, C. (1983). *Expert Systems: Fundamentals.* American Association for Artificial Intelligence, Menlo Park, CA.

Decision Techtronics Group (1983). *Modeling the Intake Process for Protective Services for Children.* Texas Department of Human Resources, Protective Services for Children Branch, Austin, TX.

DHSS (1981). Working Party Report on Alternatives to Residential Assessment. HMSO, London.

DiLeonardi, J. (1979). *The MAPS Project: an analysis of the families, service decisions and costs.* Illinois Department of Children and Family Services, Springfield.

DiLeonardi, J. (1980). 'Decision Making in Child Protective Services'. *Child Welfare*, **LIX**, 356–364.

Hartcamp, S. (1986). 'Implicit Ethics in Decision Support Systems'. Proceedings of AI BIOMED 1986. First International Conference on AI and its Impact on Biology and Medicine. Mt Pellier, France.

LaChat, M. (1986). 'Artificial Intelligence and Ethics: an exercise in the moral imagination'. *AI Magazine*, 70–79.

Mitter, P. (1986). 'Should Artificial Intelligence take Culture into Account?' in K.S. Gill (ed.) *Artificial Intelligence for Society.* John Wiley & Sons, New York. 101–110.

Negrotti, M. and Bertasio, D. 'The Archimedes Syndrome: Cultural Premises and AI Technology', in Gill, op.cit., 111–114.

Schoech, D., Jennings, H., Schkade, L.L., and Russell, C.H. (1985). 'Expert Systems: Artificial Intelligence for Professional Decisions'. *Computers in Human Services*, **1**(1), 81–115.

Schuerman, J.R. and Vogel, L.H. (1986). 'Computer Support of Placement Planning: the use of expert systems in child welfare'. *Child Welfare*, **65**(6).

Stein, T.J. and Rzepnicki, T.L. (1984). *Decision Making in Child Welfare Services Intake and Planning.* Kluwer-Nijhoff Publishing, Boston.

Texas Department of Human Resources (1983). Protective Services for Children Branch. Modeling the intake process for protective services for children (summary). Meetings at the Joe C. Thompson Center, University of Texas at Austin.

Toole, S.K., Harvey, C.K., and Winfield, M.J. (1986). 'An Assessment of Expert Systems Techniques for the Human Services'. Proceedings of AI BIOMED 1986: First International Conference on AI and its Impact on Biology and Medicine. Mt. Pellier, France.

Conference on AI and its Impact on Biology and Medicine. Mt. Pellier, France.

Toole, S.K. and Winfield, M.J. (1986). 'Expert Systems and their Implications for Social Workers'. *Computer Applications in Social Work*, 3(1), 19–22. Birmingham Polytechnic, England.

Wick, J. (1986). 'Decision Making at Child Protective Services Intake and Potential for Expert Systems'. University of Texas at Arlington (Thesis Library).

Winfield, M.J. and Toole, S.K. (1985). 'Enuraid: An Expert System to assist in Enuresis Management'. Proceedings of Microcomputer Applications Conference, University of Strathclyde, Scotland.

PART IV

FOCUS ON POLITICS AND ETHICS

Information Technology and the Human Services
Edited by B. Glastonbury, W. LaMendola and S. Toole
© 1988 John Wiley & Sons Ltd

CHAPTER 8

Empowerment

The notion of 'empowerment' and its relationship to IT is a complex one. Who and what is under consideration for being empowered? Human service administrators and their systems? Those who seek to control human behaviour? There is little doubt that IT, like knowledge, is viewed as a source of power in society, and there is a temptation for those who already exercise political and economic control to use IT as a form of reinforcement. The other side of the equation is that powerlessness is confirmed by a failure to mobilise IT. The human services are a microcosm of this societal power struggle. As earlier chapters have indicated, the first developments of IT were for the use of agency managers, and this group were able to recognise the potential of the technology as well as the importance of keeping control over it. There is little sign of parallel efforts to put IT in the hands of clients of disadvantaged sections of the community, so that the push to offer empowerment to such people has been left to small projects and self-help groups.

This chapter is about the empowerment of disadvantaged people, but before introducing the papers it is worth giving attention to the remarks made by Edis Bevan (of the UK's Open University) when he presented the theme at the HUSITA conference.

"Relevant questions for debate are: 'what do we understand by power?'; 'will information technology increase the power of clients?'; 'is this seen as desirable?'; and 'what are the realistic and practical steps human services professionals could take to facilitate empowerment?'.

"Power can be seen as a form of domination, of the ability to force your views on others. People can be pushed away from the information cores that sustain power and influence in society; they can suffer from information disability. Empowerment in this case would come where minority groups and service receivers became better able to define their own aims and set up representative and accountable organizations. They can then try to mobilize resources to access, process, store and exploit relevant information and to oblige established interests to take notice and to negotiate. Established interests in this case include the human services organisations.

"A different view of power has developed within the feminist movement; power is seen as an enhancement of the ability to live and to make one's own decisions. Here the term power is not used to mean domination over others. Power is autonomy, a sense of internal strength and confidence to face life. It involves the right to determine choices in life. It requires the ability to influence the social processes that affect our lives and to influence the direction of social change.

"From the viewpoint of service receivers, accepting Human Services can lead to the individual becoming dependent, depersonalized, defined in terms of the client status and subject to expert attempts to engineer a technical fix for the problem as seen by outsiders. How will Information Technology applications change this? On the other hand, human services professionals can help to support the 'right to communicate', a concept developed by UNESCO as part of its debate on a New World Information Order. With information being treated more and more as a commodity to be sold on the market such a right may be vital for the empowerment of the have-nots.

"The new conventional wisdom on Information Technology is that an IT-led revolution is in progress with a new kind of society emerging. This society will facilitate the empowerment and liberation of previously excluded groups of people by bringing them the power of information, a technological cure for information disability.

"I suggest that we need to examine this idea most critically. There is a strong argument for the opposite case; that the new technologies will all too easily serve to reinforce existing power relationships. There could be increased inequalities of access. The rich and powerful would have the up-to-date equipment and software, leaving the rest of us struggling to adapt yesterday's technologies. Decentralization of services may lead, not to democratization, but to more efficient centralized management control of the overall system.

"The general effect of the introduction of Information Technology could be to increase the dependency of client groups on the service providers, and therefore be the opposite of empowering. There is a danger that IT in Human Services will simply lead to the automation of existing organisational bias and create a more efficient network of fixers."

Four papers are offered in this chapter. The first is from Edis Bevan. While retaining his challenging conceptual approach to the subject, he looks at the ways in which new technology can empower, as well as enable, invigorate, enliven and enrich the lives of those with a handicap. His title is 'The Task for a New Professionalism', and as this suggests he sees considerable responsibility resting on the shoulders of human services staff to ensure the proper (in the ethical and practical senses) employment of technology. Bevan's paper offers a theoretical framework within which the role of empowerment within human servicing can be analysed.

In contrast Ames, Bentson and Denke focus with great enthusiasm on a specific project, established in Seattle to use computer technology to open up the world of print to blind individuals. Books produced in Braille have been available for many years, though only a small part of published output is available in this form. However, a modern library is much more than a shelf of books - it has a cataloguing system, a bibliographic database, a focus on local cultural news and events, and many other features. The authors have brought this in range of blind people by developing a computerised text-to-speech system.

Metzendorf's paper is also a case study of a single project, based in Philadelphia. Though too new to evaluate, the objective is to help empower disadvantaged members of the community (in this case specifically poor people, women and Black communities) by helping them to obtain familiarity with, have access to, and share in the growth of IT. The paper describes a project designed to offer hands-on computer training and experience to those who would normally have no opportunity, or perhaps be too fearful, to gain a foothold in this sector.

Cassell and Fitter describe a project which has been underway for several years, and hence already has a proven record of achievement. SPRITE (Sheffield People's Resource for Information Technology) is an action and research project designed to help non-employed people to develop useful skills and experiences. The project works through community groups (five of them by the end of 1987) who are helped to develop IT products which would be unlikely to be found in the commercial market place. A further aim is to make Sheffield City Council's IT resources more useful to community groups. The paper concludes with a discussion of some of the strategic and tactical issues in promoting community empowerment schemes.

THE TASK FOR A NEW PROFESSIONALISM

Edis B. Bevan

The empowerment of client groups requires the development of information systems beyond the confines of Human Services departments. But the Human Services have a part to play in bringing these information systems into being and sustaining them when they are in operation.

Information technology is only one part of an information system. Land (1985) argues that an information system is in fact a social system and that it is not possible to design a robust, effective information system without recognizing this fact. It follows from this that it is not possible to design a technical system according to some abstract schema and bring in 'user friendliness' as a late design feature. Furthermore, as Checkland (1981) and Nelson (1986) both argue, it is not enough to look at the information needs of an existing organisation or set of tasks. The designer of an information system needs to take into account the wider worldviews of those concerned with the situation.

The MacBride report for UNESCO advocates the recognition of a right to communicate, which it suggests is something rather more than free speech (MacBride, 1980). It involves a right to access the tools necessary for communication in any society. Many relevant questions are raised in this report that are applicable to the human services. Where do the human services see themselves in this perspective? What are the implications of moving away from the idea of the client towards that of the citizen? Who decides what is relevant about a given social problem? How could advances in information technology help or hinder this change in worldview?

In this paper I shall look at the changing worldview of disabled people and the challenge this presents the human services. I shall then try to draw on some of the lessons gained from failures and success in third world development projects and look at how approaches that work in this field could be applied to the general problems facing the human services. These approaches have certain implications as to the appropriate information systems that should be developed to support them and as a consequence what information technology applications should be supported to bring about the desired results.

This suggests that an appropriate taxonomy of software for the human services needs to include a category of 'citizen-based' as distinct from 'client-based' applications. The distinction intended here is that client-based systems concentrate on the relationship between an individual and a service. Citizen-based applications tackle the relationship between the individual and the world.

Disabled people are moving away from acceptance of a passive role in society towards being agents for change. This shift in attitude calls for a response from human services professionals that may at times be painful since it directly challenges some key assumptions about caring services.

Some forms of service provision may simply not be appropriate, may indeed reinforce passivity. Information systems that are geared to such service provisions will therefore be seen by disabled people at best as irrelevant and possibly as harmful. From this perspective information technology advances will be judged according to whether they reinforce inappropriate information systems or facilitate the evolution of systems that serve the needs of change agents. The same argument applies of course to educational institutions such as my own University!

Central to the case for a new relationship is the perception that disabled people need to find a voice of their own, and put their case forward through spokespeople responsible to a wider movement of disabled people. Henry Enns, Chair of Disabled Peoples' International, asks some theoretical questions with profound practical consequences. When looking at what happens to disabled people, he says, who defines what is a problem? What are the practical outcomes of different ways of thinking about disabilities? Where is the problem located?

"Who defines the problem. Under the old framework it was the professional. The professional defines the problem and defines the treatment. Under the new framework it is the disabled person who defines the problem. Disabled people themselves set the criteria for their involvement in society." (Enns in DPI, 1984).

This involves changing the emphasis from medical or rehabilitation outlooks on disability. The crucial factor is the relationship between people with disabilities and the world as designed for able-bodied living. The problem lies in the bad fit in this relationship.

At present when the human services concern themselves with disabled people the emphasis is on looking at how much the individual improves personal skills or adapts or adjusts to disabilities. The new goal is to empower disabled people, so that they are "in control of their own lives, in control of the decisions which affect their own lives, involved in the programs that are being planned for them, involved in the policy decisions that have implications for them." (Enns). The one process sees disabled people as clients or cases; the other as citizens with rights.

There is no doubt that information technology applications directly applied to the needs of disabled people can have a liberating effect. One of the most moving statements of liberation through technology was made by Michael Williams, speaking at Stanford University in 1982. Williams, without speech from birth, had been introduced to a speech synthesizer some two years earlier. He said:

"If, when I was a little boy, someone had told me that I would grow up and make speeches to large groups, I would have called him either a fool or a liar. Yet, here I am . . . I can only say this: modern technology has allowed me to release my creative spirit where it can soar free, high above the clouds. Without the fruits of modern technology, I would probably be stuck counting the hours to my death. To some people the synthesizer may be an ugly box with cables. To me, however, it is an analogue of freedom. Let freedom ring." (Cited in Hawkridge et al, 1984).

But many disabled people believe that this individual enablement is not enough, and that close attention needs to be paid to the way that society contributes to the creation of disability. The British activist Stephen Brisenden puts the case succinctly:

"We have been defined by what are seen as our inabilities and are given the blanket label of the Disabled . . . It teaches us a conditioned uselessness, which is not based upon our actual physical or intellectual capabilities but on the desire to make us believe that we are a drain on society's resources."

He goes on to discuss the way that medical practitioners, trapped by their medical model of disability, ignore the fact that disabled people need to make decisions about the overall quality of their lives. He contrasts this to the approach of the independent living movement. In that movement "we reject these definitions that limit and control us, because they do not describe our aspirations in society . . . Society disables us by taking away our right to take decisions on our own behalf." (Brisenden, 1986).

This parallels the arguments put forward by UNESCO in favour of a new world information order (MacBride, 1980). Under the present distribution of power in the world media, what is newsworthy is defined by media power centres in a few of the richer countries. This means that the criteria for newsworthiness are different from that of people in developing countries. Disasters and strife get reported in the third world: positive development initiatives are ignored. The debate on this world problem and how it should be met goes to the heart of the problem of empowerment faced by the human services in particular.

This approach has been recognised by the United Nations in its world program of action on disability. Disabled people are above all seen as citizens; a significant advance in official thinking. The UN initiative spells out the right to self-representation and emphasizes the strategy of equality of opportunity. In supporting this initiative, organisations like Disabled People's International lay great stress on leadership and management training and in building up representative organisations of disabled people around the world. They also stress the need to build up information resources accessible to disabled people, and which are responsible to them.

Robert Chambers, a fellow of the Institute of Development Studies at Sussex University (UK) has carried out numerous studies on appropriate development strategies in rural areas in the so-called Third World. These studies have important lessons for service providers everywhere, and guidelines for effective and appropriate action can be drawn from them.

Chambers analysis is in terms of cores and peripheries of knowledge. Where the wealth is concentrated there are cores of power and these attract a concentration of professionals. It is at these cores that the technologies for processing and spreading knowledge are developed, and such developments are in accordance with the culture of the core.

The core acts as a colonizing and standardizing force utilizing education and commercialization as well as communications media in general. The values of the core swamp the values of the peripheries where can be found people without resources. Amongst the missing resources are the means to collect, store and marshall data to support arguments against proposals made by those who do possess these resources but do not have a local appreciation of the problem. "It is alarming," says Chambers, speaking of advice given by development experts to third world farmers, "how wrong we were and how sure we were that we were right." (Chambers, 1982).

A further difficulty is that the knowledge of people at the periphery of power is often tacit, and much can be lost through attempts to verbalize the information or to formalize the procedures. Ordinary people can have a good understanding of their needs and their local situation without also having the ability to express these verbally. With the introduction of computerized systems the danger is that only the information that is easily categorized will be collected and that this information, being available in a highly prestigious form, will outweigh other and possibly more relevant information sources.

These problems are discussed in relation to the design of information systems by Howarth (in Blackler and Oborne, 1987). He argues persuasively for the greater employment of psychologists and ergonomists in systems definition and design. It is no use designing a system and tacking on a concern for human factors as an afterthought when too many fundamental decisions have been made. I suggest, however, that we need to look beyond the deployment of another cluster of experts. A new kind of expert is needed, a new professional devoted to representing the interests of the citizens, who treats the citizens as equal participants.

Chambers lists three forms of failure caused by gaps in professional perception and explicitly advocates such a new professionalism for dealing with these gaps.

There can be gaps between disciplines and professions. Important areas of study may not be a priority for any profession, so such matters are covered, if at all, only as peripheral to other questions. One consequence is that professionals may be blind to big opportunities. Another consequence can be that matters that are of central interest to the people who have to live with the problem are at best left out of the proposed solution, and too often are adversely affected.

There can be gaps where particular professions are poorly represented in a particular field, so that its expertise is simply not applied. Chambers gives the example of management in respect to rural development, and the same seems to apply to the world of disabled people. The lack of management skills at the grassroots is a prime problem for change agents. It is one of the major themes taken up by those advocating the development of centres for independent living.

There can be gaps where relevant modes of analysis are neglected. In particular there is a need to encourage a reversal in emphasis, from top down to bottom up. Chambers describes this as 'putting the last first'. This calls for a respect for the experience and knowledge of those who find themselves their clients. As Brisenden says: "Our opinions as disabled people, on the subject of disability, are not regarded with the same validity as the opinions of experts, particularly medical experts." (Brisenden, 1986).

One organization which has tackled this problem and built up a successful development strategy is the Institute of Cultural Affairs. Their approach is based on four themes which are discussed in the Guide to Rural Development Projects published by the Institute (ICA, 1986).

Firstly, direct contact between people is needed to foster successful development.

There are many projects around the world which have as their aim the activation of local power and the promotion of local initiatives. Most of these projects start from scratch with little or no knowledge of other initiatives. They learn through their mistakes and find it difficult to draw on others' experiences or to pass on their own lessons. As a consequence the major industry in self-help movements is the reinvention of wheels.

Secondly, most of these potential Change Agents feel isolated and lonely. So there is a need for an information exchange to foster vertical and lateral communications between such agents. Such an exchange would list projects and supporting organizations. It would aim at facilitating the efforts of practitioners to make contact with each other. Lateral exchanges are as important as vertical exchanges; perhaps even more important. The emphasis is on sharing through personal contacts.

Thirdly, in order to facilitate these lateral exchanges tools need to be developed to assist the construction of dialogues. These tools are the approaches that work, that have been tried out by change agents. By gathering together concrete examples in a central information exchange practitioners can select themes that apply to their own situations.

The final lesson is that there are common problems and opportunities for people around the world. The need is to identify communities and individuals innovating fresh approaches. In the words of Alec Dickson, founder of Voluntary Service Overseas: "Most directories record past achievements and present activities. This directory looks also to the future, listing aspirations of hundreds of groups, from 'women able to tackle problems created by male alcoholics' to 'wiping out dependency' . . . so here is means to create a network . . .

an indispensable aid to spread new ideas and identify communities and individuals innovating fresh approaches." (ICA, 1986).

The core information in this directory is held on a database hosted on the ECHO computer in Luxembourg, freely available to all on request. When collecting the data for this directory ICA took exceptional pains to ensure that the accounts of the projects were in line with the participants' understanding of what they were doing. The problem of omitting important tacit information was recognised.

The new professionals could adopt the same approach as ICA. They will treat the knowledge of grassroots experience as valid contributions from those who are experts at living in the given conditions. They will see their task as identifying the gaps in the current views of the situation, and work to set up and sustain information systems that facilitate study of these gaps and actions to fill them. In doing so they will not try to impose change agents from outside the community but will seek out potential change agents already living with the problem. The ICA search for approaches that work offers a model for such a procedure.

The approach to information technology implementation by such a professional will include efforts to ensure that other stakeholders in the new system do not dominate the system to the detriment of the citizens. Co-option by the formal organisation will be an ever present danger for these new systems. Stakeholder analysis is a frequently used systems development tool, but usually the citizens are represented in their role as clients and their interest in the system limited to improving the performance of a defined service. It is important that the distinction between client interests and citizen interests be understood and incorporated in systems design.

Without a wider perspective there is a real possibility that the introduction of new information technology will make no difference to the style of the organisation concerned. It will simply automate the existing bias. Dutton and Kraemer (1980) claim to have observed this in their study of the impact of information technology on local government in the United States. There is also the possibility that the introduction of new technologies will decrease the power and influence of human services professionals actually in contact with citizens; that decentralization within organisations may be of controls rather than of power (Hogget and Hambleton, 1987).

This is important because the development of a new professionalism will need to be established on the existing perception of client service and moves through more client-based strategies towards a citizen-based approach.

Some human services professionals are very aware of the need for a citizen-based approach to their tasks. The current interest in self-help groups and network intervention is one example of this (Pancoast et al, 1983). In the UK there has been considerable interest in the concept of patch teams as a means of bringing services to people in a more responsive manner. Beresford and Croft (1986) in their study of the patch system in

Brighton, UK, place great stress on the need for genuine self-management of projects and the setting up of services according to local appreciation of the situation rather than through official interpretation of needs. They go on to advocate the research style commonly known as participative research. Good communication with clients is not enough, as Hogget and Hambleton (1987) make plain in their paper on bureaucratic paternalism.

To gain benefits from technological changes we will need people in the human services capable of understanding the logic of new technologies as well as the utilization of new devices. We need people who grasp the new culture of technology. With the information technology professionals taking an interest in the human services it is the human services workers who are in the role of clients, and who need to assert their right to citizenship, to understand what is happening to them, to ensure that changes are taken in the light of wider considerations that seem relevant to the citizen, and to ensure that the technology is in accordance with the values of their own culture and with the interests of the citizens who come into contact with the services provided.

Because human services professionals at their best are concerned with people as people not as cases, with citizens not clients, they are in a position to tackle the problem of expressing tacit knowledge in the electronic age. By influencing the development of information practices from this perspective the human services could influence the development of information technology as a whole.

They could do this by fostering the growth of an appropriate culture of technology to sustain the new professionalism. The concept of a culture of technology was developed by Arnold Pacey (1983) in analogy to medical practice. Medical science is the same all over the world. To cut out an appendix or to alleviate the effects of a spinal injury require certain technical procedures.

Beyond this, however, there are assumptions about the relationship between the participants, about who makes the choices, on the priorities selected. It is not only disabled people who have discovered that western medical practice places great stress on high profile, dependency creating institutional care. Any woman trying to obtain a home birth in the UK will recognise the situation. Yet we could have a very different medical practice where the important factor is the emotional experience of the citizens involved, where the same scientific skills are applied to support women bringing children into the world in their own homes. We can make choices about medical practice. Technology practice is likewise a matter of social choice.

Any technological innovation is likely to have profound social consequences. When the technology is introduced changes are easy; there are few vested interests and relatively little investment to be written off. But our experience of the technology is too limited for the disadvantages of the innovation to become clear. It is not possible to foresee all these consequences. Later, when the damage is evident, change is very difficult. David Collingridge of the Technology Policy Unit at the University of Aston in Birmingham (UK) illustrates this through the history of the motor car. A government inquiry at the beginning of the century expressed concern over the serious problem of dust thrown up by the wheels of cars. It did not foresee the destruction of the public transport system and the consequent extra burden placed on the less well off (Collingridge, 1983).

An effective strategy for technological control, according to Collingridge, needs to involve the monitoring of the social consequences of a technology as they become apparent and nurturing the public consensus to reverse a development if it should prove harmful. This is rather easier to say than to do.

Cees Hamelink makes a similar point when he calls for an ethical decision to rid ourselves of the compulsion to take advantage of any and all technical opportunities. "We feel that what we can do we should do. It would show great moral growth if we learned to choose not to do automatically what we are capable of doing." (Hamelink, in Traber, 1986).

The task of the centre at the Open University is to build up a resource base to assist disabled people to participate in these choices. As a starting point we need to find out where the existing resources are, and what initiatives have already been taken. By collecting details of organisations and initiatives around the world controlled by disabled people or which are responsible to disabled people we hope to identify the approaches that work and the resources needed to make them work. We can then make this information available to all those who can make use of it to change the situation, whether they are disabled people or human services professionals of the new breed. We must look to information technology to help us in this worldwide search and to make the information available in an accessible manner.

Making accessible includes the establishment and support of local information networks. The centre's projects will include working with other international networks concerned with development issues that share our perspectives. We hope to link up with many electronic conferences around the world. CUSSNET is an example of such a network. The centre sees its task as presenting a view of this mass of data which will enable representative groups of disabled people to operate more effectively, to reinforce their efforts towards making disabled people around the world equal citizens in their own societies.

Appropriate information technology applications might include databases on CD-ROM discs widely distributed to local information centres. It might include the development of the so-called intelligence support systems which are being developed as part of an alternative approach to the IKBS mainstream developments in Artificial Intelligence. These allow users to explore the implications of their tacit knowledge. Appropriate applications might also include the development of co-ordinators; communications packages that take seriously the need to develop communicative competence by participants in an information system. Extremely interesting work on co-ordinators in the field of management is being done by Winograd and Flores (1986), and this could be most relevant to the management of wider communications systems. The need to foster communicative competence is a key concept in any appropriate technology practice.

As part of a university we will, of course, need to try to live up to the standards of the new professionalism outlined in this paper. We are just as vulnerable as any human services department to accusations of dependency creation, data mining and paternalism. Like the human services we can only contribute to the development of citizen-based information systems that are responsive to user needs. We cannot create them; but by adopting an appropriate technology practice we can help to foster them.

REFERENCES

Beresford, P. and Croft, S. (1986). 'Whose Welfare: Private Care or Public Service?' Lewis Cohen Urban Studies Centre, Brighton Polytechnic, Brighton, UK.

Blackler, F. and Oborne, D. (1987). 'Information Technology and People: Designing for the Future'. British Psychological Society.

Brisenden, S. (1986). 'Independent Living and the Medical Model of Disability. Disability, Handicap and Society, 1(2), 176–177.

Chambers, R. (1982). Rural Development: Putting the Last First. Longman, London.

Checkland, P. (1981). Systems Thinking, Systems Practice. John Wiley & Sons, Chichester.

Collingridge, D. (1983). The Social Control of Technology. Open University Press, Milton Keynes, UK.

DPI, (1984). 'The Winds of Change: Partnership in Development'. Proceedings of the Disabled Peoples' International Symposium on Development. Kingston, Jamaica.

Dutton, W.H., and Kraemer (1980). 'Automating Bias'. Society, 17(2).

Hawkridge, D., Vincent, T., and Hales, G. (1984). New Information Technology in the Education of Disabled Children and Adults. Croom Helm, London.

Hoggett, P. and Hambleton, R. (1987). Decentralisation and Democracy: Localising Public Services. School for Advanced Urban Studies, University of Bristol, Bristol, UK.

ICA, (1986). Directory of Rural Development Projects. Edited by Institute of Cultural Affairs International. K.B. Saur Verlag, Munich.

Land, F. (1985). 'Is an Information Theory Enough?' The Computer Journal, 28(3), 211–215.

MacBride, S. (ed.) (1980). Many Voices, One World: Towards a New, More Just and More Efficient World Information and Communication Order. UNESCO and Kogan Page, Paris.

Nelson, C. (1986). 'The Design of Well-adapted and Adaptable Computer-based Information Systems'. *Journal of Applied Systems Analysis*, **13**.

Pacey, A. (1983). *The Culture of Technology*. Blackwell, Oxford.

Pancoast, D.L., Parker, P., and Froland, C. (1983). *Rediscovering Self-Help: its role in social care*. Sage Publications, London, Beverley Hills, and New Delhi.

Traber, M. (ed.) (1986). *The Myth of the Information Revolution*. Sage Publications, London, Beverley Hills and New Delhi.

Winograd, T., and Flores, F. (1986). *Understanding Computers and Cognition: a new foundation for design*. Ablex, New Jersey.

COMPUTER TECHNOLOGY IS OPENING THE WORLD OF PRINT
TO BLIND INDIVIDUALS

Jan L. Ames, Alan R. Bentson and *Rochelle D. Denke*

Computer technology is opening the world of print to blind individuals.

In the past, a public library was not a workplace that could accommodate a blind or visually handicapped employee. A library's stock in trade was printed material, and the circulation and cataloguing systems were in print. A blind or visually impaired person who could not use print materials found little to use in a library.

Two recent changes in society brought about by technology combine to offer the possibility that eventually a blind or visually impaired individual will be able to do almost anything a sighted library employee can do. The first change is in librarianship, which has embraced the techniques of high technology to make library work faster and more efficiently. A modern library's circulation system now lies within a computer rather than on thousands of index cards, and its catalogue is in that same computer, on microfiche, or in an on-line database shared with many other libraries. Today's library is likely to include audio and video tapes, films, and records, as well as print books.

The second change is the acceptance by blind people and those who train and counsel them of the computer as an adaptive aid. The computer has proved to be a patient, obliging, and highly accurate servant to handicapped workers. Once information has been stored digitally within its memory, the computer can convey the information to a handicapped user in a usable form, whether it be large print on a screen, voice output through a speech synthesizer, or braille through an embosser.

It seems inevitable, therefore, that blind and visually handicapped people who are becoming more and more accustomed and sensitized to computer technology should come into contact with public libraries where this technology is fast becoming a means of handling ever-growing volumes of data more quickly and efficiently.

As a public library serving almost 8,000 blind and physically handicapped borrowers throughout the state of Washington with books in special formats, it is especially appropriate that the Washington Library for the Blind and Physically Handicapped take the lead in facilitating the connection between a library and the visually impaired. The following pages discuss a project which developed a way to give a totally blind staff member access to the Library's automated circulation system, thus allowing him to perform clerical functions never possible with a manual system. This was done with off-the-shelf components and readily-available software.

This program easily could be repeated at other libraries for the blind and physically handicapped, and similar adaptations could be made at any type of library.

This accommodation is a significant move toward making the Library's collection more accessible to visually impaired staff and patrons. The project has been a step in opening the doors of all libraries a little wider to visually impaired persons who might wish to use or work in a library.

BACKGROUND

The Washington Library for the Blind and Physically Handicapped has operated since 1931 as part of the network of the National Library Service for the Blind and Physically Handicapped, Library of Congress, Washington, DC. The Washington Library provides free public library services in recorded, brailled, and large print formats to blind, visually impaired, physically handicapped, and learning disabled residents of the state of Washington. Braille, large print, cassette, and disc books, along with equipment on which to play the talking books, are circulated nearly exclusively by mail via 'Free Matter' mailing. Reading materials and equipment are furnished by the Library of Congress.

One source estimates that less than one-tenth of one percent of all printed material in this country is available in a format usable for the print handicapped. In order to bridge this gap, the Washington Library also brailles and tapes local material and provides a radio reading service to broadcast current information such as newspapers, grocery ads, and special news for the disabled.

The quality of library service to the blind and physically handicapped depends directly on the scope and efficiency of its book selection and delivery system. Unlike libraries for the sighted, libraries for the blind and physically handicapped select books for users from request lists and user profiles and therefore require a unique automation system.

Until 1984 the Washington Library utilized a manual system. However, as more and more borrowers were added, the manual system became increasingly unwieldy and cumbersome. The Library reached a point where a manual system could not handle the program, even if additional staff had been available.

Therefore, the Library installed an automated selection/circulation/inventory system to replace the inadequate manual system for book and magazine selection, circulation, and inventory functions. The Library acquired a complete turnkey system designed specifically to meet the needs of the nation's braille and talking book libraries.

This system automates selection, circulation, and inventory functions. The program provides for charging and discharging materials, patron information, title information, magazine information, machine information, overdue material, multi-agency issues, security, and statistics. The system provides for on-line additions, modifications, inquiries, and deletions to the patron file, has–had file, has–now file, request file, machine inventory file, magazine holdings file, title file, reserve file, magazine publisher file, and subject heading file. Materials selection may be done manually or automatically by cyclical selection, by patron request, or from profile selection.

PROJECT ACCESS

Although the Library's automated system worked well after installation and was readily available to sighted staff, access for blind employees was impossible. Therefore, Project Access was initiated late in 1986 to explore the possibility of making the Library's automated circulation system accessible to blind users. The six-month project ran from 12 November 1986, to 12 May 1987.

A grant to pay for part of the cost of DECtalk, a voice synthesizer, was received from the Digital Equipment Corporation. In addition, money from the John B Schack Family Trust was used for purchase of a personal computer and the software programs necessary to interface with the automated system.

Alan Bentson, a blind staff member who then was working as a page and as a receptionist, was chosen to work with the project. He was selected because of his knowledge of braille, computers, and the Library's circulation system, a familiarity with authors, his ability to learn, and his good working relationship with other staff.

In addition, Rochelle Denke, the Library's computer operator, was given additional hours to work on the project. Advice in initial planning was given by staff at the New York State Library for the Blind and Visually Handicapped. Support also came from all areas of the Washington Library. For example, staff of the Braille Department brailled project information as needed.

Bentson spent the first weeks of the project learning the basics of the personal computer operations, loading the software programs, and learning to operate the library programs and the voice synthesizer functions. After he became familiar with the necessary programs, his work station was moved to the circulation desk, and tasks for the readers' advisor position were added. A readers' advisor helps library patrons with book selection, book requests, reference and referral, and book equipment and check–out. Assistance is given either by phone or in person when users come into the Library.

TECHNICAL CONFIGURATION

The Library uses a circulation and inventory system developed by Data Research Associates (DRA), St Louis, Missouri, especially for libraries serving blind and physically handicapped users. The Library's mainframe computer is a VAX-11/750, used with VT 220 terminals. An IBM Personal Computer (PC) interfaces with the DRA system. The VAX is connected to the IBM PC via cable at one of the PC's serial communication ports. Software includes the Enhanced PC Talking Program (which turns the IBM PC into a talking computer system) and PC-VT (a communication program that makes the PC work as a terminal for the VAX).

Bentson is able to access the terminal screens by receiving the information through DECtalk, which is connected to another PC serial port. Any information that can be displayed on a computer terminal now is accessible to a blind person using the DECtalk/PC setup. DECtalk is a text-to-speech system from Digital Equipment Corporation that enables people to interact with computers. This terminal device accepts ASCII test and converts it into human-sounding speech. Instead of printing the text, DECtalk speaks this data through an internal speaker, an external audio system, or over the telephone. DECtalk features eight natural quality speaking voices with variable speaking rates from 120 to 300 words per minute, as well as pronunciation controls.

The PC and synthesizer essentially are used as translation devices. The PC-VT program allows an IBM PC to emulate a mainframe terminal, while the Enhanced PC Talking program allows the user to control cursor movement, as well as data output, to the voice synthesizer. The communication speeds of the devices (mainframe, PC, and voice synthesizer) are all set to 9600 baud. Using floppy disks, the talking program and terminal emulation program are loaded into the PC. The PC then is able to translate the ASCII library programs auditorily.

The talking program speaks screen output generated by the DRA library programs. This program operates interactively with the DRA software, allowing the user to access any part of the screen without disturbing the cursor location or text. The IBM PC's function keys can be used to hear spelling of words, voicing of punctuation, or capital letters. The user can request portions of the screen to be read by column or line. This program allows the blind staff member to 'see' the screen in the same way his or her sighted counterpart does.

When necessary, data files on the VAX can be printed in braille on the Library's Thiel braille embosser. The PC-VT program will download files from a mainframe file onto the PC's floppy disk, which then can be output to the print device.

In addition, the VMS operating system of the Library's main computer system is equipped with an electronic mail utility. This allows ease of communication among all staff members. Because of its computer base, the mail system can be utilized by staff members using the DECtalk.

CONCLUSIONS AND FUTURE PLANS

Project Access had two goals: (1) to establish whether a speech unit with accompanying software could interface with the Washington Library's automated ciruclation system; and (2) to determine whether a blind employee could then use the system and perform the functions of a readers' advisor position.

Project Access proved that a blind employee can access the Washington Library's automated system and function as a readers' advisor. As a result, Bentson has been hired permanently in such a position. Although accessing reference catalogues and materials and using print forms and books remain problems, necessary accommodations have been made. Purchase of some additional equipment, such as a computer device that outputs in braille, acquisition of additional software, and the possibility of new technology should help solve some of the remaining problems.

Making the Library's automated system available to a blind employee is the first phase of making the system accessible to blind Library users throughout the State. DECtalk can also serve as an interface between a touch-tone telephone and the Library system. Therefore, DECtalk could make it possible for patrons to dial into the Library to listen to a newsletter, to hear about upcoming Library events, to listen to brief descriptions of books, and to enter requests for books.

Computer technology has definitely opened the world of print to blind individuals.

AN URGENT NEED:
EQUAL ACCESS OF COMPUTERS AMONG THE POOR

Diane Metzendorf

INTRODUCTION

This paper explores the issue of computer equity for the poor in the United States. It describes a program, Hands-On Community Computer Center Inc., located in Philadelphia, Pennsylvania, which is designed to help combat the inequities that do exist. Implementation of the center is in progress and it is expected to open during 1988.

THE PROBLEM

The Information Era is upon us. The major development of this era is the influence of the computer. The problem of computer inequity and computer illiteracy among the poor needs to be addressed as a relevant issue confronting our society today.

The concept of computer literacy defines a new type of illiteracy and the potentials for new and distressing divisions in our society. While the computer revolution has arrived, segments of our population are being left behind. According to Klaus Lenk, Educator, the most outstanding implication of the new information technology is that it is utilized first by those who can afford it.

Computer inequity appears in our educational institutions. Boys are learning about and using computers more in the schools than girls. The 12,000 most affluent schools are four times more likely to have personal computers than the 12,000 poorest schools. Findings from a John Hopkins University 1983 study indicate that predominantly white schools have twice as many computers as do schools whose students come primarily from minorities.

Computer literacy promotes computer illiteracy among the poor. Computer literacy is a needed skill for obtaining employment in service industries. Service jobs are predominantly located in urban areas throughout the United States. An article in the new York Times of October 27, 1986, reported that jobs in information processing have increased in urban cities across the US, while jobs in the manufacturing industry in urban cities have decreased. The result is a mismatch between those unemployed and employment opportunities.

Minority women, as a group, particularly those who are single heads of households, have consistently been unable to break out of the pattern of unemployment and illiteracy that living in poverty perpetuates. Long-term dependency on public assistance programs adds to this pattern. In addition, programs in job training and literacy for the single parent minority female population have experienced high dropout rates of job training participants.

Statistics gathered by InfoCorp. about who is purchasing home computers in the US support the widening gap between those that have and those that do not. There was a 10.6% increase in the purchasing of home computers from 1985 to 1986. The largest segment of users of home computers are white, male youth. These facts add to the evidence that single parent minority female headed households do not have computers in their homes and that there is one more obstacle to their gaining any competitive edge over the daily poverty they experience.

The consequences of computer inequity of poor families are far reaching and will be long lasting. It is estimated that in the next decade, eight out of every ten jobs will require computer literacy.

THE PHILADELPHIA SCENE

In Philadelphia, the population has changed. The white population has decreased while the minority population has increased from 36% of the population in 1970 to 46% of the population in 1985. There has also been an increase in the proportion of families living below the poverty level with minority females dominating those families living in poverty.

Although there has been an attempt to reach out to poor families by means of job skills training programs, the attendance rate is poor. The reasons given for the poor attendance at these programs include dislike of institutional settings and fear of travelling outside of the neighborhood.

HANDS–ON COMMUNITY COMPUTER CENTER INC.

Hands–On Community Computer Center Inc. addresses the need for computer equity. Hands–On Community Computer Center Inc. is designed to bring computers to the neighborhood of the poor population of Philadelphia. Modelled after Playing to Win, a community computer center in operation since 1983 in East Harlem, New York, the focus of the community center is to teach computer literacy to neighborhood residents. Antonia Stone, director of Playing to Win, found that the people in East Harlem were shut out from the technological society and thought of the computer as a miracle machine reserved for the privileged few – certainly beyond their reach. Their attitude changed when Playing To Win came to their neighborhood. Not only did residents in the public housing project in which Playing to Win is located use the center but in addition several are employed as computer teachers.

In a similar vein, Hands–On Community Computer Centre offers computer activities in computer literacy, basic skills literacy and job skills training.

Together, social workers and educators, with the aid of a powerful tool, the computer, work to improve the quality of daily living and to promote the human potential of Philadelphia's economically oppressed population.

THE PROGRAM

The Hands-On Community Computer program includes three major components consistent with its objectives. The first objective is to provide computer access to economically disadvantaged people. This involves educating community residents about the importance of learning to use computers.

Public speaking engagements by the Executive Director in poor neighborhoods of Philadelphia have taken place. The reception has been positive. Local support has been obtained by neighborhood residents to advocate to bring the center to their neighborhood. The location of the center is easily accessible to neighborhood residents. The hours of the center are after school and work and on weekends which encourages participation.

An outreach worker along with community members of the center communicate with local community organizations to solicit membership. Initially, it is expected that 25 families will enrol in a 15-week computer training program focusing on exposure to computers. The means by which this will be achieved is to engage the participants in computer activities which are fun yet instructional.

The second objective of the center is to train economically disadvantaged people in jobs which require computer literacy. This component of the program will focus on enrolling ten minority single-parent unemployed females for ten weeks of word processing. The goal is to find employment for 60% and to re-enrol 90% of the unemployed women completing the word processing program.

The third objective is to help economically disadvantaged people gain and maintain employment. A network composed of community center members to disseminate job openings requiring computer literacy will be formed. Neighborhood residents trained at the center will be employed by the center to teach other residents. Job training skills such as interviewing techniques and filling out applications are practiced with the aid of the computer.

The fourth objective is to offer to economically disadvantaged people computer-aided instruction in basic skills literacy and job skills training. Ten minority single-parent unemployed females will receive computer-aided instruction in reading for 15 weeks for four days a week. Those completing the program will move on to the word processing program or re-enrol for additional basic skills instruction.

The center will be available for employees and clients of neighborhood human service organizations to use on a contractual basis. Within two years it is hoped that similar community computer centers will appear in other poor neighborhoods in Philadelphia.

DEVELOPING INFORMATION TECHNOLOGY APPLICATIONS
WITH UNWAGED GROUPS: EMPOWERING THE RECEIVERS

Catherine Cassell and *Mike Fitter*

INTRODUCTION

In 1985, with financial support from Sheffield City Council and
the European Social Fund, the Sheffield People's Resource for
Information Technology was set up. Known as the SPRITE
project, its aims and objectives derive from a recognition that
Information Technology (IT) can have an important role to play
in people's lives away from the workplace. Whilst there has
been an increase in the availability and use of IT at the
workplace, there has been a substantial decline in employment.
In South Yorkshire, for example, over 50% of the adult
population are currently unwaged and therefore outside the
formal economy. These people will have little contact with new
developments in IT unless it extends into other spheres of their
lives.

As the 'Information Society' develops, so does an apparent
gap between the waged and unwaged in terms of access to
computer resources and skills (Darwin et al, 1985). Lack of
finances to invest in computer technology means that the
unwaged have minimal knowledge and little impact on developments within the area, the design of software for example is
oriented towards the commercial world and is unlikely to reflect
their needs. The computer illiteracy that results has led to some
authors speculating that society will soon be divided into two
groups: the information rich and the information poor, a society
where information is an increasingly valued commodity.

In an attempt to discover whether this gap could be narrowed
by wageless people themselves with council support, a pilot
study was conducted by Smith, Fryer and Fitter (1985).
Non-directive discussions were held with three community groups
of unwaged people: a pensioners' group, a group of young
unemployed people, and a group whose members had had some
computing experience. From content analysis of these discussions
some common themes emerged. All groups demonstrated an
acceptance of new technology and a belief that it could be
useful to their group or community in the appropriate
circumstances. Various applications were suggested ranging from
the individual, such as family budgeting and games, to the
collective. Most applications were at the collective level and
included using computers to run community centres more
efficiently, for example through electronic filing systems or word
processing. Other suggestions concerned using them to produce
better quality publicity and campaigning material (Smith et al,
1985).

The results from the pilot work provided the basis for the
application to the ESF for funding for what is now the SPRITE
project. The project was set up with the following aims:

1 to work with non-employed people in their communities to develop skills and experiences relevant to their collective needs

2 to develop information technology products useful to community-based groups, that would be unlikely to be available in the commercial market place

3 to make some of the city council's IT resources more useful to community groups, by providing them with the necessary skills and confidence to define their information needs.

The project began work in three centres in May 1986 and has recently expanded to include another two. Eventually SPRITE will be working in seven centres within Sheffield as well as maintaining links with other community groups. This paper will concentrate on developments within the initial centres which are (the following names are psuedonyms):

The Threshold: This is a centre for unemployed people that has many activities for its users and a large adult education input. The centre has a strong management committee, half of whom are users and who reflect the make-up of the local community. The centre has good creche facilities which means that it is particularly popular with women. One day a week it has a women's day where there are many activities laid on for women only. This is a particularly successful aspect of the centre.

The Frontier: This is a new community centre on the first floor of a municipal library. The centre is currently waiting for work to refurbish the building and turn it into a purposely designed community centre. The Frontier already had a computer club before SPRITE became involved with the centre. This was a games club and the users were mainly unemployed men aged 25-35. SPRITE works primarily with members of the computing club whose horizons are expanding beyond using computers for entertainment purposes only.

The Wicker: This is also a new community centre situated near the centre of Sheffield, and is purposely renovated for the city's Afro-Caribbean community. The centre has extensive facilities and many activities ranging from adult education classes to live entertainment. SPRITE works with a mixed group and has close links with the adult education computer tutor.

In each of these centres SPRITE has provided a permanent computer facility and a training programme. The first phase of the training involved workshops in computer familiarisation, introducing the users to basic concepts and the use of practical packages such as databases, word processing and publicity software. From these sessions the users then decide in which projects they are interested, for example one group is currently working on producing a database for a local tenants' association.

As well as the standard training, other workshops are provided, depending on the perceived needs of the centre. Examples are special courses for women's groups, and day schools aimed at demonstrating a specific function of the computers to other local groups. Currently the SPRITE Project Officers work in each centre one day a week running project workshops and skill-sharing sessions.

An important part of the SPRITE philosophy is user control where the users are encouraged to have as much say in the development of the project as possible. In order to be responsive to their needs and the needs of the centre, SPRITE training needs to be organised very flexibly.

THE RESEARCH

Research is an integral part of the SPRITE project. The project is being evaluated over its three years existence by a full-time evaluator. The evaluation methodology is that of action research, the major generic characteristic being that of feedback. Through the mechanism of feedback the researcher can *act* upon the results of the research by having a continual input into the project. The process of the research is therefore cyclical. The evaluation generates facts which provide the basis for devising action strategies which are then evaluated. From the results more appropriate strategies can be defined and the process continues. The evaluation therefore has an important part to play in the policy-making process.

The aim of the evaluation is to focus on the process by which the SPRITE project is implemented. This is different from much evaluation research where judgements are passed on the eventual outcomes. Process evaluation instead seeks to develop a deeper understanding about how and why certain events happen, presenting descriptions of results whilst attempting equally to explain the process by which those results were attained.

Within an evaluation programme it is important to ask who determines the criteria on which the programme is to be evaluated. Within SPRITE there will be a variety of groups involved, all with different interests in taking part. In a programme developing IT for service organisations, Fitter identified four principal groups of stakeholders: the organisation, the service providers, the clients and the IT providers. Each of these groups have their own goals and priorities within the programme that may or may not be compatible with the other groups involved. Any intervention, in this case SPRITE, will change the dynamics of an organisation and the social relationships between those groups of stakeholders:

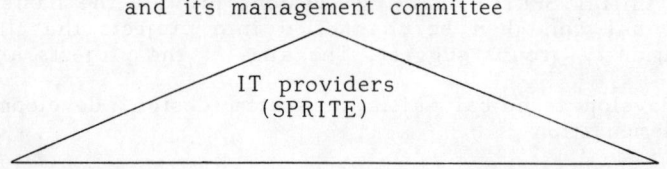

The organisation
(Community Centre)
and its management committee

IT providers
(SPRITE)

The service providers
(Centre workers/
management committee)

The clients
(Centre users)

The evaluation therefore needs to include an assessment of how a programme affects an organisation and consequently its impact on the dynamics between the different stakeholder groups involved. Within SPRITE the centre users are identified as the stakeholder group that the project is most concerned with, however, the evaluation aims to consider the impact of SPRITE on all the stakeholders. In order to do this the evaluation framework is split into three levels.

1 The individual – what impact does SPRITE have on the centre users that take part in the project?

2 The organisational – what impact does SPRITE have on the organisations in which it works? To what extent is the project implemented differently in the centres as a result of the organisational characteristics of the centre concerned?

3 The wider implications – what are the wider implications of the establishment of the SPRITE project? What are the consequences for service providers? Is IT a useful community resource?

By concentrating on pertinent questions at these three levels the evaluation seeks to understand and explain the processes by which developments within SPRITE happen in a particular way, and the impact that those developments have on the various groups of stakeholders. By presenting some of the results that the evaluation has produced so far, some of these issues can now be considered.

RESULTS

Product Development

One of the aims of SPRITE is to develop Information Technology products that are useful to the community. At first this may appear to be an over-ambitious aim; however, early results are encouraging. By working with unemployed users in community centres it has been possible to ascertain the information needs of various community groups. In line with these needs a number of projects are now developing that will lay the basis for future product development.

The initial SPRITE training sessions provide the basis of user skills that can then be channelled into projects that the users or community groups suggest. The aims of the projects are:

1 to develop technical skills in system design, development and implementation

2 to develop interpersonal skills in relating to clients and an awareness of the implications of using IT in community organisations

3 to develop socially useful products and community resources.

To illustrate the potential that has emerged for computing products that are useful to the community, a project from each of the SPRITE centres is outlined below.

The first project is being conducted by users at the Frontier centre. SPRITE were approached by a local tenants' association who were interested in using their microcomputer to keep a record of all the properties in their area. The group had no experience of using a database or evaluating to what extent particular packages would be appropriate for their purpose. SPRITE users visited the tenants association and worked closely with their representatives to define their requirements and tailor a standard software package to meet their specifications. Through regular meetings between the group and SPRITE users a system was produced that currently holds information about each property in the area and has a record structure that includes notes on repairs, benefits and re-housing where relevant. The system has now reached the testing/implementation stage. Once the testing is completed a manual will be written by SPRITE users in conjunction with representatives from the group. The tenants' association then hope to develop the database and turn it into a marketable product that will interest other similar groups.

A somewhat different project has recently been developed at the Wicker centre. The management and the workers at the centre were particularly interested in using the computer facility to manage the centre more efficiently. SPRITE users, in close collaboration with a local computing co-operative and the City Council's Computer Services Department, are working on a database system that includes payroll, cashbook and a fixed asset register. Negotiations are currently being held with a local college of further education with the intention of the college providing a course for SPRITE users in database management systems. This will provide users of the Wicker and other centres with the skills to implement accounts systems in small organisations. This is an ambitious project and the results will extend further than providing a group of users with specific skills. The further education college involved and the City Council's Computer Services Department will be working directly within the Centre, the former providing training to a curriculum negotiated with members of the community, and the latter providing advice on systems analysis to community groups. Computer Services had no prior history of direct involvement with the community and the implications of this project are quite exciting.

Users at the Threshold have been working on something quite different, concerned with how to make information about activities in the area more accessible to members of the local community. At present an individual looking for information about a particular class, for example, has to sift through piles of paper or scour a number of notice boards. SPRITE users at the Threshold have developed a viewdata program on a microcomputer that presents information in a 'user-friendly' format. The users collected the information from all the local groups in the area and divided it into specific categories such as Adult Education, Children, Computing, etc. This information was then written into a simple program. The system is now ready to be piloted with the aim that any user entering the Threshold seeking information will be able to key in and see what facilities/events are available.

Each of these projects demonstrates that there is great potential for the development of computer applications within the community by members of the community themselves. They also suggest that to be involved in a SPRITE project requires not only computing skills, but also skills such as information gathering and negotiating with other community groups. The next section of the results discusses what new skills users feel they have acquired from being involved with SPRITE.

Personal Skills

One of the aims of SPRITE is to develop the skills of people that take part in the project. Although the aim is not to train people for jobs per se, it is envisaged that some of the skills that individuals are developing may make them more employable. In the interviews that were recently held with 16 core SPRITE users each was asked the question: "Do you feel you've gained anything personally by taking part in the SPRITE project?" Responses to this question were content analysed and the results indicate that users feel they have gained a number of things by being involved.

The most important gain is that of new skills. Users now feel that they have gained a number of skills associated with using new techology, that will be relevant to them in the future. Computing skills seem to be the tip of the iceberg, indeed most users describe how they have developed other skills through being involved with SPRITE. Project work especially has led to the development of social and negotiating skills. As one user suggested:

"Before this project what I knew about databases you could have wrote on a postage stamp. Now I'm learning a lot, plus I'm learning a lot of things at other times, getting on with people and their organisations, that kind of thing."

Some of the projects have required demonstrating computers to other groups. This necessitates an understanding of the most effective way of communicating technical information and an awareness of the initial difficulties that people face when first using computers. Skills such as these that are developed through SPRITE are perceived as enabling users to feel more confident. As one woman suggested:

> "I've got more confidence with computers now, I've never been involved with them before. As computers are getting more into day-to-day jobs, when you've been out of work for a long time, once you go back into work everything has altered so much. I think you'd feel a lot worse if you didn't have that confidence behind you . . ."

For a lot of users an equally important outcome is meeting new people, being involved with different groups and making new friends. Such experiences within SPRITE are important, as one user suggested:

> "I think I've gained an attitude now so that I can go out and get more involved with things instead of just shying away, it's the social aspect of it too. I mean with meeting different people, getting to know them, new and, well valuable friends, if you can give somebody something then they give you something back . . ."

Being unemployed can often be an isolating experience and being involved with a community group can offset the feelings of alienation. Taking part in purposeful activity is also attractive for the users involved, the following quote from a Frontier user sums it up:

> "I feel I'm actually helping somebody for the first time, I've never had an opportunity to do so through computers, I don't know about the others . . . I just feel I've actually done something and you know, I'm proud of it . . ."

People often suggested that being involved with SPRITE got them out of the house for a change and being involved with projects that they perceived to be useful was particularly rewarding compared to their everyday activities:

> "If I hadn't known about SPRITE I'd have been sat in the house now, just laying on the sofa watching the school programmes, that's what I used to do. All day."

Despite acquiring new skills and feeling more confident, users in general do not feel that taking part in SPRITE makes them more likely to get a job. Although SPRITE is seen to provide them with the relevant skills to enter new fields two major barriers are usually described. The first is that as SPRITE does not provide any formal qualifications or certificate such experience would be difficult to demonstrate to an employer.

Secondly, there is a general feeling amongst the users that there aren't really any jobs available for the skills that they have acquired. Such beliefs are based on a realistic appraisal of the local labour market. Some users have, however, got jobs through being involved with SPRITE, though these jobs tend to be part-time or temporary. SPRITE has also generated work for some of the users who have taught introductory courses for the project in new centres. These have been funded by a Workers' Education Fund. Other users have progressed into more formal forms of computer education.

Overall then, SPRITE users feel that they have developed a number of new skills through being involved with the SPRITE project including those that extend beyond the technical. This has various implications for the project as a whole that will be discussed in the next section.

IMPLICATIONS FOR FURTHER DEVELOPMENT

Process Evaluation

The philosophy behind the SPRITE project is that of user pro-activity and participation. The focus of the evaluation on the processes at work is designed to encourage the understanding of how pro-activity and participation can be achieved. But to what extent are action research methods successful in ensuring that the project is responsive to the users' needs?

The experience of the SPRITE project has demonstrated that community centres are dynamic organisations whose users and activities can be changing all the time. A project based in community centres needs to be flexible enough to take into account changes as they occur. Many community projects rarely have the time to consider such issues because other concerns usually achieve a greater priority. In these circumstances the advantages of independent feedback are numerous.

Unlike other methodologies action research enables an evaluator to make interventions when they are perceived as necessary. A concrete example is that over a period of two months there was a decline in the number of users using the facility at the Threshold. In those circumstances the research spent extra time at the centre talking to centre users and attempting to discover the causes of this decreased in use. As a result of these discussions a programme of development work was devised for the centre. SPRITE sessions were provided for particular groups within the centre who as yet had had no contact with the project. Also certain key individuals in the centre were trained in how to use the computers. Finally a computer games club was set up with help from users from the Frontier Centre. The club was designed to involve some of the young men in the centre who were only interested in that particular aspect of computing.

In this example information from the evaluation was used to design the intervention programme. This intervention is currently being evaluated and its impact assessed. In such instances the action researcher can be an additional resource in the development of the direction of the project by responding to changing circumstances.

Within SPRITE feedback from the evaluation has operated at two distinct levels:

1 at any everyday level, for example by modifying the training in a particular centre as a response to feedback

2 at a more strategic level, for example helping to determine the criteria on which future centres would be selected to become involved in SPRITE.

It is anticipated that towards the end of the project the evaluation will also be operating on a third level: that of reviewing the overall SPRITE philosophy and describing lessons that will be useful for future implementations.

An important feature of the SPRITE project is its continual evaluation of the implementation. As action research techniques have shown themselves to be useful, it is interesting to consider how other programmes or projects can build such techniques into their 'normal' method of development. Alternatively, it is relevant to examine the other mechanisms by which projects attempt to make themselves aware of how they are progressing from their user/client perspective. These are issues that the SPRITE project will need to consider as the evaluation comes to an end.

Pro-activity and Participation

Both pro-activity and participation can be considered at two levels – within the SPRITE Project and within the local community. Evidence from within the SPRITE Project suggests that given a suitable framework users can make a considerable input into the direction of the project. Through this input there can be active participation in the development of computer applications within the local centres, and consequently within the community. The pertinent question is what characteristics define the suitable framework.

The framework of computer training that SPRITE provides seeks to de-mystify technology, to be of an informal nature and to be easily modifiable depending on what the group wants to learn. As one user suggested:

"With SPRITE in particular, they haven't made me feel like an idiot, they've helped me to understand, they've made it so its become a tool and not something that's got a load of mystique to it. There's a rule they taught me: if you put rubbish into a computer then you get rubbish out of it. In other words you have control of what goes in and out of it and there's nothing to be afraid of . . ."

The description of the products that SPRITE users are developing suggests that active participation within computer developments can be facilitated providing that it is relevant to the community's needs. Typical images of unwaged people present them as passive and impoverished consumers of technology. Early indications are that this balance can be re-adjusted if there is the opportunity for some form of control over development. This is possible outside the economic relationship of employment and within the community setting. An organisation like SPRITE can lay the basis for pro-activity and participation within the development process.

New ideas and beliefs about computing can lead to users becoming more pro-active as regards information in the local community. Technology is no longer something to be scared of, and computers are no longer accepted to be the causes of non-payment of benefit or delay in housing repairs, despite staff assurances to the contrary. Instead they can become tools to further the cause of community groups.

In practice, then, SPRITE is beginning to demonstrate that the less powerful groups within society can be empowered through participation in the design of IT applications to define their own information needs and question the needs of larger organisations like the City Council. At the current stage of the SPRITE project this potential needs to be harnessed and developed. In order to do this appropriate action strategies need to be devised.

Autonomous versus Participative Development

Through the mechanisms of its evaluation procedure SPRITE is currently developing a strategic plan for continuation beyond the initial three year experimental project. There is considerable demand from the current users for the project to be established on a more permanent footing.

An important, and as yet unresolved, question is the extent to which SPRITE should, in the future, maintain an autonomous structure and work independently from major public institutions such as the local authority, or alternatively become more directly involved in working with, and influencing the developers of public information systems. Computer literate community users would be in a position to become involved with designers of community information systems and to bring their own perspective and experience into the design process. However, the structures for such an involvement do not currently exist and their creation would require careful consideration. In contrast there is a demand for the development of autonomous information systems under the direct control of community groups. These can be used to support a group in its negotiations with the local authority or health services. This point was made by a user from an organisation for people with disabilities:

"I'll give you an instance: if the City Council turn around and say to you, 'yeah but how many wheelchairs have you got?', and then we start going 'er, er er' it looks bad, it's almost as though you're searching ahead for a justification, whereas if you've got the facts at your fingertips, it impresses them that you've got them and know what you're doing . . . (otherwise) they will have marshalled their forces, they've got their arguments ready. Therefore I see a good database as a means of matching them at their own game . . ."

This path of autonomous development may, in the long run, prove more effective for promoting the interests of unwaged groups than becoming 'submerged in the bureaucracy of public service organisations in an attempt to make those services more responsive and appropriate to user needs. Strategic decisions on the most appropriate balance between autonomous and participative development have yet to be made.

The Relationship between Service Providers and Receivers

If successful one consequence of empowering users of community centres is likely to a change in their relationship with service providers. There may be more occasions on which the view of a professional service provider is challenged or an account of why something is or is not happening is required.

This change in relationship may happen in two ways. The development of a telecommunications infrastructure linked into community centres, if it were to happen, would make possible the provision of new services, and new patterns of work organisation. Currently services are provided independently by different agencies (welfare rights centres, libraries, job centres, social service departments, housing departments, health centres, etc.). In recent years there has been a demand to decentralise many of these services. With the aid of information technology the potential exists to provide many of these services from a single neighbourhood centre. However, this would have profound implications for the role of service providers. There would be a need for more 'generalists' in the neighbourhood but linked to specialist centres elsewhere.

Another way that the role of service providers may be challenged is through the availability of better information for community groups. This was demonstrated by the quote above by the user from the organisation for people with disabilities; it is also illustrated in Figure 8.1.

As SPRITE users become skilled in their activities they can make a substantial and valuable contribution to developmental projects. This is 'unpaid labour', and there is a general recognition within SPRITE that it should not be used to undermine employment relationships or pay rates agreed with established trade unions. Yet the problem is a deep one. At what position should the dividing line between unpaid educational activity and paid work be drawn? There are no easy solutions. As the SPRITE project develops these concerns are likely to become greater, as is illustrated in an interview with a user who was talking about another unpaid user:

"The thing that annoys me is that you've got people like S.... who's brilliant and you would have to go out and pay for men who are probably not as talented. OK, it's great that he's got a means of expressing his talent but to me it's criminal that such talent has got to stay marginalised instead of being able to be used. You get computer operators in the Town Hall that probably don't know half what he knows . . ."

Figure 8.1

CONCLUSIONS

Initial results from the SPRITE Project suggest that given an appropriate framework, unwaged community centre users can take an active role in the system's development process. The projects in which SPRITE users are currently involved suggest that IT can have a productive impact within the community.

Users have emphasized that SPRITE is more than a collection of hardware and software. It is a complex 'support' package including training, development work and the basis for a federation of local groups involved in community computing. A foundation stone of the project is the philosophy of user control which, supported by the evaluation process, is creating a pro-active and participative environment for user groups.

The next year of the project will be crucial in determining the strategies by which the information needs of unwaged groups are most satisfactorily met. The wider implications of the project such as its impact on service providers, and the provision of community information generally, could be substantial. If SPRITE continues to flourish, and the pro-active and participative environment continues to provide support to the development of individuals and groups, the consequence would be a fundamental challenge to the way work is organised and services provided.

REFERENCES

Darwin, J., Fitter, M.J., Fryer, D. and Smith, L. (1985). 'Developing Information Technology in the Community with Unwaged Groups'. Proceedings of Working Conference on the Development and Use of Computer-based Systems and Tools, Aarhus, Denmark.
Smith, L., Fryer, D., and Fitter, M.J. (1985). 'A Study of Computing Needs of Wageless People in Sheffield'. For Sheffield City Counil. MRC/ESRC SAPU Memo 708, University of Sheffield.

Information Technology and the Human Services
Edited by B. Glastonbury, W. LaMendola and S. Toole
© 1988 John Wiley & Sons Ltd

CHAPTER 9

Privacy, Information Ownership and Codes of Practice

The technical ability to store, manipulate and transmit vast quantities of personal data has provoked a major moral issue surrounding the circumstances in which such material should or should not be used. It is widely acknowledged that, with the exception of some specific areas of information such as criminal records, this kind of material cannot be treated like any other market commodity, but must be subject to some limitations on its exploitation. As a broad generalisation, two approaches have been taken, while a third is badly in need of consideration. One approach, a theme of Chapter 8, is to empower those who are the subject of personal data, so that they can exercise some control in their own right, or at the very least have access to and knowledge of what information is held about them. The second approach, which is covered in the larger part of this chapter, is to develop formats for protecting data, so that it is only available to authorised users (though that begs the question of who should be so authorised).

The third theme, reflected in this chapter in some discussion of codes of practice for keepers and users of personal data, is concerned with developing a comprehensive social and ethical framework for IT. From a number of viewpoints it is possible to observe how technology has outstripped the human capacity to handle it. At its most specific this can be seen in the chronic problem of finding enough trained staff to develop and apply the technological potential. In a world entering a second decade of high unemployment, some of it blamed on the replacement of human labour by machines, IT remains a rare sector of the economy in which there are massive job vacancies.

At its most panoramic, IT has been bolted onto society, and has become an indispensible part of many economic processes, but it has yet to become socially integrated. This is not the place to get into a detailed argument about the characteristics and processes which lead to social integration, but it can be suggested that for such a development to take place it must be possible to find qualities of familiarity, dependability, and acceptability. Passage of time may also be an important factor. On all counts IT falls short. Familiarity is concentrated at the bottom end of society's age range, and is often no more than superficial. Dependability is widely questioned. Indeed, one of the few aspects of IT to become fully integrated is the excuse that something is not available, doesn't work, or cannot be done 'because the computer is out of action'. Acceptability of IT is also rather narrowly based in the community, and is challenged by a countervailing spread of fear and suspicion.

The idea of establishing a social and ethical framework for IT is closely associated with making those modifications which will lead to social integration. In part this requires action to educate communities, and present the technology more effectively. In part, and this is the more substantial sector, there is a need for those who control and exploit IT to democratise their activities, to become publicly accountable for them, and to behave and be seen to behave according to a set of rules which are in harmony with basic human rights.

This is the context for human service developments, so professionals and their managers start from a somewhat treacherous and insecure foundation. And because the business of the human services is to collect personal information as the necessary basis for offering help, the issues achieve a starkness and immediacy which may not be experienced elsewhere. In his paper overviewing the handling of personal information, Dolan is concerned to establish that a vital need is to give the foundation more security, initially by ensuring a potentially useful legal framework for data protection. However, within that framework a great deal of responsibility remains with service staff. He argues that IT, despite its limited incursion to the human services to date, is acting as a long overdue catalyst to the re-examination of how information is conceived, created and used. There is a task to reconceptualise our notions of how 'information' is formulated in professional theory and practice, and to assimilate appropriate codes of practice.

The next two papers, from McKinley and Rodwell, are very different, but both express a profound suspicion about IT. McKinley is a psychotherapist who writes as though he has a love/hate relationship with the expert systems becoming available to his profession. He spells out the polarities of good and evil within new technology, and the seductiveness of computer programs. He warns us not to be taken in by the enjoyment of them, or their apparent contribution to efficiency, unless and until we have clarified for ourselves that they conform to important ethical standpoints about the rights of individuals. In short, his message is to beware of empowering the service professional at the expense of castrating the consumer.

Rodwell takes us into what for some will be the unfamiliar subject of hermeneutics, which he defines as concerned with the interpretation of meaning. He argues that in normal communication between people, meaning is derived both from the formal content of the language used, and from the context in which the communication takes place. His view strongly supports the human service professional value of the uniqueness of each individual, and of each individual's way of conveying meaning. However, he then goes on to cast doubt on the value of computers, which can be programmed to respond rigidly and reliably to a precisely defined language, but cannot respond to the unique context of each human situation. His argument is that at best computers severely limit the processes of communicating accurately, and at worst lead to extensive misunderstandings of communications.

Visser and Monasso focus their combined papers on the use of informatics in social work education in the Netherlands. Visser outlines the development of a special project to computerise and network schools of social work, and feed into the network a curriculum database. Monasso then turns to some of the ethical issues in this project, which he views as a form of automation. Using some less familiar terms (for example 'registration system' for the more widely known 'information system'), Monasso reports on interviews with and experiences of staff involved in the project. He pleads for new and clearer agreements on the collection, transmission and use of data, and stresses the responsibility of management.

The final paper in the chapter, from Rush et al, raises an issue which is every bit as important to the human services, but has been rather overshadowed by other concerns in the debate to date. That is the extent to which IT has failed dismally to conform to any reasonable notion of equal opportunities. Many of the points they make could have been set in the context of racial discrimination, third world politics or disadvantaged minorities: they choose to set them in the context of the role (or lack of it) of women in handling communication and information. They establish that communication and information are not solely the preserve of IT, but are more broadly based, putting IT in with the rest of the media, especially the press. The paper is a strong feminist statement about IT as a male dominated development (as instanced by the exclusive use of the male gender in the majority of papers in this book, and the fact that most of the authors are men), and reinforces the picture of a narrowly based and elitist place for IT in society. In the context of power politics the issue is one of empowerment: but at root it is a matter of fundamental social values.

PRIVACY, INFORMATION OWNERSHIP
AND CODES OF PRACTICE

Paul Dolan

INTRODUCTION

The concept of privacy is ancient, if of changing composition. From a wide-ranging analysis of privacy, Moore (1984) argues that personal privacy and private rights are linked by the notion of 'intrusion'. The idea of 'property' is historically quite recent, at least in the individualised form prevalent in Anglo-Saxon countries.

'Information' has, as a concept, recently had to live alongside the notion of 'data'. The latter term has a semantic and philosophical history: we perhaps need to learn from the way that 'sense-data' have become discredited as ultimate components of perception. Crudely speaking, data have been seen as inherently structured by the mode of perception, and the perceiving organism. Geiss and Viswanathan (1986) define data as "the raw material produced by observation or measurement – that is, facts or that which the senses perceive – and that produced by thought – inferences, calculations, and specula-tions". This definition seems to fail the distinction proposed by Keen and Scott Morton in the same publication between "data being facts and information being facts that are necessary for some purpose, and that have meaning and significance". This seems to duck the question of what are the conditions to be met for facts to be adjudged theoretically relevant, as data. Indeed, some philosophers (e.g. Taylor, 1985) argue that "the activities of searching for, creating, espousing and rejecting theories" are too little understood as we concentrate on the content of theories.

The concern of this paper is with what is called personal data; in the definition of the UK's Data Protection Act this is data relating to a living individual who can be identified by the data, or by the data and other information. Personal information can be constituted out of data, by a process of decision and manipulation. For the social worker or worker in human services this is an everyday process, governed by theory, and yielding professional knowledge. This kind of knowledge may be tentative and limited: but it does need to refer back to concepts of data and information for empirical content. This is why there is a logical reason why a changing conception of data and information will necessarily change the professional knowledge base of practitioners and educationists. A specific example may illustrate this. Social work education, and practitioner codes of ethics seem to have responded (or be in the process of responding) to information regulation and control through conventions or laws, rather than change being initiated from within. External pressure, and change due to fear of technology have been dominant, at least in the UK.

THE EFFECTS OF REGULATION

In Sweden there are positive duties of openness laid on social workers by the Social Services Act, 1980. Section 52 requires that: "Individual persons should be kept informed of logbook entries and other records maintained concerning them". Also regulations exist on storage of information in security, "so as to be inaccessible to unauthorised persons" (Section 51). In Sweden there is also a weeding-out process applied to notes and other particulars in personal dossiers five years after the final entry – a major administrative task. These seemingly elaborate regulations have clearly been influenced by the presence of a Data Inspection Board since the early 1970s. Another general effect of regulations is to require the development of more stringent rules limiting the use of data to specific purposes in the given case. The Data Protection Act of the German State of Hesse illustrates this: "In principle personal data shall only be obtained from the data subject with his knowledge . . . When data are obtained from the data subject without his knowledge, he shall be notified of this fact as soon as the legitimate accomplishment of the tasks is no longer thereby put at risk. Notification shall include specification of the relevant legal basis . . ." If personal data are to be processed for purposes other than those for which they were collected certain conditions must be satisfied: it must be necessary to process an application lodged by the subject, or to prevent substantial prejudice to public safety or life, danger to health or personal freedom, or if there are indications suggesting criminal offences . . .

The effect of regulation, for the individual, is to seek to make the process of data collection and use more transparent. "As a matter of principle, the individual shall at all times know which authority wishes to obtain what information about him and the reasons for the data collection."

IMPLICATIONS OF LEGISLATION

In Sweden it is too soon to see what the results of legislation have been. Elis Envall (personal communication) argues for scepticism as to whether bureaucratic behavior has changed much in Sweden. The Metropolit scandal might appear to gainsay this assessment: long-term collection of personal information unbeknown to the subjects was terminated despite the protests of the researchers.

One element common to regulatory systems is the presumption of literate, rational, inquisitive, responsive citizens, who are fairly knowledgeable about the services holding information in their files. Clearly, many social work clients are none of these things: even citizenship may be legally doubtful. Yet this is the kind of audience addressed by the leaflets of the UK's Data Protection Registrar. After 11 November 1987 the effectiveness of this will be seen in terms of direct requests to give effect to the new right of access. Effects seem to be more likely to be felt indirectly in agencies, through their Codes of Practice. Such codes are being encouraged by the Registrar: no doubt agencies or groups of agencies can set up their own codes to guide their staff and specify the rights of their service users. One wonders how many will actually involve service users in the process of drawing up Codes of Practice, for example, elderly people, people with a mental illness . . . Further, what assumptions are going to be made by professionals designing such agency codes, about service users' wishes and behaviour; the use of computer-based information networks; the extent of control of such networks by agency professionals or others? How far does it make sense to design agency-based Codes of Practice if there is exchange of information with other agencies? How much control and responsibility can the individual agency exercise?

Answers to these questions have led, at least in the UK, to national recommended Codes of Practice rather than legislation. Also, at least in the UK, The Social Services Code of Practice has been devised by a group of human services professionals and information technologists, under the auspices of a local government advisory body on computers (LAMSAC). The Code is therefore advisory and does not have effective support from the Data Protection Registrar. It has been issued to recently to evaluate its impact, though it is being supplemented by specific codes for specific areas of work, such as child protection. I suggest the impact of this Code will be felt only over years, rather than months, partly because it has been produced by active professionals, whose thinking may not be representative of routine practice.

QUESTIONS OF CHANGE

A debatable question of Codes of Practice is whether they actually change behaviour, or at best register changes that are under way independently. For example, a test of the Swedish Social Services Act's approach to data handling is currently being debated, raised by the issues of AIDS notification. My first hand observations in Sweden were that some social workers still kept, rather guiltily, personal case notes on service users, although these are prohibited in favour of official dossiers. In the UK an action-research project found that where social workers were committed to openness with service users, few problems were experienced where detailed and focused recording was wanted.

Macarov reviews later (in the conference) the history and some of the changes in the uses of confidentiality, particularly illustrating how confidentiality has been used to protect the human services professional. Does there exist a right to professional privacy (as opposed to professional secrecy)? What would be the limits on that right?

I have avoided the concept of a 'right' to privacy so far, but it is worthwhile exploring whether positive legal rights might have a part to play alongside professional codes.

In Europe the most notable outcome of an international initiative has been the European Convention for the Protection of Individuals with regard to Automatic Processing of Personal Data. This, it should be noted, aims at the protection of individuals, not data; it covers access and the specific grounds for holding data. Nevertheless it assumes rather than explores the nature of a right to privacy. A major drawback of the Convention mechanism is that there is no direct enforcement procedure of the Convention itself where national legislation is in force, except eventually through the Commission and the Court of Human Rights. National legislation (or a State law, as in Hesse) can be progressive or limited, as in the case of the UK's Data Protection Act. This contrives not to mention privacy except when quoting the European Convention . . .

FOR FURTHER DEBATE

We need to consider whether there might be a long-term use for directly enforceable standards of personal information protection, with a range of accesssible codes of practice governing particular areas of work. The European Convention on Human Rights provides a more general model than the Data Protection Convention, and its scope is not limited to Europe. The re-conceptualisation of information within a system of information management in agencies is a more diffuse goal. But benign individuals within structures of information management that are incoherent can be lethal professionals.

REFERENCES

Moore, Barrington, jr. (1984). *Privacy: Studies in Social and Cultural History*. New York.
Geiss, Gunther and Viswanathan, Narayan (1986). *The Human Edge: Information Technology and Helping People*. New York.
Taylor, Charles (1985). *Philosophy and the Human Sciences*. Philosophical Papers 2, Cambridge.

DESIGN AND ETHICS OF 'PSYCHOTECHNIC' SYSTEMS

Tom McKinlay

I wish to put forward recommendations regarding the proper design and good use of high-tech psychosocial perception/analysis/response systems. This primarily regards computer driven expert systems and the emerging artificial intelligence systems as they are applied to social service work and psychotherapy. These recommendations are offered from the particular perspective of a long-time residential psychotherapist and designer/developer of a unified diagnostic and treatment awareness system.

The original motivation for development of such systems typically seems to come from a desire to increase our success in helping people. However, out of the relatively high percentage of psychotherapeutic failure, and from our attempts to reduce that percentage, will come unexpected threats to our original purpose. With the greater knowledge and power we will soon have in hand, will come greater forms and degrees of the use *and* abuse of tools for psychosocial change. As an example, psychotherapy is only relatively 'inadequate' now. By way of a well intended solution, we run some considerable risk of moving it to 'monstrously effective'.

In the foreground of this discussion is the development of computer-aided expert systems and artificial intelligence systems, generally for diagnosis and treatment, which will afford as much effective and efficient abuse of human rights as they will empowerment of human rights. These systems are much needed tools indeed. They should be developed and welcomed into use. And yet, they are in great need of responsible, forward-looking awareness and control.

It is becoming quite clear that the power of these perception/analysis/response systems in respect of information and actual behavior change is rapidly, yet quietly, becoming immense. And most importantly, the power of the systems is undifferentiated as to positive or negative use.

We must therefore appreciate that by effecting greater change in ourselves with these tools than has been generally possible, we become open to errors of two main kinds: poor design and wrong use.

We can expect to see a lot of poor design. Systems that basically just track a collection of interesting data on behavior and treatment yet lack a meaningful framework and a comprehensive and substantive data base, and systems that lack any real holistic framework or unified awareness: these are poorly designed systems of a superficial and seductive kind. Poor design may also include logistic interference with the user's prime purpose, that is, the therapist tending to focus on responding to the data system rather than treating the client.

The effect of these poorly designed systems will be to discredit fine systems (because they can appear to be so much alike), and more importantly, their effect will be to mislead users into following and responding to arbitrary and disjointed information. Essentially, they will abuse the client by promoting discordant and off-target treatment actions. If the information with which we work and on which we rely is wrong or misleading, and worse still, convincingly and seductively presented, our judgement and actions will be wrong and misguided to the same degrees.

We can also expect to see a certain amount of wrong use; that is, the immoral, unethical, or simply thoughtless use. This danger of wrong use is somewhat paradoxically proportionate to the quality of design in that wrong use of fine systems is the most threatening combination. Fundamental human rights and the dignity and worth of the human person will be at issue, and not only with outright and conscious immoral use. There will be much grey area between right and wrong use. There may initially be a general disregard for the 'change agent' power of these systems, and simply the thoughtless user or one without relevant ethical guidelines may wander into wrong use.

In the helping professions we may be accustomed to seeing individual failure and the failure of some treatment programs. We may even be accustomed to seeing isolated 'change agent' tools or modalities inflicting pain or injury in degrees disproportionate to the benefits. But, as yet, we are not accustomed to seeing our professions becoming, at will, imbued with systems threatening the very concepts of human freedom, responsibility, and worth as we hold them. Let's not jump from the 'frying pan of inadequacy' into the 'fire of misguided power'.

The goal is to offer excellent benefits to all involved. The challenge is to build these psychosocial change systems well and use them properly. The key is prevention of wrong use, not reform.

DESIGN

The basic advance in psychotechnic systems is not so much one of diagnostic or response modalities, and certainly not one of computer hardware, it is rather an advance of clarity, insight, and communication. The advance is in bringing perceptually isolated aspects together, the broad and precise, the intuitive and empirical, all through a holistic framework into a unified awareness.

Holistic frameworks yield a more realistic perspective of behavior and conditions as they actually are, that is, with all characteristics fundamentally related within relatively larger, unified fields of dynamics. Such frameworks will make use of naturally organized data, both empirical data as well as the critically important, intuitively produced data. With both types, the essential inter-relatedness of the content and process of the represented patterns is there for the user. This offers a unified appreciation, and the effects through our response are, in turn, more resonant with and more potentially considerate of the individual.

From the complete and integrated framework presented by such holistic systems, intrinsic behavior patterns clearly emerge and suggest specific targeting of treatment work where it can most effectively resolve, for example, entire negative syndromes. The essential dysfunctions become more apparent and accessible to direct treatment focus. Treatment modalities and overall strategies can be suggested and implemented with far greater respect for the integrity of the individual.

ETHICS

If we are to bear the power of far more effective psychosocial change tools, we will also bear the responsibility of their effects. The very kind and degree of power involved in these emerging systems insists that we thoroughly consider the humanitarian implications. It is exactly because these systems offer so much efficiency by design, that we must look beyond that efficiency and better clarify our work's purpose and meaning. We will need such clarification of purpose to stay on track at 'higher speeds'.

The astoundingly beneficial rewards of psychotechnic systems will be accompanied by an increasing vulnerability to human rights abuse. A true accountability of the finest of treatment will be accompanied by the deceptive legitimization of wrong treatment. A far greater ability to respect and respond to each individual as a unique and complete being will be accompanied by the depersonalization and devastation of individual integrity. A far more perceptive insight and intuitive response will be accompanied by the potential of convincing disinformation. Human rights are certain to be violated through the misuse of high-tech psychotherapeutic tools. The abuse is hand in hand with the power. We must rise to this momentous opportunity for power with good judgement, foresight, and control.

The once tortured and imprisoned Soviet psychiatrist Anatoly Koryagin, who has seen first hand the workings of a 'repressive psychiatry', stated very simply upon his recent release that: "Our profession should not be an accomplice to torture and repression". This principle is not frivolously stated and is best kept close at hand as we increase the power of this and allied professions. The cruel effects of unrestrained 'therapeutic' tools is known and acknowledged to exist now, yet those cruelties might become ever more present as the power of the tools increases.

To keep clear the potential 'blurring of perception' of who's a healer and who's a torturer, Koryagin recommends the help of an international humanitarian counsel and the clear definining of the profession's ethical position. He rightly identifies and criticizes wrong use of his profession's tools and modalities. What Koryagin has seen is bad enough. After 'super-charging' psychotherapeutic tools and modalities, such wrong use could actually be more prevalent and less detectable.

Our helping professions' prime purpose of empowering fundamental human rights and upholding the dignity and worth of the human person may actually be in precarious relation with a new-found interest in empowering the profession per se, that is, good professionals becoming distracted with efficiency and losing a sense of original intent.

At the very least, the helping professions must anticipate the increase in psychosocial control, be very discriminating in their selection and use of high-tech psychotherapeutic tools, and have their use openly accountable to basic ethical standards.

The human impact of psychotechnics should be open to ongoing assessment and should operate within parameters of generally correct and humane effect. This humane accountability should apply to government as well as private sector supported systems and always be fully considerate of the point of view of the affected persons and their inalienable rights.

COMPUTERS AND THE HERMENEUTIC
DIMENSION OF HUMAN SERVICES

Graham Rodwell

The analysis of the limitations of computers in the human services has been developed largely by those who retain a belief in their beneficial potential. The problems which they identify are mostly attributed to surmountable failures such as management failure or inadequate software (Glastonbury, 1985). The philosophical debate generated by research into artificial intelligence, however, suggests an alternative, more cautious view based on the impact of computers on the hermeneutic dimension. From this perspective, the inherent structure of computers carries a persistent risk of systematic distortions of communication and a loss of meaning in human services irrespective of the efficiency or value basis of the software.

This discussion is developed in five parts. the first part summarises the hermeneutic approach to understanding. The second part describes the hermeneutic dimension of human services. The third part argues that computers are structurally incapable of modelling this dimension. The fourth part discusses the communicative deformations which may result when computers are used to replace hermeneutic understanding. Finally, the fifth part considers whether it is possible to expand the contribution of computers in human services without such consequences.

THE PERSPECTIVE OF HERMENEUTICS

Hermeneutics has been described as the theory or philosophy of the interpretation of meaning (Bleicher, 1980). In its modern form it can be traced back to writings of Dilthey (1958) and his attempt to establish a systematic basis for the cultural sciences. In recent years, the theory has been reconstructed by writers such as Gadamer and Apel through an analysis of language (Gadamer, 1976; Apel, 1967). The argument presented here is derived from the interpretation of this tradition by Habermas (1972; 1979; and 1984).

Central to the hermeneutic tradition is the recognition that meanings are never quite identical. They always contain an essential element of particularity. This particularity is derived from a continuing relation to the concrete circumstances of life. The interpretation of meaning involves a coherent understanding of what is unique as well as what is general.

Dilthey explored this problem through an analysis of the understanding of individual life histories. To understand the personal significance of events, the individual draws on commonly available symbols in a way which establishes an individuality of meaning. The interpretation of autobiographical accounts requires not only the reconstruction of these inter-subjective symbols but also an understanding of their individual application.

For Habermas, this hermeneutic analysis poses a fundamental methodological question: "How can the meaning of individuated life structure be grasped and represented in inevitably general categories?" (Habermas, 1972). His answer to this question is based on the analysis of language use. According to this line of argument, ordinary language involves a continual gap between a linguistic expression and what is meant by this expression in the context of individual life relations. This gap is closed by forms of interpretation which draw on sources of indirect communication such as symbolic actions and gestures. In reaching an understanding, the participants in communication rely on this inter-relation of language and activity to establish particular meanings.

THE HERMENEUTIC COMPONENT OF HUMAN SERVICES

It is a characteristic feature of many human services that they are organised to respond, in part, to accounts of the needs and problems of individual clients or client groups. These accounts are constructed through a hermeneutic process of interview and interpretation in which a welfare professional uses ordinary language to try to understand a particular situation. The interpretation of the specific meaning of events constitutes a key element of the process of assessment and may be used to evaluate the significance of any outcome.

The hermeneutic basis of human services is evident where the service is organised in accordance with a client centered approach, where the symbolic categories may be derived from the client's own account. But even where the assessment categories are largely predetermined by fixed theories or organizational requirements, the professional may be expected to construct accounts of the specific way that the general categories apply to each individual. For example, if an elderly person is judged to be at risk, the professional may be expected to provide an interpretation of the particular nature and meaning of that risk for that individual in that specific context. Unlike forms of medico/biological assessment, the construction of such accounts requires the use of reflexive and open ended language. The human service professional must supplement the fixed process of categorisation with symbolic expressions which point to the particularity of the client's circumstances and experience.

This hermeneutic element in human services is intended to recognise the individuality and identity of each client and client group. It enables human services to respond to individual and particular needs rather than just to general categories of need. The hermeneutic dimension established in the interview can only be preserved, however, if assessments can be presented in a communicative forum which preserves the dialogic properties. For example, the interpretation of risk may be presented at a case conference in such a way that an understanding of the

specific nature and meaning of this risk can be established as
the basis for action. If, on the other hand, the agency employs
a fixed set of responses for any situation categorised 'at risk',
irrespective of the individual meanings, then the hermeneutic
component of interpretation is undermined.

COMPUTER LANGUAGE AND HERMENEUTICS

Many of the potential uses of computers in human services
involve the transfer of linguistic symbols from the hermeneutic
context of ordinary language into the domain of computer
languages. Irrespective of the computer language employed, this
involves the translation from a non-formalised language into one
which is, by definition, formalised. Computer languages must
have a defined and finite set of expressions in which the
possible relations between these expressions can be established
in advance. In order to change language into the pieces of
information that can be manipulated, it must be stripped, at
some stage, of the particular empirical content derived from the
specific context. To transform meanings into general categories
of information necessarily removes their particular and individual character. This makes it impossible to preserve or model
hermeneutic understanding.

The nature of this problem has been touched on most
frequently in the philosophical discussion surrounding Artificial
Intelligence (AI). Dreyfus has stressed the concrete component in
knowledge and argued that knowledge-based systems misrepresent
knowledge by reducing it to the abstract representation of
information (Dreyfus, 1979). Searle has used hypothetical
examples to appeal to a shared pre-understanding of the
intrinsic difference between the pragmatic concept of understanding and language processing (Searle, 1984). Some writers in this
field are now cautious about their claims for the potential of AI
and for the manipulation of language by computer. Jones (1987),
for example, carefully avoids the use of the term 'understanding', noting that no current system can understand that 'I'm
working' could mean 'be quiet'. Other writers, however, have
defined the problem away by simply excluding the hermeneutic
dimension from the outset. Raphael dismisses the hermeneutic
concept of understanding as inferior and irrational:

"In fact, we might define understanding as the ability to
re-express the concept in terms of concrete mathematical
expressions of computer algorithms. Calling a method 'informal' merely masks the fact that we do not know how it
works." (Raphael, 1976)

Rich reduces the problem of understanding to a question of fixed
responses:

"To understand something is to transform it from one
representation to another where this second representation has
been chosen to correspond to a set of available actions that

would be performed and where the mapping has been designed so that for each event an appropriate action will be performed." (Rich, 1986)

Even where some aspect of the hermeneutic problem is recognised, it tends to be treated as a difficulty which is limited to programs that are designed to simulate intelligence or linguistic interaction. However, the argument applies equally to all software which takes symbols from contexts of ordinary language where they are used to establish particular meanings and transforms them into symbols of a formal language for the purpose of manipulation. The structural inability to preserve dialogic understanding applies equally to a wide range of monitoring and information systems and not just those designed to interact or draw inferences.

THE DISTORTION OF COMMUNICATION

This structural inability to sustain hermeneutic understanding does not place a fixed limit on the range of application for computers in human services. Computer use can be extended into any area where languages can be formalised. In many areas of service partially formalised languages are already in use. Income maintainance and benefit systems, for example, use formal languages to a high degree, although they still retain a dialogic component in the application of rules to individual circumstances which resists computer modelling. Existing information systems based on formal languages provide evidence and data of the same kind as quantitative social sciences.

The extension of formal languages may bring a number of benefits in terms of consistency, objectivity and explicit reasoning. Nonetheless, it can also be argued that the increasing dominance of formal languages distorts communication. The existing tendency for 'facts' which are constructed in a formal language to be given priority over hermeneutic interpretation in decision-making may be further legitimated. The growth of formal languages provides the ground for an increasing bureaucratisation of services.

Bureaucratically organised services not only fail to recognise the individuality of clients but also, according to Habermas, serve to undermine their ability to make sense of the world. The accountability of services is increasingly seen in terms of following set rules rather than acting sensibly according to the interpretation of particular conditions. Formal languages may become the basis for new forms of management by objectives. Success is assessed independently of the specific meaning of the outcome, and systems of services are monitored independently of the understanding of the clients.

THE INTERPRETATION OF COMPUTER INFORMATION

The dangers of the bureaucratic use of computers have been discussed by Sharron (1986.) He has recognised the dangers of decision-support programmes becoming decision-making systems and stressed the need for the professional to retain the ability to interpret computer produced information. Following LaMendola (1986), however, his argument tends to suggest that software which is designed and controlled by professionals can incorporate different values from those of business information systems.

The hermeneutic argument above suggests that welfare clients at least should be cautious about this solution. The design and control of information systems by professionals may protect professional autonomy without preventing formal language from becoming dominant. In a sense, computers are not neutral. They depend on and promote one form of reasoning, irrespective of who controls the decision, and irrespective of the hierarchical structure of the organisation. As information- and knowledge-based systems are developed, social workers may still be drawn away from their hermeneutic role towards new forms of technical expertise. Such an outcome would retain the power of the professionals while reducing their ability to reach an understanding of individual experience and meaning.

The possibility of developing cmputer systems while preserving the central hermeneutic component of human services ultimately depends not on the design process but on the growth of new forms of assessment and accountability. The beneficial use of decision-assisting systems requires social institutions in which computer-produced information can be interpreted for each individual circumstance. It is possible, however, to envisage software which facilitates such interpretation and which can be used more readily in conjunction with hermeneutic understanding. Such software need not wait for the development of highly sophisticated programs intended to mimic natural language or reasoning. On the contrary, simple systems which make clear use of formal logic and fixed categories are less likely to disguise the need for hermeneutic interpretation. Software of this kind might provide structured opportunities to redefine the categories and reconsider meanings for individual cases. It would promote an understanding of both the value and the limitations of information processing in formal languages.

REFERENCES

Apel, K-O. (1967). *Analytic Philosophy of Language and the Geisteswissenschaften.* D. Reidel, Germany.
Bleicher, J. (1980). *Contemporary Hermeneutics.* Routledge & Kegan Paul, London.
Dilthey, W. (1958). *Gesammelte Schriften.* 18 vols, 2nd edition. Verlag B.G. Teubner, Germany.

Dreyfus, H. (1979). In M. Ringle (ed.) *Philosophical Perspectives in Artificial Intelligence.* Harvester Press, Brighton.

Gadamer, H-G. (1976). *Philosophical Hermeneutics.* California University Press.

Glastonbury, B. (1985). *Computers in Social Work.* Macmillan, London.

Habermas, J. (1972). *Knowledge and Human Interest.* Heinemann, London.

Habermas, J. (1979). *Communication and the Evolution of Society.* Heinemann, London.

Habermas, J. (1984). *The Theory of Communicative Action.* Heinemann, London.

Jones, K.S. (1987). In T. O'Shea et al (eds.) *Intelligent Knowledge Based Systems - An Introduction.* Harper and Row, London.

LaMendola, W. (1986). 'Software Development in the USA'. *Computer Applications in Social Work and Allied Professions,* **13**(1), 2-7.

Raphael, B. (1976). *The Thinking Computer.* W.H. Freeman & Co., Oxford.

Rich, E. (1986). *Artificial Intelligence.* McGraw Hill, Maidenhead.

Searle, J. (1984). *Minds, Brains and Science.* Reith Lectures, BBC, London.

Sharron, H. (1986). 'Can Machines Replace Social Workers?' *New Society,* 21 March, 502-503.

INFORMATICS IN SCHOOLS FOR SOCIAL WORK
AND SOCIAL SERVICES

Albert Visser and *Jan Monasso*

Part I
The Educational Background

In Holland almost 50% of the institutes of Higher Professional Education with departments for social work and social services (about 40 in total) have some kind of computer system for teaching the use of information technology in the field of social work. Since the Ministry of Education and Science launched a 4-year Special Plan on Informatics, 15 pilot projects were started at schools for social work and social welfare within the framework of that scheme. The Plan, known as INSP, is being carried out between 1984 and 1989.

The first aim was to give an additional training to teachers, and secondly to students and for professionals in the form of a post-graduate course. We had a strong barrier to overcome. Social work students and teachers chose this study to work with people, not to work with machines! But when they got over this barrier some would get so excited about computers that they almost turned into computer-junkies. This, however, made a further step necessary: to reflect thoroughly what exactly you want to do with the computer, why you need it, when and with what purposes.

That is why some other assignments are the development of curricula for:

- social effects of automation
- social and organisational aspects
- managerial and supervisory support of social welfare institutions and those involved in social and development work
- telematics and the use of external databases for social purposes.

The schools selected for these projects received material and financial support from the Ministry of Education to set up the further training schemes and curriculum development. The results are supposed to have a mediating effect on informatics development in other schools for social studies. It is very important that the schools *share* their results! In addition, there are several other schools which, on their own initiative and at their own expense, began experimenting in the sphere of informatics education.

There is a small group of professionals and teachers in the field of social work who put a lot of effort into integrating and stimulating the initiatives in both the professional and educational field. In the field of Higher Professional Education for Social Work and Welfare this is done by the Curriculum

Development (CD) Team, financed by the Ministry of Education and supported by the Council for Higher Professional Education.

This CD team has just recently investigated some trends on the use of information technology applications in the professional field. Also, a survey of the state of the art was made, with respect to information technology applications in the schools for social work and social welfare, including the pilot projects. Based on the findings of these investigations and in addition to the already existing projects there will be started new projects for curriculum development on informatics applications which will be co-ordinated by the CD team.

Since the start of the four-year Special Plan (INSP) there have been some changes in the policy of the Ministry of Education. There is a change from more broadly orientated projects towards in-depth projects, concerning more advanced technologies and applications. They also intend to stimulate the networking of all institutions for higher education and universities. This new approach will most probably mean that there will be no further separate stimulation for informatics education in the schools for social work. Just recently there has been a trend towards more commercialising education, which means that there will be a lesser Ministry influence on education and a bigger role played by commercial firms. In Holland we are not familiar with this. It is rather unusual to be sponsored by business firms and to sell and buy educational programs and software from colleagues.

If there is no further special stimulation in the welfare education sector, and the trends towards commercialisation continues, this could result in the schools for social work and social welfare falling behind in learning to use and develop new information technology applications. We do, of course, hope that it will still be possible to finance the CD team. This would mean that we can keep a rather unique feature in the educational field: a co-ordinating point for the development of social applications of information technology.

We are now raising funds to keep the (text)database up to date, which means that the institutions in the survey regularly update their factsheets. Then every school that wants to set up a program or wants to develop a course does not have to carry out its own research but can look in the (text)database and retrieve the relevant information. Curriculum development will then be actually based upon the trends and needs in the professional field.

In Part 2, Jan Monasso will explain how we did the survey for our research, and will also consider some of the ethical issues arising from it.

Part 2
Automation and Registration

REGISTRATION SYSTEMS: ENDS AND MEANS

Performing the work of registration in pre-computer times was a controversial affair. It took months for the value of the relationship between the registration of facts and the conclusions reached from them to be realised. The introduction of computers reduced considerably the time required for the feedback of registered facts and summaries. This is very much appreciated by both the directing staff and their employees. Furthermore it appears that computer output, provided that it is quantified and well explained, gives valuable information about the practice itself. Nevertheless, our research revealed that many automatic registrations were faulty. According to De Graaf (1982) important conditions for the success of a registration system, generally speaking, are:

1 the goal, or the objectives of a registration system must be precisely specified

2 exclusive attention must be devoted to a registration system by a person who controls the system, maintains it and takes charge of the performance of the task in hand.

In certain respects the input and output methods of data and information are restricted to predetermined procedures; nevertheless the modern database software makes it possible for the individual user to manipulate information and decide for himself how to proceed. Given that this requires prior training, it still opens up prospects that will have many features: not only made-to-measure automation but electronic screening of the functioning of the organisation concerned comes within reach of the relevant employees. So the question is: who are those authorities? And what are the implications for the work sphere, for collegiality, for professional autonomy and work methods? In practice, conceptions of what these elements imply already exist; new agreements are needed as to who can claim what.
     In the first place, institutes must refuse to accept requests from financiers and governments for indiscreet information. A so-called 'Information Statute' could solve this problem. An agreement is arranged between the (more powerful) government and those actually engaged in the storing and processing of data. Disputes over proposed information procedures and data distribution could be settled by reference to the Statute or by the intercession of a committee of good offices.
     In the second place, a clear distinction must be made between two types of policy information, these being: information necessary for the management of the organisation, and information to meet the differing needs of executives and work-teams. A revision of the automation concept is necessary here: each worker or functionary should have his own isolated access to

part of the information system for special ends. The central system can be, in effect, decentralised through the use of access codes and passwords. It must also be possible for workers to have their own 'digital space' to dispose of, so that personal requirements can be satisfied by, for example, creating files for their own use. In this connection it is important to draw attention to a different attitude to the method of setting about automation and system development.

Van den Berg (1986) declares that a more realistic approach of automation processes is required. Among other things, he points out the problem of the unforeseen: changes in circumstances bring changes in information needs with them. The subjectivity problem must also be recognised: differing (favourite) notions of organisation dictate different demands of the information system. Both problems are notorious among those concerned with automation, but nowadays they can be more easily faced, thanks to the growing number of technical possibilities afforded by both hardware and software.

Finally, the use of data within an institute must be regulated by co-operation between organisations working together and professional unions. It is desirable that the agreements for this purpose be given the importance of a professional code of ethics.

REGISTRATION AND PRACTICE

In previous years, the automation of client registration within two types of work (social case-work and ambulant mental health services) (AMW and RIAGG) was stimulated and conducted from above. In the meantime, the vast majority of the institutes within these spheres of activity have actually adopted automated client registration. In the juvenile-assistance area a similar development has been initiated. Many other fields of activity and individual initiatives in the work being carried out develop their own registration systems, with the help of database programmers (health care, community development, neighbourhood and educational work).

The distinguishing characteristic of a registration system is a certain (screen) form, which displays a number of categories showing the data related to clients or patients and sometimes to members of the organisation.

Through modern (relational) database programming, it is possible to create various functions for the use of institutes with differing goals. At this point, the rapid introduction and expansion of the system becomes understandable: 'You can do so much with it'; and 'It is convenient to have all kinds of data about our clients constantly available'. Practical experience shows that the possibilities of database technique are still only partly exploited.

The following are the functions principally involved.

1 The daily consultation of client data, on behalf of the administration and/or the executive staff members of the

institute. The principal concerns in this regard are administrative: production of address labels, supervision of appointments, waiting list information and the supplying of innumerable other useful and daily informational requirements. From this viewpoint, registration is preponderantly experienced as profitable innovation, by those who utilise it.

2 Provision of justificatory data to the authorities, such as health insurance institutions and government bureaux; the introduction of summaries in annual reports.

3 The production of surveys and lists that can be used as information in the forming of policy, for example, to investigate how actual practice of the service rendered looks as set out in numbers and tables. Here, great variations between summaries serve to set up ingeniously arranged outputs, which can stimulate the imagination and provide specific information about the practice actually in use. This function is being more and more used in making annual reports or in producing material for the benefit of discussions related to work and the team.

4 Policy information, designed to support the management or administration of the institute - registration systems that provide specific management information are not yet generally operational. The question is whether this practice will develop out of client registration. Within RIAGG (ambulant mental health services), for instance, differences of opinion exist. Much policy and justificatory information is incontestably relevant to the directing of an institute. The refining of this database function, coupled with time registration, will be a hot issue among those affected, for it makes a new kind of control possible of the work of production and makes very real the question of competence in the use of data.

5 Statistical processing of registration data takes place also, especially through the co-ordinating national branch organisations, or by the bigger institutes. This concerns specially set tasks that are seldom met with in small automation personal computer systems. But it is just here that the possibilities arise, with the help of statistical database functions or programming, to transform the institute's clients into 'calculable proportions'. Trends in the practical field can be established quickly and dependably. It appears, moreover, that a new way of evaluating objectives is possible (statistical profile method).

6 Countless applications are possible by means of database technique, especially by matching files and records against one another (also from other information systems). In this way widely differing informational requirements can be satisfied, which for traditional storing methods would be impossible, or only possible through excessive effort. This technique permits also a new control policy or administration regime.

CONSEQUENCES AND PROSPECTS

Different automation experts and registration operators point to the fact that institution management is changing; there is talk of the imposition of more order and control. It is difficult to establish whether a direct effect from automation is concerned or whether, through the decline in financial means, and the accompanying change in mentality ('new objectivity' in Holland), a new management regime has come on the scene. It is the case, in any event, that any trend of this kind is strengthened by automation.

It is interesting that the advent of automation coincides with a period when there is much talk of a turnaround in political and social values. From support policies (emancipation work and social action) to market policies; from social concern to preoccupation with professional concerns and with changing ideas of how support programs and welfare schemes should function in society.

This is the climate in which the question of automation in the welfare sector is settled. The 'internal logic' of automation promotes a rationalist view of the world. It is precisely this compelling influence that suits many management and government groups, so that automation often becomes the image of success and quick-wittedness.

If it is established that automation strengthens a control regime, then it is important to safeguard the professional character of the organisations in the various work areas from this effect, and resist bureaucratisation. Social services that can be directed through registration systems ought, therefore, to be regarded with some degree of suspicion.

As the database technique has up to now been applied only partially to work practices and the management of institutes, the need for new agreements affecting the use of data is not yet generally realised. This will change quickly, as soon as the users sense that they are being watched, and management observes the wide variations among those actually doing the work as regards their way of working and the rate of performance.

There are also reasons to assume that there will be more searching around in other people's affairs, if these are accessible. This curiosity will be nourished by the ease with which data can be displayed on the screen. In this connection it is regrettable that as far as the safeguarding in the work area is concerned, there is still little regulation of operational practices. This question is made even more urgent because of the fact that many groups of clients cannot exert any influence upon registration practices.

Interesting is the remark of an official from a juvenile work organisation that workers "compelled to electronic reporting, will direct their efforts more on short term gains, rather than invest in their clients in the long term". That is to say, a relationship is suggested between the registration system and the way the work is done. In future registration systems to be applied in residential assistance there will be little room for the inclusion of biographical data, so that attention will be diverted to the immediate circumstances of young people that must be applied in the present rather than giving attention to what happened in the past.

The foregoing remarks indicate a possible effect that is not the consequence of a technical determinant but that results from decisions made by the principals. It is thus important to the identification of certain effects of automation that we establish whether they can be related to human (and political) choice procedures, or whether they are directly, and necessarily, connected with whatever technique has been applied. In reality, there will often be interference, so that a reactive control will be required to forestall undesired consequences (Holvast, 1986).

An approach to such an investigation, which will review these effects and consequences systematically and with consideration for the future, can be defined as 'Technology Assessment'. The actual investigation would then be concentrated on the relationship and interaction (actual or possible) between the techniques applied and the social and cultural environment.

As to the 'curiosity factor' mentioned earlier, a technical solution is the best: each worker to have his own protected access to the information system with his own files and (filtered) records, and an authorised access to specified data stored in the central unit.

Where registration systems include broader distribution of data for institute activities, for example in connection with treatment procedures, it is important that effects detected will be noted and described. In this way a new field of knowledge comes into existence, so that the interested groups and professionals can proceed deliberately towards progressive automation. In this respect we can speak of 'sociale informatiekunde', that is sector-minded automation knowledge (van Dinten, 1986) for the social services and allied professions.

Finally, practical experience has revealed two more dangers arising out of the setting up of, or changes in, registration systems. These are not directly related to automation as a technical determinant of human relationships, but to:

1 the mentality of some people in power, who want a transparent practice, 'because the liberties that social workers permit themselves must be abolished'

2 automation 'boys' who insist on proceeding according to the notions, peculiar to their own specialised functions, for the reason that, as they put it, 'the field workers don't know what they want'.

In such a climate, a real risk exists that automation will become a straitjacket, and will give rise to unacceptable working conditions.

REFERENCES

Berg, F. van den (1986). 'Over Automatisering, Management-informatie en Problemen', in *Informatie en Informatiebeleid*, April, uitgave Otto Cramwinckel, Amsterdam.
Dinten, W.L. van (1986). 'Communicatie, Informatiewetenschap, Informatietechniek en de invloed er van op strategievorming', in *Informatie*, jgn 28, no. 1.
Graaf, H. de (1982). *Pas op je tellen*, uitgave NIMAWO.
Holvast, J. (1986). *Op weg naar een riscoloze maatschappij?* Academic Service, Schoonhoven.

TECHNOLOGY OVER TIME: (COMMUNICATION/INFORMATION)
LESSONS WE SHOULD HAVE LEARNED

*Ramona R. Rush, Elizabeth B. Shear, Janrose C. Zingg,
Judy A. Goodrich, and Linda A. Porter*

"From there you can't call out, you can't shout loud enough
to be heard." (Elena Bonner, exiled to and isolated in Gorky,
USSR) (1986)

"Woman herself must judge of woman . . . man as man is
still as obtuse of yore . . . He yet fails to see in her a
factor of life whose influence for good or evil has even been
in direct ratio with her freedom. He does not yet discern her
equal right with himself to impress her own opinions on the
world. He still interprets governments and religions as
requiring from her an unquestioning obedience to laws she
had no share in making . . . man has assumed the right to
think for woman." So wrote Matilda Joslyn Gage in 1893 (Lynn
Spender, 1983).

These two quotes, in the minds of the authors of this paper, set
the tone we want for the discussion which follows. It continues
to be an amazement to us, as we approach the end of this
century, that more than three-quarters of the world's population
(in 'developing' countries); diverse, 'dissident' groups in
'developed' countries; and the 'better half' of both of those
populations (women) have been treated as 'minoritized majorities' and kept out of war and board rooms where most of the
decisions about technological advances are made.

In addressing the question: "Women and the Communication
Revolution: Can we Get There from Here?" in the early 1980s, we
wrote that one of the more important communication reality
checks has to do with outworn concepts, formulae, models and
language (Rush, Buck and Ogan, 1982). We noted that when the
concepts of 'development' and 'change' are preferred, we might
have one mindset. When 'equity' is offered along with
development or change, we have quite a different viewpoint.

One aggregates, the other specifies. That theme is as worth
exploring today as it was in 1982. When data concerning humans
are aggregated, as often happens with indicators of and
statistics for the concepts of development, communications, and
change, the interpretation and/or implementation usually follows
dominant models or the traditional thinking. We lose sight of
individual, secondary, or tertiary group differences which might
have suggested a modified model or even a completely different
one.

As a case in point, aggregated models for communication and
development sometimes do include women, but women's problems
and issues are seldom the focal point; the aggregation is
usually done at the expense of those very matters. Elaborating
on this basic and crucial point, Canadian sociologist Thelma

McCormack, citing Papanek (1978) and Wolf (1966), points out that most theories of development have little to say about women; generalized constructs like 'the peasant' presumably refer to both men and women, although the empirical studies more often than not look into the fields and see only men (McCormack, 1981).

It should come as no surprise, then, even if it always seems to, when we read statements such as this:

"While women represent 50 per cent of the world adult population and one-third of the official labour force, they perform nearly two-thirds of all working hours, receive only one-tenth of the world income and own less than 1 per cent of world property." (UNESCO, Medium-Term Plan 1984-1989).

When aggregation masks specificity (or, more accurately, diversity), the result is often inequitable distributions of power, money, technology, 'goods' of all kinds. It should not escape our attention that the dominant economic model/myth system is the one which largely benefits from such aggregation.

It is largely for such reasons that E.F. Schumacher's 'Small is Beautiful: Economics as if People Mattered' (1973) has collected such a following over the years, and why futurist Hazel Henderson has sub-titled two of her books 'The End of Economics' (1978, with a foreword by Schumacher), and 'Alternatives to Economics' (1981).

Current occupational situations and trend projections would indicate that men (usually white and in the so-called 'developed' countries) will continue to dominate the future production and distribution of information and knowledge. In this most recent communications revolution, there are indications that women's and other voices are not going to be heard this time either, especially given the unique nature of the revolution – the new information technologies (e.g. cable TV, computers, communication satellites) have advanced so recently and rapidly that they are converging with each other, and with traditional mass media. If consumer and user opinions weren't solicited in earlier times with less complex and singularly-advanced communication technologies, the outlook isn't good for the focal era of information and communications.

A quick flashback to women's roles when other revolutionary technologies came on the public scene indicates that men have always played the more active role in shaping these technologies and determining their use, while women (and minorities and other oppressed majorities) have generally been the passive recipients of what has been offered or trickled down after the 'real' needs were met. The needs and intentions behind many of these successive communications technologies arose from male-dominated commercial and military enterprises.

Women will have to guard against becoming the sure-footed workhorses of the 'Information Society', and/or underemployed and unemployed functional and technical information illiterates. Indeed, the outlook for women in the communications revolution from a standing point within the present communications

industry, including the US computer workforce, only reinforces
the idea that revolutions have come and gone but the relative
power and status of the actors have remained the same (Rush,
Buck, and Ogan, 1982).

In the 1982 article 'Women and the Communications Revolution:
Can we Get There from Here?', Rush, Buck, and Ogan pointed to
an interesting phenomenon which looks as if there is some kind
of a mystical 'ceiling' (or, more accurately for women, a
'flooring') effect in the form of a ratio of concentration in
symbolic representation, occupational status, and/or salary
levels for women. The ratio usually resides around a 1/4:3/4 or
1/3:2/3 proportion, female to male or vice versa (see also Rush,
1983a).

For example, of officials and managers in television stations
about 75 per cent were males the other one-quarter were
females; women represented about 36-38 per cent of the US daily
press workforce; and in the computer industry, women earned
about 74 cents for every dollar earned by the male peers, and
men still outnumbered women by a factor of three to one except
in the lowest paying operative area where 63 per cent were
women, and so on. This ratio holds in the latest benchmark
study done about women in the media by Jean Gaddy Wilson
(forthcoming) – women reside around the one-third figure in
employment and in management in newspapers, television and
radio. The only exception is management in newspapers where
about one quarter are female.

Few studies or reports in the last ten years of women's
employment and portrayals in the mass media have painted
anything but a dismal picture about women's progress, if
progress means rising out of the lower echelons of hierarchical
job patterns and from behind the commercialized dirty rings
around the collars (Gallagher, 1981; Rush, Buck, and Ogan,
1982). There are discouraging reports about hi-tech electronics
companies, including communication, moving their manufacturing
plants to third world countries in order to exploit low-salaried
labor (mostly young, single females wanting and needing their
first jobs or mothers needing income to support families). And
the ripple effect increases unemployment among other (exploited)
females back in the 'developed' home country, which also does
not bode well for future social change. However, there are
random research reports which do allow some optimism about
women's roles with the new technology (Hanson, forthcoming).

DIFFERENT VOICES/DIFFERENT APPROACHES TO COMMUNICATION

Obviously any time of change, of transition, or disruption, is
also a time of questioning. But the questions need to come from
our 'new brains', not our old ones. First we have to de-myth,
re-tool, and then re-fit the human condition. Communications
student, Janrose C. Zingg (1987), points to an example of such
intervention:

"'Re-tooling' is a process of building knowledge. Specifically, women must refine their understanding of science and its applications, for from this base hard tools are wrought, machines built, and technologies grown. The physical and natural sciences must become as familiar to us as our own perceptions of ourselves. For indeed, we know there are consequences from 'the boys playing with gasoline in the garage'. We must be able to communicate information from the feminist view on probable consequences of appropriate technology and use of the earth's resources."

Different voices with a call for different communication approaches are coming from many quarters.
The Women's Institute for Freedom of the Press, located in Washington DC, has a research and publishing program based on seven assumptions for a new philosophy of communication which answers some of the calls for a redefinition of the news, and challenges barriers to media access. These assumptions are:

1 people make their judgements on the basis of the information they have at a given time

2 each person is the best judge of her or his own best interests

3 media owners give us the information they think important for us to know

4 media do not mirror society (they represent the owners' views)

5 for the public to obtain the information of the majority, people must be able to speak for themselves

6 power is based on the number of people you can reach with your information

7 equalizing power among us would require that we all have equal means of reaching the public to communicate our information when we wish, in the way most suitable to our message.

(WIFP, 1977)

As the infamous 1984 got under way with the possibility of Big Brother continuing to watch us, there appeared to be convergence phenomena occurring, as was noted earlier, because of the rapid advances in communication technologies as new media mix with one another and with traditional media in ways heretofore unconceived. But there is also a convergence of minds, of kindred spirits, much in the way that the Reverend Jesse Jackson in the USA envisions his Rainbow Coalition. What remains to be seen is whether the technical efficiency of the communication systems will connect with human communication needs and development (Rush, 1983b).
In many ways, communications is at a crossroads. And, in as many ways, so is feminism. The overlapping, the convergence,

of these ways is a crucial question, at least for some of us. The centerpiece issue is one of language, information, communication, and knowledge - and factors of their production, distribution, and consumption.

And somehow, in the widely-heralded 'Information Society' or 'Communications Era', the focal issues seems not only appropriate but commanding. For those concerned, approaches vary but the message is much the same - that "while theories can be used to oppress, they also can be used in the interest of liberation - that one sex alone should not control information and the production of knowledge in our society". (D. Spender, 1983).

Women, heretofore the world's 'minoritized majority', have the appropriate experiential equation to lead efforts toward a New World Order, based on a democratization of language, information, communication, and knowledge.

In testing this premise, women must primarily rely upon our own insights, intuition, language, experiences, research, interpretations, philosophy, and theory-building as the bases for world views and world hypotheses. To effect this, networks of women's coalitions in all fields and endeavors need to be expanded and linked, especially to the distribution of communication power which will come (but not to women unless we intervene) with the new technologies.

Priorities for future efforts need to be assessed. For example, there is an extensive documentation about inequities between the sexes in the workplace and in symbolic representation. A continual re-substantiation of this paramount evidence provides a necessary check on reality. But it is also necessary to intervene in the underlying structure and dynamics of social and cultural reproductions if we are to influence the sources of change and contestation when there are prevailing distributions of power and control in society (Golding and Murdock, 1980).

'Who constructed and continues to construct the social and cultural reality?' leads to questions of management, training, access, participation, manipulation, etc., and thus to some understanding of the distributions of knowledge in a society.

The inequality in access to production of information is brought out by the gaps - by what is not said, by those who are silent. It would seem logical that women in all communications fields are the appropriate persons to beat the drum for diversity. And we are talking here about *diversity* . . . of viewpoints, perceptions, experiences - the so-called 'marketplace of ideas'.

Kessler (1984) uses several quotes to underline the necessity of diversity through expression. One, which echoed Milton and Mills' defense of minorities, was used by the US Commission on Freedom of the Press (also known as the Hutchins Commission, which submitted its guidelines for operation of a free and responsible press in 1947): "Valuable ideas may be put forth first in forms that are crude, indefensible, or even dangerous. They need the chance to develop through free criticism as well as the chance to survive on the basis of ultimate worth." The

First Amendment, wrote the Commission, "was intended to guarantee free expression, not to create a privileged industry".

Kessler writes that accumulated evidence over the years overwhelmingly points to a closed marketplace within the popular conventional press and a routine denial of participation – access – to those who held aberrant beliefs. This lack of access has taken at least three forms:

1 complete exclusion from the popular media marketplace of the (dissident) group, its ideas and goals

2 exclusion of ideas, goals, and programs of the group, but inclusion of events (e.g. marches, strikes, demonstrations) in which the group participated

3 ridicule, insult, or stereotyping of the group and its ideas rather than discussion, explanation, and debate.

"Merely mentioning a group does not constitute access," Kessler writes. "What the group stands for, what it is fighting for (or against) – its ideas – also must receive a forum . . ."

If women's and other diverse voices aren't heard, if those important contributions do not get through to the public, then those persons will continue to build from and extend the system we have already used to communicate with each other – a variety of channels including person-to-person communication, conferences, newsletters, organizations, music, cable, columns, film publishing, computer networking, video cassettes and discs. The ultimate challenge is not to be 'separate but equal'; rather, the goal is to be 'connected and equal'. But first, women's and other issues, identified as such on a world-wide basis, have to be resolved according to criteria established by and within a public agenda planned and set by women and other, now silenced, voices. This is the basis of the 'gender gap' connection and other 'gap' connections.

What this envisions at the start is a communication system or systems which build on the foundation of women's 'herstory' and other oppressed persons' histories, on *our* world views and *our* current experiences of the world; systems of communication where the language and knowledge generated reflect our metaphors of the world, our psychology, politics, economics, and culture.

Several writers make crucial points that the implications of integrating women (and, by extension, other groups) into either present communication structures or a New Order yet to be created must be carefully analyzed. Otherwise, women may end up being integrated into a new international order as detrimental to themselves as their 'integration' into development has been (Isis, 1983).

As McCormack (1987) points out, what we need is a multi-media approach with different systems of communication reinforcing each other:

"But I think it is essential that we put a great deal of effort and resources into the approach, for in countries that are developing, women are looking for new understandings of themselves in the various public and private roles they play. If modernization means overcoming a psychology of dependency, then it would be ironic if women exchanged one form of dependency (traditional) for another. Communication can make a big difference in the scenario. If the problem is ignored, if women become even more invisible in a situation of rapid change, there can be a serious form of pathology which develops among women, a deep alienation from themselves."

What, then, are we to do? Women, individually or collectively, have not historically been known to have access to sufficient economic bases to obtain and maintain far-flung world-wide communication systems, as do the Associated Press or the UPI. However, women are recognizing the human potential possibilities in the transition from the Industrial Age to the Information Age and taking an inventory of where women are, what women need to do, and where women need to be, to ensure that any future silences in 'herstory' are there for the correct reasons (Rush, 1986).

WOMEN HAVE IMPRESSIVE COMMUNICATION/INFORMATION INVENTORIES

The results of a world-wide assessment of women's communication/information inventories are quite revealing even though they are most likely conservative estimates, given the traditional tendency to not include in most counting estimates or procedures anything belonging to the 'fugitive' world of women.

The Sheer Impact of Numbers – The immense social change which is taking place with increasing numbers of women in the work force has general and specific ramifications for women and the traditional mass media. The general media agenda must include messages and marketing strategies to reach an increasingly-powerful consumer. One message is that women live a long time, and more than ever are single heads of households. These female heads of households are important consumers even if corporate and government policies have driven many of them and their children into recurring poverty.

Networks are in Place – Included in women's notable communication achievements – because this particular form of non-hierarchical, decentralized communication has been developed and relied upon by women throughout history for information, education, protection, friendship entertainment – is networking. Women network in and out of the traditional mass media, and they have networks only for women's communication. All channels of traditional communication and especially **new communication technologies** are used. Networking has increased within general populations and networks certainly have increased in number for women's communication purposes.

An example of women's connections is the US-based, computerized National Women's Mailing List with 70,000 self-reported women and 10,000 women's groups networking via this channel of communication (1986). The NAWML was started in 1981 as the first project of the San Francisco-based Women's Information Exchange. Its purpose was to demonstrate that feminist technology was both possible and practical, and that computers could be used to strengthen the women's movement.

A further example is the separate but collective networking efforts of Isis Women's International Cross Cultural Exchange (WICCE) in Geneva, and Isis International in Rome (Cottingham, forthcoming).

In the early 1980s, Isis had around 10,000 contacts in more than 100 countries of the world, and a documentation center of about 100,000 items. Isis had produced 29 Isis International Bulletins with information from women from all over the world in the first seven years, after starting in 1975 with $3,000. It has also organized or helped to organize international conferences on many global topics, including women and new technology, and it has developed the International Feminist Network (IFN).

Internationalism as a Mindset – Women's experiences have pointed them in the direction of connections for the 'general good' and 'community' – this extends to international concerns, especially since women have been able to overcome learned biases and stereotypes from male-driven concerns about national security, economics, and politics. These experiences are realized in many ways, but certainly through international travel to international meetings. The numerous governmental and non-governmental meetings held nationally, regionally, and internationally during the UN Decade for Women, ending in Nairobi in 1985, have had resounding impacts worldwide. Sociologist Jesse Bernard (1986) has a related point:

". . . The activities of most such (international) meetings, further, are slow-breaking news so that they are not likely to be widely reported in the media. Like so much else in the female world, they remain as yet almost wholly invisible – except when they cannot be ignored, patronized, or ridiculed. Press reports are usually limited to meetings at which male-world issues are highlighted, as in the UN-sponsored meetings in Mexico City and Copenhagen.

"Still, such ignorance may, it has been argued, have a benign side. It is probably just as well that the press ignore the complex systems of networks in process in the female world, creating and expanding consciousness of a shared global female world. It gives the process a period of grace, a chance to learn by mistakes, an opportunity for trial-and-error without too much outside interference, without too much fear of failure, without loss of face when goals are not reached. A time to achieve the self-confidence that will be urgently needed when the male world discovers it and attempts to take it over. Or co-opt it. The thinking and research and sharing in which women scholars are engaged may have an analogous impact which will also surprise the status quo with a so-called sleeper effect when the rays of the Feminist Enlightenment finally reach it."

Women's literature and other forms of communication have reflected and are increasingly reflecting this global feminist connection.

Women are serious about finally being visible, audible, and meaningfully included, because women intend to supply the other half of the dialogue in this current one-sided global monologue.

The truly integrative model to which we can point is the result of women's efforts to get their information circulated and included. A first-level outreach has been established where issues needing public attention are raised, debated, and articulated in women's newspapers, newsletters, magazines, journals, television and radio programs, videotapes, throughout the world. Then women employed at the second-level, mainstream mass media include information in those channels about all of these issues for the general public (Allen, forthcoming).

For some persons, this means a 'gain-gain' situation in that women's experiences, intuitions, and knowledge can be added to those of men for a human approach to seemingly inhuman and inhumane global issues. For others, not much will change . . . noticeably . . . for a while.

But perhaps the most important point that can be made is that women are actively involved in communication and community at all levels, but especially locally and internationally. That may prove to be the most successful integrative combination and model for women, communication, and development – *thinking globally and acting locally*.

REFERENCES

Allen, Donna (forthcoming). 'From Opportunity to Strategy: women Contribute to the Communications Future'. In R. Rush, and D. Allen, (eds.) *Communications at the Crossroads: The Gender Gap Connection*. Ablex Publishing Corporation, Norfolk, NJ.

Bernard, Jessie (1986). Personal correspondence.

Bonner, Elena (1986). *Alone Together*. Knopf, New York.

Boulding, Elise (1976). *The Underside of History: A View of Women Through Time*. Westview Press Inc., Boulder, Colorado.

Cottingham, Jane (forthcoming). 'Isis: A Decade of International Networking'. in R. Rush and D. Allen (eds.) op.cit.

Gallagher, Margaret (1981). *Unequal Opportunities: The Case of Women and the Media*. The Unesco Press, Paris.

Golding, Peter, and Murdock, Graham (1980). 'Theories of Communication and Theories of Society', in Wilhoit and deBock (eds.) *Mass Communication Review Yearbook*, vol.1. Sage Publications, Beverley Hills, CA.

Hanson, Jaris (forthcoming). 'Women in Telecommunications: The Executive Woman in Informatics'. In R. Rush and D. Allen (eds.) op.cit.

Henderson, Hazel (1978). *Creating Alternative Futures: The End of Economics.* Perigee Books, New York.

Henderson, Hazel (1981). *The Politics of the Solar Age: Alternatives to Economics.* Anchor Press/Doubleday, Garden City, New York.

ISIS, Women's International and Information and Communication Service (1983). *Women in Development: a Resource Guide for Organization and Action.* Geneva.

Kessler, Lauren (1984). *The Dissident Press.* Sage Publications, Beverley Hills, CA.

McCormack, Thelma. (1981). 'Development with Equity for Women', in Naomi Black and Ann Baker Cottrell (eds.) *Women and World Change: Equity Issues in Development.* Sage Publications, Beverly Hills, CA.

McCormack, Thelma (1987). Personal Correspondence. April.

National Women's Mailing List, PO Box 68, Jenner, CA 95459, USA.

Papanek, H. (1978). 'Comment on Gusfield's Review Essay on Becoming Modern'. *American Journal of Sociology,* **83**, 6, 1507–1511.

Rush, Ramona R. (1983a). 'A Different Call to Arms: Women in the Core of the Communications Revolution'. Paper presented to the Association for Education in Journalism and Mass Communication, Oregon State University, August.

Rush, Ramona R. (1983b). 'Efficiency AND Equality: Confronting an Age–Old Tradeoff in the Information Age'. Unpublished manuscript. Department of Communication, University of Kentucky, Lexington, KY.

Rush, Ramona R. (1986). 'From Silent Scream to Silent Scheme: The Role of Women in International Communications'. Paper presented to the First Canberra (Australia) Conference on International Communication, December.

Rush, Ramona R., Buck, Elizabeth, and Ogan, Christine. (1982). 'Women and the Communications Revolution: Can we get there from here?' *Chasqui* (publication of the Centro Internacional de Estudio Superiores de la Comunicacion para America Latina (CIESPAL), July–September.

Schumacher, E.F. (1973). *Small is Beautiful: Economics as if People Mattered.* Harper & Row, New York.

Spender, Dale (ed.) (1983). *Feminist Theorists: Three Centuries of Key Women Thinkers.* Pantheon Books, New York.

Spender, Lynne (1983). 'Matilda Joslyn Gage: Active Intellectual'. In D. Spender (ed.) op.cit.

UNESCO. 'The Status of Women'. *Medium-Term Plan,* 1984-1989. XIV.

Wilson, Jean Gaddy (forthcoming). 'Future Directions for Females in the Media'. In R. Rush and D. Allen (eds.) op.cit.

Wolf, E. (1966). *Peasants.* Prentice-Hall, Englewood Cliffs, NJ.

Women's Institute for Freedom of the Press, 3306 Ross Place, NW, Washington, DC 20008. Dr Donna Allen, Director.

Zingg, Janrose C. (1987). Personal Correspondence. May 1.

Information Technology and the Human Services
Edited by B. Glastonbury, W. LaMendola and S. Toole
© 1988 John Wiley & Sons Ltd

CHAPTER 10

Technology Transfer and the Third World

The paucity of papers from third world participants at HUSITA reflected the difficulty experienced by those from poor countries who wanted to attend. Only a handful were able to come. In sharp contrast the conference debate about technology transfer and the third world was extensive, high–profiled, and characterised by strong assertions of principle. The position of the third world provoked widespread feelings of guilt and concern from representatives of wealthier nations. The dominant principle was undoubtedly that of 'help thy neighbour', with calls to do everything possible to enable poorer countries (or poorer communities) to share in the benefits of IT. In many of the poorer countries Export Production Zones have been established where the natural and labour resources of the country are being used to produce technology cheaply, yet rarely is it being made available to the indigenous population. At the same time this positive and creative urge was surrounded by a web of issues, some practical, some of principle, about the nature of the rich/poor relationship. Could Western IT be taken 'off the shelf' and used to advantage by countries and groups which lacked a basic technology infrastructure? What adaptations were needed? Would the transfer of technology pass on the unsolved problems as well as the benefits of IT? What would be the cultural and ecological effects? Should third world countries make a bid for 'state of the art' hardware and software, or start at a less advanced stage? Would the wealthy nations be prepared to hand over the latest developments, or use the third world to dump obsolete equipment and ideas? Should the poorer nations, in exchange for technology transfer, stop undermining developmental work (especially of multinational corporations) by banning cheap cloning? Could many of us from the wealthier countries survive without the benefits of Far East cloning? Was the very notion of technology transfer a paternalistic extension of traditional colonial relationships? Should action be taken to ensure price structures in third world markets which reflected the incomes of potential buyers of IT? Should all software be free or very nearly so?

No considered answers have yet been formulated to many of these questions, but if HUSITA leads to the start of an International Organisation then its members will need to address them, and to produce a coherent policy which will encourage third world people to join in.

The issues themselves can be clustered under a number of themes, two of which are taken up in the papers offered in this chapter. One theme concerns the readiness and ability of a poor country to make good use of IT opportunities. Daniel, writing from Tamil Nadu State in southern India, describes the sort of IT facilities to be found in a poor setting. Essentially it is a story of hardware which is inadequate for the job (and in Western terms obsolete), handling simple data analysis projects. The projects themselves are of vital importance to India, and output could be substantially improved with quite small incremental boosts in hardware and applications software. In his description there are some aspects of IT which are significant by their absence – most notably communications – and this serves to illustrate the plight of poor countries, and point up the 'taken for granted' value it has been for wealthier nations to have solid dependable infrastructures in such areas as power supplies and telephone links.

Another Indian contributor, Rao, from Bombay, seeks to analyse the problems for IT uses in India. Specifically she looks at local government, and the ability of computers to handle planning and information services. She sees potential, but many limitations, the latter mostly associated with socio/political attitudes towards the control of technology. She suggests that to date in India computers have not been made available to those who need them and would use them, but as status symbols to top officials. Her paper is a vivid illustration of the issues of empowerment and access discussed in earlier chapters. She is also concerned about internal political corruption and the exploitation of database material, as well as the widespread practice of a suspicious population in providing government information gatherers with false data. For Rao successful IT is primarily a political issue, and her research supports the view that IT, far from alleviating, is likely to enhance those bad practices which are already entrenched in a system. In India's case the bad practices have to do both with the standards of conduct of some officials, and with a long-standing tendency to clog a system with information overload. In short, too many officials collecting too much information, some for dubious purposes, some for no purpose at all.

The final paper in this chapter, and appropriately the last one in the book, is from Philippine philosopher Joaquin Tan. He raises the second theme, that of the social, political and economic price the third world countries are asked to pay for technology transfer, whether the transfer comes from wealthy countries or as part of the business activities of multinational corporations. Tan's concern is partly with technology transfer as a continuation of colonisation, but more fundamentally with the institutional arrangements and value systems that come with the package. He argues that ill-conceived technology transfer, however well motivated, establishes "the West as destined to cast the rest of the world in its own image". For him, placed in an ex-colony torn by internal dissent, and viewing the enormous power of the industrialised world, acceptable technology transfer is a matter of understanding and sharing different cultures and value systems as an integral part of sharing technology.

USE OF COMPUTERS IN HEALTH SYSTEMS RESEARCH IN INDIA

J. Christopher Daniel

Every individual has the right to life and health and to the necessities of life including proper medical services, which in turn depends on the equitable distribution of health resources and appropriate health care systems. In India, the delivery of health care services is mainly through the complex of State Government owned primary health centres and hospitals in rural areas. In fact, primary health care occupies a pivotal position in the national health care system. India lives in villages, which are inhabited by 80 per cent of the population. The overall picture of health in India during the last 30 years is a mixture of light and shade, of some outstanding achievements whose effect is unfortunately more than offset by grave failures. Unfortunately, health projects and programmes undertaken by governmental institutions in particular and voluntary health organisations in general have suffered for want of an effective system for integrated planning, scheduling and control.

HEALTH SYSTEMS RESEARCH

Health systems research is one of the inputs to a study of health problems, and to the improvement of the health status of the people. It is found to be very useful in developing health indicators on the basis of which any health care or development projects and programmes could be planned, implemented and monitored.

According to the World Health Organisation (1986), health systems research is concerned with strengthening the means of health promotion and health care. It begins with existing field problems and uses a variety of research disciplines to apply scientific knowledge for improving health care and health status, bridging in this way the wide gap that now separates knowledge and action in health.

Problems of health, their causation, and approaches to handling health problems, could be studied by conducting health systems research. Particularly, it is necessary to promote research on the social and economic aspects of medicine which are the main concerns of social workers, health educators, community organisers, and medical social workers. One of the priority areas in research is the problems of the under-privileged and poor in urban slums and villages in India whose health status has to be improved.

INFORMATION NEEDS AND COMPUTATION

It is said that information is power. The power is generated through the virtue of knowing what is happening around, what is likely to happen, the correct assessment of the factors responsible, accurate judgement and choice of actions out of those feasible and the capacity to intervene and implement corrective actions (Ramaiah, 1979). For planning of any project and programme in the health sector, data collected through sample surveys or field studies on its goals and objectives, the characteristics of the population living in the community, the socio-economic bases of the community, degree of health consciousness, problems of health, prevalence of disease, knowledge, attitude and practice of health care services, etc., are required to be collected and analysed. Based on the data analysis and interpretation, information becomes available for planning and policy level decision-making. Computation of data helps the programme managers, planners and policy-makers to monitor and evaluate the health project programme. The computer has an important role in the delivery of health services. Among its various applications, the computer is useful for data processing tasks which help provide information not only for the transaction of day-to-day operations and the implementation of programmes, but also for planning and policy-making at high levels of health programme management. It is found to be very useful in health system research for improving the quality and quantity of health care. The use of computer-based data processing is of great importance: without it the health management personnel will be seriously handicapped for want of reliable **data** and **information.**

Use of computers in health systems research helps to:

1 find out or assess the health needs of the community by computing data relating to certain health indicators such as infant and child mortality, life expectancy, maternal morbidity (incidence and prevalence rates), disease-specific death rates, disability, etc.

2 determine the conditions for, and the effects of alternative patterns of health care delivery, in terms of feasibility, quality and costs

3 analyse and quantify the dynamics of the economics of health systems

4 analyse management problems i.e. health planning, administration and regulation for achieving greater managerial efficiency

5 analyse the structure, functions and deficiencies of health systems

6 evaluate effects of health programmes by analysing their structure, process and outcome.

Computer applications are possible mainly in the following health programmes undertaken by both governmental institutions and voluntary health associations in India:

1 integrated child development services

2 family planning programmes

3 nutrition rehabilitation projects

4 environmental improvement services project.

COMPUTER APPLICATIONS IN THE DELIVERY OF HEALTH SERVICES IN INDIA

Computers are used in monitoring child survival and development through the National Sample Survey Organisation (NSSO) established by the government in India. This organisation undertakes surveys covering social and economic aspects of the life of the people. Most of the surveys are centered around infant and child mortality, childhood disability, morbidity, nutrition, and family planning. The data collected on the various health indicators are sent to the processing division of the NSSO, where tabulation and computation work is done. Another governmental organisation which uses computers in health surveys is the National Nutrition Monitoring Bureau (NNMB). The Bureau aims at collecting and processing data on food consumption, providing a nutritional profile of representative segments of the population on a continuous basis, and conducting impact evaluation of ongoing national nutrition programmes. Computation is used by the Bureau for publishing state-wide data and providing information on the following aspects:

1 average levels of food and nutrient consumption according to per capita income

2 adequacy status of proteins - calories

3 prevalence of nutritional deficiency signs in different physiological, age and sex groups

4 average body measurements according to age and sex

5 extent of growth retardation among pre-schoolers (1-5 years) on the basis of weight-for-age status.

One of the development programmes implemented by the Government of India is the Integrated Child Development Services (ICDS). The objectives of the ICDS are to improve the nutritional and health status of children in the age group 0-6 years, to lay the foundation for proper psychological, physical and social development of the child, and to reduce the incidence of mortality, morbidity, malnutrition and school drop-outs, etc. The package of service provided to children and pregnant and nursing mothers includes:

1 supplementary nutrition

2 immunisation

3 health check up

4 nutrition and health education

5 referral services and non-formal pre-school education.

Right from the inception of ICDS there has been greater emphasis on proper monitoring and evaluation for getting feedback on the implementation and co-ordination of the programme. Data relating to key indicators such as demography, mortality, nutritional status, supplementary nutrition, morbidity, health services, number of children (3-6 years) receiving pre-school education, proportion of children receiving pre-school education, status of health and nutrition education provided to women and community participation (status of community participation and status of women's organisations) are collected from various project areas and sent to the computer unit for processing and analysis.

Primary Health Centres (PHC) are the focal point of government health delivery services in rural India. Programmes undertaken at the PHC level are monitored periodically on the basis of a variety of data collected and compiled through 13 different types of registers and forms such as village record, family folders, health card, records relating to pre-natal, natal and post-natal services, vital events register, daily diary, etc.

The Central Bureau of Health Intelligence collects data from various health centres and forwards them to the National Information Centre for processing and providing relevant tables for monitoring the health programmes. The National Information Centre is responsible for computation and analysis of the data and making information available to policy-makers on time.

A few schools of social work in India have been entrusted with the responsibility of developing a comprehensive system of monitoring and evaluation of social components of the Integrated Child Development Services. They utilise the services of computer centres for processing and analysing data relating to pre-school education, health and nutrition education and community participation.

CONCLUSION

India, a developing country, is slowly but steadily moving towards 'Computer Culture'. Though 'computerphobia' and 'technophobia' seem to prevent people from using computer technology, its far reaching advantages cannot be gainsaid particularly in the context of health care delivery systems in

India. The awakening of 'computer applications' in health systems research is yet to catch up in a big way in India for want of computer facilities. Computers have an important role in this information age, but their use in India is yet to be explored in many areas of health care where data handling is of paramount importance. Governmental institutions, voluntary health care agencies and schools of social work in India engaged in human development use computers for effective planning, monitoring and evaluation of health projects and programmes and for foreseeing future design needs.

With regard to computer applications by the school of social work in India in health systems research, it is observed that only a very few institutions go in for computer consultancy for processing and data analysis.

Many schools have been facing the 'problem of affordability' to equip them with computers. Furthermore, we have failed to realise the importance of developing software literacy in social work education. Knowing the significance of human service information tchnology, it is felt that schools of social work should attempt to create a software literacy awareness among students and teachers and develop programming ability and computer creativity in them. It is being increasingly realised that there is a dire necessity for including information technology as a social work component to support humanity especially in the delivery of health services which will benefit not only the people but also help develop health indicators for monitoring progress towards health for all by the year 2000 in India.

REFERENCES

Ramaiah, T.J. (1979). 'Health Programme Management through PERT'. Abhinav Publications, New Delhi.
World Health Organisation (1986). 'Health Research Strategy'. WHO, Geneva.

IMPLICATIONS OF COMPUTERIZING DISTRICT ADMINISTRATION

Vidya Rao

The preparation and implementation of programmes of self-sustaining development is not necessarily a long-term task. It is more so because India is a traditional society in which there are pockets of rural population that are yet to join the mainstream. Planned development was accepted many years ago as the only way to bring about changes. The planners have been introducing a variety of programmes to pass on the benefits of developments to local communities with varying degrees of success. Panchayat Raj Institutions, as an important unit of local self-government, are entrusted with the task of implementing the development programmes. The unevenness of obtaining the benefits of development is partly due to the intermittent nature of inter-sectoral, and forward-backward linkages. The programmes for developing a people are basically multi-disciplinary; linking different sectors in a region and co-ordinating the process of development of different sections of a traditional society is a complex task. District administration in the process generates a great deal of information that can potentially facilitate balanced development.

This paper will briefly describe the organizational set up of the local self-government, the concept of decentralized planning and the Integrated Rural Development Programme. Finally, there will be discussion of some of the important socio-political implications of computerization. Let me briefly describe the organizational set-up of the local self-government in India.

LOCAL SELF-GOVERNMENT IN INDIA

The emergence of local self-government as the main instrument for development in independent India is the result of several factors - India's history, the teachings of Gandhiji, the directive principles of the Constitution, the Five Year Plans with their endorsement of people's participation, and several pre-independence experiments in community development. There was a well-developed system of village panchayats in ancient India, and they have existed in one form or another throughout the history of India, although they were dormant during the seventeenth and eighteenth centuries.

The elected councils, which have come into existence as a result of the introduction of the three-tier system of Panchayat Raj, are the village panchayat, Panchayat Samiti (Block Council), and the Zilla Parishad (District Council). These institutions have four distinct purposes:

1 to elicit local knowledge and wishes

2 to provide a means of local administration

3 to create a local political system

4 to effect social change.

Their executive counterparts are the Block Development Office (BDO) at the intermediary level and the District Administration at the district level.

After the initial enthusiasm following the creation of these institutions, there has been stagnation and decline in their functioning in many parts of the country. Wherever Panchayat Raj institutions have been actively involved, the implementation of development and anti-poverty programmes has been decidedly better, and the selection of beneficiaries and designing of schemes have been more satisfactory. These institutions need to be revitalized and endowed with necessary resources and power to discharge the functions and responsibilities assigned to them.

RURAL DEVELOPMENT PROGRAMMES

Impetus for rural development was provided by planning. First, it took the shape of community development programmes in the early 1950s. Community development programmes emphasised that all-round development of rural areas should be maintained, and that the initiative was to come from the community itself. The programmes related to agriculture, communication, co-operation, and rural housing. The integrated approach to rural development, however, got gradually diluted mainly due to the importance given to self-reliance in food. The emphasis shifted almost exclusively to increasing agricultural production. Through the 1960s, the original community development programme went through several changes.

The launching of some of these rural development programmes has been accompanied by the creation of new programme-oriented and often overlapping structural mechanisms. Small Farmers Development Agencies, Drought Prone Area Agency, and so on were created in the form of registered soceities. Special budgets, and posts of specialist extension officers were created by taking them away from the Block Development Office (BDO).

By the early 1970s the need to take special measures for the benefit of the poor was sharply felt. A large number of programmes was introduced and have thus been operating for the past fifteen years. In practice, these programmes were reduced to mere subsidy. The realization of the situation led to the formation of a simple programme integrating all development-related activities to achieve sustained social and economic development of the area. Thus the concept of Integrated Rural Development was evolved during the Fifth Plan period in an attempt to consolidate different development programmes into one single package.

The Integrated Rural Development approach aims at developing the area and the people by bringing about the necessary institutional changes and enhancing the receptiveness of the people by delivering a package of services to encompass not only agriculture and rural industries, but also health, nutrition, education, basic civic amenities, family planning, etc., with the ultimate objective of improving the quality of life. By the late 1970s the block machinery was in shambles, and at the district level there was a multiplicity of special and sectoral institutions competing to serve essentially the same target group.

The District Rural Development Agency (DRDA) was created during the Sixth Plan period to co-ordinate the planning and implementing agencies at the district level. The DRDA co-ordinates the implementation of Integrated Rural Development Programmes (IRDP), Training of Rural Youth for Self-Employment, National Rural Employment Programme, Rural Landless Employment Guarantee Programme, Drought Prone Area Programme, etc. However, there is no uniformity in the actual staffing pattern of the DRDA in the country. The IRDP is a package of programmes closely integrated to achieve spatial balance in social and economic development, based on community participation in the process of development. The approach contains some new elements in addition to earlier concepts of community development and agricultural extension. The main objects of IRDP would be to evolve an operationally integrated strategy for the purpose of increasing production and productivity in agriculture and allied sectors, based on the resource and income development blocks in the country. It aims at improving the productivity of the existing assets as well as creating new productive assets. Since the bulk of the rural poor are landless or marginal farmers, a significant part of the activities for their benefit would be in the non-farm sector. It is a dynamic concept, continuously changing with respect to conditions and requirements of rural society.

The IRDP strategy has the following main elements: a five-year development profile is the framework of action; a specific farm guidance programme is to be provided; a special programme of assistance for the economic upliftment of the poorest rural households is to be implemented; a credit plan is developed; a single agency is to implement the 114-odd programmes offered by more than eight departments.

DECENTRALISED PLANNING AND INFORMATION NEEDS

While efforts have been made to strengthen the delivery mechanism for rural development, there is considerable attention being given to the decentralization of planning as an important function of the district administration. Strengthening district planning, it is believed, will result in the correction of regional imbalances in development and will go a long way in meeting the aspirations of the local people. Apart from the massive increase in the volume of work, the intricacy and diversity of work parameters would require a much greater intensity of systematic planning. At present, planning is centralised at the State and the Central levels. In this context, the critical importance of district planning has been pointed out by a number of committees set up by the government. In the history of planned development in India, the Fourth Plan period (1969–74) stands out as a significant milestone. The most important development was in relation to the pattern of devolution of plan funds to the state level. Since then, the state level planning machinery and their methodologies have become well established. The next step is to take this decentralization process further down to the next appropriate level below the state, namely the district. There is now a broad consensus that the basic unit for policy planning, project formulation and implementation at the sub-state level would be the district.

Essential prerequisites of decentralized district planning call for sustained action from the state-level. They include, apart from political commitment, some measures for disaggregation of allocations, delegation of administrative and financial powers, reorientation of attitudes and relationships, building up of capabilities and instruments of control, establishment of participatory decision-making structures, and training/retraining of personnel. The process of development planning proceeds in several phases, namely, pre-planning, planning, implementation, monitoring and evaluation. The planning phase itself has the following steps:

1 formulation of the objectives of the district plan
2 compilation of data
3 preparation of district profile
4 formulating the main strategy and thrust of the plan
5 analysis of existing programmes with reference to the above, and to:
   (a) modification of the ongoing programme
   (b) proposals for removal of inter-block disparities
   (c) assessment of unemployment/underemployment for manpower planning
   (d) formulation and inclusion of new projects
   (e) working out the interlinkages between sectors
   (f) organizing the monitoring
6 assessment of resources for allocation
7 statement of spatial dimensions
8 resource allocation.

WHAT CAN THE COMPUTER DO?

It stands to reason that the district planner will need in depth data and information for planning. This data/information is structured under the following sets: (a) resources; (b) demographic data; (c) agro-economic data; (d) socio-economic data; (e) infrastructure data; and (f) sectoral data.

In order to appreciate the status level of a district in its regional setting as well as in its developmental level vis-a-vis the state and the country, a district profile has to be developed which would give the planner the status position in regard to potentialities, problems and constraints. The outline of the district profile is given below:

1   location
2   historical perspective
3   administrative set-up
4   political climate
5   level of leadership available
6   climate and environmental setting
7   natural resource endowment
8   drainage, land cover, ground water, and land use
9   demography/income distribution
10   agriculture/irrigation/water-supply
11   industry/employment
12   electricity/additional sources of energy
13   transportation/communication
14   institutional finance and co-operative societies
15   education
16   health services
17   livestock and veterinary services
18   social welfare/other welfare
19   state level projects in operation
20   central level projects in operation.

Indicators of development include a set of seven demographic indicators, a set of ten agro-economic indicators, and a set of 13 infrastructure indicators. An attempt has also been made to develop a tentative list of projects and schemes available from the district administration. The respective outlays, including spatial components, plan allotment and institutionalized credit, are worked out according to this tentative list of programmes in the states where district planning has made some strides. Software has been developed to create a database and a process to arrive at the developmental and potentiality indicators. Procedures have been developed to arrive at inter-block variations and accommodate the relative backwardness of the areas. This package is operational on microcomputers.

The complexity of district administration arises out of the multiplicity of institutions and processes operating simultaneously, criss-crossing each other. Being too close to the people, public accountability is a real pressure. District planning bodies are primarily a forum where district level functionaries explain the rationale for their proposals and actions and the people's representatives make the necessary modifications/adjustments. Thus it is a forum for negotiation to finalize plans. However, our experience is that district planning has fallen prey to the monopolisation of power by a rural elite, and adherence to the Panchayati Raj system has not guaranteed people's participation.

While co-ordination is a problem at all levels of planning, its complexity and intricacy is particularly acute at the district level precisely because of the power structure. Co-ordination here stands for integration in planning and co-ordination in implementation. Since district planning bodies in the country today have only limited planning powers, integration at the planning stage has not materialized in any significant way. For integration at the planning stage to come about in an ideal manner, the entire planning activity touching on all aspects should be undertaken by one single planning body, which will prepare comprehensive plans for all activities in an objective manner, untrampled by the vested interests.

District developmental administration in the country, despite the variations, has some features of uniformity. Apart from the Panchayat Raj institutions, there are District Rural Development Agencies, Lead Banks, District Industrial centres, etc. They will have to be assigned some role in planning. In this context, one way of making the optimum use of funds available under different schemes could be breaking down a scheme into its several components and utilizing the funds from different agencies for different aspects of the same programme. This, however, is a cumbersome procedure. If this could be done it would be a major breakthrough in our efforts at integrating the efforts of multiple agencies. This would enable co-ordination between regular plan programmes with special programmes, between complementary activities, their sequencing, location, etc. Co-ordination between area levels, integration of district credit plan with district plan urban-rural integration also have to be arranged.

Decentralized planning at the district level thus calls for an immense amount of data and information. This would mean making improved arrangements for the collection, storing, processing and retrieval of data quickly. The introduction of computers and the development of relatively cheap standard software for district planning purposes seem to hold great potential for district planning.

The information revolution, which is currently storming the Indian scene, has the potential to make available new, fast, accurate and effective tools and techniques for processing and analyzing information for district administration. There is unlimited scope for the use of data processing equipment to help speed up decision-making and service-delivery. District administration collects information at various operational levels about a variety of beneficiaries and events. Very often the bulk of this information collected is not put to appropriate use due to problems in the existing information system. Firstly, there is no uniformity of information collected even within one department. Different functionaries use different types of forms for collection of the same information. Different departments dealing with inter-related services have their own systems which differ from each other. There is no uniformity in the pattern, in terms of frequency, source, etc. There is delay in passing the information collected to different levels resulting in non-comparability and non-usability of the information collected. There is delay and distortion in writing, legibility and comprehensiveness due to inappropriateness of the information system, including collection and storage.

Accurate, complete, detailed, relevant information has to be available on time to policy-makers and planners, to the District Development Commissioner for monitoring, control and co-ordination, and to front-line functionaries for efficient programme implementation and service-delivery. Use of a computer has certain advantages, for they can handle large volumes of repetitive, routine, standardized data and can put the data through complex processes at high speed. Use of a computer is justified in the interests of uniform, extensive, accurate coverage of services and will reduce human errors and delays.

LIMITATIONS

A computer is a symbol of modernity. If one has power, one has access to high-tech modern equipment. In a way, if one has a personal computer, it means that one has 'connections' in high places. Whether one knows how to use it or not, it is a required status symbol in the political context. Besides, it makes you an intellectual among administrators. The decisions to computerize district administration, or at least district planning, gives rise to an important political question – who will have computers and who will have access to computers? In government, all facilities go by 'entitlement' and not 'need'. In the district all decisions are taken at the highest level, namely the District Development Commissioner or the District Collector. All the basic work of analysis gets done at the level of most minor technical officers. In deciding who should have a computer, we must look at the various sectors, their importance in contributing to the economic growth of the district, and the social inputs necessary to maintain the growth rate. And within the departments/sectors, computers should be used by those responsible for basic calculations and analysis. The general trend of supplying computers to higher officials would not increase efficiency by itself.

Before supplying a computer to anyone in the district administration, it should be decided which system should be adopted. Integrated systems would be too ambitious at this stage because this would require fundamental changes. Political exigencies, time, inconvenience to public and cost are major reasons why we cannot go in for integrated systems right from the beginning. Process or decision-oriented approach is the next alternative to be considered. Decision-making process at the district level is highly complex. The possibility of choice of location, identification of beneficiaries, etc., slipping out of control is real. The decisions will have to be rational and based on facts. There will be a great deal of resistance from elected representatives and their hamstrung district adminis-trators to this system because they cannot dole out favours. Naturally the choice would fall on a data base system. A database system would be least threatening, although a great deal of preparation would be required in standardizing various aspects of the design of the database and training of personnel.

There is, understandably, a lot of resistance to computeriza-tion because it is a threat to the existing social structure. Computerization is also not a panacea to solve the problems of efficiency and effectiveness. The elite, who are in positions of power, can easily use the information as a device to exhort co-operation and compliance because more than 50% of the rural population is illiterate. And the position of the rural elite may be threatened by the unemployment of local people and entry of trained outsiders. Introduction of computers at the district level is ominous from another point of view. When narrow sectarian, communal feelings are being fanned for political ends, one cannot say to what use the computer will be put. No organization can be 100% secure from wanton misuse of the system. Interruption, disclosure, modification, removal, and destruction are some of the forms of misuse that the system should be protected against. The system should be designed to detect, locate, correct errors; must provide measures for the reconstruction of the file; must provide arrangements for back-up in case of failure; and must control access to confidential data at low cost.

We, as a people, are fascinated by secrecy and mystique. In a highly competitive society, government as well as the people are secretive. Though the essence of democracy is open administration, the government finds it difficult to collect accurate, true, relevant information. The people supply inaccurate, distorted, irrelevant information to the government and there is no way to check this. In fact, sometimes there is an overload of inaccurate, distorted, irrelevant information at the data-capturing stage itself.

Land records are important because they are the formal records of the social structure of the district. However, records are never updated. Any attempt to update them would amount to updating/changing the social structure. There are strong forces which prevent any attempt in this direction. Revenue collection is also a touchy subject. As a result, only health, education, social welfare, and such other sectors would be amenable to computerization in the beginning. Every district has a district credit plan which will also lend itself to computerization. However, inter-linkages between the social service sectors and the credit plan would pose certain problems.

Health statistics, unemployment figures and poverty statistics will have to be read together to develop a meaningful analysis that would indicate future courses of action. Computerization of inter-sectoral correlation and inter-district comparisons would be useful. Interpretation and interpolation of each one of these parameters would be a sub-routine, and interlinkage of these sub-routines will have to be compatible. Normally, this should not be a problem. But, with a large number of computer illiterates, data-capturing of inaccurate, distorted, relevant/irrelevant data is a real obstacle. In as much as the social service sector is a big vote-catcher, compatability becomes a useful tool. For instance, finding out whether water-logging as a result of an irrigation scheme has increased the incidence of malaria among women may be relatively easy with the help of a computer, but finding out the correlation between the availability of landless labour, migration and infant mortality/crime against women is a sensitive issue, and the computer may not be of much help. The computer can be useful only if there is political will. A simple matter such as the list of voluntary organizations engaged in rural development is not available with district administration. The reasons given are not convincing. On the other hand, district officials maintain a list of voluntary organizations patronized by politicians.

In this context, computerization poses a threat to the very network of rural elite and power centres. Hence, it is too ambitious to aim to computerize all aspects of district administration at one go. It will have to gradually evolve over a period of ten or more years. At this stage, whether efficiency of the district administration, specifically IRDP, will increase and corruption would go down just because some aspects of the IRDP are being computerized is a moot question. The pace of technology use must match the state of Indian society.

MAKING TECHNOLOGY SERVE HUMANITY

Joaquin G. Tan

The use of western technologies does not seem beneficial to the majority of the people in both first and third world countries. Its most obvious result is industrial growth and to Ivan Illich (1973) this produces the "modernization of poverty . . . the experience of frustrating affluence that occurs in persons mutilated by their overwhelming dependence on the mass-produced goods and services of industrial productivity". Poverty here refers not only to the material want experienced by the third world countries but also to the spiritual needs lacking in the first world societies.

TECHNOLOGY TRANSFER AND ITS CONSEQUENCES

Johann Galtung has pointed out that:

> "Technology is not merely a mode of production with hardware (tools) and software (skills and knowledge) components. It is also a carrier of codes – economic, social, cultural and even cognitive. The economic code that adheres in western technology demands that industries be capital-intensive, research-intensive, organization-intensive, and labor-extensive. On the social plane, the code creates a 'center' and a 'periphery', perpetuating a dependency-forming structure of inequality. In the cultural arena, it sees the West as entrusted by destiny with the mission of casting the rest of the world in its own image. In the cognitive field, it sees man as master of nature, the vertical and individualistic relations between human beings as normal and natural, and history as a linear movement of progress."

Susantha Goonatilake further elaborated, saying that technology acts as a "social gene", i.e. "as a carrier of social relations from one society to another . . . (It) tries to recreate aspects of the social system which produced it in the first place." It is no wonder that in third world societies one can see replicas of not only the technologies found in western societies but also social systems and institutions, their problems and diverse effects on both the human population and the environment.

I would like to note at this point that 'tools' here denotes not only simple hardware and large machines but also institutions that produce tangible commodities and systems, like schools and hospitals, and intangible ones such as education and health.

To continue perpetuating the industrial society with all its wanton destruction of the environment, centralized control of decisions, and the legalized exploitation of third world economies, to name just a few, would take its toll on the very survival of our civilization on the planet. Much has already been said about the impending collapse of the world ecosystem (e.g. Weaver, 1986) and the ever-growing threat of superpower annihiliation of all the creatures on this earth. Most of us are already numb to it, helpless in the face of the seemingly enormous and uncontrollable situation in which we find ourselves. Almost always we blame others, i.e. the system, for the wrong things we see and experience around us. Unknowingly, in our own mind set and life habits, the very same systems, beliefs and practices to which we point an accusing finger are operating. This should not be a surprise. We have been conditioned by the materialistic and mechanistic world view on which the present civilization operates.

THE CLASSICAL REALITY

To understand the condition in which our minds have been programmed by society, we need to briefly look into the historic processes that modern science and technology underwent. Modern science and technology have an implicit worldview that operates a hidden inner logic. Rene Descartes, the father of modern philosophy, gave birth to the methodology of a new science of nature. His "philosophical approach also brought a mechanistic dualistic view into the world by making sharp ontological and epistemological divisions between mind and matter. Matter, consisting of things 'out there' was separate from, but could be observed, manipulated and commented upon by the realm of the mind. This separation was essential at that time to remove the hand of God, moral fear, faith and revelation from the sphere of the new science. Descartes felt that animals, including humans, functioned on the mechanical principles and were therefore machines." (Goonatilake). The new methodology developed into a precise knowledge of nature that laid the basis for a technological revolution. This in turn created the industrialized lifestyle and culture of the west and other countries which have adopted western values. Descartes continues to permeate the collective consciousness of the population today. He is still the driving force of the majority of today's population. He lives in the institutions, systems, professions which we have developed over the last 300 years of industrialism.

I cannot avoid feeling anxious over the direction taken by the advancement of software in computers. Computer softwares mostly cater to traditional institutions and professions that serve traditional and conditioned human needs in the present society. Going through the list of softwares in human services that CUSS network published, one will instantly get the impression that most of the work done to make the new information technology support humanity is to continuously legitimize existing structures, institutions and professions. Not much has been done to look into how computers can liberate man from the materialistic and mechanistic world or at the least help solve the disparities between and within our countries.

CLEAVAGES IN OUR SOCIETY

Before I go on with my ideas about how the new information technology can best serve the needs of humanity, I would like to describe how the cleavages between the first and third world societies came about. Most third world countries have a history of being colonized. During that period, a number of alterations were made to their political, cultural, social and economic situation. Political boundaries were set arbitrarily without due consideration to ethnic diversity, language, topography and the like. Land use patterns were altered to suit the markets of the West at the expense of the self-reliance possessed by the indigenous peoples. Thus, products of third world countries are heavily affected by the fluctuations in the world market. Worst of all, much of the content of the educational system of the former colonies were moulded and directed by the colonial masters. As a result, those who went through the educational process became alienated from their own culture and traditions. This capturing of the minds of an elite segment of third world countries ensures the continuity of control exerted by the former colonizers upon the destinies of their former colonies. The political independence granted to them is not genuine. In other words, third world economies, even education and culture remain tied down to the institution and systems of their former colonizers. This relationship is now manifested in their dependence on transnational corporations (Constantino, 1978).

I do not intend to point an accusing finger at anyone or at any nation for the ills that we experience today. We inherited this situation from our forefathers who have failed to realize the need for change which we perceive now. My intention is to find a common ground for us to start working together to heal the cleavages that separate us from ourselves, from each other, and from our environment. This paper is presented by an individual from the third world who has assimilated the culture, lifestyle and thinking habits of the first world. We live in between two worlds, the affluent industrial and rural poverty societies. We understand both of them only to the extent that we interact with them. Communication is constant among us but the variation in its quality and accessibility (facilities and abilities) is one of the key factors that distinguishes the privileged from those who lack the amenities and basic sense of control over their lives. As a reaction to the state we find ourselves in, we create alternative structures, systems and ways of thinking with the less privileged in our society. We hope to slowly erode the control of exploitative transnational activities in the communities we serve. The main vehicle for this is organized people's actions through non-government people-oriented organizations. We find in the first world various experiences of service work similar to the above mentioned. I read of solidarity groups, relief agencies, peace movements, alternative lifestyle communities and other efforts to change the current trends of development. I also know of initiatives to reorient the consciousness of individuals from affluent countries on the effects of our various lifestyles.

SETTING THE PROBLEM ASIDE

I do not have to belabour the point regarding the consequences of technology transfer (especially the new information technologies) to our societies. They will definitely be similar to those of the other technologies that have been developed. We have to realize that the innovations in information technologies is still directed mainly towards the urban population and the highest income group; not those social groups, particularly the rural areas (comprising about 70% of most third world populations) who are mostly in need of the benefits derived from these innovations. The disparities in economies both between and within our societies is very much related to the inefficient communication infrastructures we find in poor countries. The relevance and timeliness of information can make the difference between survival and disaster for millions who live on or below the poverty line. Going back to Galtung's point, it will demand intensive capital, research and organization and extensive labor. Socially, a center-periphery relationship will perpetuate a dependency-forming structure of inequality. We will perceive the West as destined to cast the rest of the world in its own image. Worst of all, our indigenous innovative capabilities will continually be suppressed with the influx of more technological innovations from the outside. Our government will persistently rely on the experts from the first world to solve our problems, unaware of the fact that the very model of western development is the source of their problems.

We can set aside the various symptoms of our problems and concentrate on what we can do together to eradicate their sources. The first step is to change our mental set. Current studies point out that the mechanistic and materialistic view of the world can no longer be the driving force in our everyday living. The holistic view of the world now expounded by new physics and quantum mechanics has reconceptualized science and totally altered the meaning of classical reality (Augros and Stanciu, 1986). It is now up to us to incorporate this new instrument of thought into our present way of life, in our everyday consciousness: to view reality as an unbroken wholeness and not that of separate entities. Likewise, we must view humanity as an unbroken wholeness acting on the world with a purpose: in this day and age to realize itself as one humanity and practice it as a reality. There is no they and we but only us.

A LIMITED PHILIPPINE EXPERIENCE

The limited experience we have had in the Philippines indicates the potential for appropriating the new information technology for the service-oriented work that we do. A group of non-governmental people-oriented organizations is now in the process of utilizing them in the following fields: human rights, economics, appropriate science and technology, labor, rural developoment, alternative institution building, micro industry building and the like. Generally, word processing has liberated our minds to articulate more perspective and viewpoint at a faster rate. We discussed and decided to develop a program that may be used to catalogue basic bibliographic information on important materials. This effort enables us to have access to each other's library. Thus, less time is spent searching for specific materials leaving us with more time to accomplish other tasks. Others are using video recorders to document the people's life situations, struggles and aspirations and inform the rest of society about it. Right now we are learning to make use of the FIDO bulletin board to link us more. This will help us exchange more thoughts and ideas about ourselves and our work with the indigents. Since no-one can afford to host a bulletin board on a full 24-hour basis, we have devised a scheme whereby 4 or 5 groups will handle the board. Each group will allot $2\frac{1}{4}$ hours of their computer time to accept calls from other similar oriented organizations. There will be a 15 minute overlap between hosts to ensure that the messages in the previous host will be transferred to the next. During office hours, anybody can call up the scheduled host to leave messages or send one. This is still a plan though. Its implementation is blocked mainly by the lack of modems (a modem costs 2 months of an average Philippino salary, as against less than 1 week's earnings in Europe or North America). At present, only 6 of us have acquired modems. Other groups are still unfamiliar with the benefits they can derive from this system. Gradually, we demonstrate to them its use and advantages in our work. Hopefully, we can implement the whole scheme as planned. There are other efforts being made by groups to appropriate the technology such as computer communications using radios, community radio programs, and the like.

An important point based on this experience is the capability of the use of the new information technology to be more readily appropriated for service work than other technologies we have used before. It has the potential to overcome the adverse side effects usually associated with transfer of technologies coming from the developed countries. "Communication is the glue that permits decentralization without fragmentation", as Dr Soedjat-moko (1985) points out. It can be used to broaden the views of the users instead of developing in them a narrow perspective. Inter-relationships can be developed even with persons we do not know. There could still be problems difficult to overcome like cost (which means that it can not be democratized), and the issue on control. However, it still seems that the new information technologies have more potential over other technologies.

CONSCIOUSNESS AND THE PROCESS OF APPROPRIATION

Another observation we made is that the level of consciousness of the user is crucial in the process of technology appropriation. We are here today because of our common cause which is to learn more from each other about who we can support humanity and achieve the illusive peace and unity to which we all aspire. The new information technology may be able to bridge the disparities among our societies. The experience of developing the FIDO software strikes me to a great extent. There was really the effort to decentralize and make the program available to anyone who needs it. No-one imposed conditions for its use. The general attitude which prevailed is that of sharing and the urge to communicate and to reach out. The decentralization of networks and the conviviality in the use of the network (the individual uses it as much and as little as he sees fit, one of the conditions postulated by Ivan Illich, 1973) are indications of the action of our consciousness to make a technology serve humanity.

Communication softwares, tools, techniques and hardwares are essential ingredients in the learning processes of development. However, development does not only mean the acquisition of these technologies. It means the creative employment of these tools within the appropriate cultural framework of the audiences the technology is meant to serve. While the form is being established the substance needs to be worked on. I suggest that the substance incorporates the following.

1 The establishment of solid lines of communication and information flow among peoples of the world defining various audiences and addressing expressed needs. We may start with alternative groups who are in service work and have reached a certain level of planetary consciousness, who view the wholeness of the world and are ready to act it out.

2 The development of databases that would support the actions of people to neutralize the excessive control and illegal activities of transnational corporations, as well as foreign policies of governments that legitimize exploitation of the economies of others.

3 The sharing of experiences of evolving alternative structures and systems that are going on in our societies such as alternative lifestyles, appropriate technologies, sustainable agriculture and peace efforts.

A TURNING POINT

We are at the threshold of change. Some call it 'post industrial society', while others refer to it as the dawning of the 'new age'. Whatever it is named, what remains is that we have a choice. On one hand we can proceed to the logical conclusion of today's society as predicted by a number of scientists which is the collapse of the world ecology due to our indiscriminate wasting of resources (trees, energy and the like), the pollution of the environment, or a nuclear holocaust. (This is the consequence of our prevailing attitude toward the adoption of the armed solution to resolve conflicts.) On the other hand, we can use what we have now to understand more of each other, develop better human relationships, practice goodwill, and protect and regenerate the one planet which nourises us all.

British psychologist Peter Russel (in Weyler, 1983) "see(s) humankind as a sort of global nervous system connecting the planet together in a vast planetary leap . . . If you look at the last three decades of growth in telecommunications, telephone systems, computers, databanks and satellites, it is quite obvious that we have begun to interconnect and interrelate in a much more complex manner . . . We have the potential to evolve . . . as a unified system, a 'global brain'." The increase in consciousness brought about by the practice of interconnectedness and interrelation would lead to greater understanding among ourselves. The cleavages which separate us from realizing our oneness and wholeness would one day disappear as we increase our practice of linking ourselves and learn again to participate in the constructive evolution of the planet.

Still more work remains to be done. The next steps to be made promote the worry that we might be 'worshipping a false god' (Darrow and Saxenian, 1984). But we know that we must use all we have to create a situation where everyone will realize the need to heal and regenerate the earth, to make amends on the abuses we made on each other and to leave our affluent but wasteful lifestyle in favor of voluntary simplicity. Everyone's immediate action is important. This way we can truly make use of the new information technologies to serve humanity.

REFERENCES

Augros, R.M. and Stanciu, G.N. (1986). *The New Story of Science*. Bantam Books, London.

Constantino, R. (1978). *Neocolonial Identity and Counter Consciousness*. Merlin Press, London.

Darrow, K. and Saxenian, M. (1984). *Worshipping a False God?* Development Forum, October.

Galtung, J., in Gonzales, R. *IT in the Eighties: In Search of a Philosophy.*

Goonatilake, S. *Aborted Discovery: Science and Creativity in the Third World*. Zed Books Ltd., London.

Illich, I. (1973). *Tool for Conviviality*. Perennial Library, Harper & Row, New York.

Soedjatmoto (1985). 'Communication for Development in a Time of Crisis'. *Jakarta Post*, December 7.

Weaver, Don (1986). *Solar Age or Ice Age: Which will you work for?* The International Permaculture Species Yearbook, 16–25.

Weyler, R. (1983). 'Conversation with Mystic Scientist Peter Russel'. *New Age Journal*. Rising Star Associated Ltd., June.

Information Technology and the Human Services
Edited by B. Glastonbury, W. LaMendola and S. Toole
© 1988 John Wiley & Sons Ltd

CHAPTER 11

The Way Ahead

The astonishing assortment of work offered in this volume and the larger array presented at the HUSITA Conference is in itself convincing evidence of the formative activities currently under-way to apply information technologies to the human services. Progress is uneven in each of the topics covered in the book, and while there is certainly a need for a continuing infusion of technical capacity, an underlying factor is that the uneven distribution of IT resources throughout the world is, in the long term, a problem of high priority in the developed countries, and as much a crisis for third world countries as other, better publicised, hardships.

In the short term, the effects of the lack of IT resources in the human services may not be seen to be as compelling as starvation, nor as motivating as the likelihood of ozone depletion or pollution, but, nonetheless, each of these problems is related to the others, each carrying its own vector of serious consequences. Information technology, like any other technology, is not a solution to unspecified problems. Yet the purposive use and application of IT may, and indeed can, support problem solutions, and in fact is being so used. But in the human services, there is a reluctance by funding bodies to support the development, use, and application of these technologies. One could argue that information technologies are tools of power or dominance, and are only shared when a government or state must share them. One could argue that information technologies supply business and commercial interests with a competitive edge and therefore are considered to be instruments of profit, and for this reason are not shared. One could argue that the human services are considered to have low status and low social value, and that they therefore are not considered seriously for project funding. In fact, these arguments are not sensitive to the real needs of human services in developed countries, while for the third world it is the critical lack of financial resources to support any human service activity that is often the more telling explanation.

In most of the developed countries, human service organiza-tions can be seen to support at least three social functions. First, they assume major responsibilities to socialize the members of society. They socialize them with the values, roles, and goals of a society, its aspirations, shortcomings and hopes. Second, human service organizations provide social control functions, with important tasks in the implementation of laws to cope with offenders and protect vulnerable people. Third, they enable the integration and smooth functioning of individuals, families and communities by providing information, social support, therapy, and counselling. These resources are critical to the citizen and fundamental to society.

Simultaneously the human services have gone through a decade or more of criticism, for not responding well enough to the needs of the populations they serve, for using techniques which were sometimes seen as inconsistent, ineffective, and inexplicable, for adopting policies and practices which were dehumanizing and stigmatizing, and for poor management, waste, and inefficiency.

A NEW STANCE

Information technology applications in the human services were, to a degree, developed either because of these criticisms, or as solutions to the problems these areas of complaint present. For example, calls of poor management have hastened the development of management information systems in the larger human service organizations, particularly those in the public service. The early experience with such systems was that they could themselves be wasteful, at times unmanageable, and often prone to inaccuracy; overall they were ineffective in providing support to the provision of human services. The report in this book on their continued development in Europe illustrates the innumerable worker and consumer difficulties many of these systems present, and, in some cases, such as in the area of privacy, the real danger they constitute to the public interest. It is clear, in this case, that IT is not a solution to the complaints about human service organizations and their work. If anything, such applications may emphasize, exaggerate, and highlight organizational and work-related difficulties.

We suggest a new stance. We propose a major reorientation of the issue which moves the focus away from areas of complaint, be they real or imagined, to the social functions which must be performed by human service organizations and their workers. This is a stance which emerges from the work reported both here and at HUSITA. Human service reflects an aspect of everyone's life in a developed country, not one that necessarily proceeds from the effects of a free market, or from State legislation, but from the rights and abilities of individuals to pursue their own individual welfare. This reorientation permits the human service professional to develop IT applications which are proactive in terms of the purposes, values, and goals of their organization, their discipline and the social mission they feel they must perform. There are a number of such activities reported here, and their emergence must be nurtured, supported, and actively pursued. However, they are plagued by a common set of problems.

CONTINUING PROBLEMS

The first of these problems, as already identified, is funding. In each of the areas discussed in this volume, the ability of the project managers to secure appropriate resources has and will be limited. The investment potential of such projects can be significantly enhanced when supranational co-operation between work groups is possible, particularly when the number of people working in any one area in the human services is relatively small. Only a few of the papers here report such co-operation. A linked concern is the problem of increasing the level of technical expertise amongst the human service IT application developers. Unlike other application developers, human service personnel have often not had funding for training in technical areas, and are, for the most part, self-taught. The net effect is slower application development, less skill generalization, and, often, limited knowledge and use of available tools.

This argument about resources for staff training can, and perhaps needs to be extended beyond the limited group of IT developers to all agency personnel, whether clerical, professional or managerial. The jump into IT is commonly easiest for clerical staff, in large part because the obvious comparability of the typewriter keyboard with the computer keyboard establishes a point of contact, and helps overcome fears. Managers and professionals perhaps have a bigger leap to make, but what use is a manager who has to make overall planning and deployment decisions if he or she cannot understand the IT-based information available to facilitate the decision? Or more directly for customers of the human services, what value can be attached to a service professional who is unable to handle the computerized benefits calculator, or the proven aid to decision-support?

The lack of implementation of IT applications by the human service worker is an issue which cannot be ignored. Yet it is not only a worker problem: it is also an organizational weakness. For example, while large public systems may spend exorbitant amounts of currency on centralized computer systems, the actual service workers (those at the 'front line' of service provision) may not have sufficient access to terminals, except in closely regulated situations, and may find any request for IT devices to assist in their own work given a low priority ranking, or rudely turned down. On the other hand, small organizations may simply not have enough money for equipment, and may not be able to convince anyone that such a piece of equipment has anything to do with helping them in their work.

While it may be fair to comment on the lack of training opportunities for staff, or their reluctance to make use of IT, what could turn out to be a more deeply entrenched problem concerns the knowledge base and practice method of the human service professional. The manner in which human service professionals go about their work and their decision-making is complex. Work which continues to delineate the knowledge base of the disciplines involved would facilitate progress, whether in the context of IT development, workload management, moving forward the theoretical framework of professional activity, or in other associated areas. The obstacles to be overcome, and the compromises to be made, are to be found both within technology and professional practices. Many of the available IT tools are not yet adequate to the task of human service work. For example, much direct service work is done in a textual, free form method. It is difficult to find a tool that would support the development of a computer-based application which could scan such materials and produce a summary of the worker's judgements, client's problems, and alternative evaluation or treatment plans. The flexibility and individualised responsiveness of much human service work is extremely difficult to encompass within a computerized system. Issues have to be raised about the validity and reliability of IT applications so far developed for use by humans in problem solving. At the same time, just because much of the work of professionals is done in a face-to-face manner, and the benefits of the encounter are largely provided through human contact and physical presence, does this justify an attitude that IT is intrinsically unsuited to large areas of human service activity? Or is it fair to expect practitioners to share in a thorough and pragmatic examination of their work, to see exactly where IT applications have a valuable role?

A further area of controversy concerns the public issues around IT applications. If a computer system is used to violate personal privacy, or if inaccurate information denies a client his or her due, then human service workers have both a professional responsibility to do something about it to assist the client, and a value commitment to oppose systems which violate human rights and dignity. This conflict must be joined by human service workers, however, by focusing on the just and fair application of the technology as assessed by its users. Some applications may not be warranted at this time, simply because of their potential for abuse.

THE HAVES AND HAVE NOTS

It needs to be recognized that most third world countries are in an entirely different situation, and have little chance to enjoy the luxury of getting involved in the issues discussed in previous paragraphs. The work presented at the HUSITA conference demonstrates that most of the undeveloped country participants simply have little or no access to IT. In one case, a participant described a situation in which only a few computers were in use in the entire country. Other countries reported that despite having access to devices of IT, the skills to utilize those devices would have to be imported. Under these circumstances, unless a special international effort is made, technology transfer cannot take place. If technology transfer cannot take place, neither can we hope to empower human service workers and their clients in these countries to participate in their own destiny. In a sense, the undeveloped countries are a clear example of the consequences of not transferring important technologies to other populations.

Perhaps more importantly, it is critical to note that the situation of the poor and the disadvantaged in every country, regardless of its state of development, is similar. Amongst the papers which caused the greatest stir at the HUSITA conference were those analyzing the effect of being deprived of IT access in circumstances where it could have been of obvious benefit. Issues of deprivation and empowerment, often raised in a general philosophical way, were taken up by physically handicapped and other disadvantaged people who were able to speak with depth, feeling and authority from their own experiences. The fact that there are people whose vital daily needs can and are being met by IT-based solutions should itself be sufficient justification and motivation for keeping technology moving and funds coming in.

ISSUES EMERGING FROM HUSITA

The analysis of ongoing problems, and the particular difficulties facing disadvantaged individuals and communities, have already exposed many of the dominant issues arising at the HUSITA conference. These issues are in effect the obstacles facing society before even a small part of the presently available technological potential can be realised. There would remain an enormous task for the human services even if there were no more forward moves at all on the technological front. In attempting to provide a framework for a more broadly based and forward looking analysis of IT in the human services, the editors of this volume began by grouping conference papers under four headings, according to their focus:

Consumers
Agencies
Technology
Politics and Ethics

These headings are reflected in the four parts of the book, and do indeed indicate the range of concerns amongst those who have espoused the cause of IT, whether to praise, condemn, or keep a watching brief over it. A point to make very clear is that HUSITA was not a gathering of IT fanatics, committed to pushing forward their obsession regardless of other factors. There are perhaps a few such people around, just as there are a few who can see no potential benefit whatsoever for IT, and would like to see it vanish from the face of the earth. If there is a general description covering the majority of participants, it would incorporate something about enthusiasm and commitment to the technology and its application, balanced by substantial caution and an awareness of wider concerns, and of 'wheels within wheels'. The innocence of early IT lovers has gone, to be replaced by reflective maturity, some scepticism, and a willingness to think deeply about where societies are being led.

This was most obviously present at HUSITA when the focus was on consumers, and the political and ethical framework for IT implementation. The consumer problems emerging from the papers in the book indicate that when IT applications are developed in the public interest to fulfil social needs, the most important requirement is that the general public must have a major role in making decisions about the application of the system at the level of ordinary people. The public through legislation if necessary, must participate in the decisions about the data contained in the systems, the use of the data, and the consequences of the system. Furthermore, it is arguable that the developers of IT applications for the human services must now go through the same trauma which many groups of scientists have had to face (in nuclear physics and genetic engineering, for example), of establishing a code of practice to incorporate a socially acceptable ethical framework for their activity.

Violations of human rights, privacy, and dignity are increasingly possible through the use of IT applications. Privacy, particularly IT-based problems of privacy, pushes forward the notion that there is a human right to protect personal secrets, which in turn must be balanced with the public right to knowledge. Within the human services serious consideration must be given to delineating the circumstances under which systems can and should be designed which give autonomous control to those whose data is being filed. In the last resort this is clearly a responsibility for a nation's leaders and legislators, but human service workers can pioneer such efforts in the workplace, ensuring that citizen controlled, value-led systems alone are undertaken and their consequences examined. This is not a new task for human service staff, since they have traditionally been linked with the social conscience of a community, and with advocacy for the less privileged or more vulnerable members. In this context it is important that the human service worker supports universal access to information technologies, while at the same time studying and reporting on the evolution of IT assisted social support systems, the impact of IT on self-development, and behavioral changes related to participation in an IT environment. Social systems as a consequence will be noticeably more complex, and the mobilization of resources for problem solving more complicated, but unless these matters are tackled head-on then we must expect public resistance to grow in proportion to the inadequacy of insensitive technological solutions.

A linked issue to emerge here is that the way that people behave is changing, and their expectations of life enhancement are growing, in part (perhaps a very large part) due to participation in the use and application of IT. There is an indication from the HUSITA discussions that people are much more concerned with self-realization. Since IT can support participatory decision-making through electronic networks and communicating, as well as through aids to improving personal performance and self-sufficiency, human service workers who favour such developments will need to master the technology available to support new varieties of decision-making, help educate populations who have been excluded from its use, and join in the promotion of participatory democracy whenever possible. Of course, such participation means that more information will be made public and can be shared. Substantive issues for human service workers will arise around such questions as: how can we create and share fair and accurate data? How can people participate in public decision-making if it cannot always be done in a face-to-face fashion? How can public decisions be reached by electronic means which respect the needs and values of a population at risk?

The range of difficulties arising from the technological impoverishment of third world countries has already been aired in this chapter, but the gap between haves and have nots bears reiteration. The technological gulf which exists between countries and within countries with regard to devices of IT, hinders any attempt to establish ethical frameworks which cross national or regional frontiers (though we need to keep in mind that computerized data, much of it personal, crosses such boundaries incessantly). The issue may focus around the establishment of a system of international co-operation, a part of which is committed to providing technical assistance. Within such a system, the introduction of information technologies cannot proceed without consideration being given to developing national information structures in social services in the various countries. This is a point to be picked up later in this chapter, when considering the idea of forming an international organization.

In scrutinizing notions of consumerism and empowerment at HUSITA it soon became clear that few of the issues were unique to the human services, but rather were embedded in humanity-wide challenges. Nevertheless, human service staff have a long tradition of involvement in topics concerned with promoting human welfare, and for that reason are in the vanguard of the broader debate. The position is somewhat different with regard to agency and technology matters. Two reasons are worth citing. One concerns the nature of human service organizations and the people who work in them. The organizations are not self-contained manufacturing or distributive units, so much as agencies seeking to inter-relate with and help those in the surrounding community who need help and protection. The raw material of human service agencies is human lives, the output human futures. Furthermore, while the organizations may have a structure which has superficial similarity to other sectors of the economy (a hierarchy of authority, for instance), they have a 'production line' which is staffed not by skilled or unskilled employees, but by trained professionals. In short, there are factors which make human service organizations unique.

The second reason is more of an observation, that despite the efforts of a minority of staff, the human services have not taken to IT with the speed and determination of most of the rest of a developed economy. The excuses may be substantial, such as the intrinsic problems of adapting technology to human service practices, but the reality is that from a technological viewpoint, agencies are amongst the camp followers rather than in the vanguard of progress.

Given the context, then, that human service agencies have some unique characteristics, and do not have a position of technological leadership to maintain, what ideas emerged from HUSITA for a way forward? With regard to an agency focus, the main theme has to do with taking a much more flexible, open and imaginative approach to IT. Contributors praised the success of agencies in establishing highly effective management information systems, and then pleaded for applications which would give comparable levels of help to practitioners and consumers. Put another way, information systems, primarily if not exclusively for the use of agency accountability, were in widespread and full operation: in contract applications at the front line, designed to help processes of therapy and service giving, were much less common and almost all chronically experimental. For a variety of reasons (lack of funding, unsupportive attitudes, etc.) applications within human service process, as opposed to management, appeared to get stuck at the prototype stage. Furthermore, the stagnation had less to do with basic technological difficulties than with the unwillingness of agencies to deploy the resources and show the determination to succeed.

Some of the problem can be put down to the isolation of IT specialists from the rest of the agencies' staff, to the extent that although their influence on specifically IT matters was enormous, it was minimal in other sectors. The result was a lack of balance and integration in agency policies. Those human service agencies which had made real progress, many in North America, appeared to have done so because managers had got a sensible balance in policies and resource deployment.

A trend at HUSITA to see shortfalls in IT applications as also reflecting technological weakness was particularly noticeable amongst participants who were employed as agency staff. A view was expressed that despite incredible advances in core technology, applications technology lagged far behind. This could be instanced by looking at the papers on such topics as systems development or expert systems, and noting how frequently they were describing applications with more promise than performance. A vital step for the future must be to get some solid achievement with systems which are different to or more than straightforward management information systems. Several papers pinpointed more precisely where these achievements could come.

One thrust would be in the more intelligent use of the vast stores of data already available, to facilitate decision-making, draw attention to trends, or suggest tentative conclusions from cumulative data, such as what presumably will occur when we are able to integrate the computerized knowledge base of an agency with the agency database. Another initiative would be in the development of computerized knowledge-based systems to the point where they became an easily usable intelligent interface at the disposal of staff or consumers. Before this goal is attained the technology needs to be developed to the point where knowledge can be obtained from the agency staff and success-fully modelled in the system. So far, the first generation expert systems have been demonstrably inadequate in fulfilling this task, usually because they employ only production rules of so-called expert systems shells. The difficulties in successful model building relate to two separate problems: one involves knowledge acquisition, and the other representing the knowledge within the system.

The most promising work to resolve the first difficulty involves the use of an intermediate language between those who have the knowledge and the system itself. However, we must be aware that this is in the main a philosophical problem involving the question "What is knowledge?". The difficulty in transposing one form of knowledge to another has a longer history than computer systems development in human services! Knowledge representation problems will be resolved when systems are developed using more than just rules to model the knowledge. Work incorporating what systems developers call 'frames' and 'semantic net structures' has shown some promise in dealing with knowledge representation problems, and need to be experimented with in the human services. Both knowledge acquisition and knowledge representation require attention to procedural matters – that is, how the information system developments and the expert systems are produced. Human service systems are not technologically easy to develop.

Several contributors stressed the importance of a profound and prolonged relationship between systems designers/developers and service professionals, even suggesting that some staff should seek to gain expertise to carry out the entire activity. Whatever the arrangement, the objective has to be to produce applications which 'strike a chord' and have real meaning to practitioners, by modelling the entire helping process, and using the worker/client transaction as the starting point.

AN INTERNATIONAL ORGANIZATION

Human service IT development is both public and international in character. The globalism of its progress is evident in any reading of the work contained in this book, in the nature of the contacts made between HUSITA conference participants, and in the public usage and utility of the implementations described here. Work in the human services clearly indicates that it may be possible to form an international organization which can help identify projects throughout the world human service community, disseminate information, link both project members and expressed international needs, and commit itself to co-ordinating the dialogue between human service IT system developers, application developers, and theorists on the one hand, and the human service workers throughout the world on the other hand.

An international organization can also help explore and articulate principles which will guide human service work in IT development. From the work presented here, it would seem that a few of these principles may be emerging. For example, in all cases, human service IT work seems to honour the principle that the right of usage is predominant in IT, not the right of ownership. A second principle which emerges is that IT applications must be self-controlled, or contain principles which allow for control at the individual level. Another is that participation will be voluntary and co-operative, and that co-operation and fairness become the basis on which to foster participation.

Establishing and running an international organization would be a time-consuming and costly task, but providing it held to principles of the kind mentioned above, and had objectives concerned with promoting technology transfer, and supporting the less favoured services and nations, it must surely be of considerable worldwide benefit.

CONCLUDING REMARKS

When those who initiated the HUSITA idea first got together they posed a number of questions. Do people who are involved in the application of IT to the human services ever come together? Are there any national organizations representing them? Were there enough interested people to come to an International conference, given that wherever it was located some would have a formidable travel problem? Did people around the world, especially on either side of the Atlantic, have enough in common to warrant meeting together?

The answers to these questions indicated that there were some gatherings, noticeably in the UK and USA (subsequently there have been more, such as the one towards the end of 1987 in the Netherlands), but no national organizations specifically for IT in the human services. There were some focal points for activity (*Cussnet* and *Computing in Human Services* in the USA, *Computer Applications in Social Work* in the UK), and some national organisations were favouring IT-focused special interest groups. Overall there were enough signs to justify quiet optimism about the potential audience for an international gathering, though some concern as to whether the North Americans would be willing and able to finance the high cost of coming to the UK. For HUSITA the North Americans did themselves and everyone else proud, by travelling across in large numbers and making an enormous contribution to the success of the event. European and other developed countries also managed good sized contingents, and the only people missed were those from the third world and from minority communities (especially ethnic minorities) everywhere. There were small and much valued third world and minority groups, but any plans for a repeat will need to address the task of increasing that representation considerably.

The question about interest in common was based on what now, with the benefit of hindsight, seem to be some rather crude views. Causing most worry was the idea that the North Americans were so far ahead in IT applications that they would feel held back by the rest of us, and the rest of us would be left floundering in the face of North American expertise and experience. Reality only partly validated this view, and in ways which may be wholly unimportant. Certainly we were made aware that in terms of access to the latest technology North America had a clear lead, while perhaps only the Netherlands appeared willing to match the level of investment in developmental research. Yet the issues which have featured throughout this book came forward as common to all of us, whatever the country of origin. It came as no surprise that after the formal end of HUSITA 87 many participants stayed on to give their support to the notion of an International Organization, and the development of networks to keep everyone in touch. Since HUSITA 87 the Government of the Netherlands has come forward with funding for a feasibility study on the scope for an international organization.

These are the immediately tangible outcomes. In a less tangible but equally real way, the motives which supported future international gatherings have also promoted the start of a new relationship. For some human service workers this may be too precipitate. The developmental history of IT in the human services is one too recently involved with denial and withdrawal, argument and cynicism, irrelevance and unreliability, to embrace the beginnings reported here with the passion they deserve. For others the new relationship cannot come too soon, and is vitally needed to provide the thrust to further forward movement. Perhaps it can be the task of these latter to bring their colleagues and other members of their communities, their inventions, and their values into a convergence that enhances progress, and at the same time paces exploitation, and sets standards for future conduct.

The contributors to HUSITA and this book were moved by a common understanding of human service work, its principles and values, and their juxtaposition with IT. It is an exploration which will encumber them with both creative responses and responsibilities, an encumberance most of the contributors seem to accept willingly. In many ways, the growth in the experience of human service practitioners with IT is a consequence of the use of these technologies in personal ways, and in the areas of socialization, social control, and social integration. These are areas which touch the worklives of most human service workers and the everyday life of the people with whom they work.

It is also clear that, in a fundamental way, IT is both public and international. This work documents two serious problems in this regard: the invasion of privacy, and the IT gap between those who have, use and apply these technologies and those who do not. The invasion of privacy is documented in the consumer studies included here, particularly in terms of large public systems. The information gap is never more clear than in the situation of the third world, but it also exists world wide, among the poor of all countries, among the oppressed populations; even, to some extent, among the human service professions. This gap means that there is a relative absence of the tools of IT among these populations, and a risk of the consequent enhancement of antagonism and cultural disparity. These are obstacles more formidable than the financial imbalances which already exist, and which will continue to plague all attempts at technology transfer, mutual understanding, and effective human services. We strongly suggest and advocate that these problems take priority in both human service efforts and the public agenda.

We have also attempted to delineate in this book a wider range of major issues which face the human services and IT. Through those issues, a beginning set of philosophical and practical principles have surfaced which are largely undocumented in any other literature. We consider those principles to reflect the initial development of a much needed hermeneutic, a science of understanding which involves humans, information technologies, and their context; it is an area in which human service work can lay claim to discovery, knowledge building, innovation and a degree of pride.